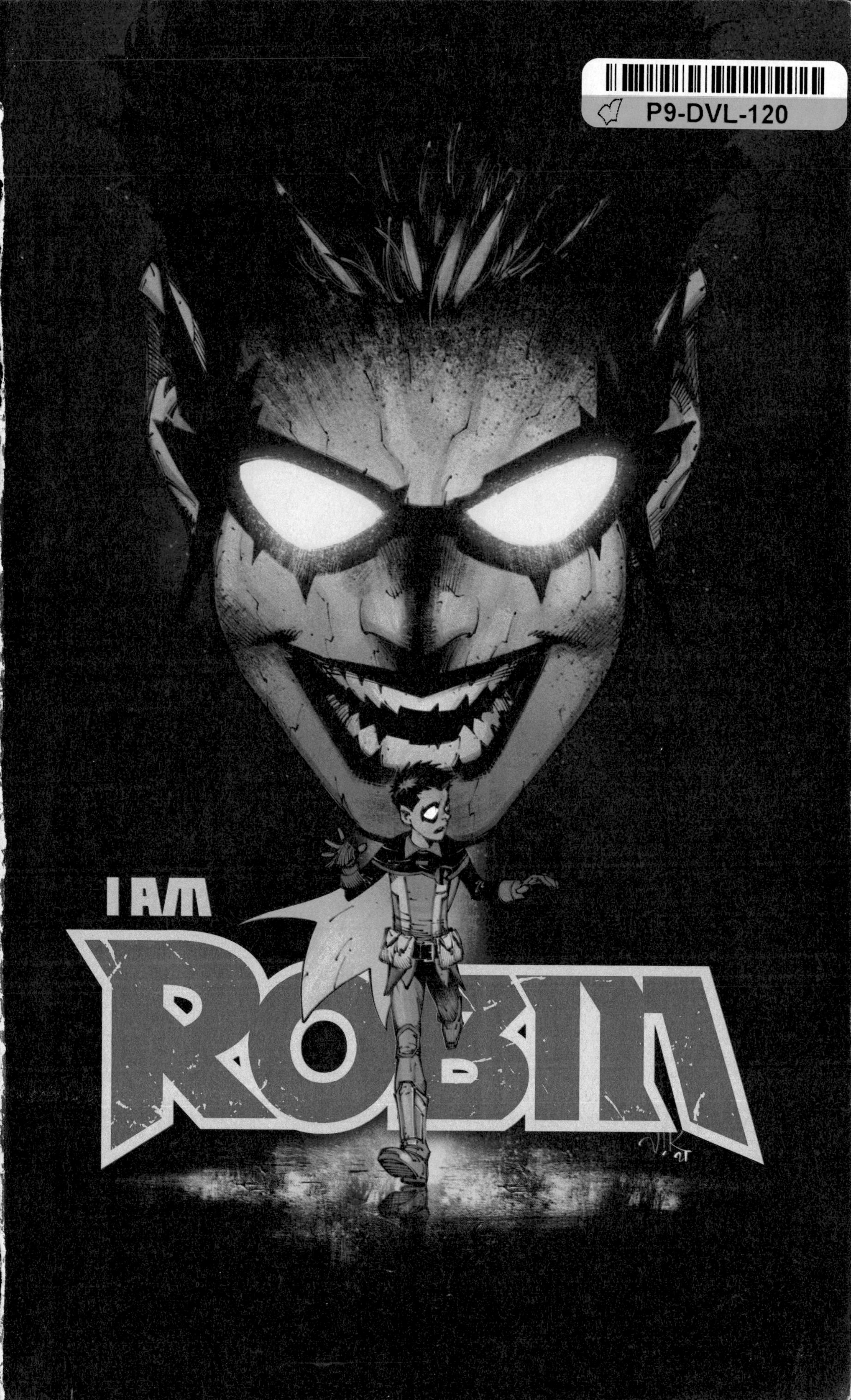
I AM
ROBIN

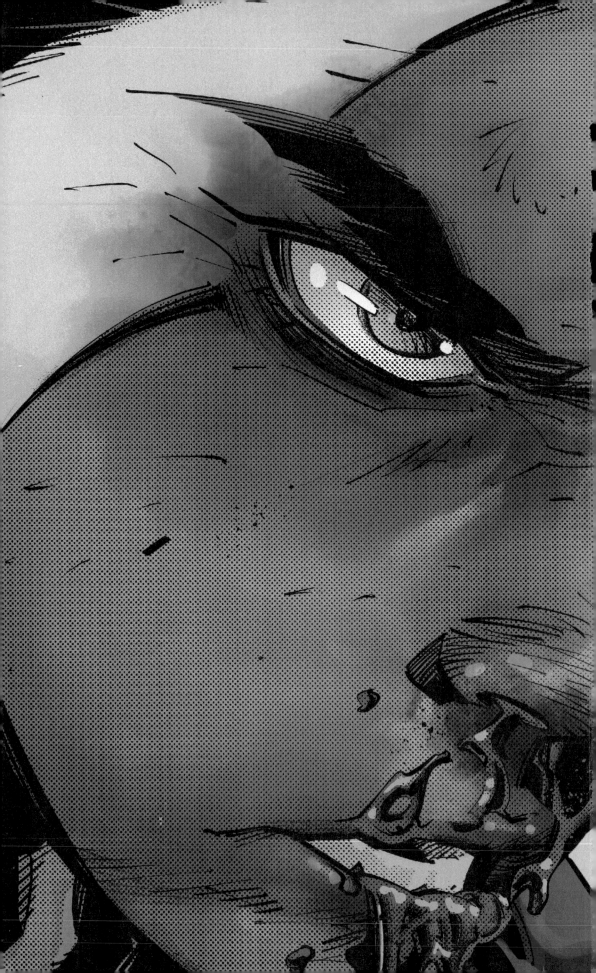

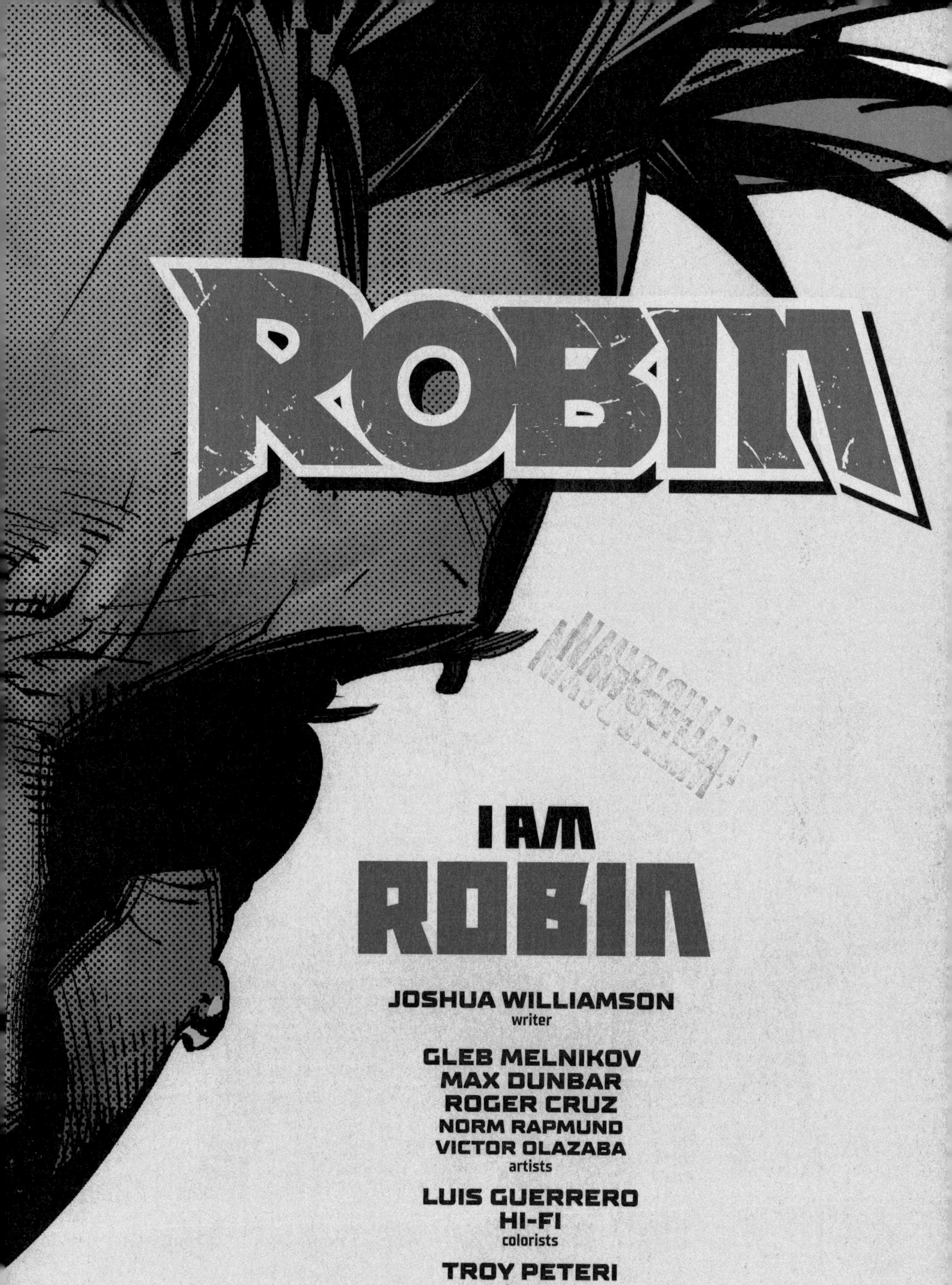

ROBIN

I AM ROBIN

JOSHUA WILLIAMSON
writer

GLEB MELNIKOV
MAX DUNBAR
ROGER CRUZ
NORM RAPMUND
VICTOR OLAZABA
artists

LUIS GUERRERO
HI-FI
colorists

TROY PETERI
letterer

SIMONE DI MEO
collection cover artist

SUPERMAN created by **JERRY SIEGEL** and **JOE SHUSTER**
By special arrangement with the Jerry Siegel family

PAUL KAMINSKI Editor – Original Series & Collected Edition
DAVE WIELGOSZ Associate Editor – Original Series
STEVE COOK Design Director – Books
CURTIS KING JR.
DAMIAN RYLAND Publication Design
RYANE LYNN HILL Production Editor

MARIE JAVINS Editor-in-Chief, DC Comics

ANNE DePIES Senior VP – General Manager
JIM LEE Publisher & Chief Creative Officer
DON FALLETTI VP – Manufacturing Operations & Workflow Management
LAWRENCE GANEM VP – Talent Services
ALISON GILL Senior VP – Manufacturing & Operations
JEFFREY KAUFMAN VP – Editorial Strategy & Programming
NICK J. NAPOLITANO VP – Manufacturing Administration & Design
NANCY SPEARS VP – Revenue

ROBIN VOL. 2: I AM ROBIN

DC Comics, 100 S. California Street, Burbank, CA 91505
Printed by LSC Communications, Owensville, MO, USA. 8/12/22.
First Printing. ISBN: 978-1-77951-673-2.

Library of Congress Cataloging-in-Publication Data is available.

PEFC Certified
This product is from sustainably managed forests and controlled sources
PEFC/29-31-337
www.pefc.org

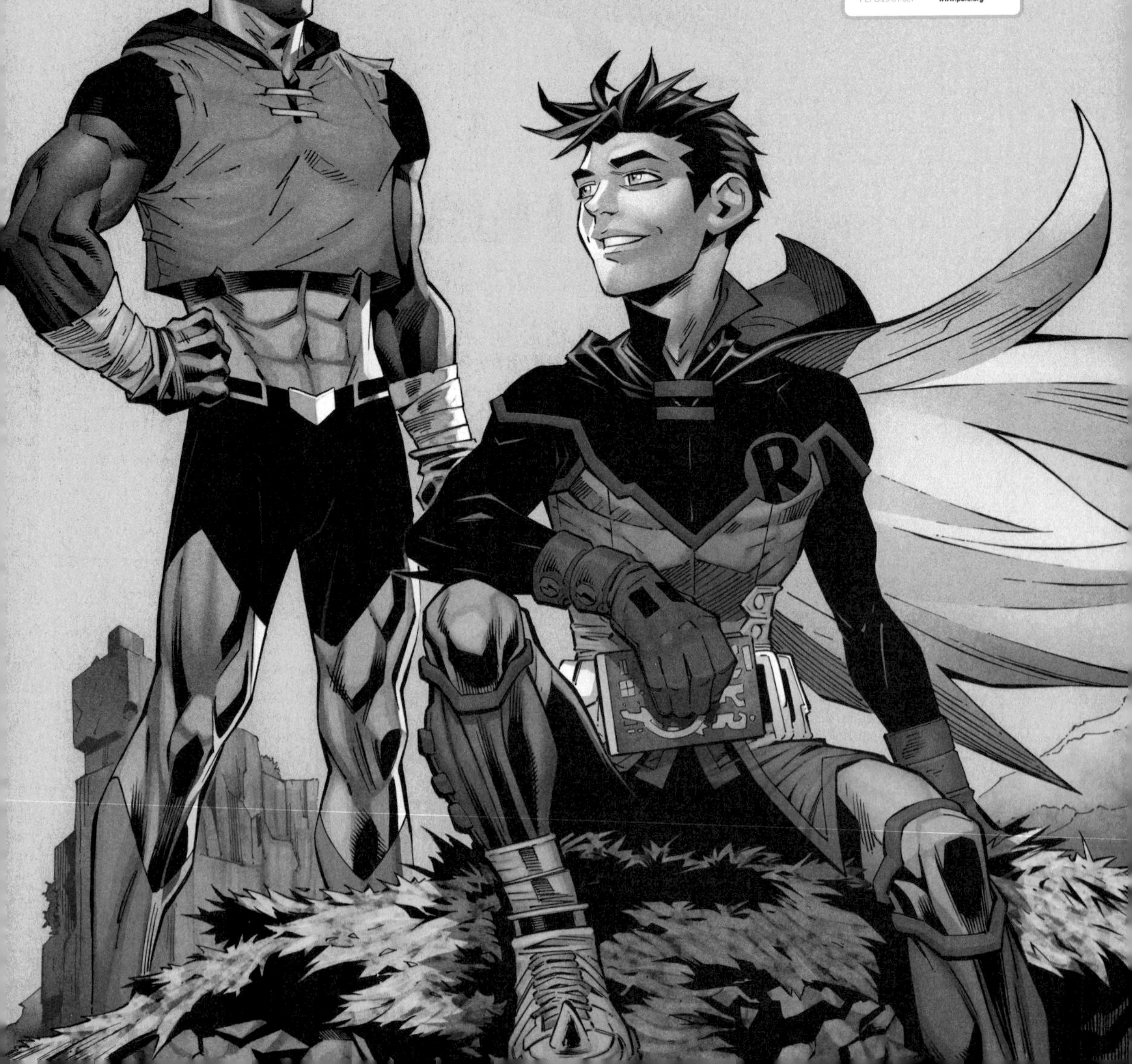

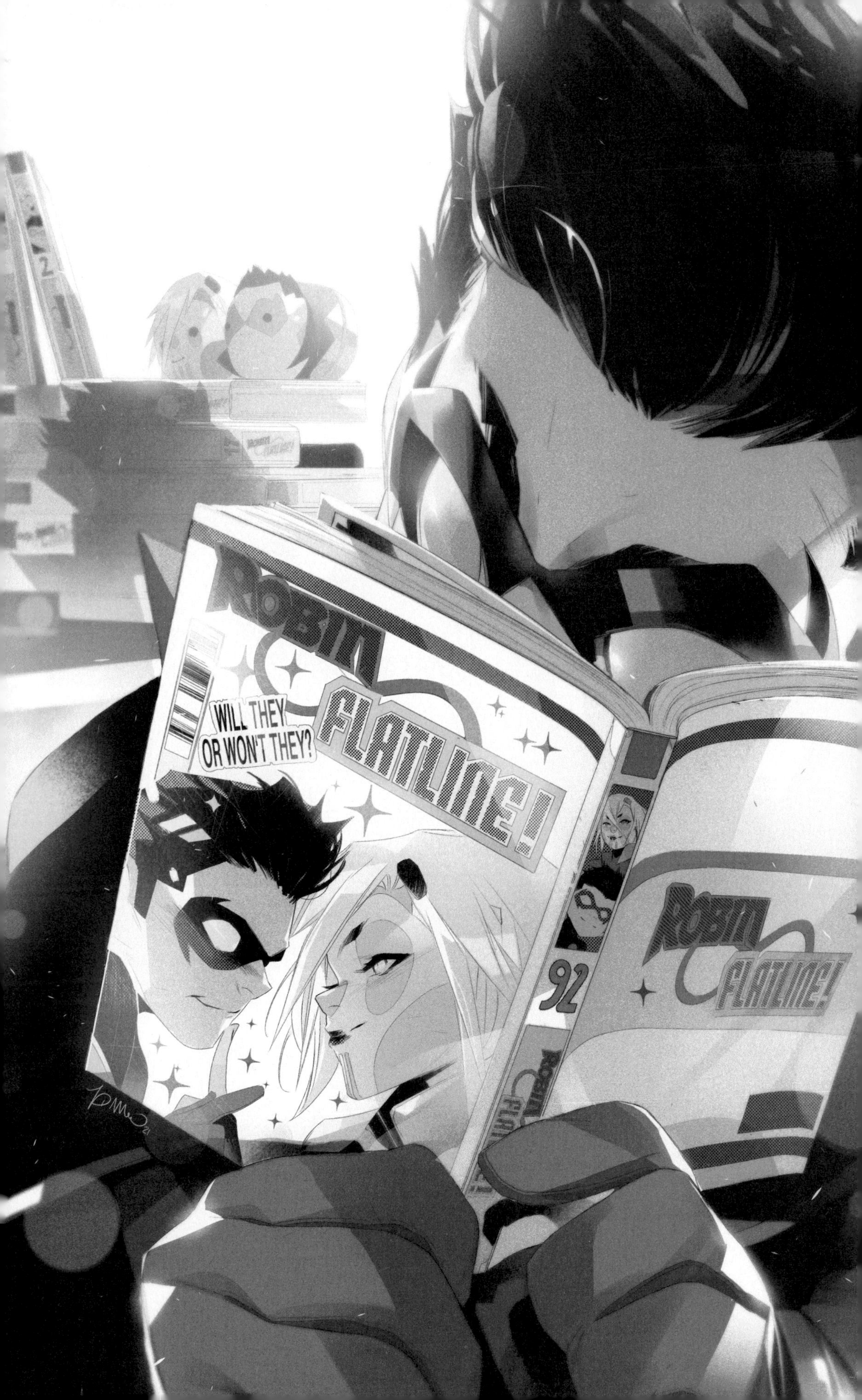

ROBIN
WILL THEY OR WON'T THEY?
FLATLINE!
92
ROBIN
FLATLINE!

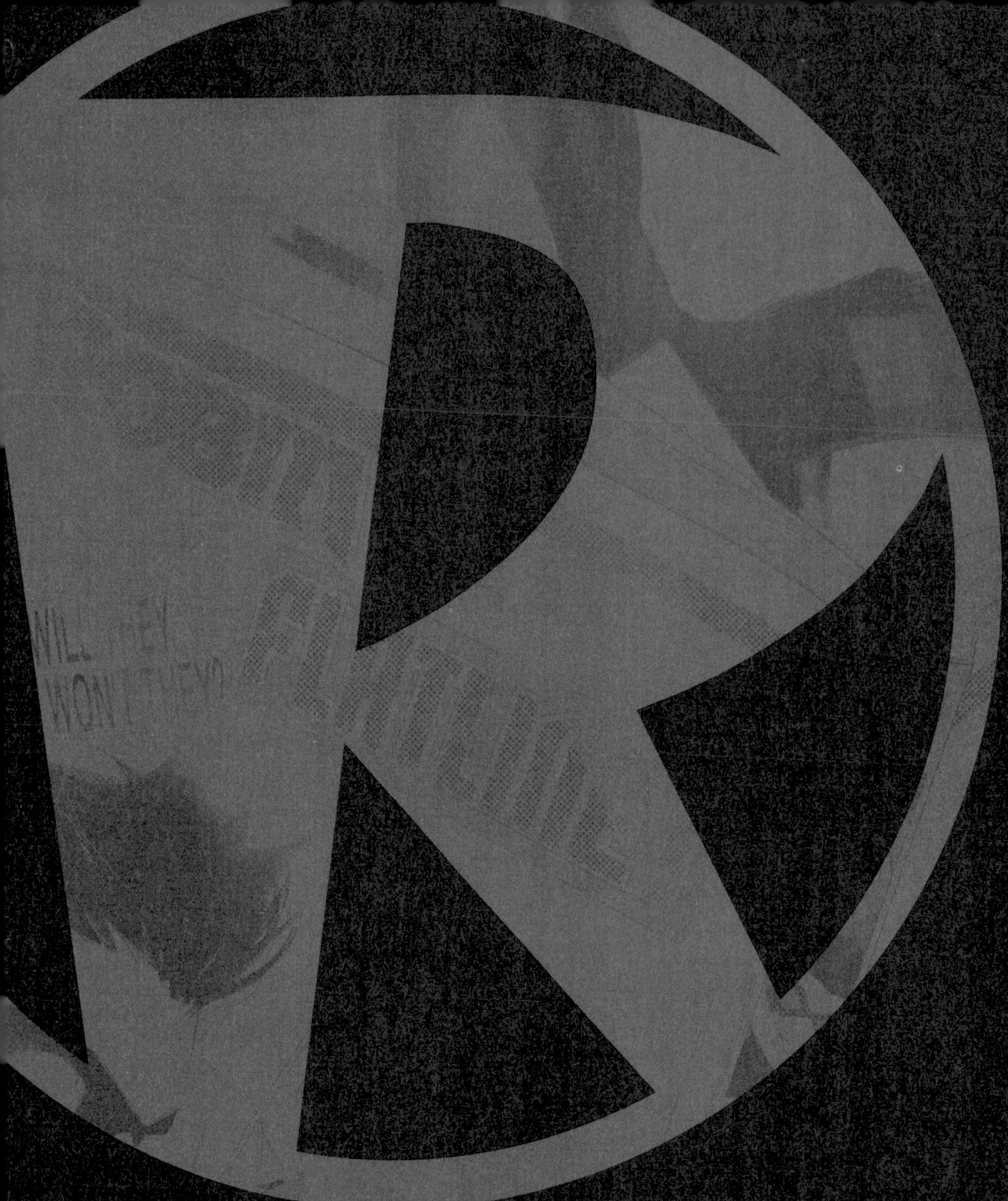

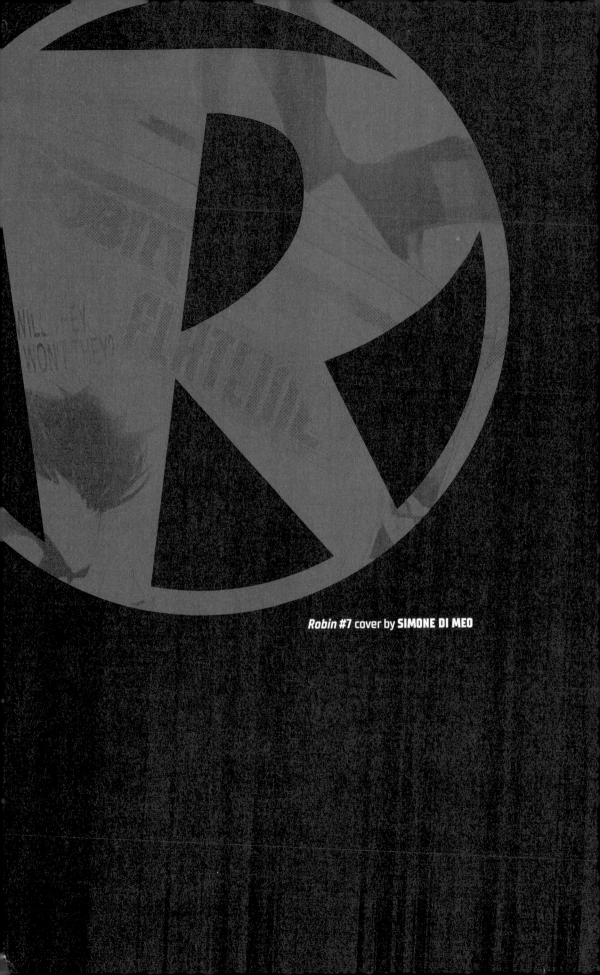

Robin #7 cover by **SIMONE DI MEO**

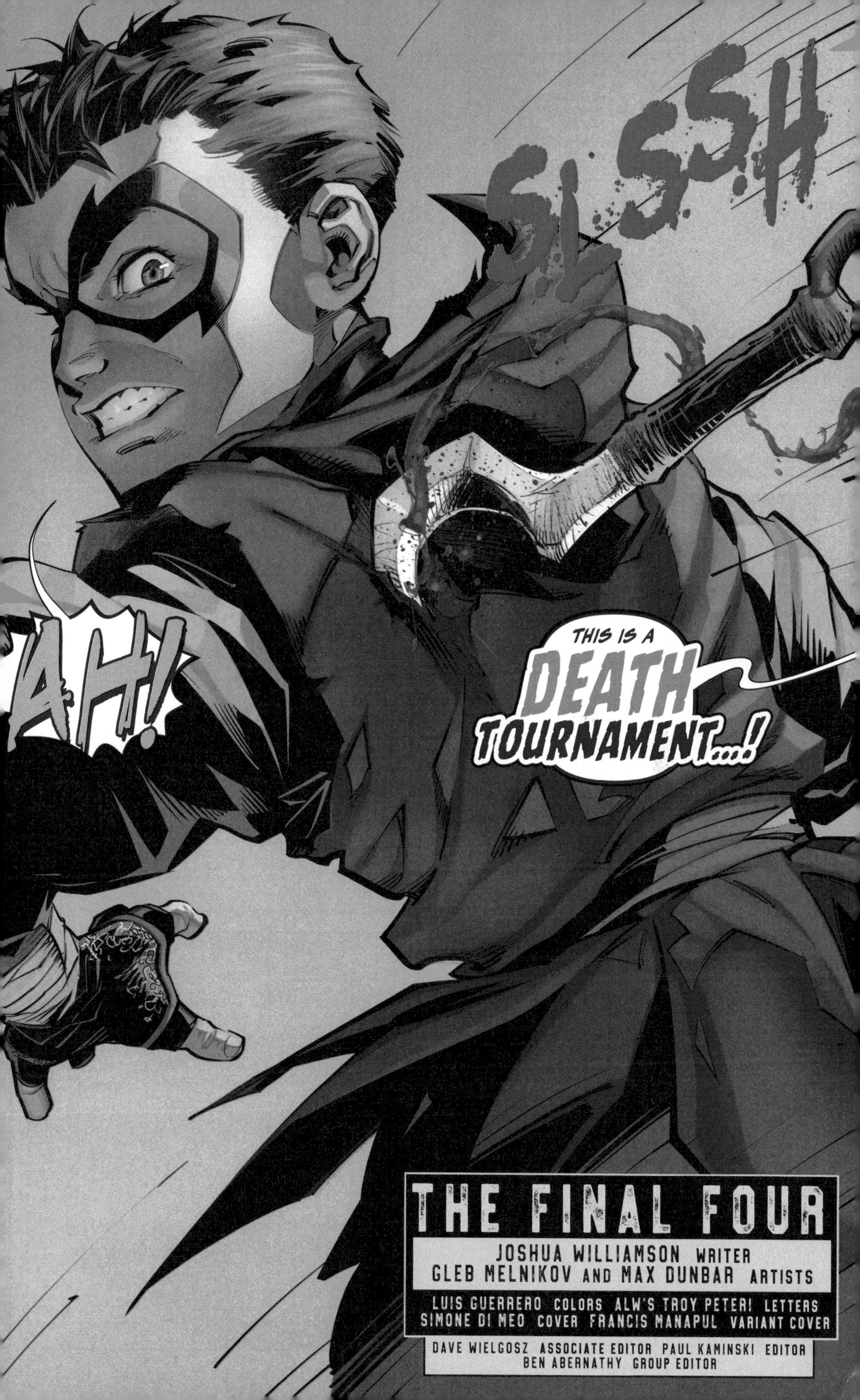
SLSSH
AAH!
THIS IS A DEATH TOURNAMENT...!
THE FINAL FOUR
JOSHUA WILLIAMSON WRITER
GLEB MELNIKOV AND MAX DUNBAR ARTISTS
LUIS GUERRERO COLORS ALW'S TROY PETERI LETTERS
SIMONE DI MEO COVER FRANCIS MANAPUL VARIANT COVER
DAVE WIELGOSZ ASSOCIATE EDITOR PAUL KAMINSKI EDITOR
BEN ABERNATHY GROUP EDITOR

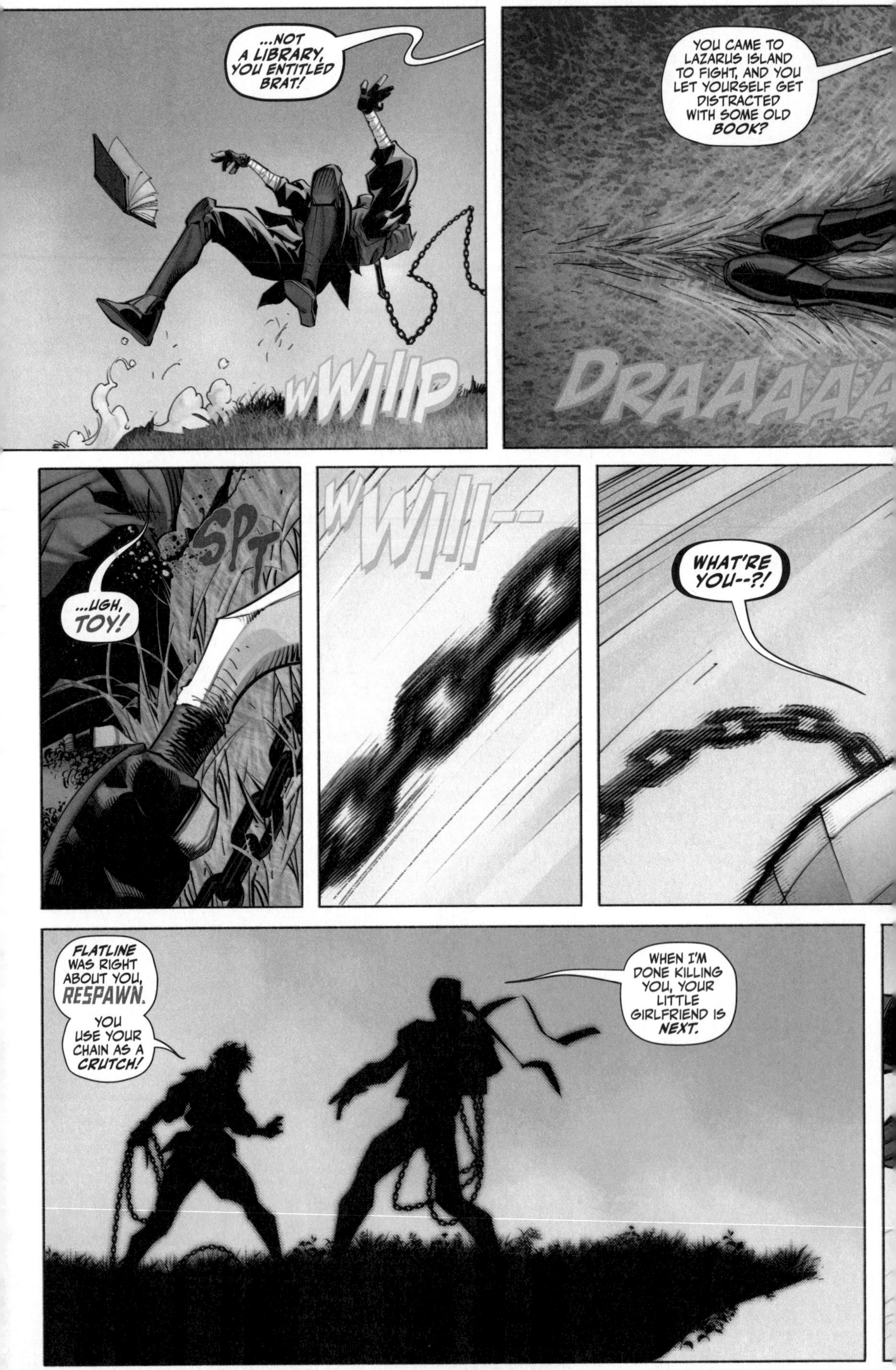
...NOT A LIBRARY, YOU ENTITLED BRAT!
WWIIIP
YOU CAME TO LAZARUS ISLAND TO FIGHT, AND YOU LET YOURSELF GET DISTRACTED WITH SOME OLD BOOK?
DRAAAAA
SPT
...UGH, TOY!
WWIII--
WHAT'RE YOU--?!
FLATLINE WAS RIGHT ABOUT YOU, RESPAWN.
YOU USE YOUR CHAIN AS A CRUTCH!
WHEN I'M DONE KILLING YOU, YOUR LITTLE GIRLFRIEND IS NEXT.

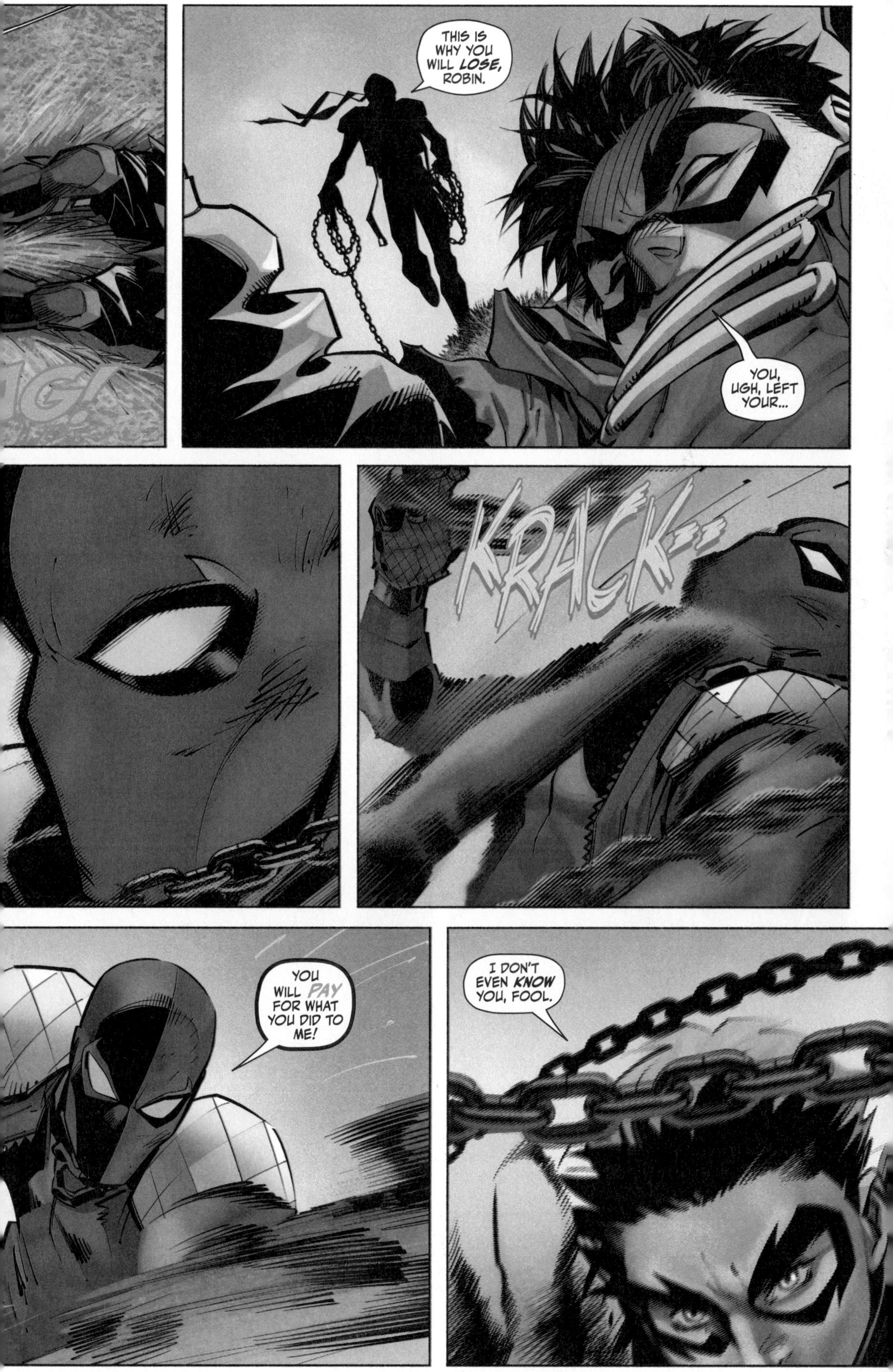
THIS IS WHY YOU WILL *LOSE*, ROBIN.
YOU, UGH, LEFT YOUR...
KRACK--
YOU WILL *PAY* FOR WHAT YOU DID TO ME!
I DON'T EVEN *KNOW* YOU, FOOL.

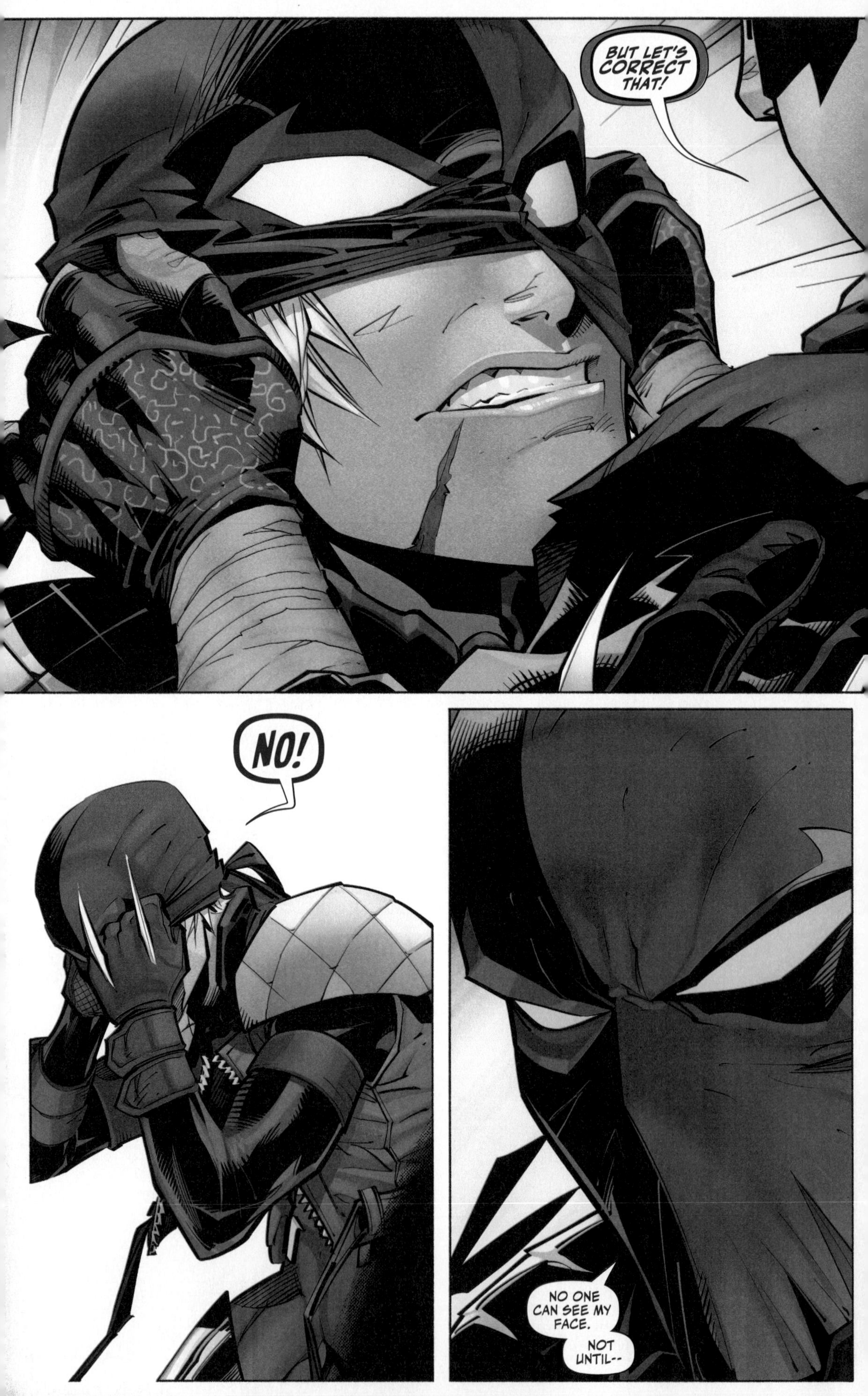

BUT LET'S CORRECT THAT!
NO!
NO ONE CAN SEE MY FACE.
NOT UNTIL--

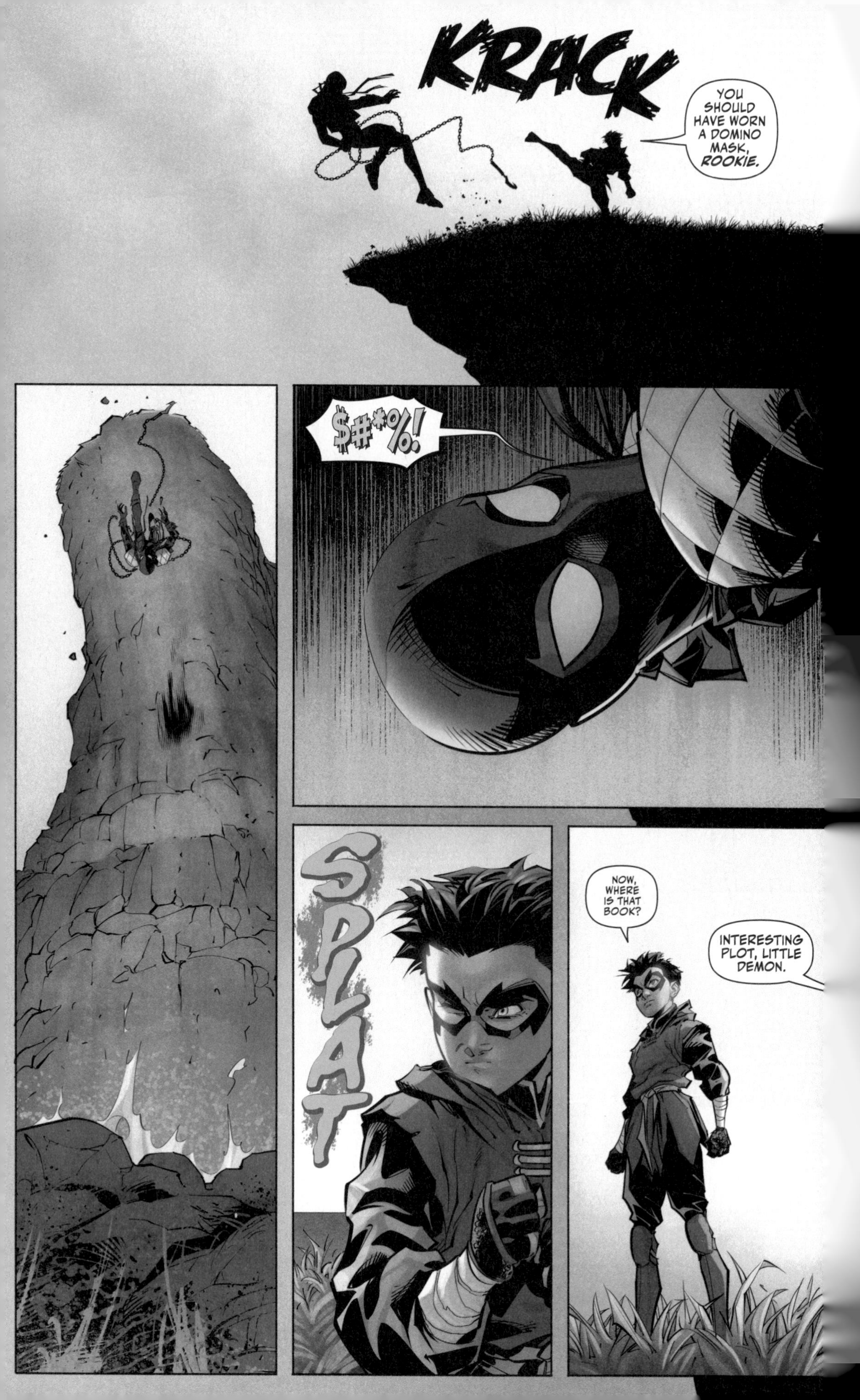
KRACK
YOU SHOULD HAVE WORN A DOMINO MASK, ROOKIE.
$#*%!
SPLAT
NOW, WHERE IS THAT BOOK?
INTERESTING PLOT, LITTLE DEMON.

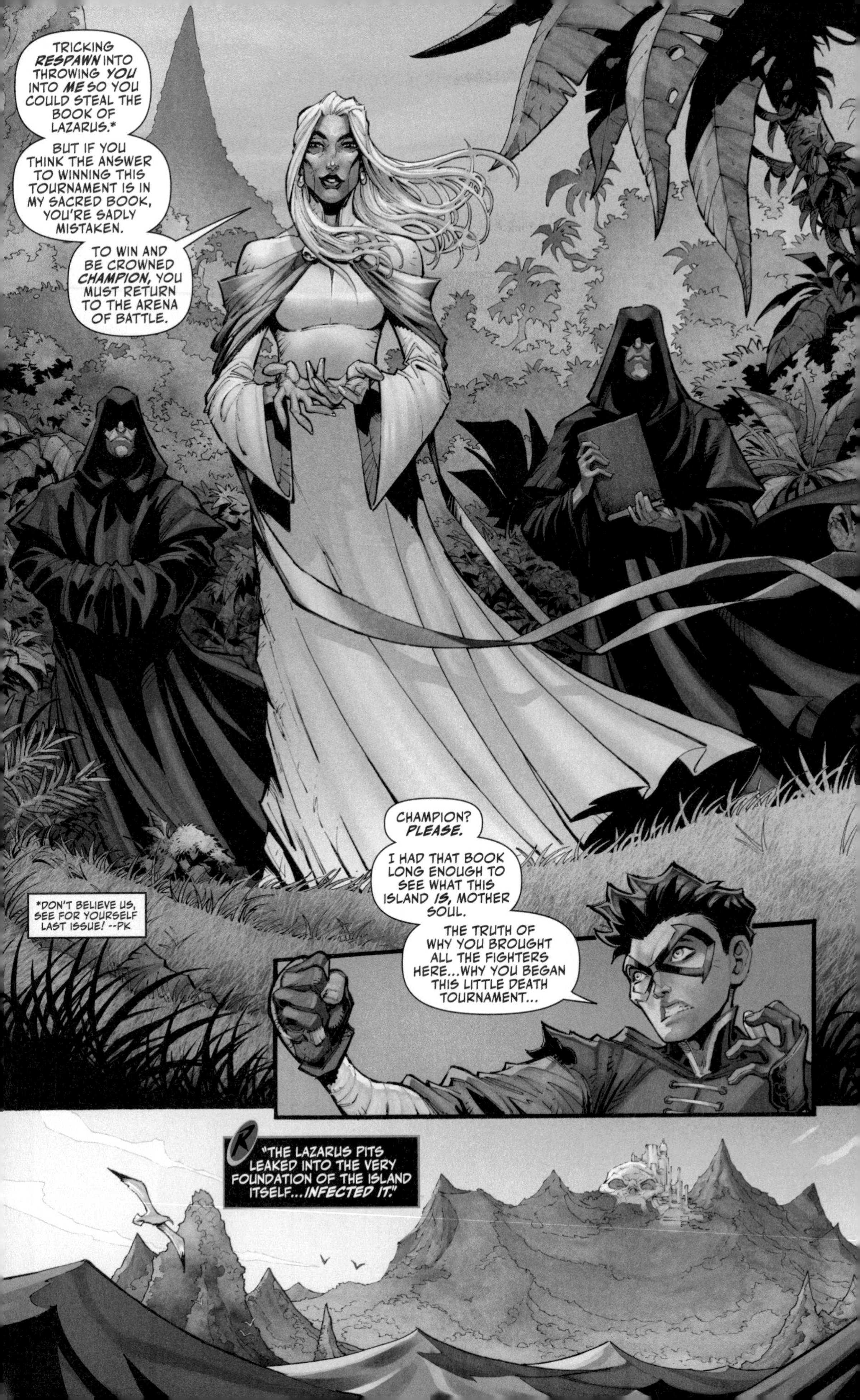
TRICKING RESPAWN INTO THROWING YOU INTO ME SO YOU COULD STEAL THE BOOK OF LAZARUS.*
BUT IF YOU THINK THE ANSWER TO WINNING THIS TOURNAMENT IS IN MY SACRED BOOK, YOU'RE SADLY MISTAKEN.
TO WIN AND BE CROWNED CHAMPION, YOU MUST RETURN TO THE ARENA OF BATTLE.
*DON'T BELIEVE US, SEE FOR YOURSELF LAST ISSUE! --PK
CHAMPION? PLEASE.
I HAD THAT BOOK LONG ENOUGH TO SEE WHAT THIS ISLAND IS, MOTHER SOUL.
THE TRUTH OF WHY YOU BROUGHT ALL THE FIGHTERS HERE...WHY YOU BEGAN THIS LITTLE DEATH TOURNAMENT...
"THE LAZARUS PITS LEAKED INTO THE VERY FOUNDATION OF THE ISLAND ITSELF...INFECTED IT."

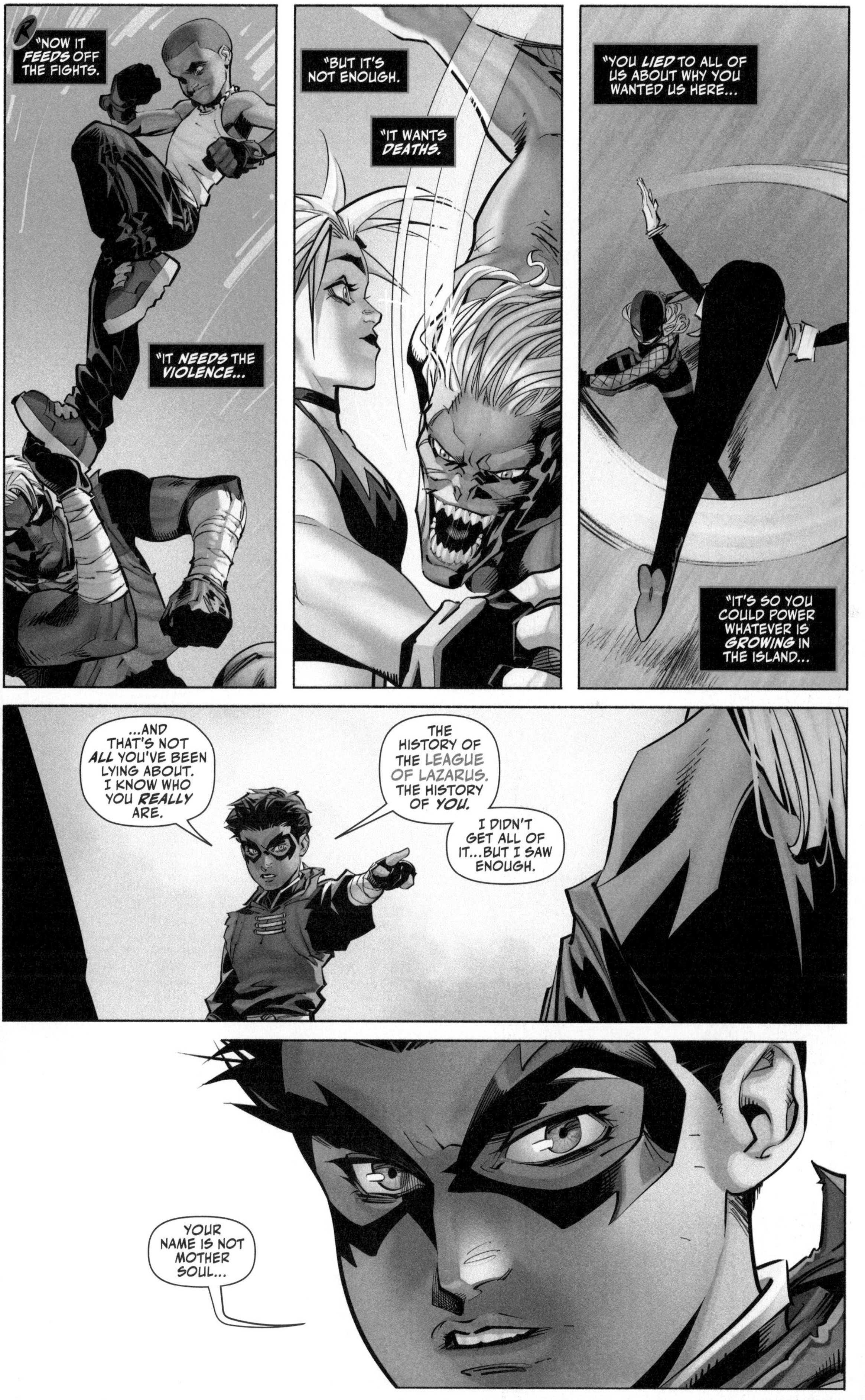

"NOW IT FEEDS OFF THE FIGHTS.
"IT NEEDS THE VIOLENCE...
"BUT IT'S NOT ENOUGH.
"IT WANTS DEATHS.
"YOU LIED TO ALL OF US ABOUT WHY YOU WANTED US HERE...
"IT'S SO YOU COULD POWER WHATEVER IS GROWING IN THE ISLAND...
...AND THAT'S NOT ALL YOU'VE BEEN LYING ABOUT. I KNOW WHO YOU REALLY ARE.
THE HISTORY OF THE LEAGUE OF LAZARUS. THE HISTORY OF YOU.
I DIDN'T GET ALL OF IT...BUT I SAW ENOUGH.
YOUR NAME IS NOT MOTHER SOUL...

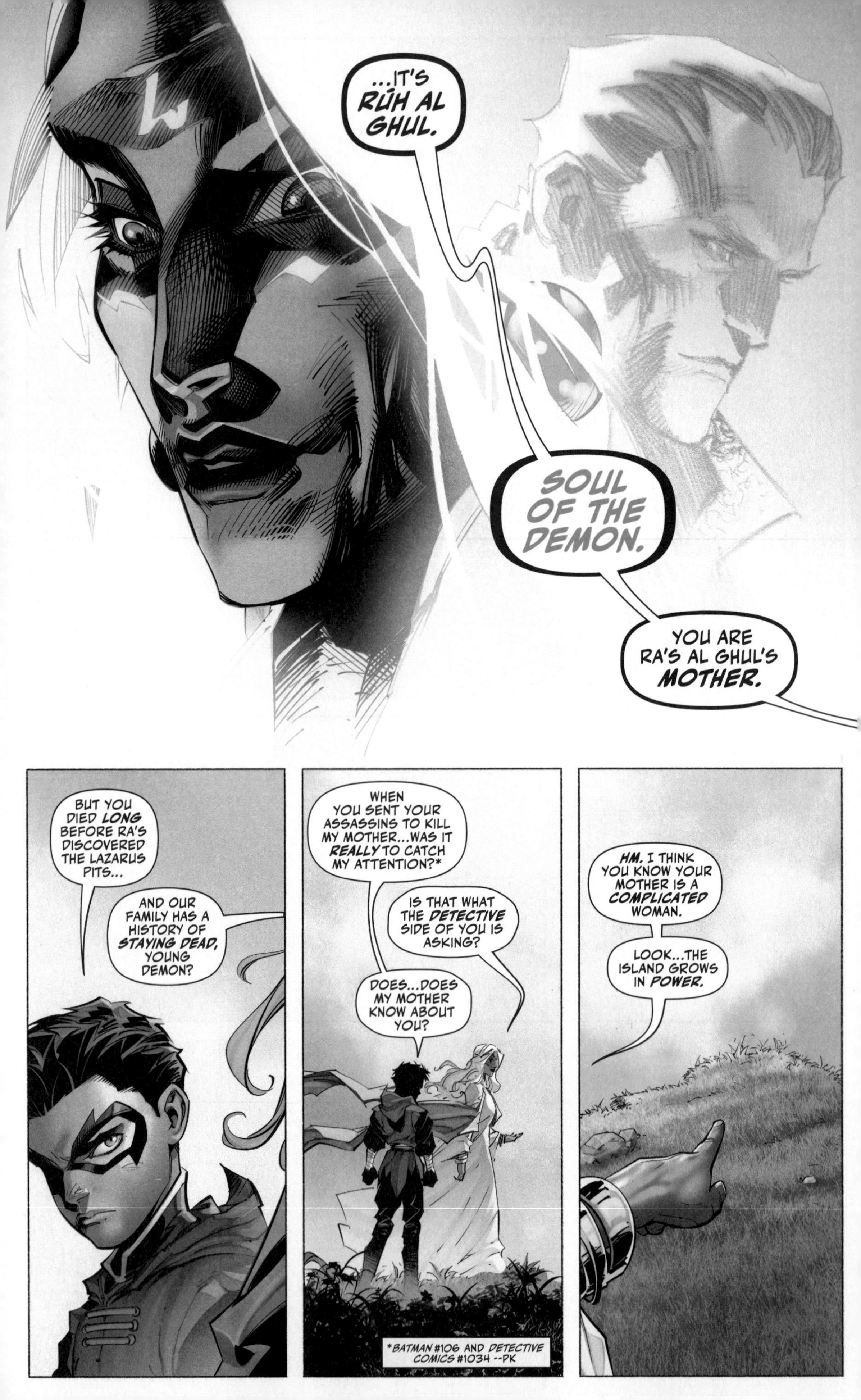
...IT'S RŪH AL GHUL.
SOUL OF THE DEMON.
YOU ARE RA'S AL GHUL'S MOTHER.
BUT YOU DIED LONG BEFORE RA'S DISCOVERED THE LAZARUS PITS...
AND OUR FAMILY HAS A HISTORY OF STAYING DEAD, YOUNG DEMON?
WHEN YOU SENT YOUR ASSASSINS TO KILL MY MOTHER...WAS IT REALLY TO CATCH MY ATTENTION?*
IS THAT WHAT THE DETECTIVE SIDE OF YOU IS ASKING?
DOES...DOES MY MOTHER KNOW ABOUT YOU?
*BATMAN #106 AND DETECTIVE COMICS #1034 --PK
HM. I THINK YOU KNOW YOUR MOTHER IS A COMPLICATED WOMAN.
LOOK...THE ISLAND GROWS IN POWER.

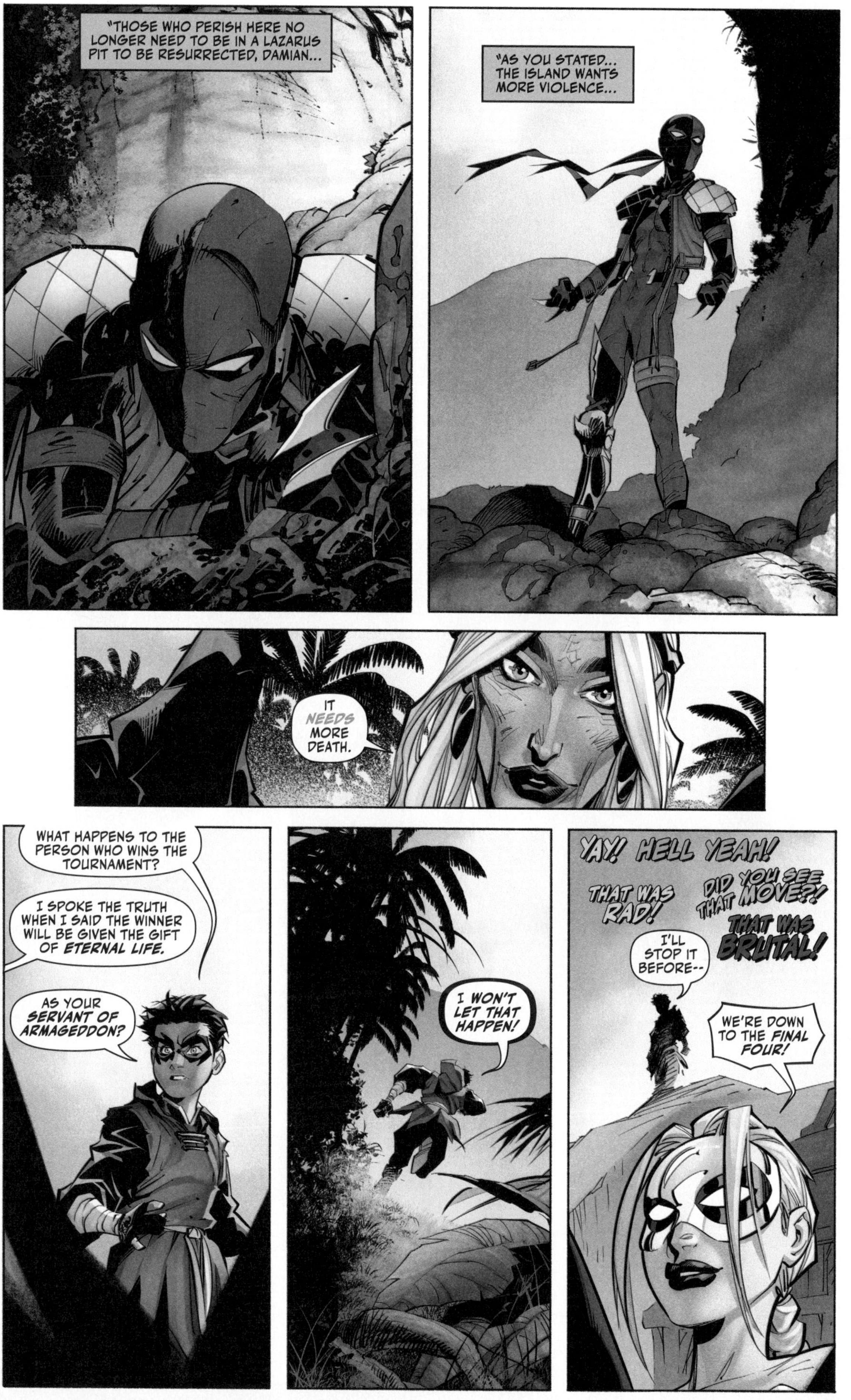
"THOSE WHO PERISH HERE NO LONGER NEED TO BE IN A LAZARUS PIT TO BE RESURRECTED, DAMIAN...
"AS YOU STATED... THE ISLAND WANTS MORE VIOLENCE...
IT NEEDS MORE DEATH.
WHAT HAPPENS TO THE PERSON WHO WINS THE TOURNAMENT?
I SPOKE THE TRUTH WHEN I SAID THE WINNER WILL BE GIVEN THE GIFT OF ETERNAL LIFE.
AS YOUR SERVANT OF ARMAGEDDON?
I WON'T LET THAT HAPPEN!
YAY! HELL YEAH!
THAT WAS RAD!
DID YOU SEE THAT MOVE?!
THAT WAS BRUTAL!
I'LL STOP IT BEFORE--
WE'RE DOWN TO THE FINAL FOUR!

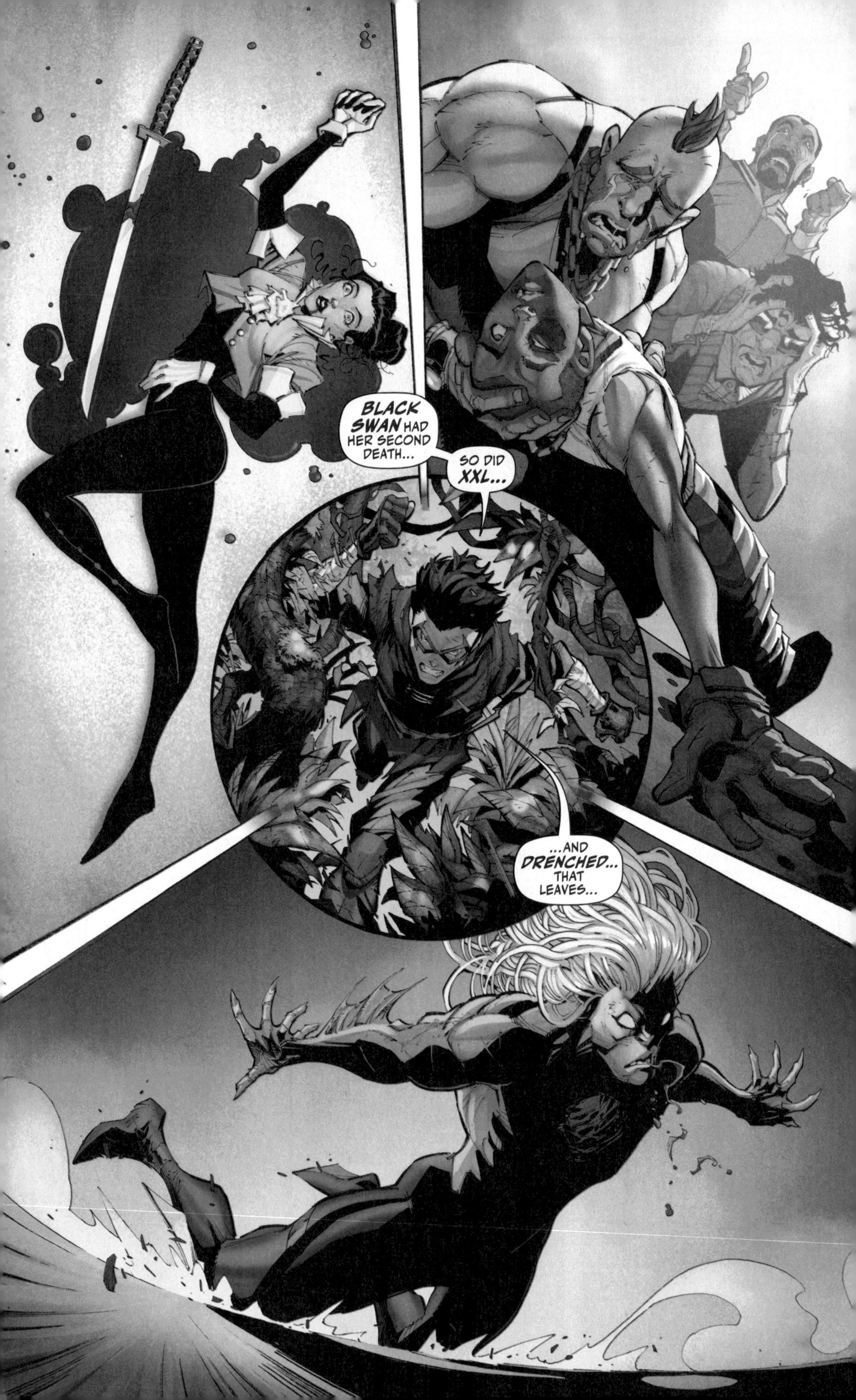
BLACK SWAN HAD HER SECOND DEATH...
SO DID XXL...
...AND DRENCHED... THAT LEAVES...

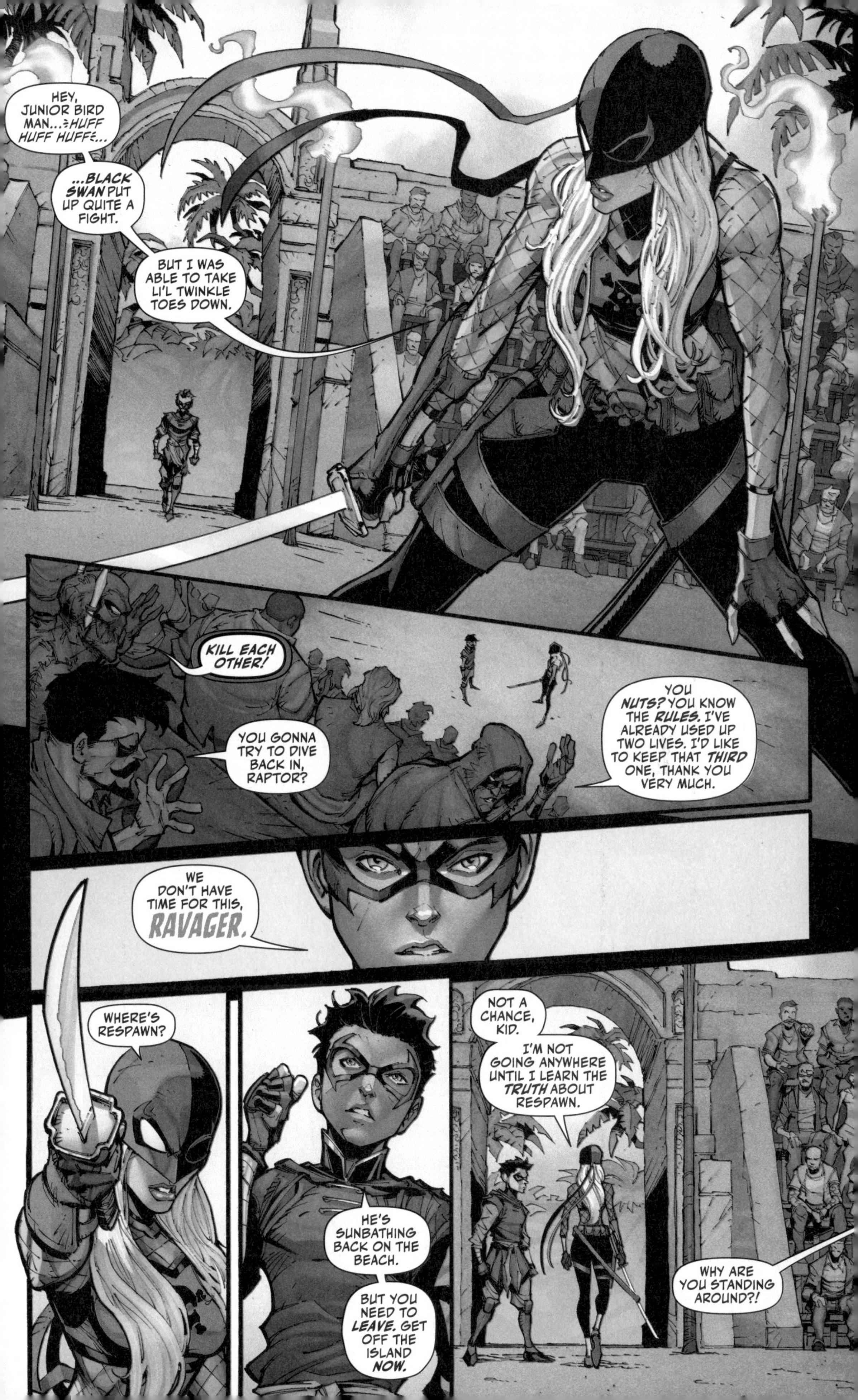
HEY, JUNIOR BIRD MAN... ≈HUFF HUFF HUFF≈...
...BLACK SWAN PUT UP QUITE A FIGHT.
BUT I WAS ABLE TO TAKE LI'L TWINKLE TOES DOWN.
KILL EACH OTHER!
YOU GONNA TRY TO DIVE BACK IN, RAPTOR?
YOU NUTS? YOU KNOW THE RULES. I'VE ALREADY USED UP TWO LIVES. I'D LIKE TO KEEP THAT THIRD ONE, THANK YOU VERY MUCH.
WE DON'T HAVE TIME FOR THIS, RAVAGER.
WHERE'S RESPAWN?
HE'S SUNBATHING BACK ON THE BEACH.
BUT YOU NEED TO LEAVE. GET OFF THE ISLAND NOW.
NOT A CHANCE, KID.
I'M NOT GOING ANYWHERE UNTIL I LEARN THE TRUTH ABOUT RESPAWN.
WHY ARE YOU STANDING AROUND?!

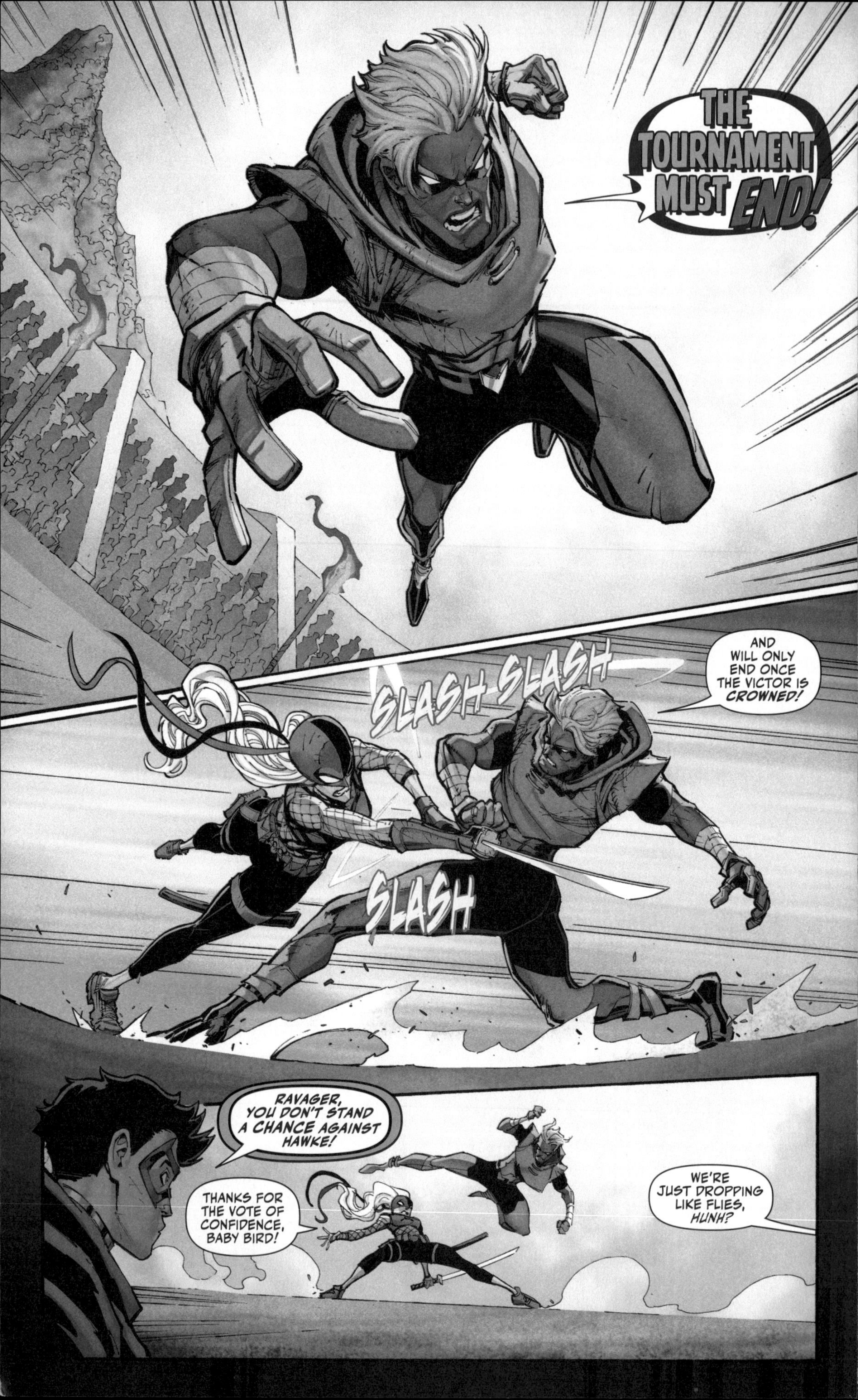
THE TOURNAMENT MUST END!
SLASH SLASH
AND WILL ONLY END ONCE THE VICTOR IS CROWNED!
SLASH
RAVAGER, YOU DON'T STAND A CHANCE AGAINST HAWKE!
THANKS FOR THE VOTE OF CONFIDENCE, BABY BIRD!
WE'RE JUST DROPPING LIKE FLIES, HUNH?

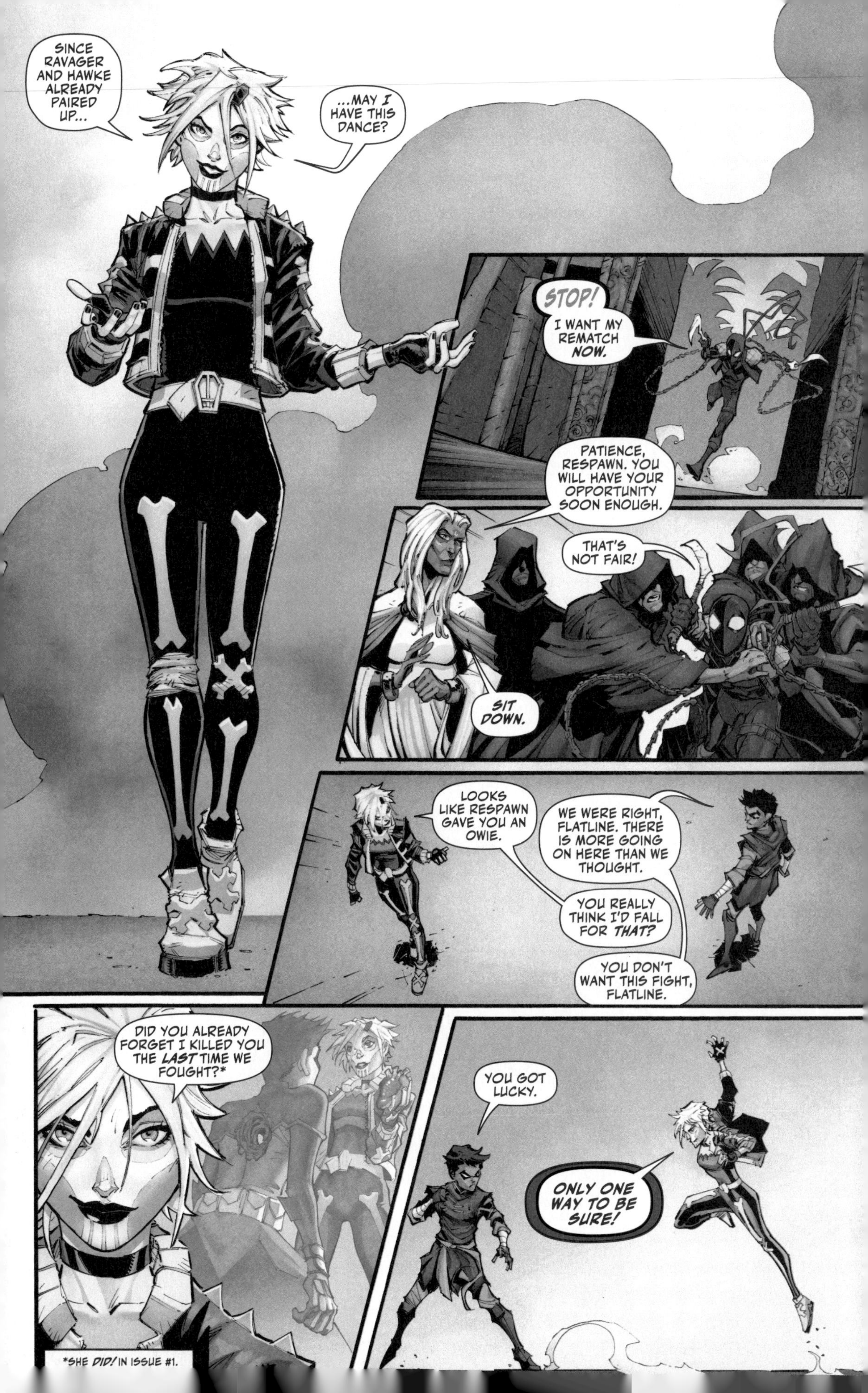
SINCE RAVAGER AND HAWKE ALREADY PAIRED UP...
...MAY I HAVE THIS DANCE?
STOP!
I WANT MY REMATCH NOW.
PATIENCE, RESPAWN. YOU WILL HAVE YOUR OPPORTUNITY SOON ENOUGH.
THAT'S NOT FAIR!
SIT DOWN.
LOOKS LIKE RESPAWN GAVE YOU AN OWIE.
WE WERE RIGHT, FLATLINE. THERE IS MORE GOING ON HERE THAN WE THOUGHT.
YOU REALLY THINK I'D FALL FOR THAT?
YOU DON'T WANT THIS FIGHT, FLATLINE.
DID YOU ALREADY FORGET I KILLED YOU THE LAST TIME WE FOUGHT?*
*SHE DID! IN ISSUE #1.
YOU GOT LUCKY.
ONLY ONE WAY TO BE SURE!

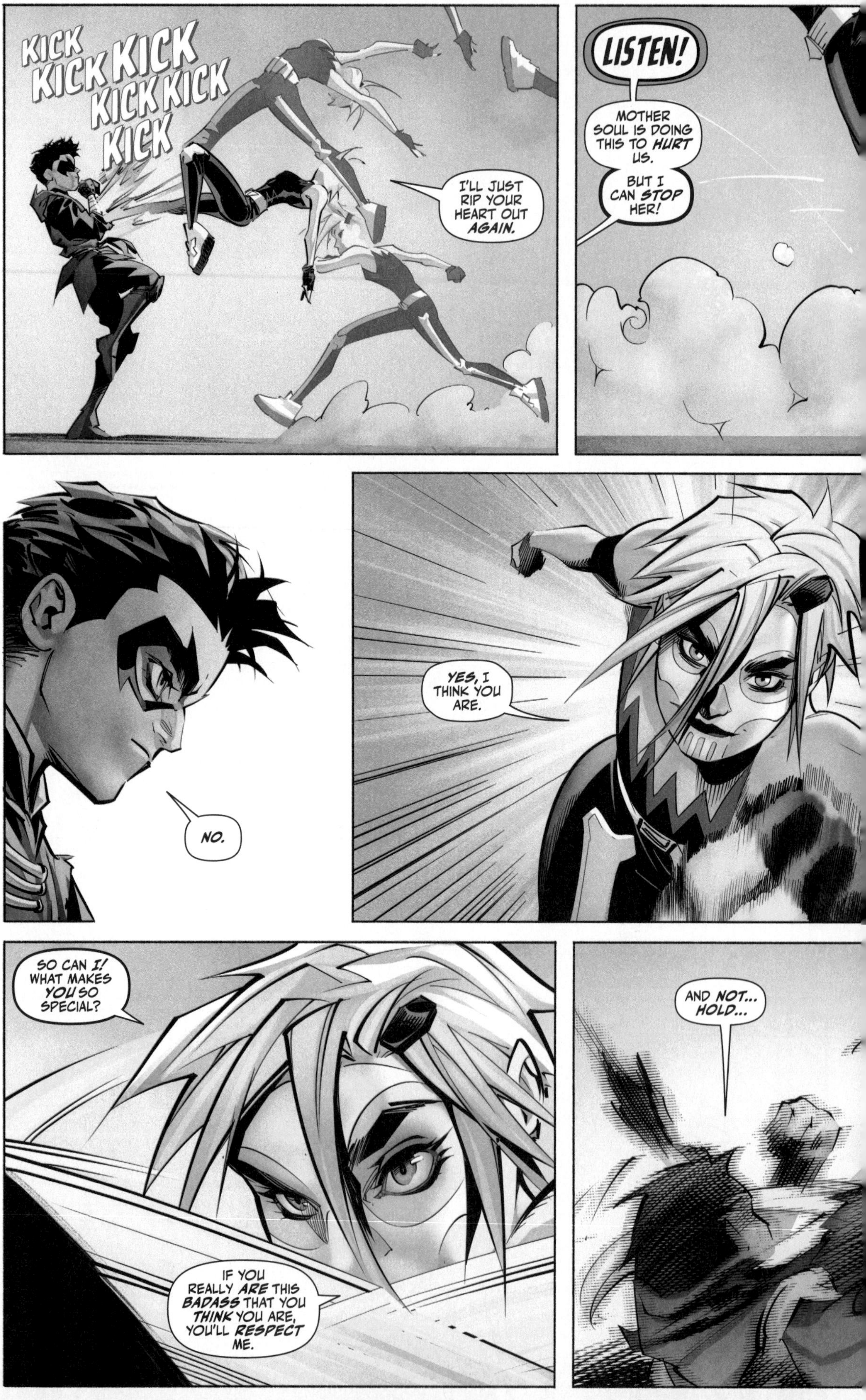
KICK KICK KICK KICK KICK KICK
I'LL JUST RIP YOUR HEART OUT AGAIN.
LISTEN!
MOTHER SOUL IS DOING THIS TO HURT US.
BUT I CAN STOP HER!
NO.
YES, I THINK YOU ARE.
SO CAN I! WHAT MAKES YOU SO SPECIAL?
IF YOU REALLY ARE THIS BADASS THAT YOU THINK YOU ARE, YOU'LL RESPECT ME.
AND NOT... HOLD...

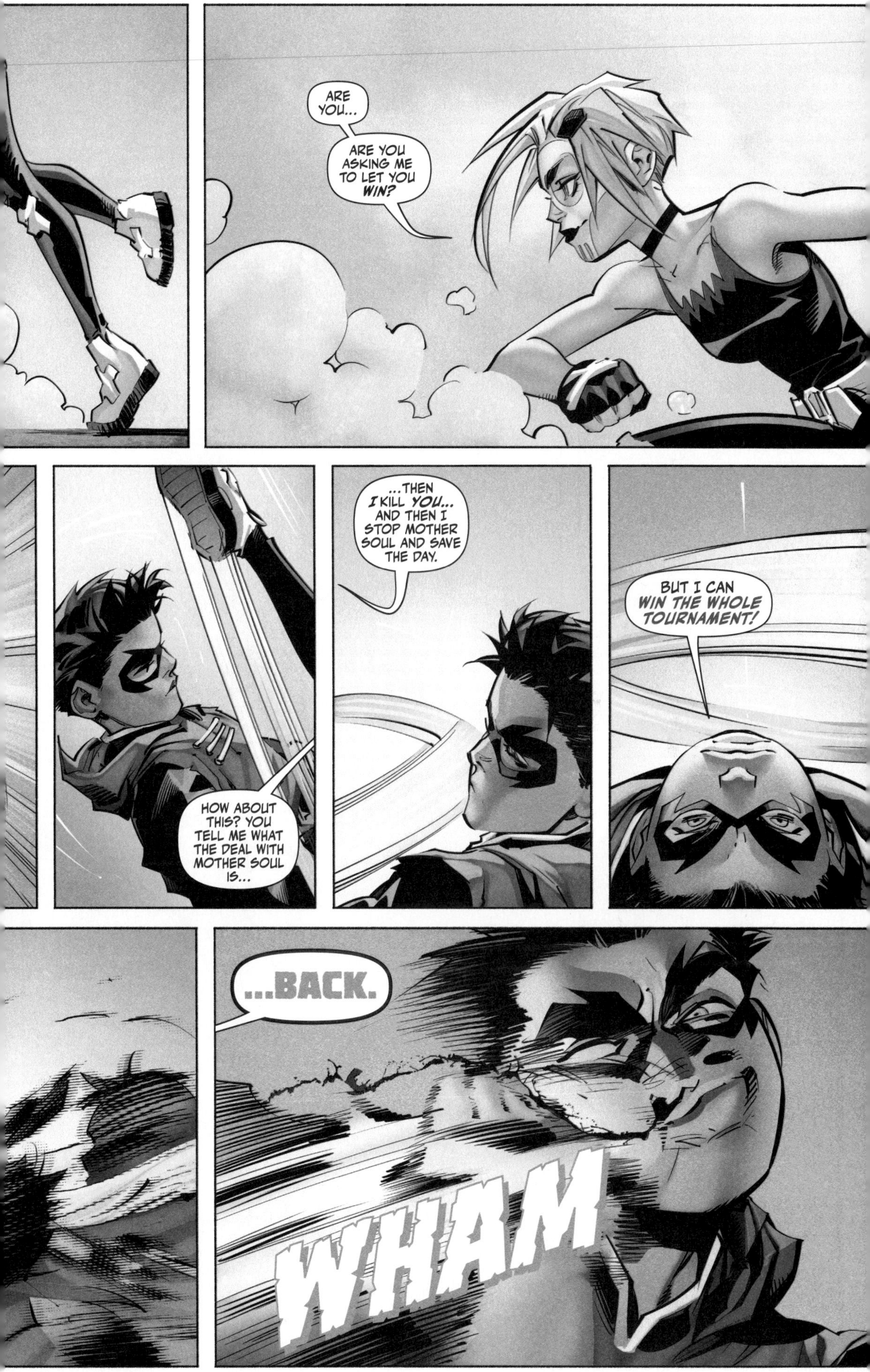
ARE YOU...
ARE YOU ASKING ME TO LET YOU WIN?
HOW ABOUT THIS? YOU TELL ME WHAT THE DEAL WITH MOTHER SOUL IS...
...THEN I KILL YOU... AND THEN I STOP MOTHER SOUL AND SAVE THE DAY.
BUT I CAN WIN THE WHOLE TOURNAMENT!
...BACK.
WHAM

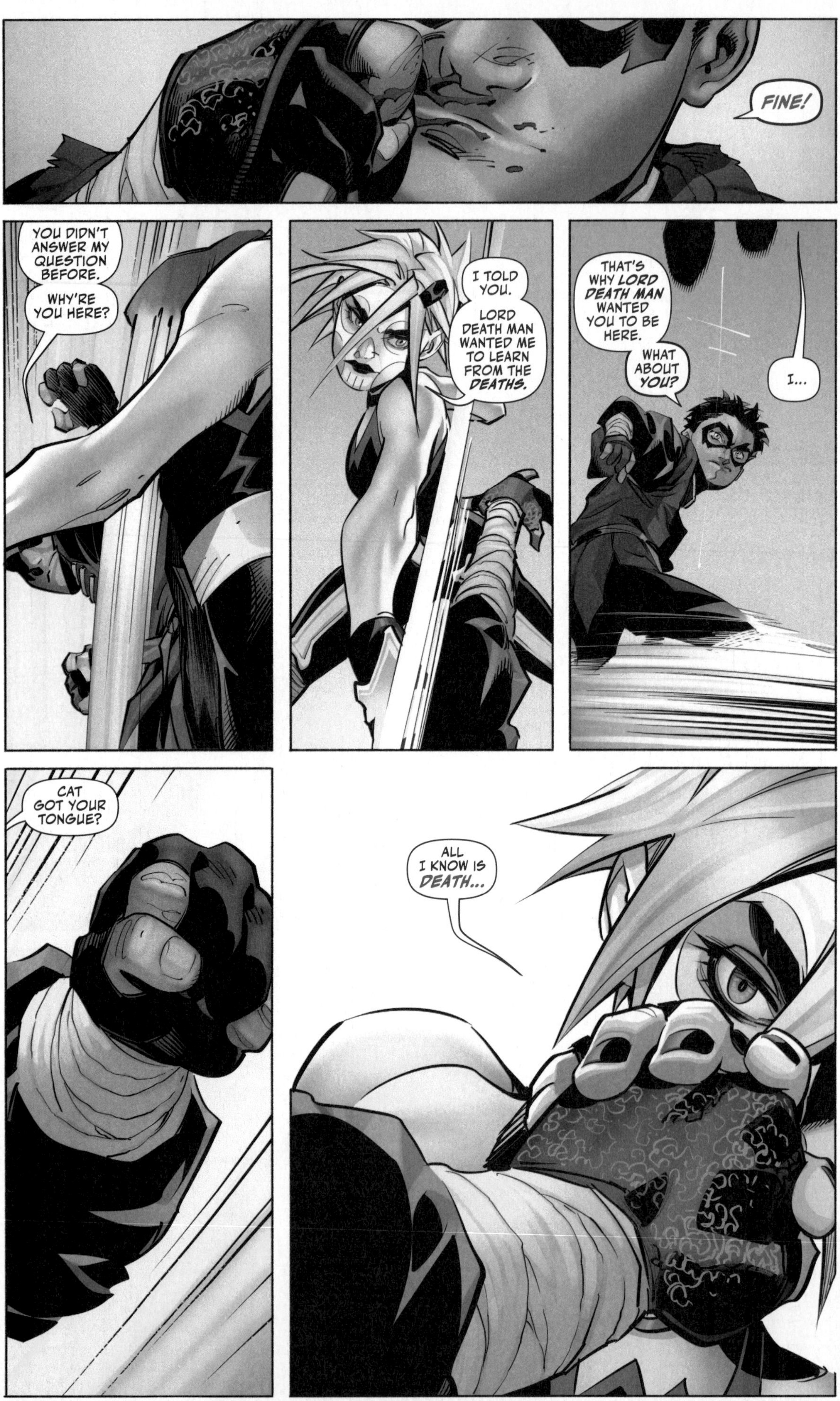

FINE!
YOU DIDN'T ANSWER MY QUESTION BEFORE.
WHY'RE YOU HERE?
I TOLD YOU.
LORD DEATH MAN WANTED ME TO LEARN FROM THE DEATHS.
THAT'S WHY LORD DEATH MAN WANTED YOU TO BE HERE.
WHAT ABOUT YOU?
I...
CAT GOT YOUR TONGUE?
ALL I KNOW IS DEATH...

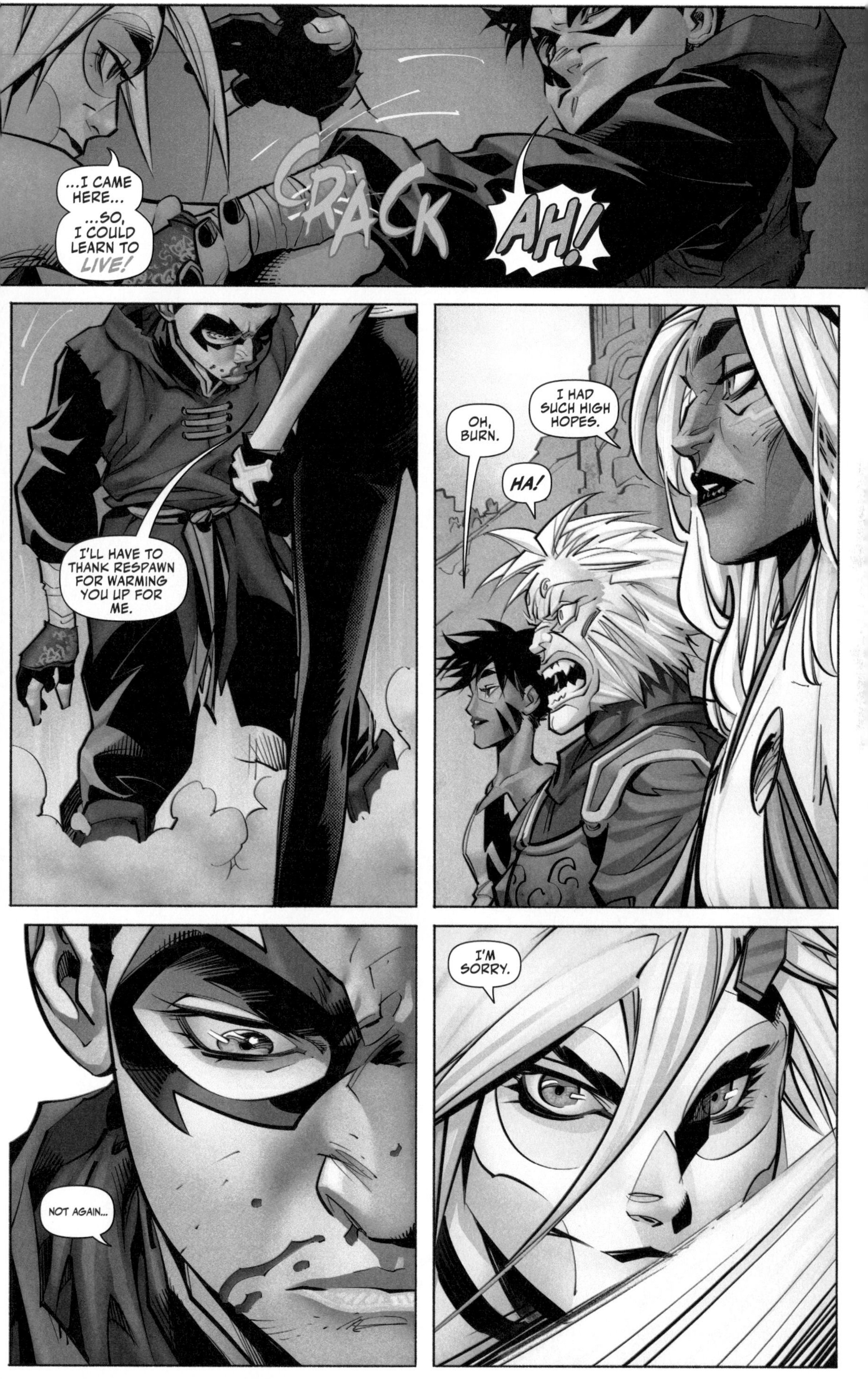
...I CAME HERE...
...SO, I COULD LEARN TO LIVE!
CRACK
AH!
I'LL HAVE TO THANK RESPAWN FOR WARMING YOU UP FOR ME.
I HAD SUCH HIGH HOPES.
OH, BURN.
HA!
NOT AGAIN...
I'M SORRY.

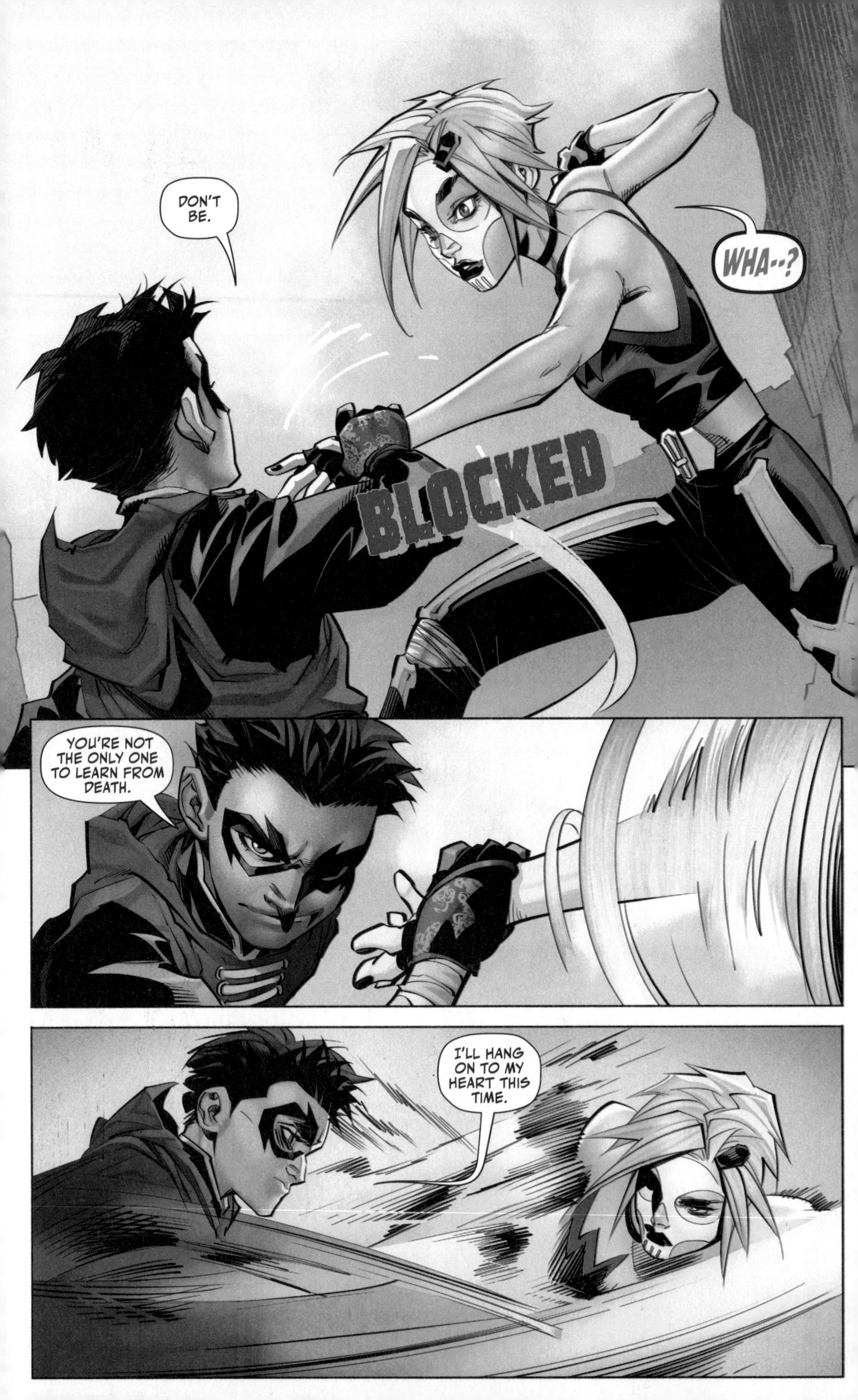
DON'T BE.
WHA--?
BLOCKED
YOU'RE NOT THE ONLY ONE TO LEARN FROM DEATH.
I'LL HANG ON TO MY HEART THIS TIME.

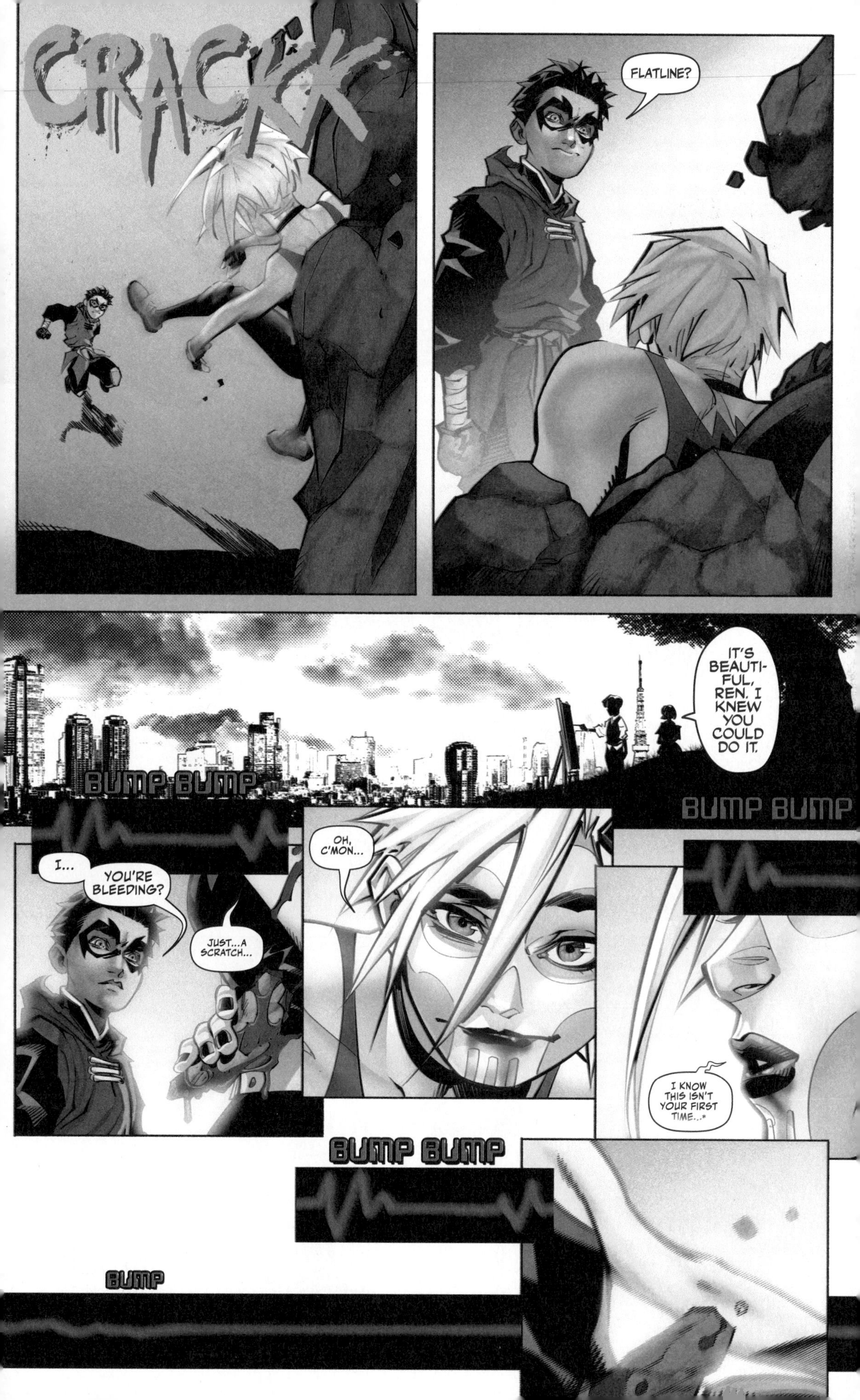
CRACKK
FLATLINE?
IT'S BEAUTIFUL, REN. I KNEW YOU COULD DO IT.
BUMP BUMP
BUMP BUMP
I...
YOU'RE BLEEDING?
JUST...A SCRATCH...
OH, C'MON...
I KNOW THIS ISN'T YOUR FIRST TIME...*
BUMP BUMP
BUMP

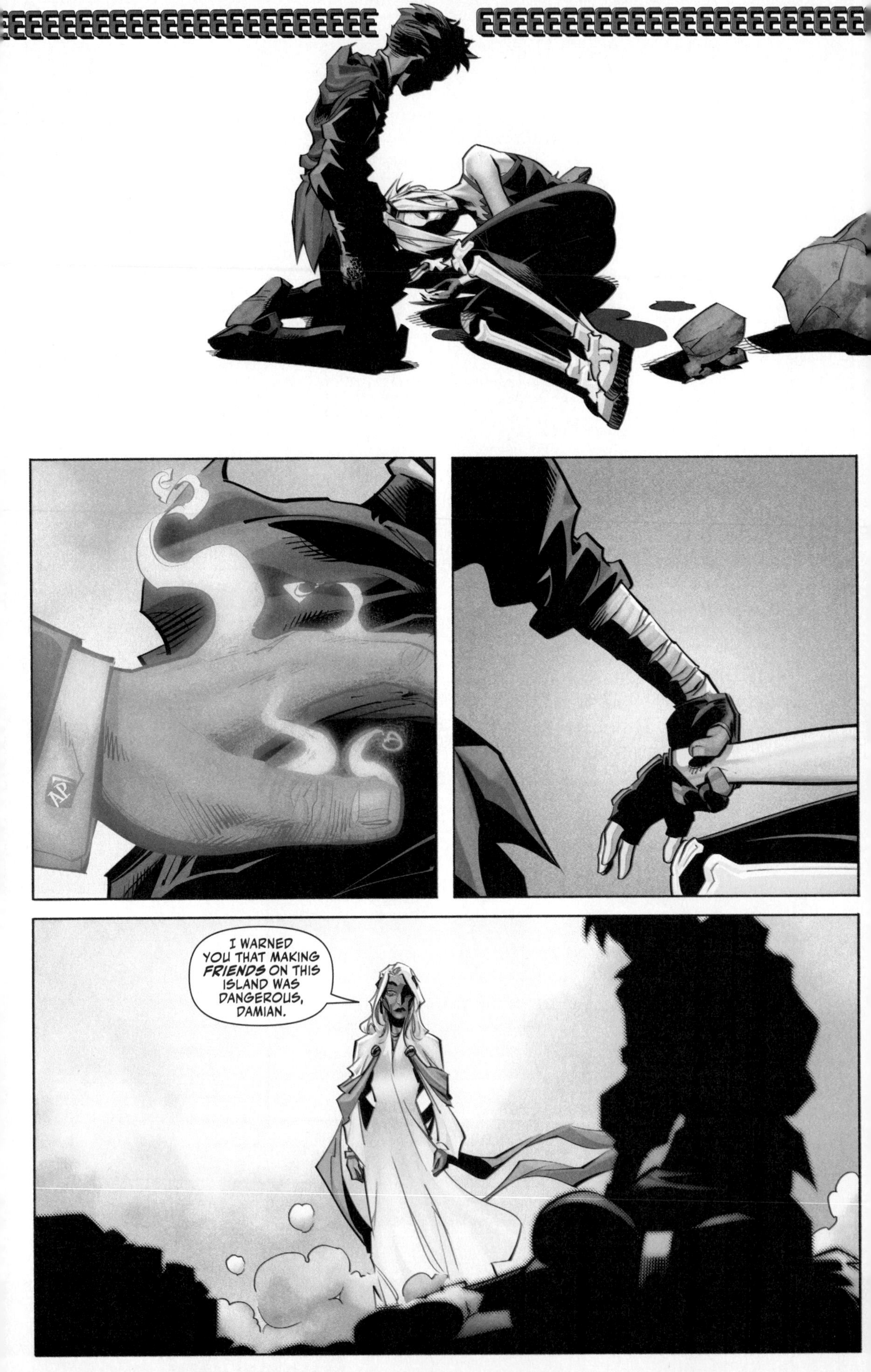
EEEEEEEEEEEEEEEEEEEEEEEEEE
EEEEEEEEEEEEEEEEEEEEEEEEEE
I WARNED YOU THAT MAKING *FRIENDS* ON THIS ISLAND WAS DANGEROUS, DAMIAN.

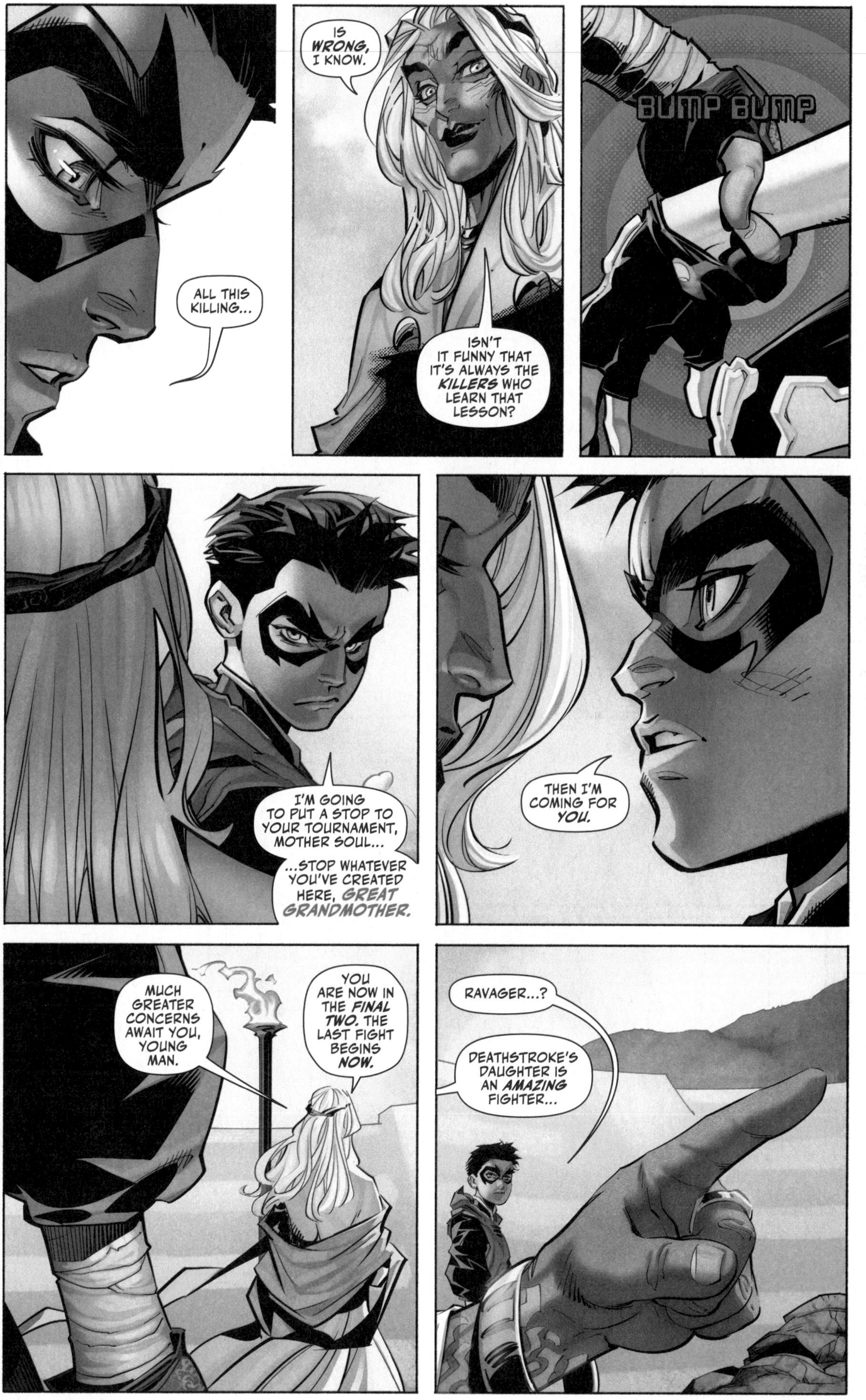

ALL THIS KILLING...
IS WRONG, I KNOW.
ISN'T IT FUNNY THAT IT'S ALWAYS THE KILLERS WHO LEARN THAT LESSON?
BUMP BUMP
I'M GOING TO PUT A STOP TO YOUR TOURNAMENT, MOTHER SOUL...
...STOP WHATEVER YOU'VE CREATED HERE, GREAT GRANDMOTHER.
THEN I'M COMING FOR YOU.
MUCH GREATER CONCERNS AWAIT YOU, YOUNG MAN.
YOU ARE NOW IN THE FINAL TWO. THE LAST FIGHT BEGINS NOW.
RAVAGER...?
DEATHSTROKE'S DAUGHTER IS AN AMAZING FIGHTER...

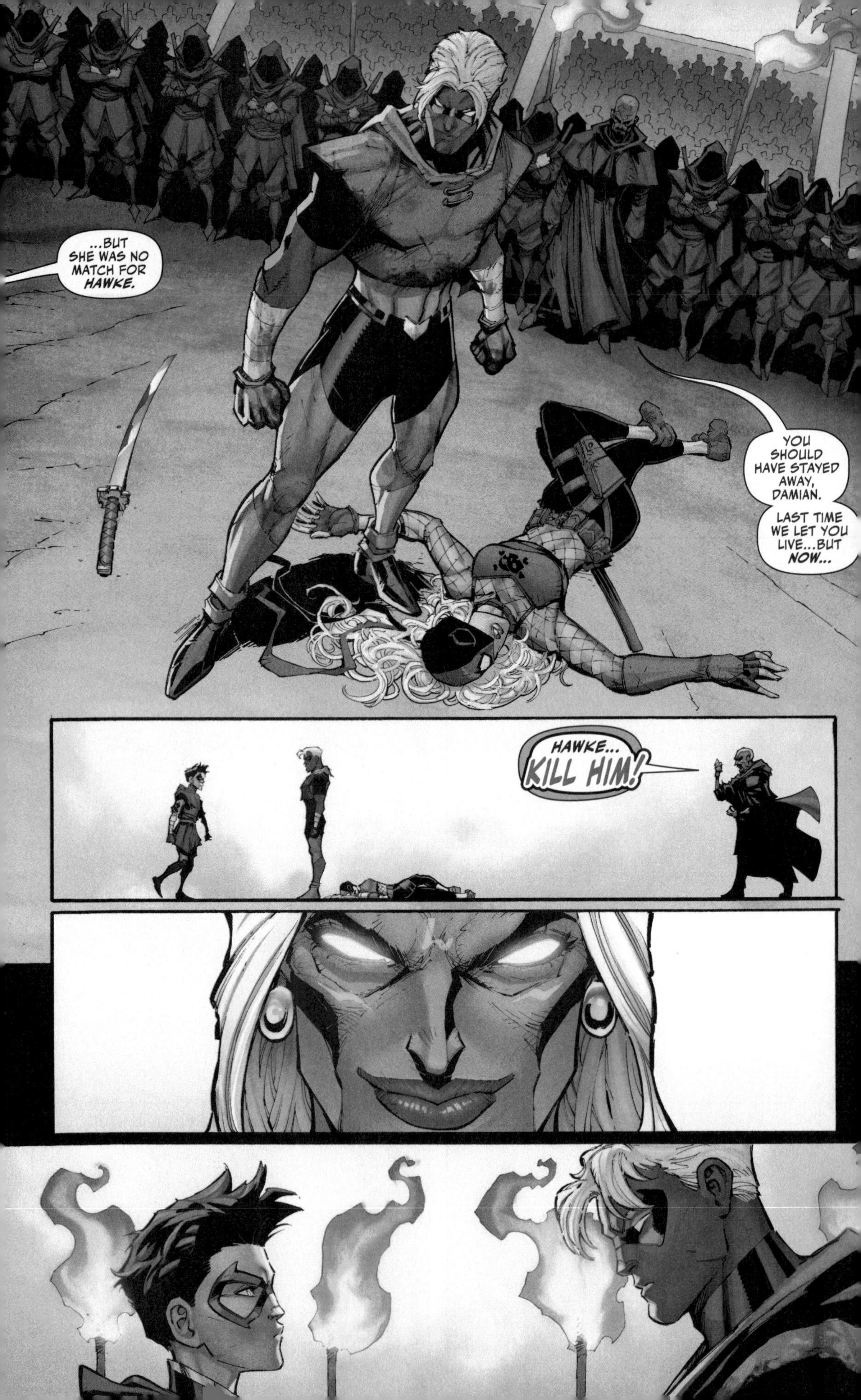
...BUT SHE WAS NO MATCH FOR HAWKE.
YOU SHOULD HAVE STAYED AWAY, DAMIAN.
LAST TIME WE LET YOU LIVE...BUT NOW...
HAWKE... KILL HIM!

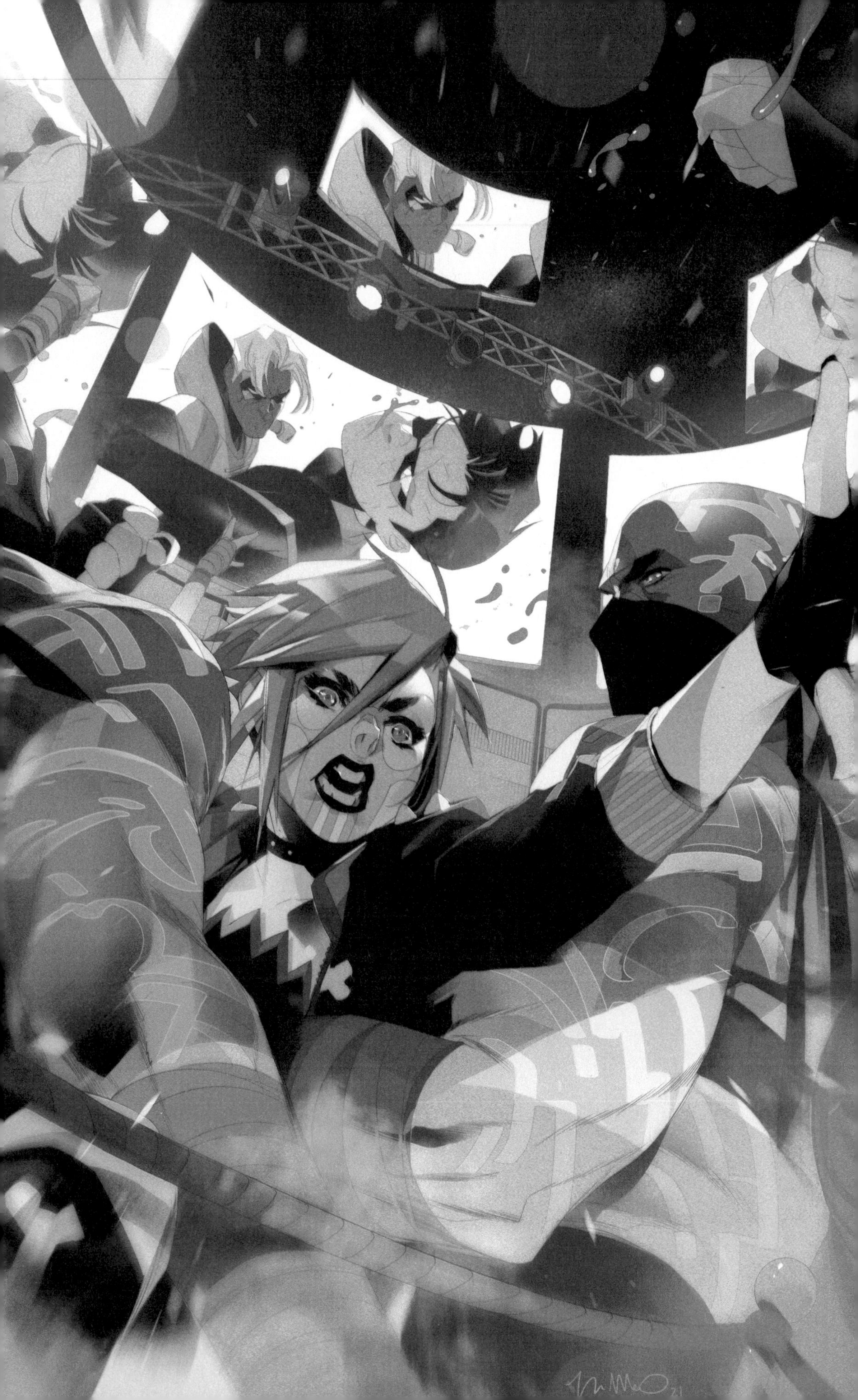

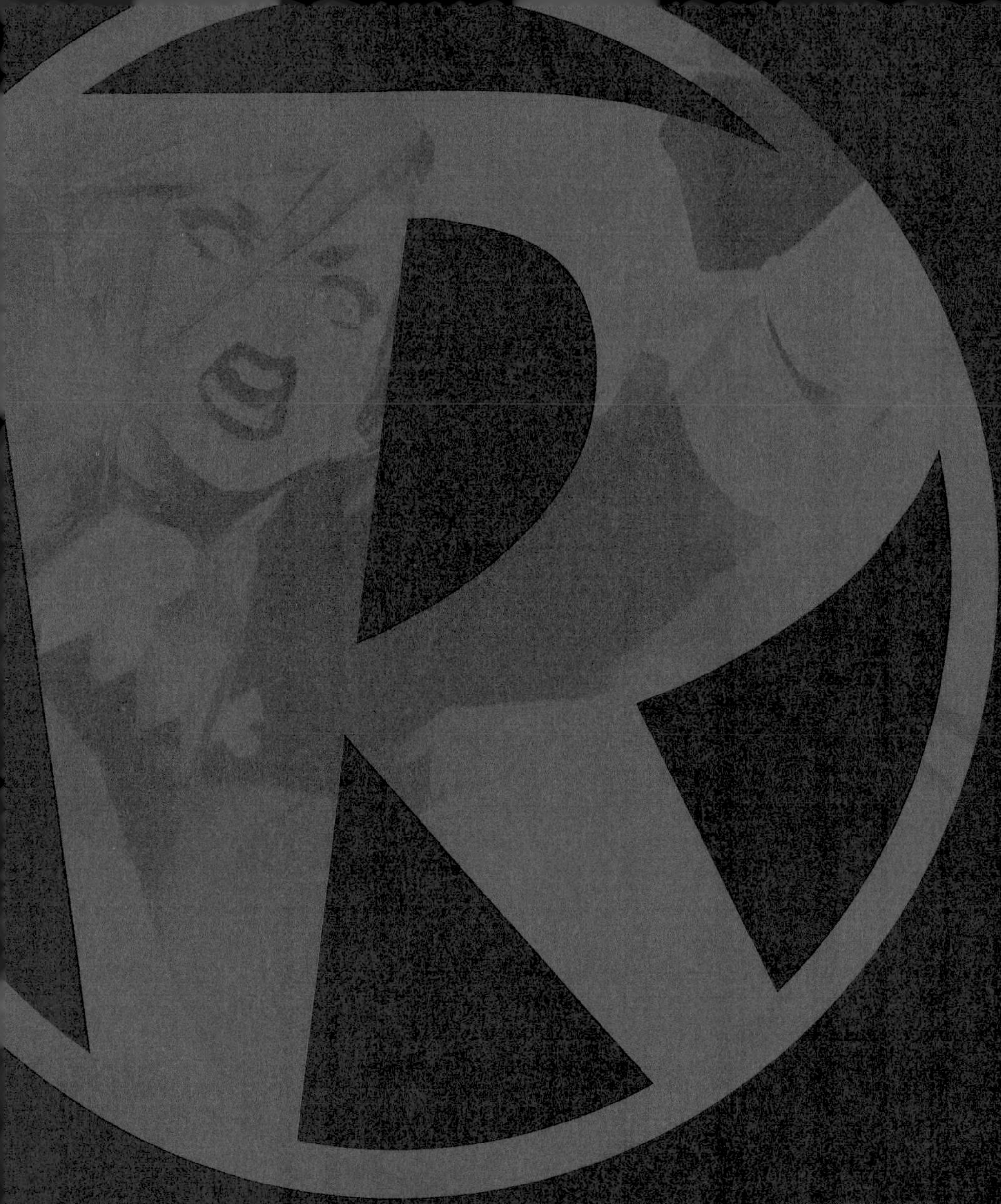

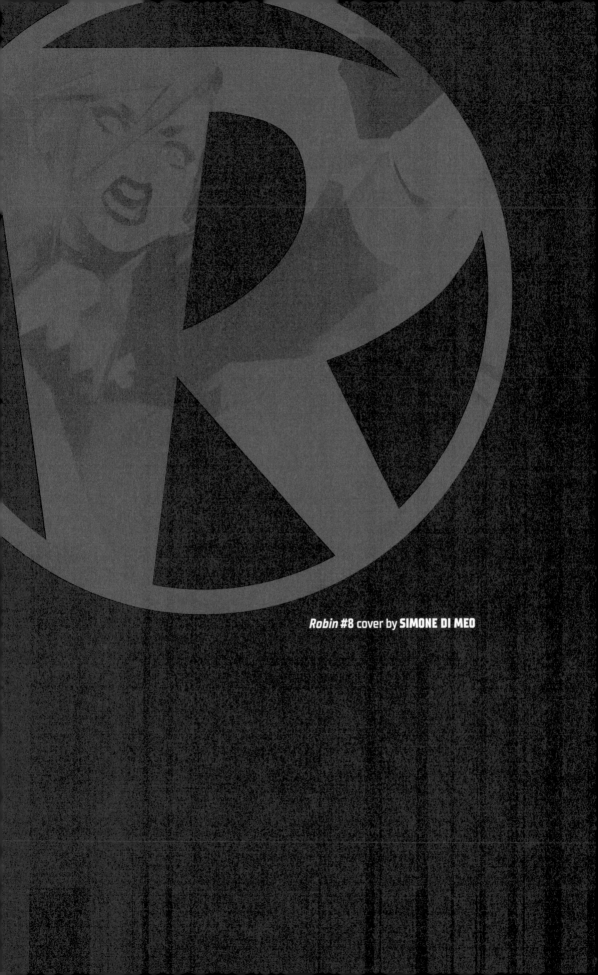

Robin #8 cover by **SIMONE DI MEO**

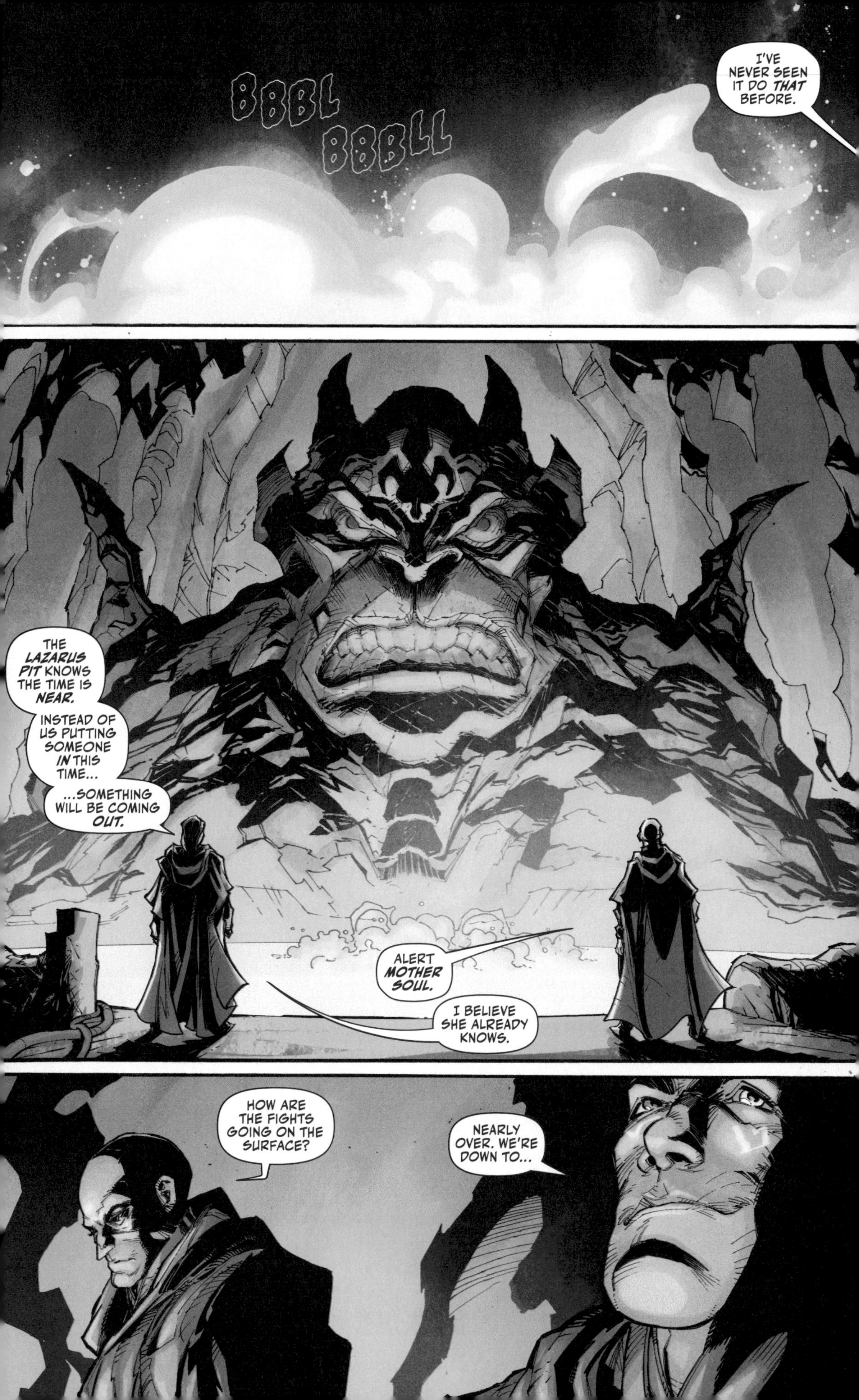
BBBL
BBBLL
I'VE NEVER SEEN IT DO THAT BEFORE.
THE LAZARUS PIT KNOWS THE TIME IS NEAR.
INSTEAD OF US PUTTING SOMEONE IN THIS TIME...
...SOMETHING WILL BE COMING OUT.
ALERT MOTHER SOUL.
I BELIEVE SHE ALREADY KNOWS.
HOW ARE THE FIGHTS GOING ON THE SURFACE?
NEARLY OVER. WE'RE DOWN TO...

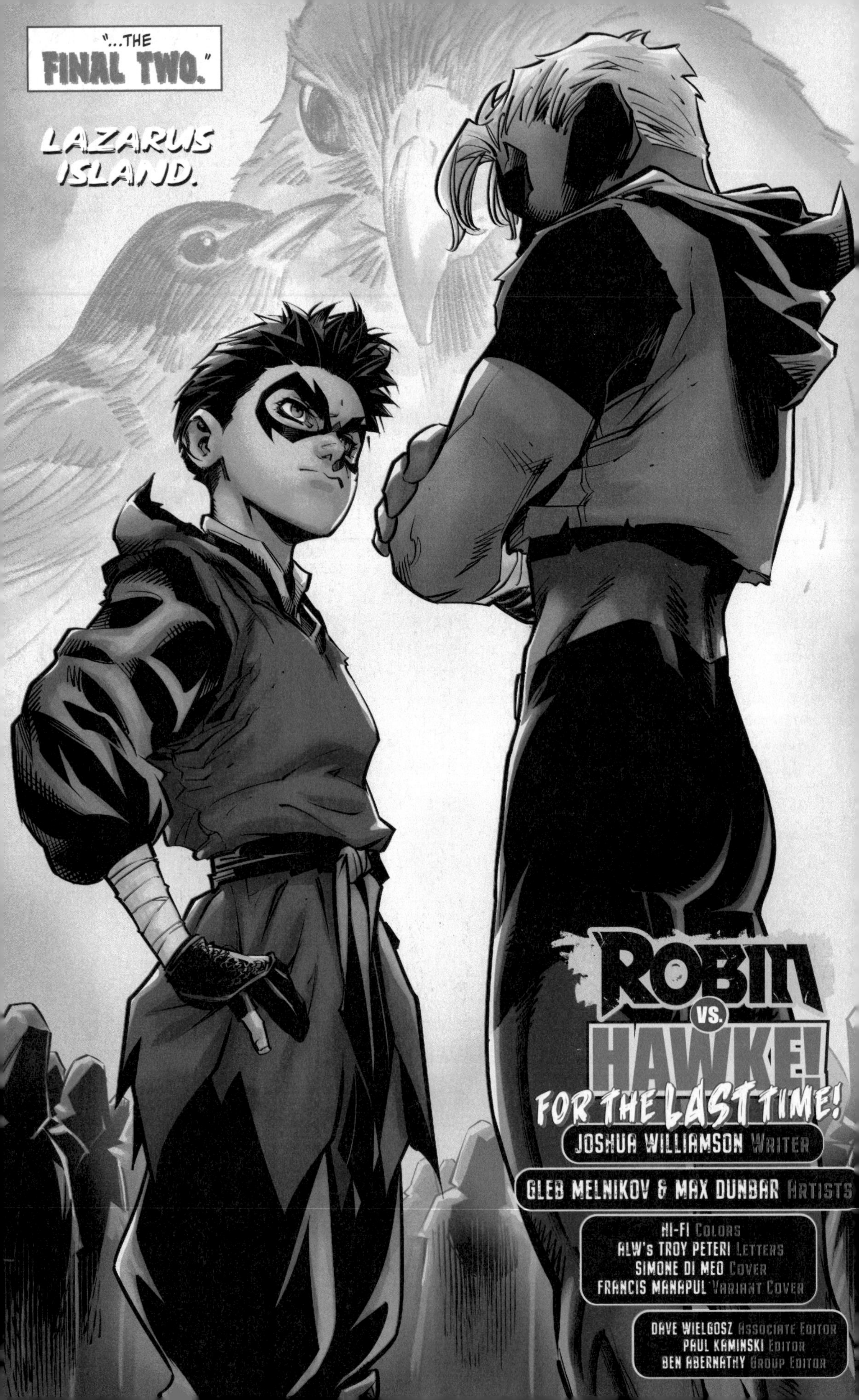
"...THE FINAL TWO."
LAZARUS ISLAND.
ROBIN VS. HAWKE! FOR THE LAST TIME!
JOSHUA WILLIAMSON Writer
GLEB MELNIKOV & MAX DUNBAR Artists
HI-FI Colors
ALW's TROY PETERI Letters
SIMONE DI MEO Cover
FRANCIS MANAPUL Variant Cover
DAVE WIELGOSZ Associate Editor
PAUL KAMINSKI Editor
BEN ABERNATHY Group Editor

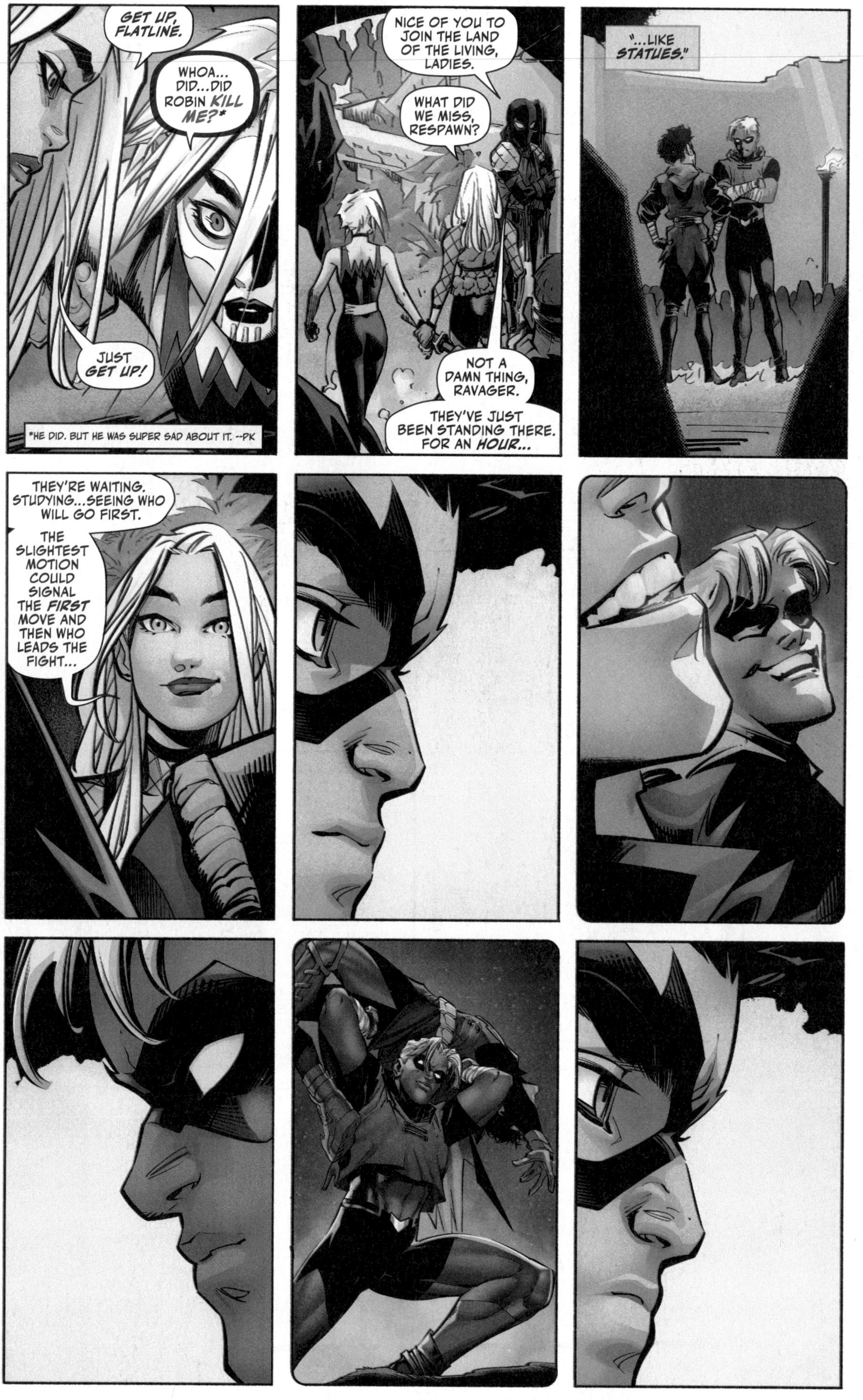
GET UP, FLATLINE.
WHOA... DID...DID ROBIN KILL ME?*
JUST GET UP!
*HE DID. BUT HE WAS SUPER SAD ABOUT IT. --PK
NICE OF YOU TO JOIN THE LAND OF THE LIVING, LADIES.
WHAT DID WE MISS, RESPAWN?
NOT A DAMN THING, RAVAGER.
THEY'VE JUST BEEN STANDING THERE. FOR AN HOUR...
"...LIKE STATUES."
THEY'RE WAITING. STUDYING...SEEING WHO WILL GO FIRST.
THE SLIGHTEST MOTION COULD SIGNAL THE FIRST MOVE AND THEN WHO LEADS THE FIGHT...

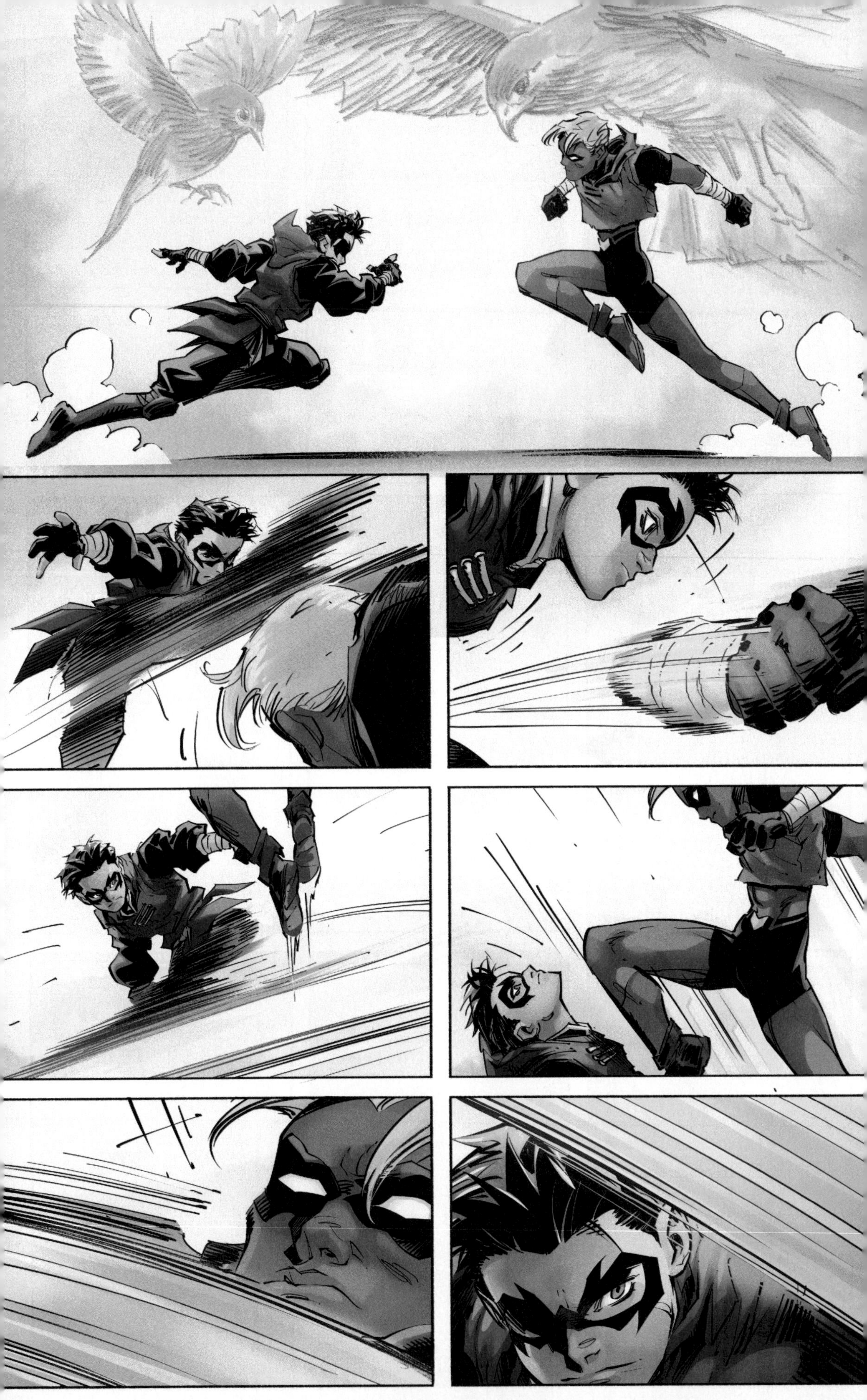

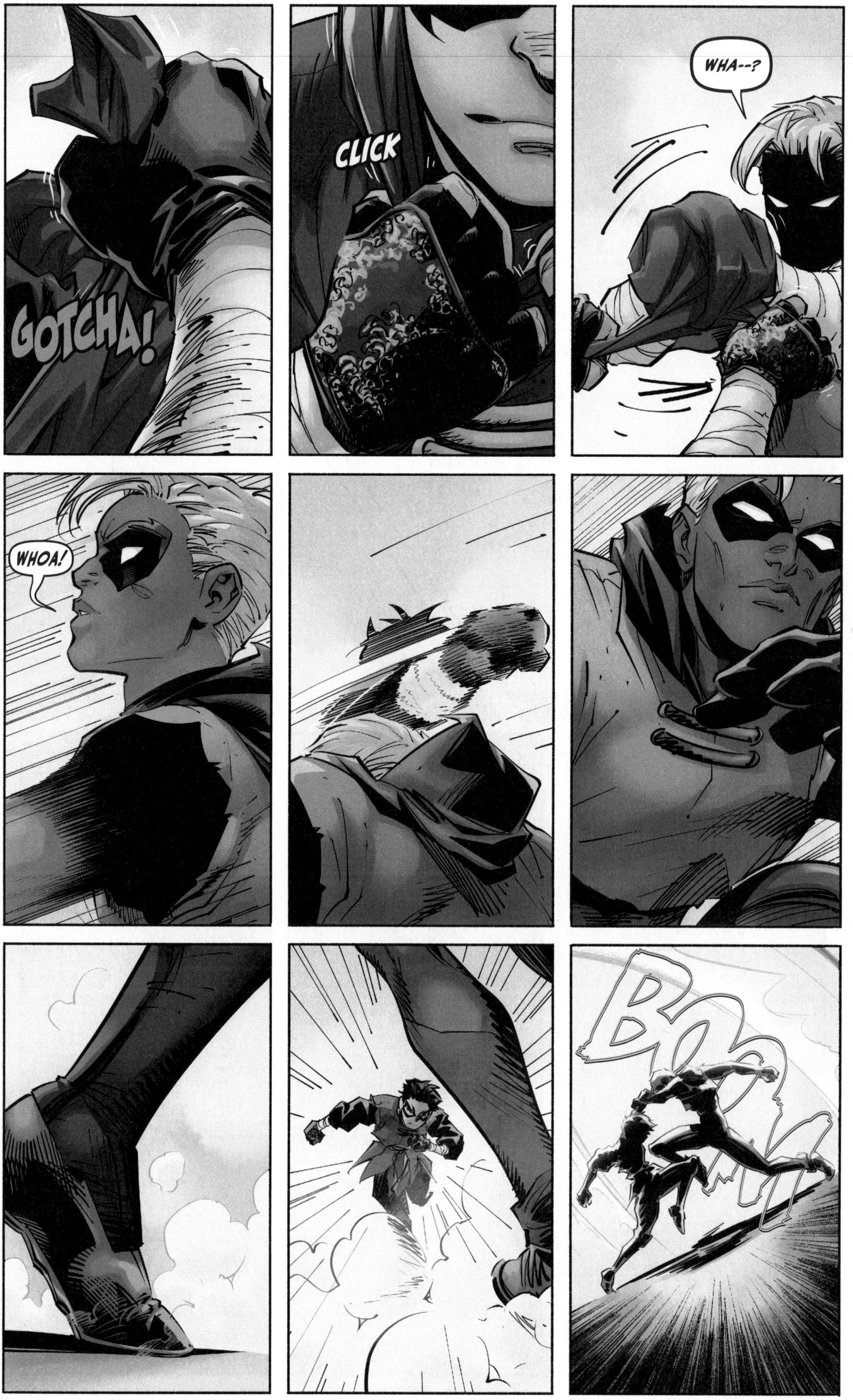
GOTCHA!
CLICK
WHA--?
WHOA!

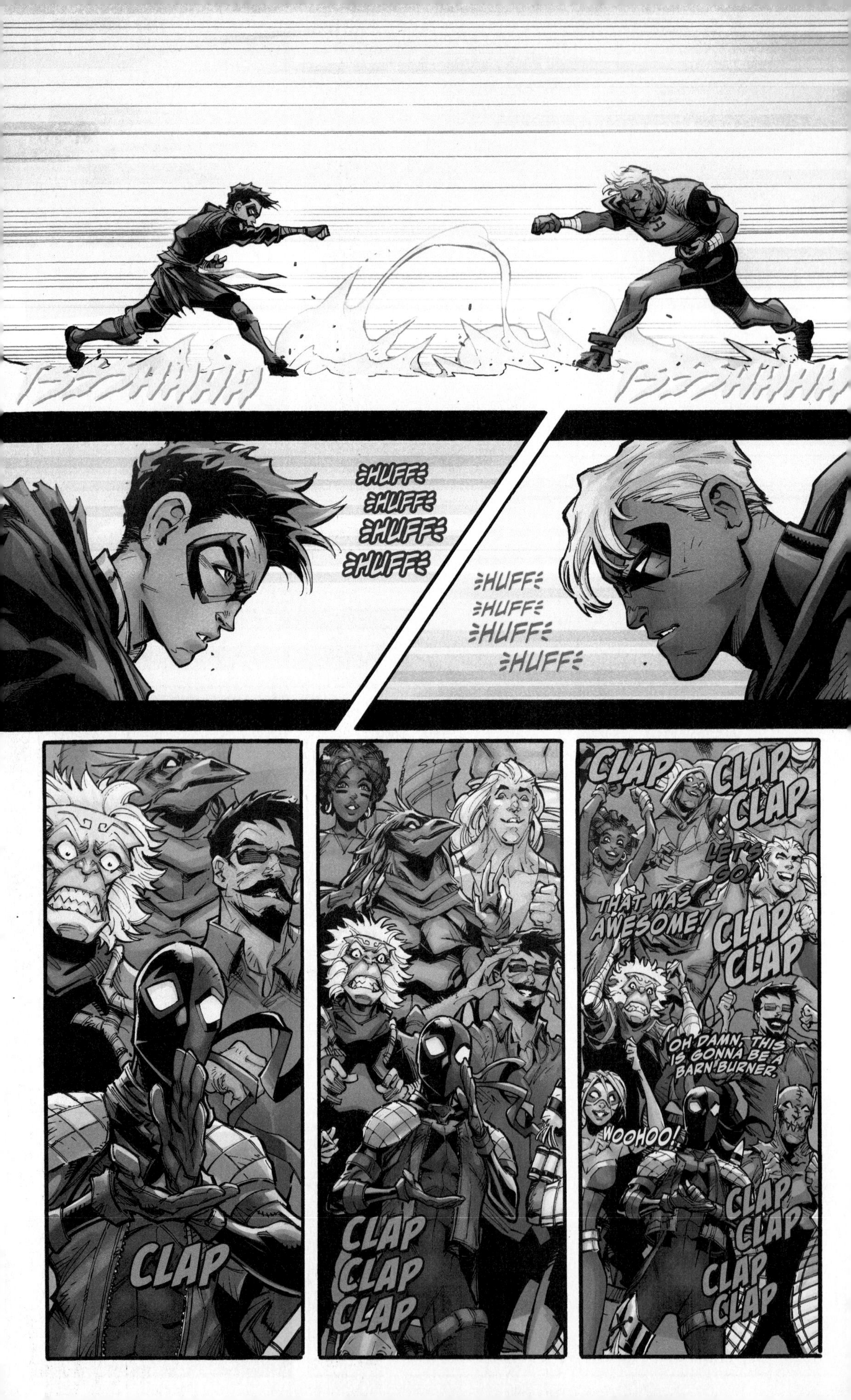

HUFF
HUFF
HUFF
HUFF
HUFF
HUFF
HUFF
HUFF
CLAP
CLAP
CLAP
CLAP
CLAP
CLAP
CLAP
LET'S GO!
THAT WAS AWESOME!
CLAP
CLAP
OH DAMN, THIS IS GONNA BE A BARN BURNER.
WOOHOO!
CLAP
CLAP
CLAP
CLAP

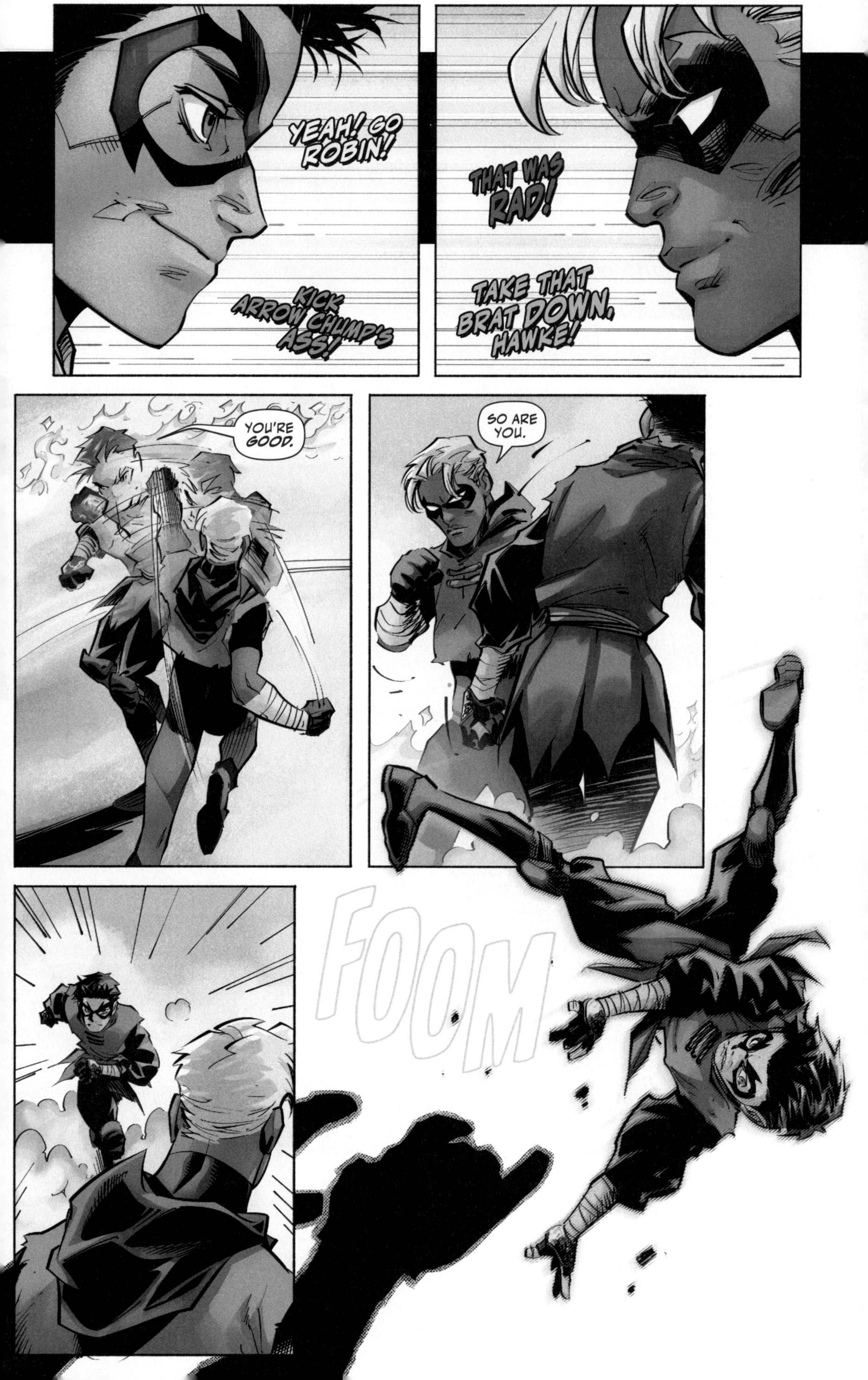
YEAH! GO ROBIN!
KICK ARROW CHUMP'S ASS!
THAT WAS RAD!
TAKE THAT BRAT DOWN, HAWKE!
YOU'RE GOOD.
SO ARE YOU.
FOOM

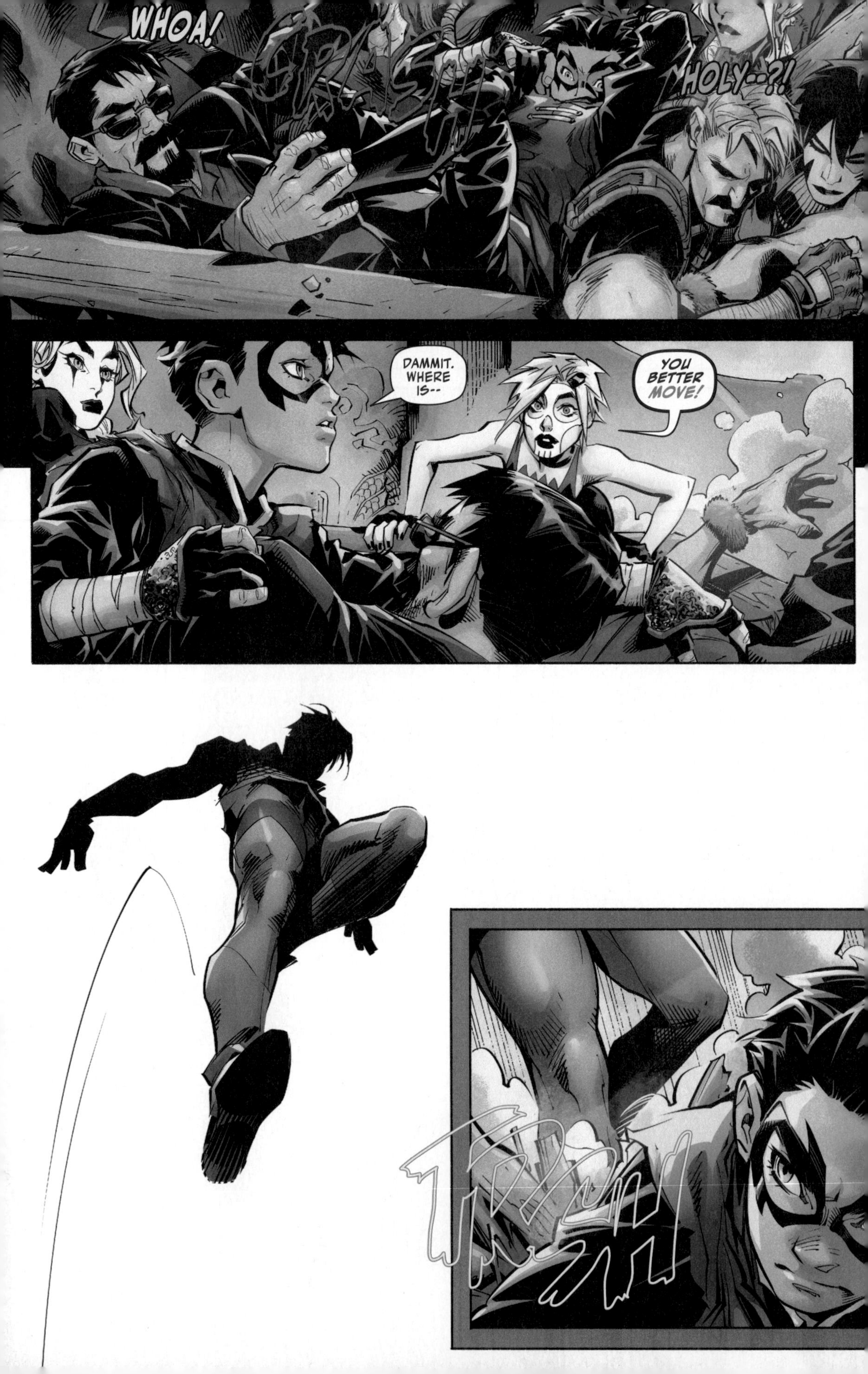
WHOA!
CRASH
HOLY--?!
DAMMIT. WHERE IS--
YOU BETTER MOVE!

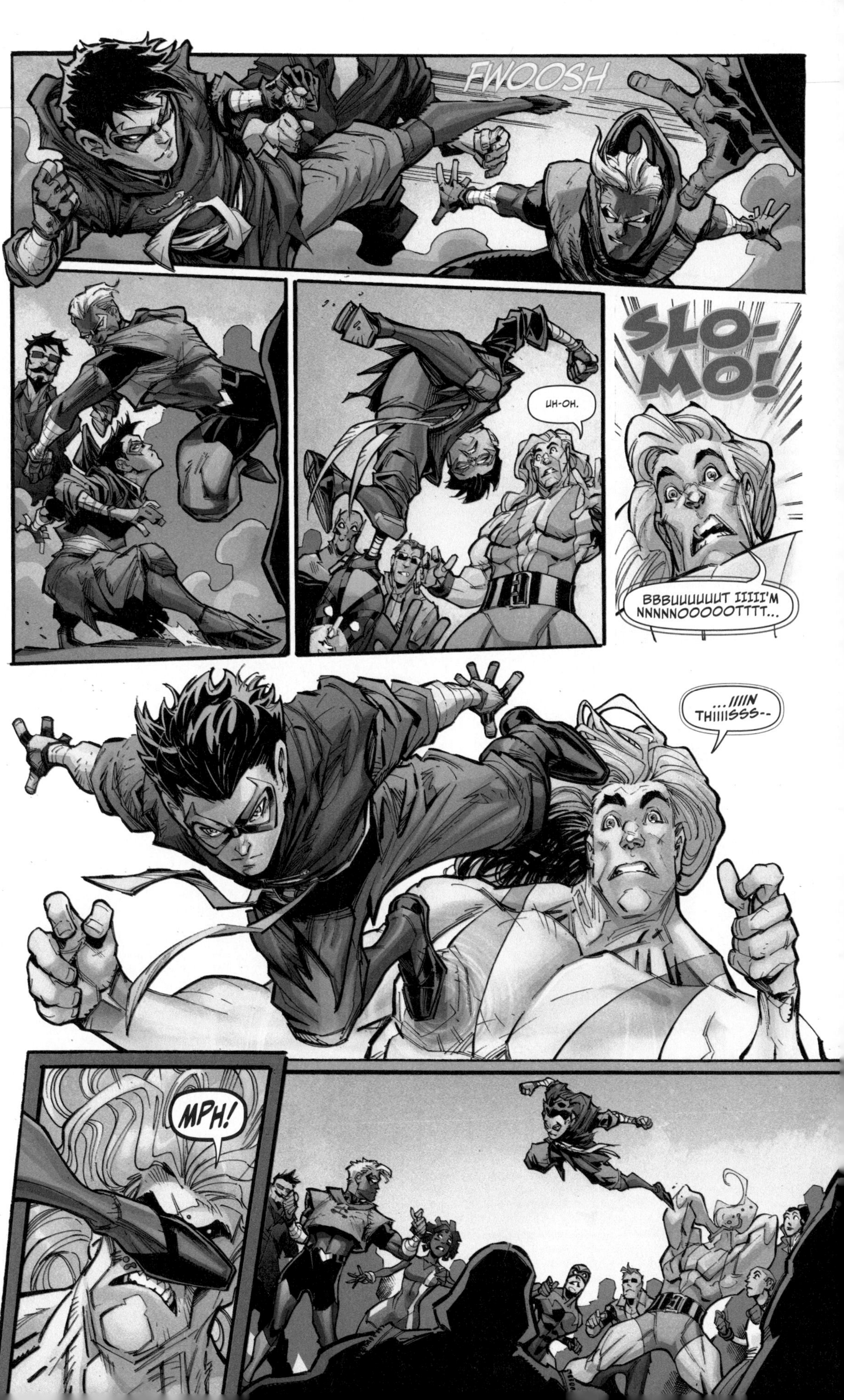
FWOOSH
UH-OH.
SLO-MO!
BBBUUUUUUT IIIII'M NNNNNOOOOOTTTT...
...IIIIN THIIIISSS--
MPH!

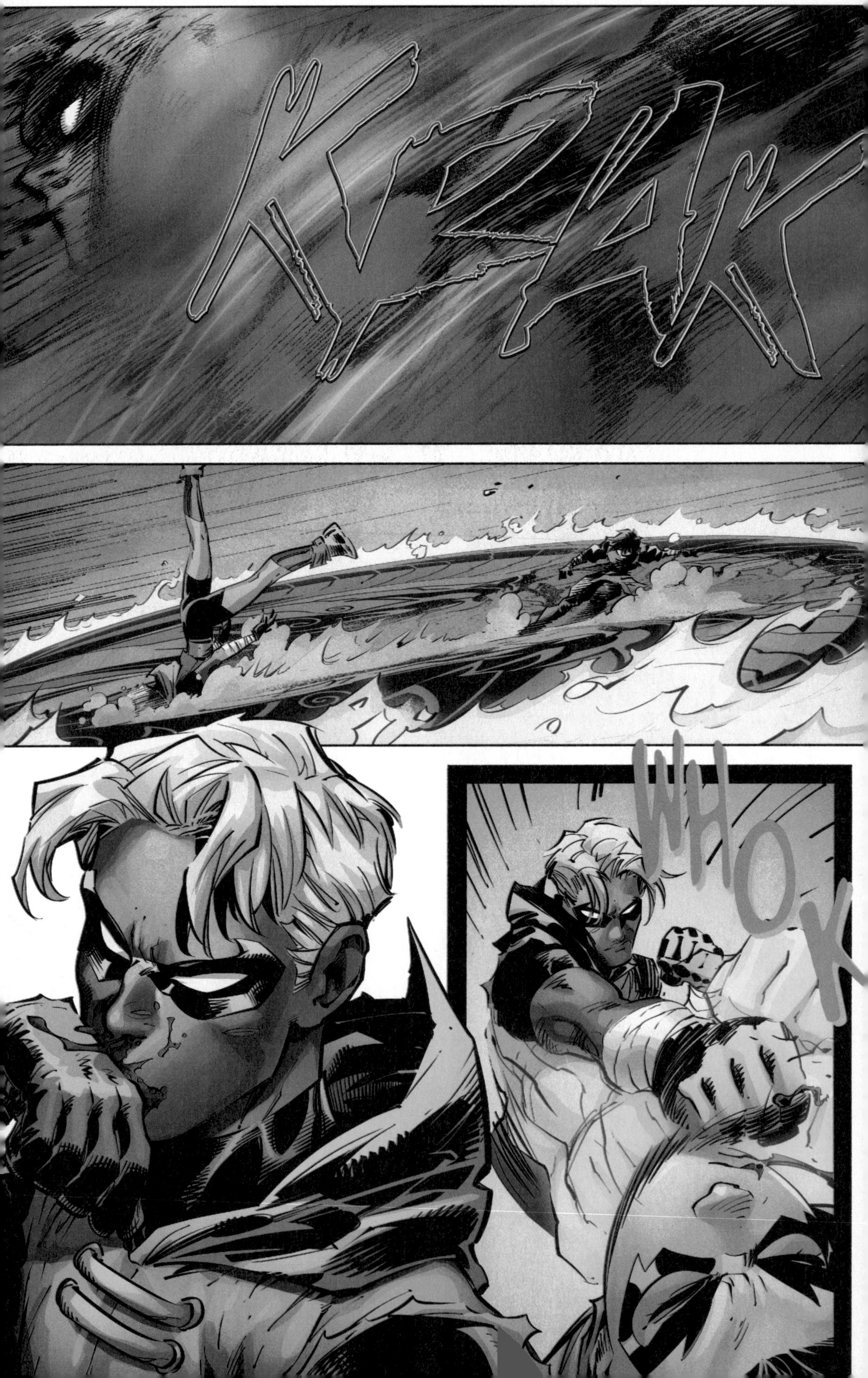
WHOK

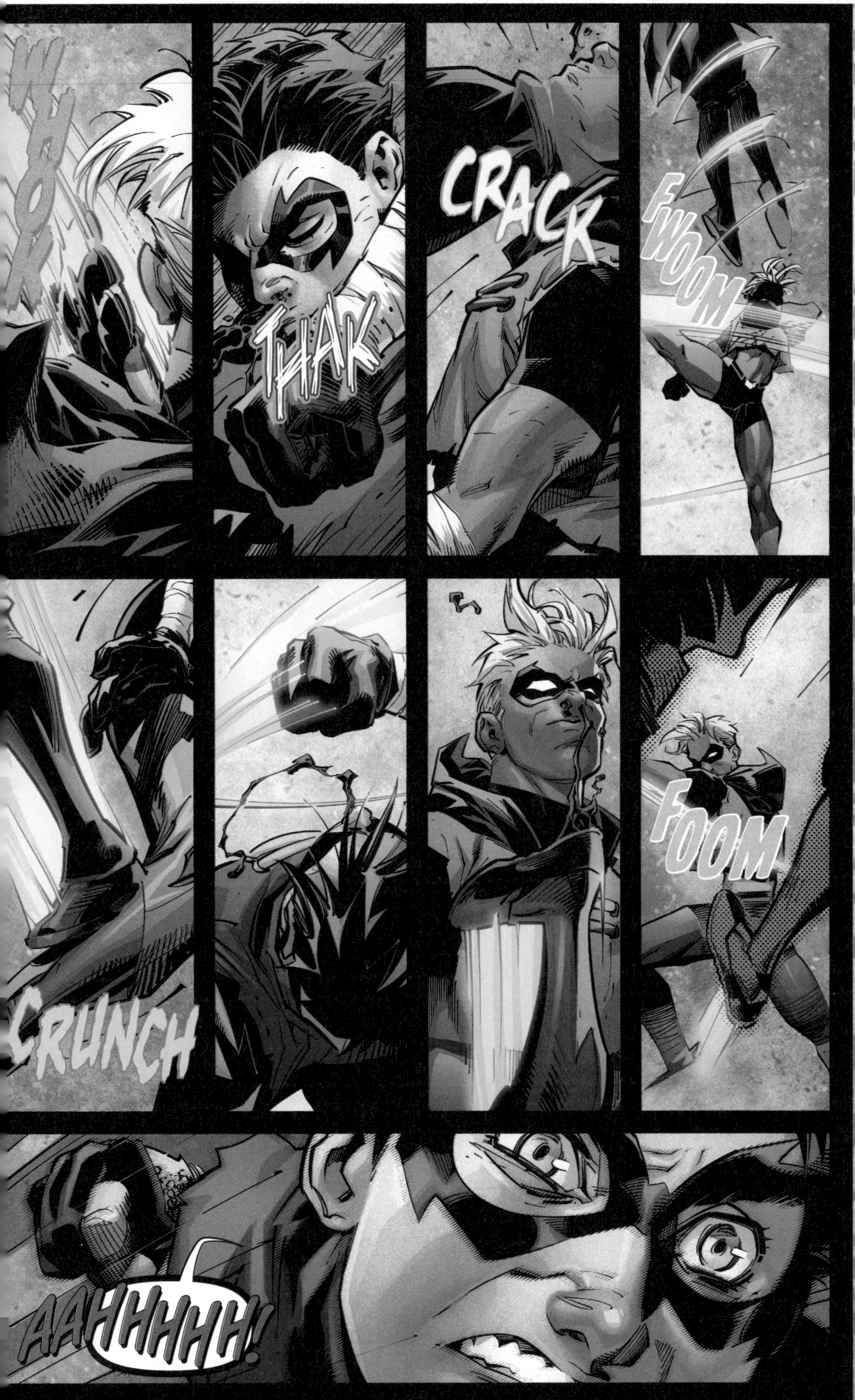
WHOK
THAK
CRACK
FWOOM
CRUNCH
FOOM
AAHHHHH!

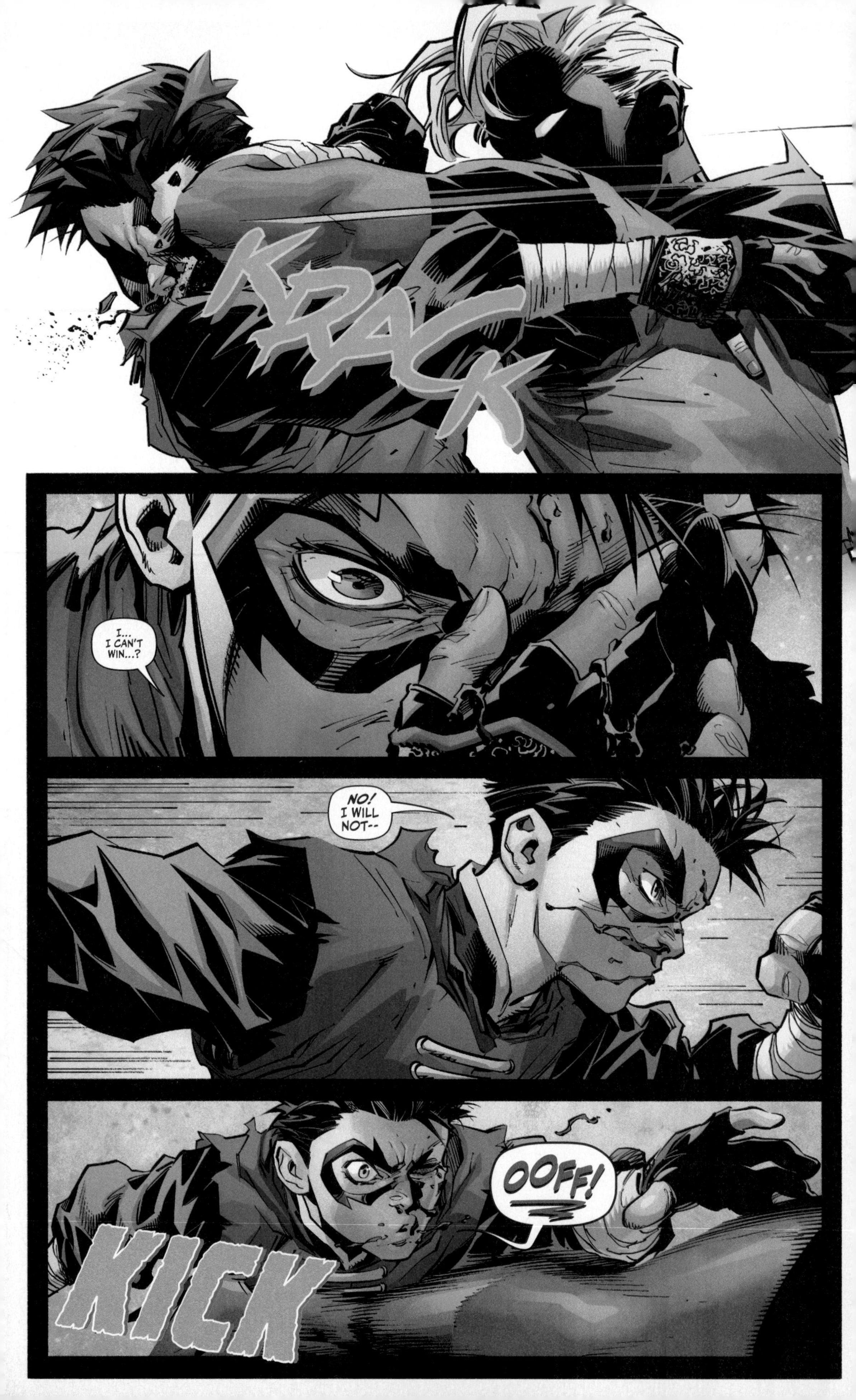
KRACK
I...
I CAN'T
WIN...?
NO!
I WILL
NOT--
OOFF!
KICK

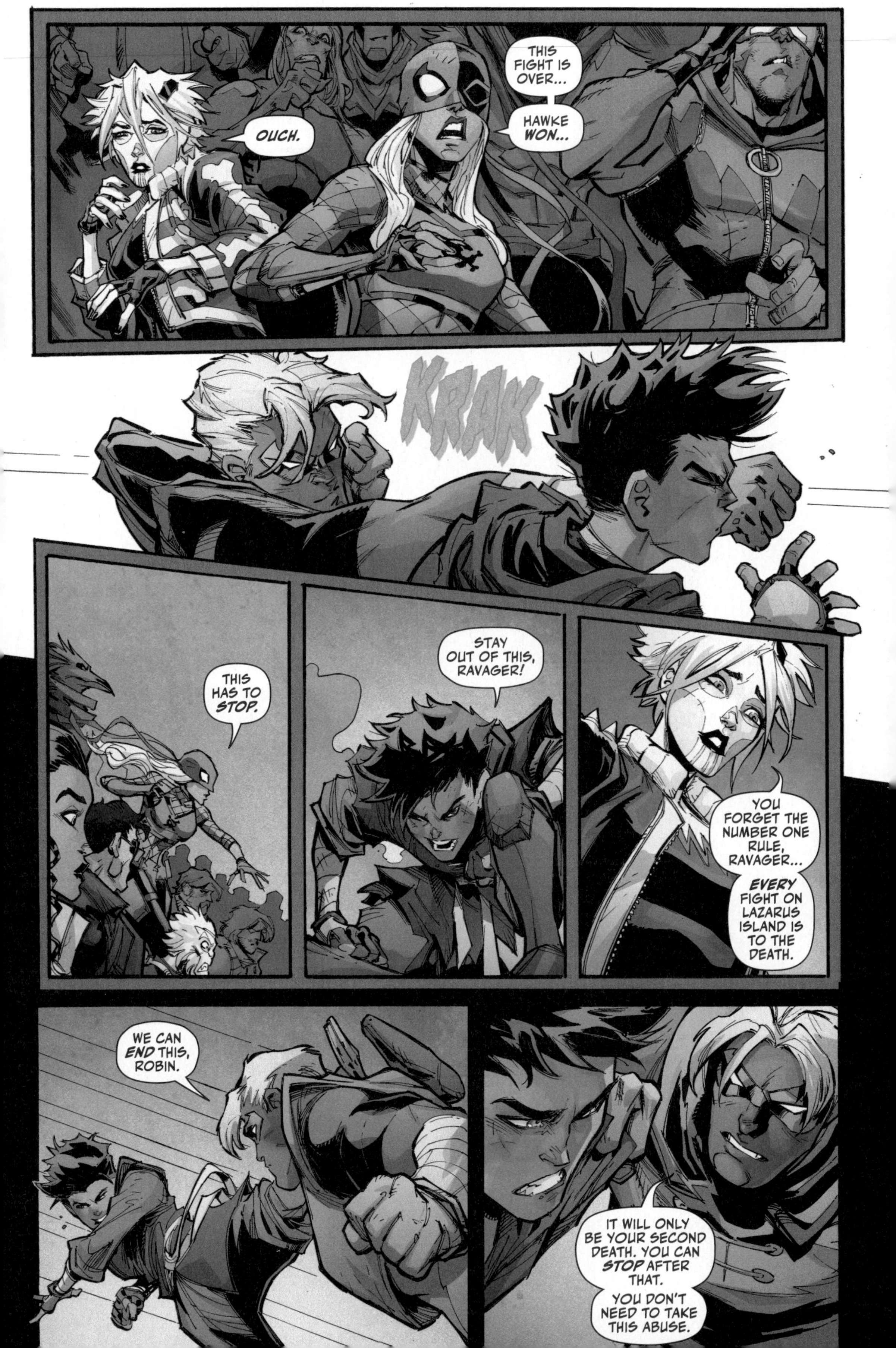
OUCH.
THIS FIGHT IS OVER...
HAWKE *WON*...
KRAK
THIS HAS TO *STOP*.
STAY OUT OF THIS, RAVAGER!
YOU FORGET THE NUMBER ONE RULE, RAVAGER...
EVERY FIGHT ON LAZARUS ISLAND IS TO THE DEATH.
WE CAN *END* THIS, ROBIN.
IT WILL ONLY BE YOUR SECOND DEATH. YOU CAN *STOP* AFTER THAT.
YOU DON'T NEED TO TAKE THIS ABUSE.

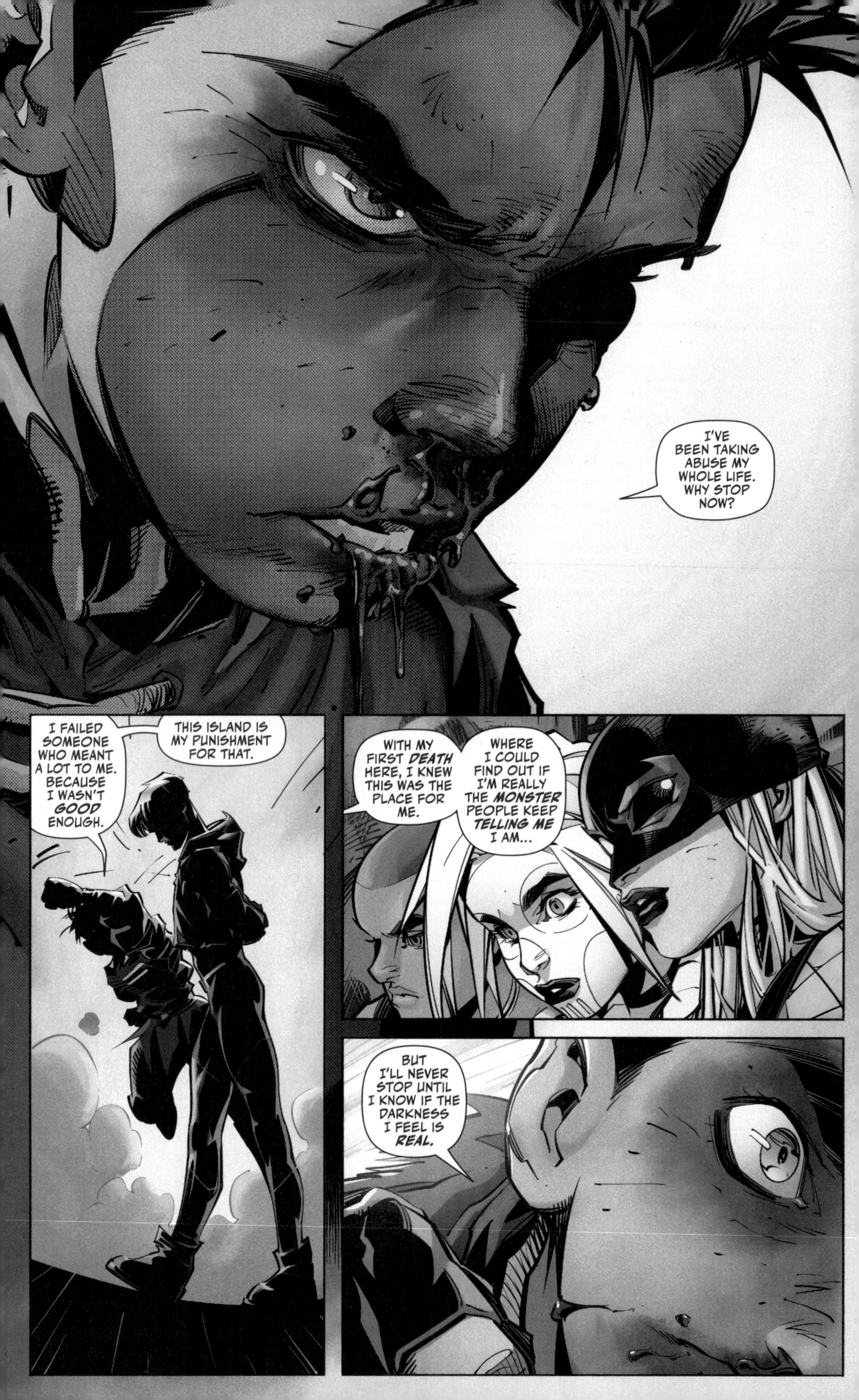
I'VE BEEN TAKING ABUSE MY WHOLE LIFE. WHY STOP NOW?
I FAILED SOMEONE WHO MEANT A LOT TO ME. BECAUSE I WASN'T *GOOD* ENOUGH.
THIS ISLAND IS MY PUNISHMENT FOR THAT.
WITH MY FIRST *DEATH* HERE, I KNEW THIS WAS THE PLACE FOR ME.
WHERE I COULD FIND OUT IF I'M REALLY THE *MONSTER* PEOPLE KEEP *TELLING ME* I AM...
BUT I'LL NEVER STOP UNTIL I KNOW IF THE DARKNESS I FEEL IS *REAL.*

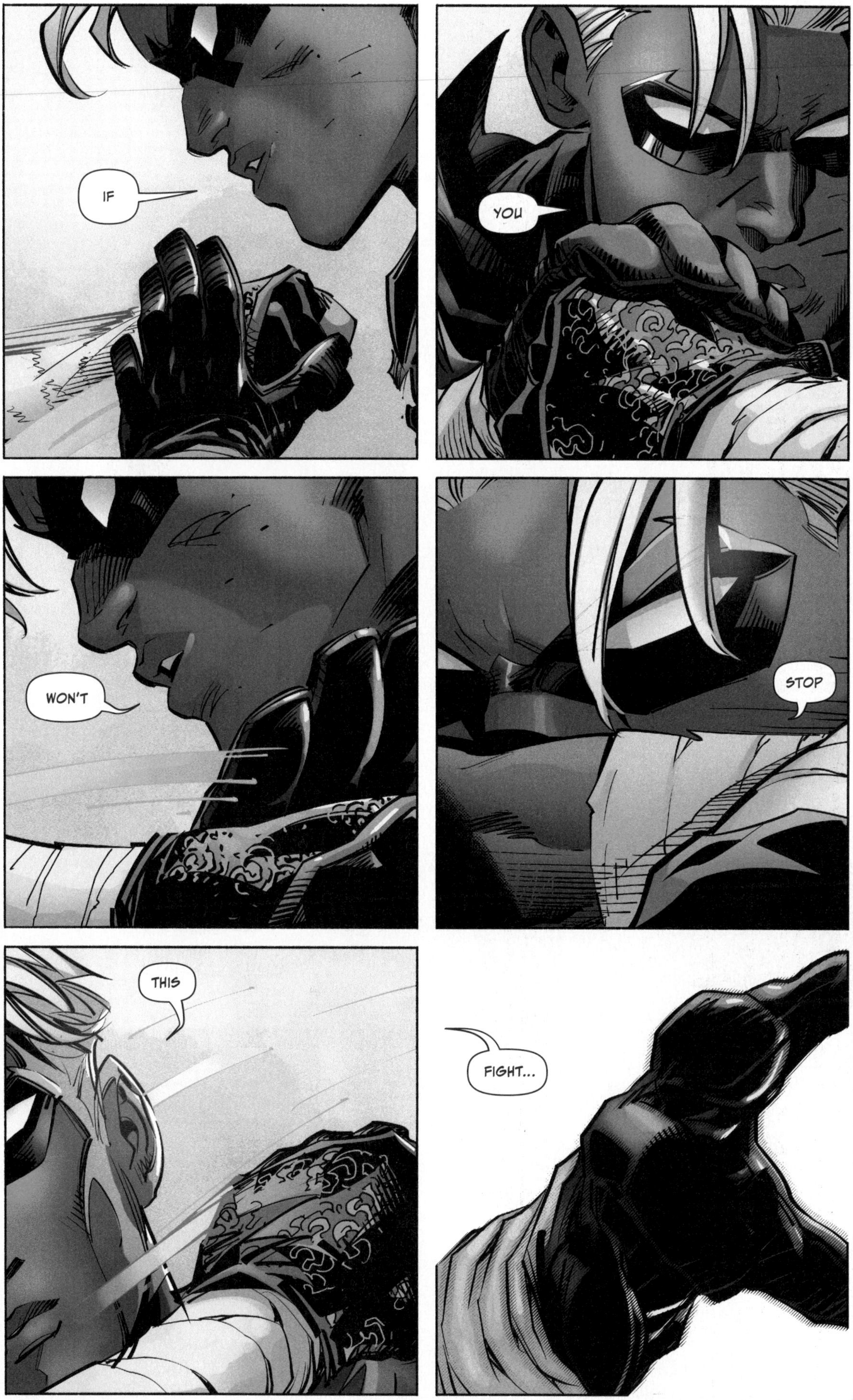
IF
YOU
WON'T
STOP
THIS
FIGHT...

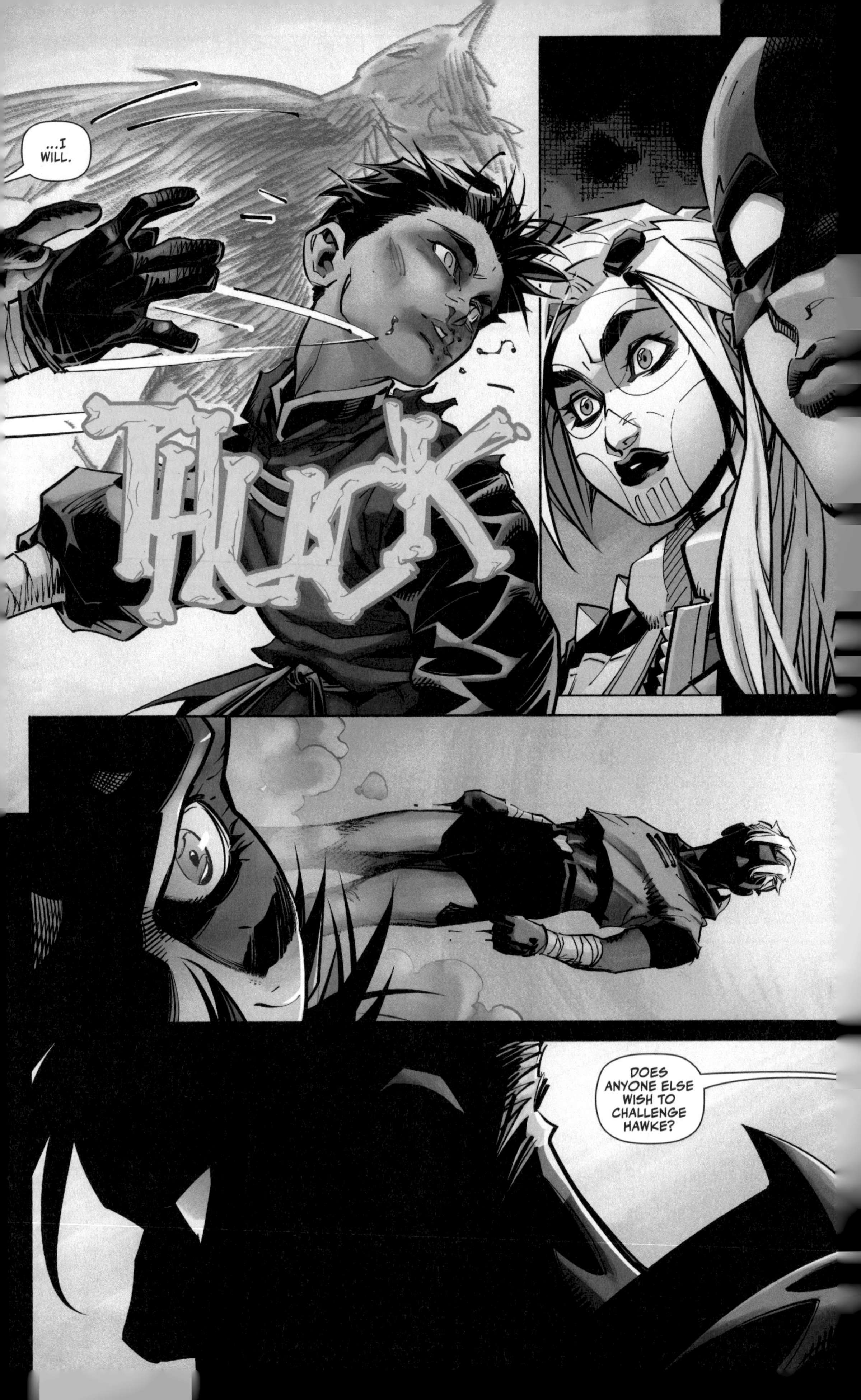
...I WILL.
THUCK
DOES ANYONE ELSE WISH TO CHALLENGE HAWKE?

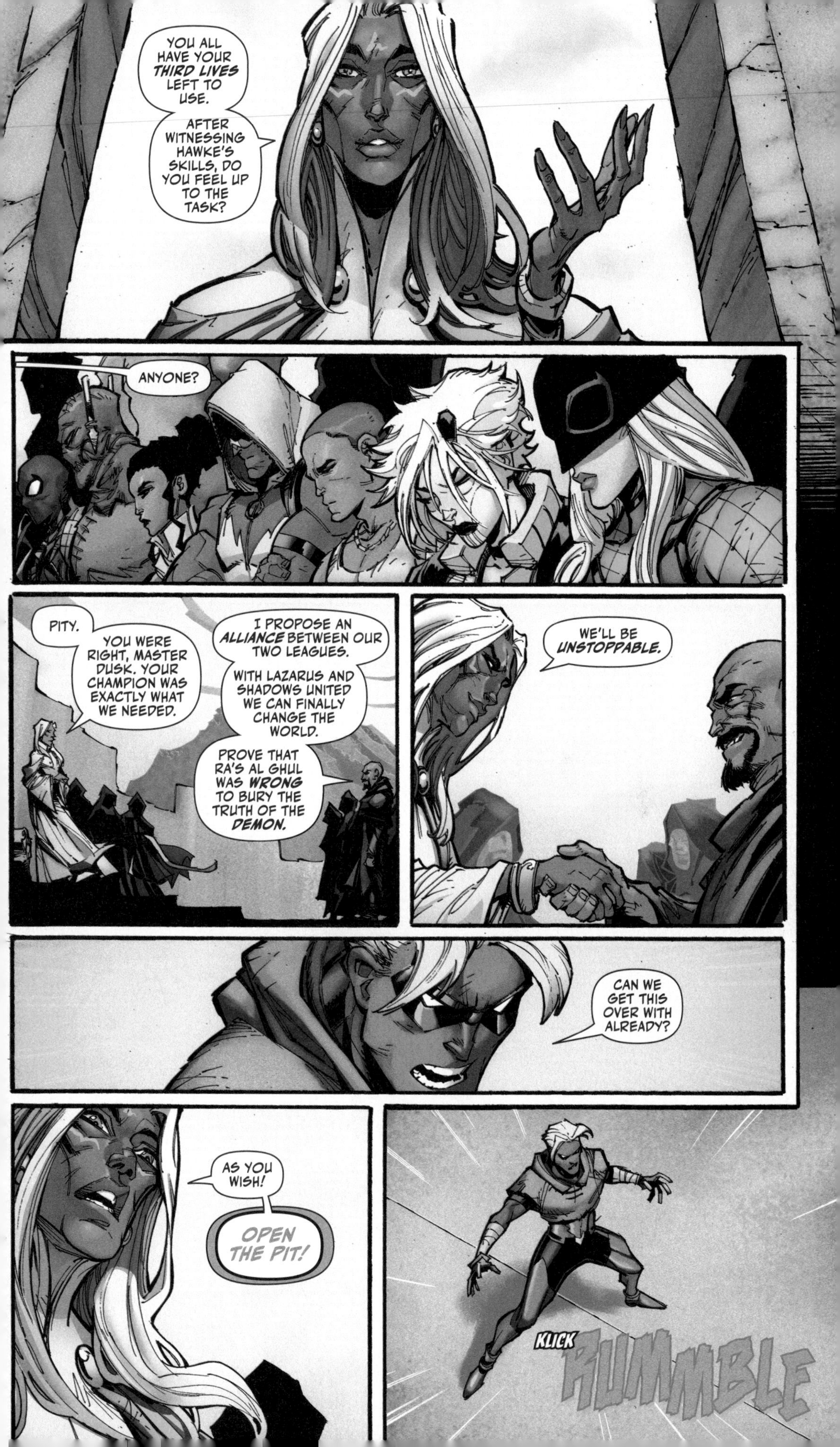

YOU ALL HAVE YOUR THIRD LIVES LEFT TO USE.
AFTER WITNESSING HAWKE'S SKILLS, DO YOU FEEL UP TO THE TASK?
ANYONE?
PITY.
YOU WERE RIGHT, MASTER DUSK. YOUR CHAMPION WAS EXACTLY WHAT WE NEEDED.
I PROPOSE AN ALLIANCE BETWEEN OUR TWO LEAGUES.
WITH LAZARUS AND SHADOWS UNITED WE CAN FINALLY CHANGE THE WORLD.
PROVE THAT RA'S AL GHUL WAS WRONG TO BURY THE TRUTH OF THE DEMON.
WE'LL BE UNSTOPPABLE.
CAN WE GET THIS OVER WITH ALREADY?
AS YOU WISH!
OPEN THE PIT!
KLICK
RUMMBLE

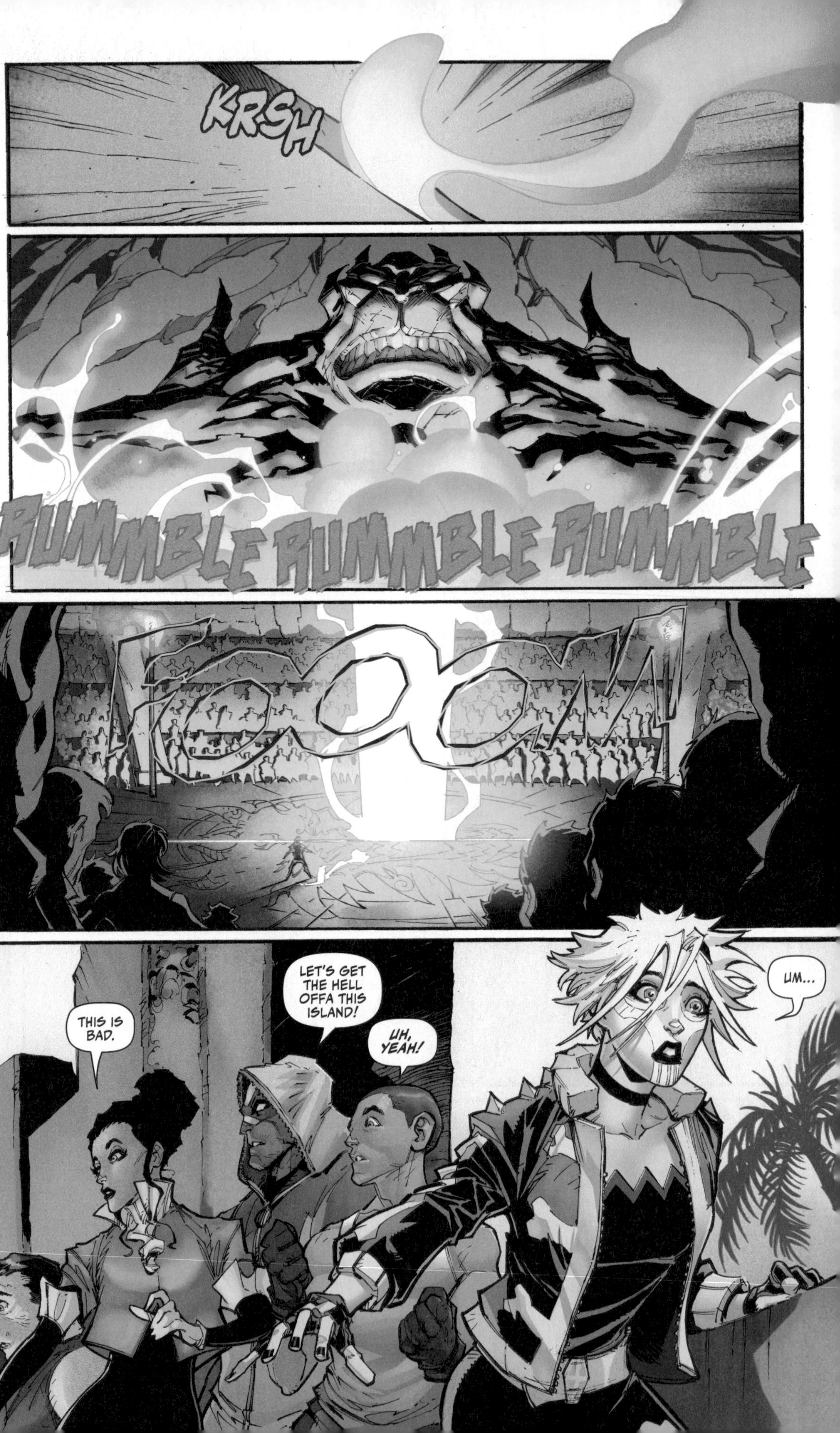
KRSH
RUMMBLE RUMMBLE RUMMBLE
FOOOM
THIS IS BAD.
LET'S GET THE HELL OFFA THIS ISLAND!
UH, YEAH!
UM...

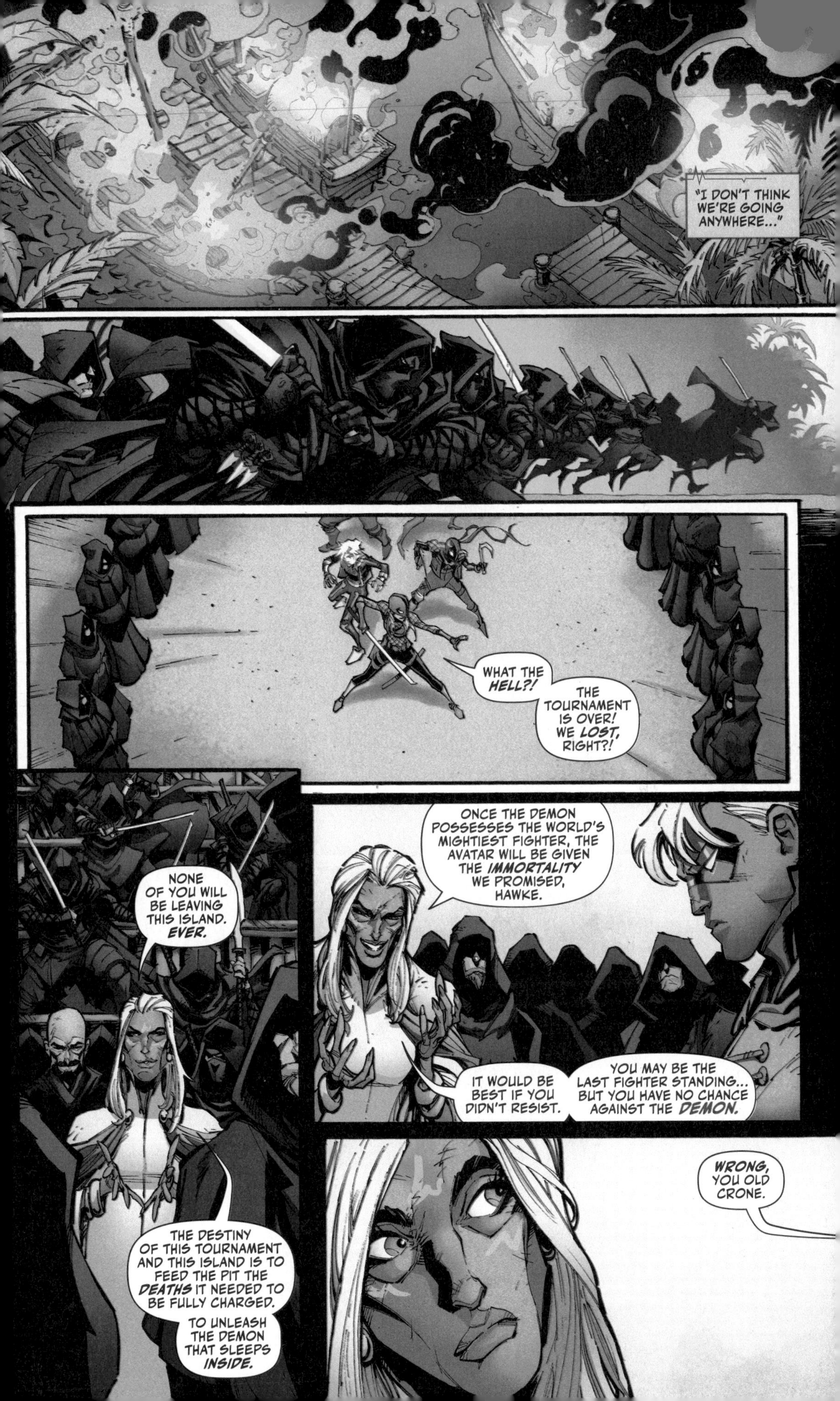
"I DON'T THINK WE'RE GOING ANYWHERE..."
WHAT THE HELL?!
THE TOURNAMENT IS OVER! WE LOST, RIGHT?!
NONE OF YOU WILL BE LEAVING THIS ISLAND. EVER.
THE DESTINY OF THIS TOURNAMENT AND THIS ISLAND IS TO FEED THE PIT THE DEATHS IT NEEDED TO BE FULLY CHARGED.
TO UNLEASH THE DEMON THAT SLEEPS INSIDE.
ONCE THE DEMON POSSESSES THE WORLD'S MIGHTIEST FIGHTER, THE AVATAR WILL BE GIVEN THE IMMORTALITY WE PROMISED, HAWKE.
IT WOULD BE BEST IF YOU DIDN'T RESIST.
YOU MAY BE THE LAST FIGHTER STANDING... BUT YOU HAVE NO CHANCE AGAINST THE DEMON.
WRONG, YOU OLD CRONE.

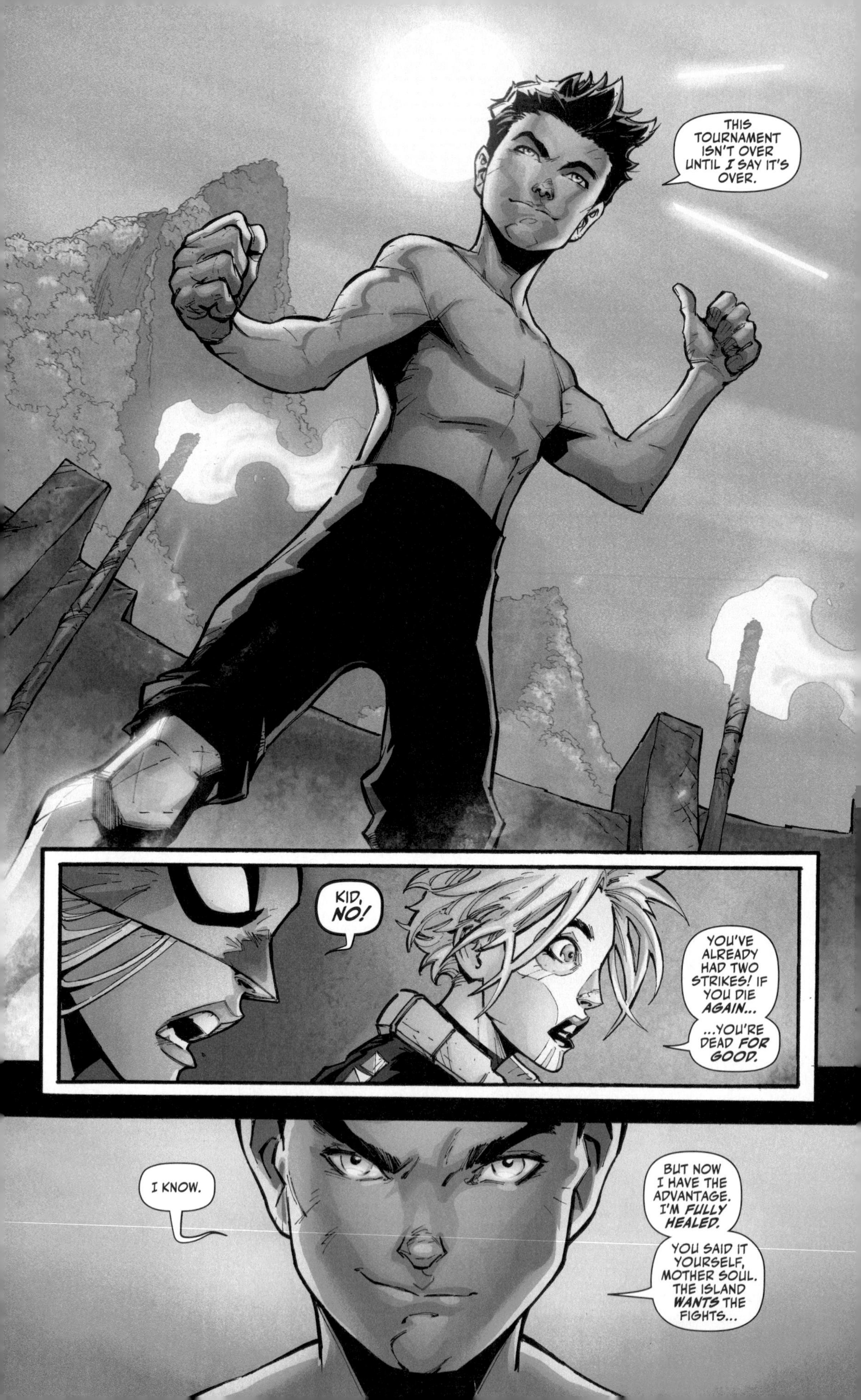
THIS TOURNAMENT ISN'T OVER UNTIL *I* SAY IT'S OVER.
KID, *NO!*
YOU'VE ALREADY HAD TWO STRIKES! IF YOU DIE *AGAIN*...
...YOU'RE DEAD *FOR GOOD.*
I KNOW.
BUT NOW I HAVE THE ADVANTAGE. I'M *FULLY HEALED.*
YOU SAID IT YOURSELF, MOTHER SOUL. THE ISLAND *WANTS* THE FIGHTS...

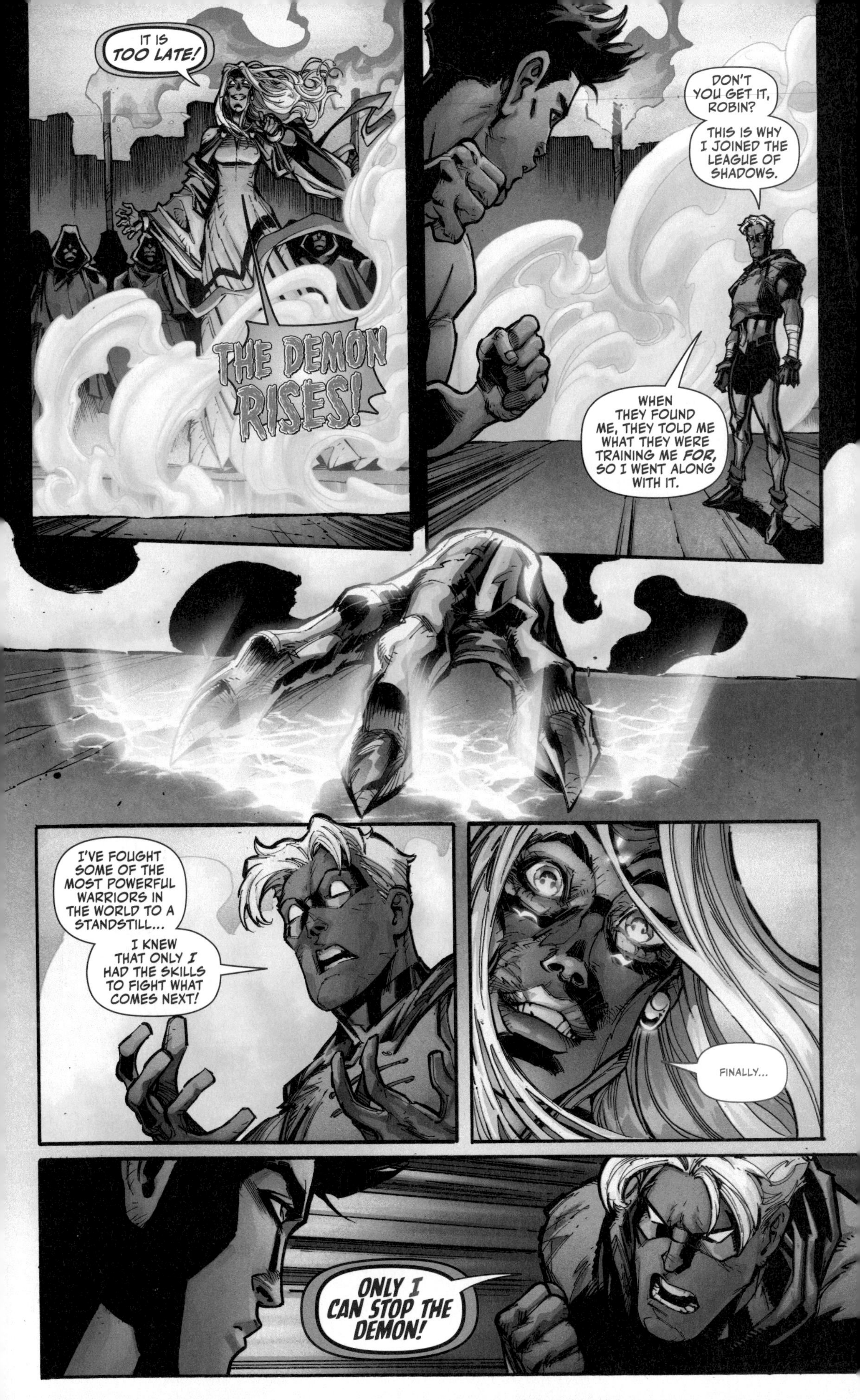
IT IS TOO LATE!
THE DEMON RISES!
DON'T YOU GET IT, ROBIN?
THIS IS WHY I JOINED THE LEAGUE OF SHADOWS.
WHEN THEY FOUND ME, THEY TOLD ME WHAT THEY WERE TRAINING ME FOR, SO I WENT ALONG WITH IT.
I'VE FOUGHT SOME OF THE MOST POWERFUL WARRIORS IN THE WORLD TO A STANDSTILL...
I KNEW THAT ONLY I HAD THE SKILLS TO FIGHT WHAT COMES NEXT!
FINALLY...
ONLY I CAN STOP THE DEMON!

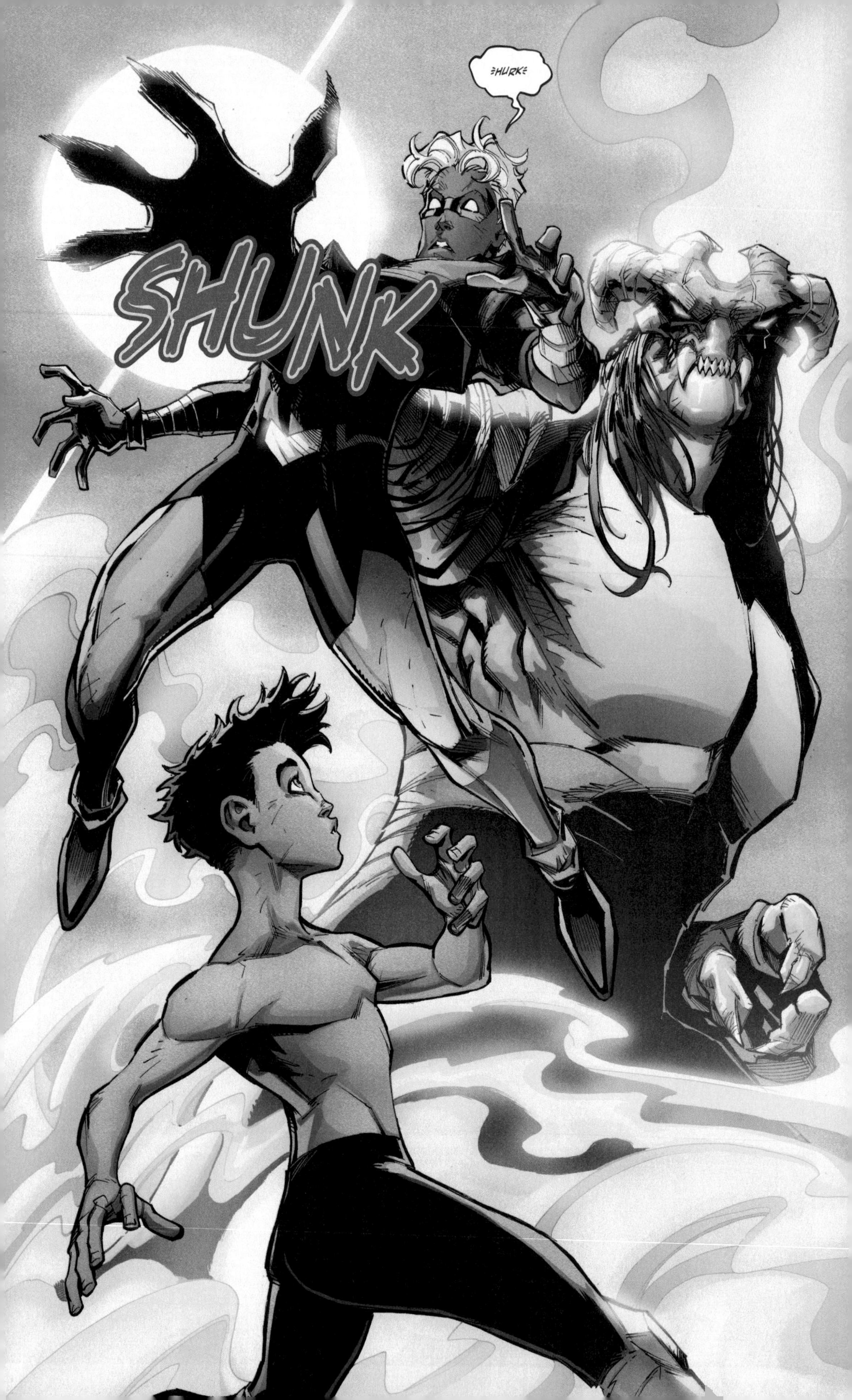
HURK
SHUNK

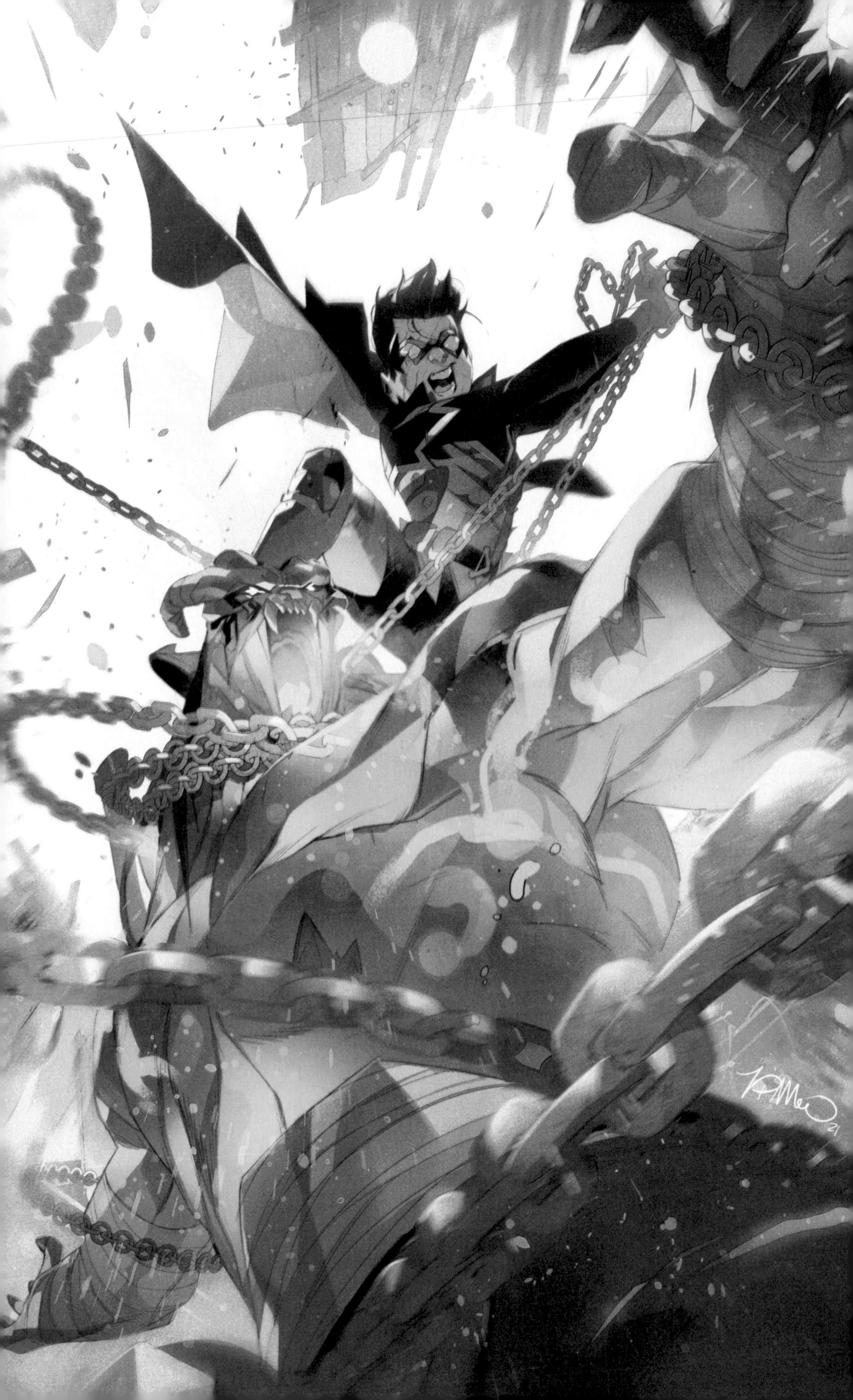

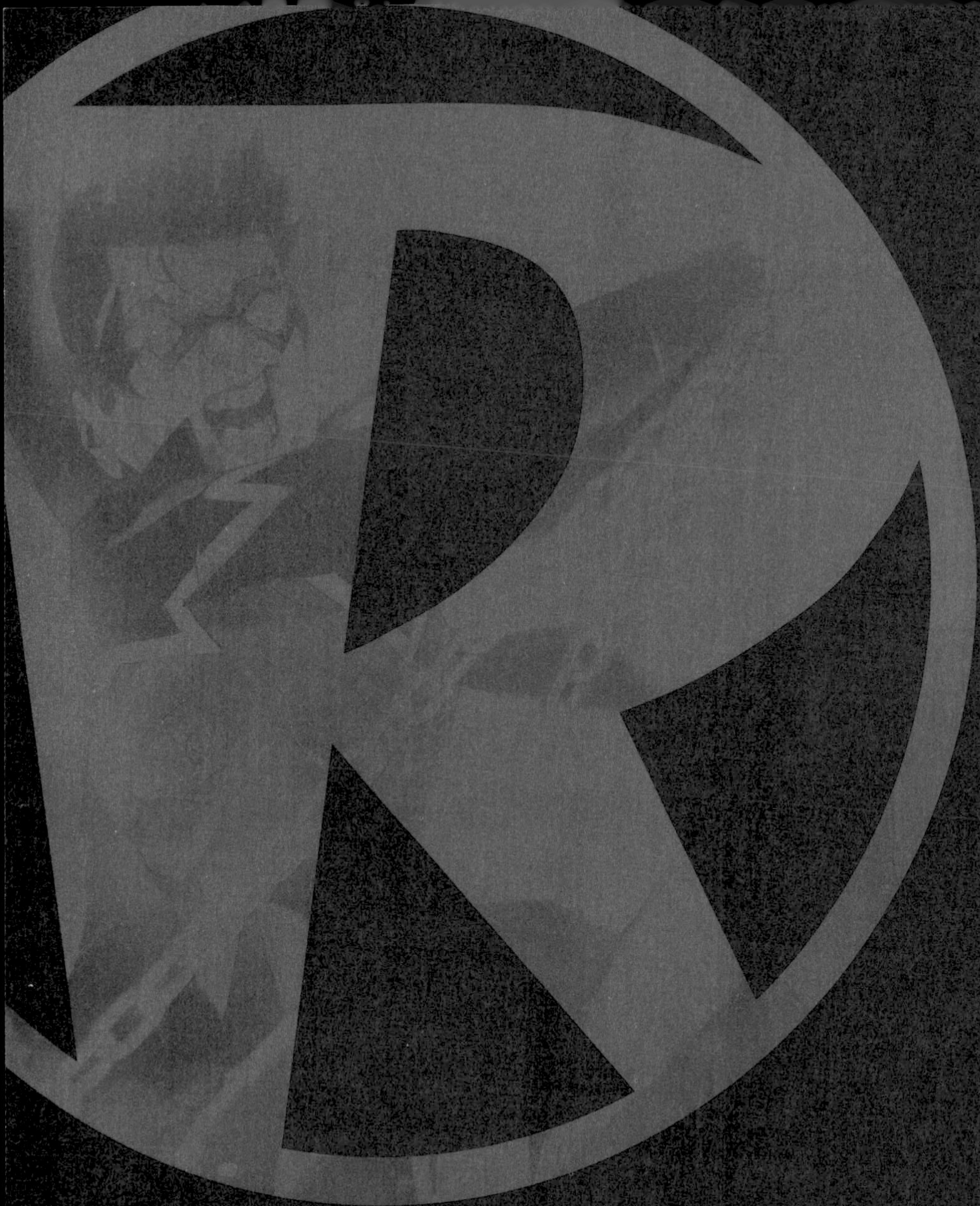

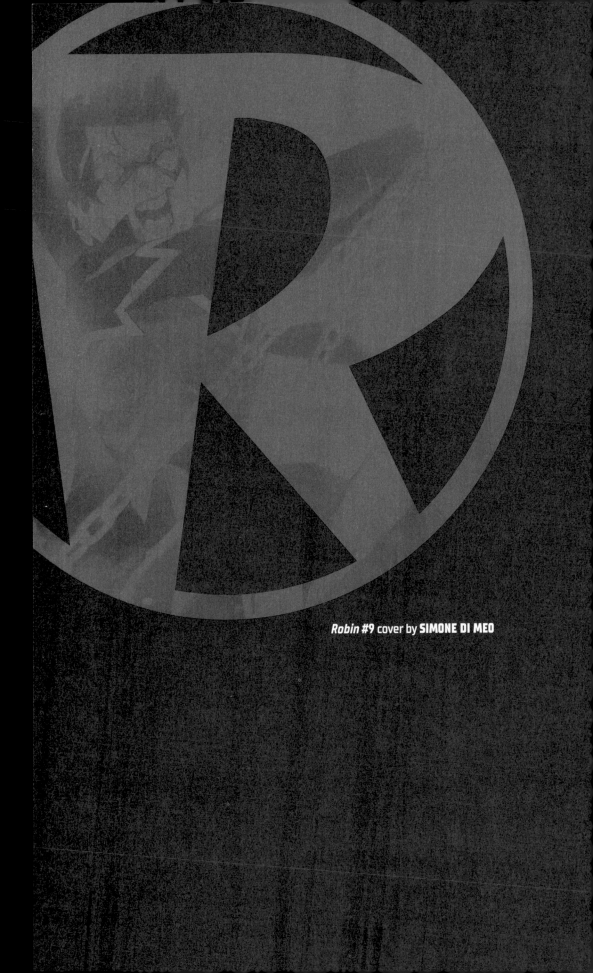

Robin #9 cover by **SIMONE DI MEO**

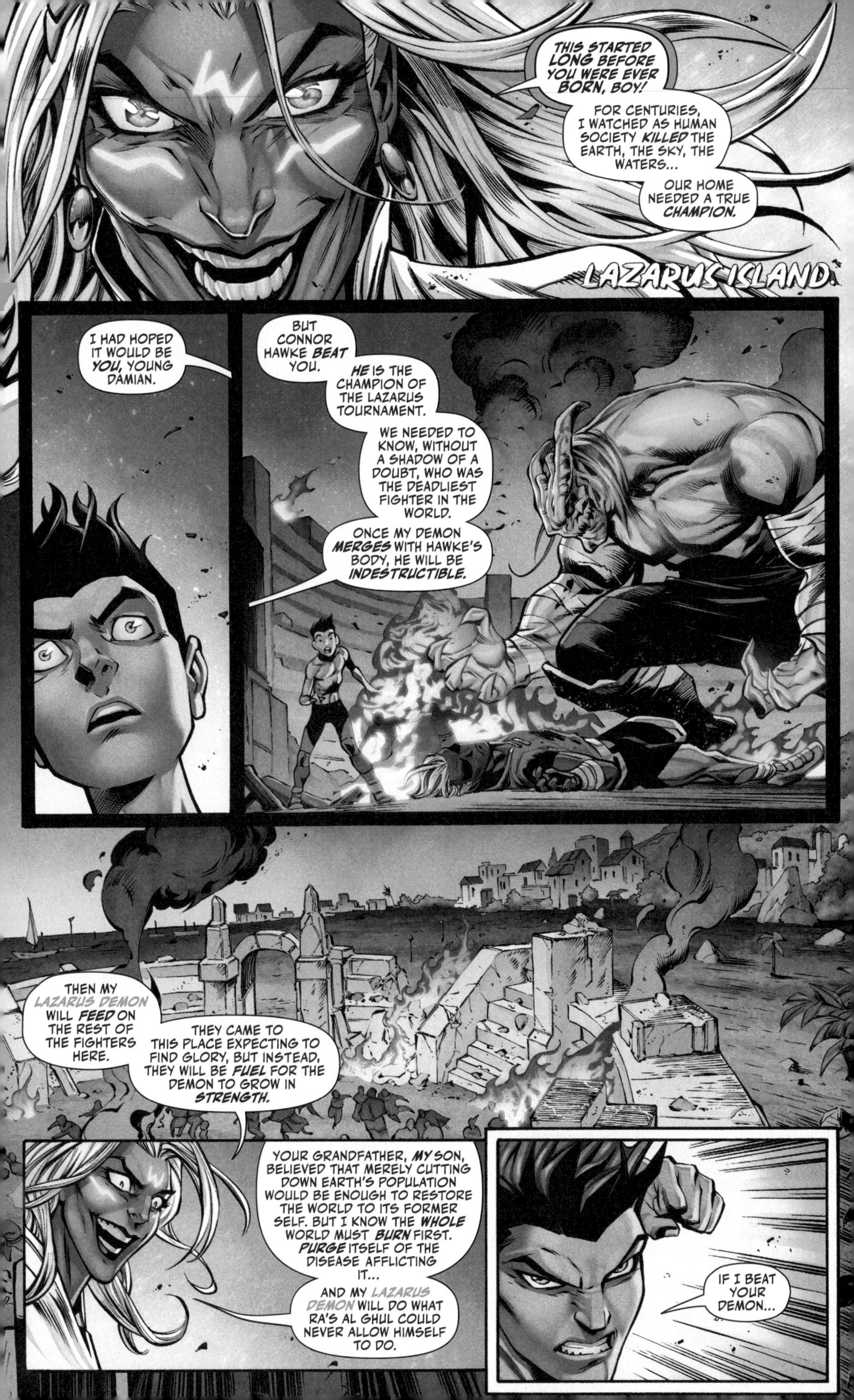
THIS STARTED LONG BEFORE YOU WERE EVER BORN, BOY!
FOR CENTURIES, I WATCHED AS HUMAN SOCIETY KILLED THE EARTH, THE SKY, THE WATERS...
OUR HOME NEEDED A TRUE CHAMPION.
LAZARUS ISLAND.
I HAD HOPED IT WOULD BE YOU, YOUNG DAMIAN.
BUT CONNOR HAWKE BEAT YOU.
HE IS THE CHAMPION OF THE LAZARUS TOURNAMENT.
WE NEEDED TO KNOW, WITHOUT A SHADOW OF A DOUBT, WHO WAS THE DEADLIEST FIGHTER IN THE WORLD.
ONCE MY DEMON MERGES WITH HAWKE'S BODY, HE WILL BE INDESTRUCTIBLE.
THEN MY LAZARUS DEMON WILL FEED ON THE REST OF THE FIGHTERS HERE.
THEY CAME TO THIS PLACE EXPECTING TO FIND GLORY, BUT INSTEAD, THEY WILL BE FUEL FOR THE DEMON TO GROW IN STRENGTH.
YOUR GRANDFATHER, MY SON, BELIEVED THAT MERELY CUTTING DOWN EARTH'S POPULATION WOULD BE ENOUGH TO RESTORE THE WORLD TO ITS FORMER SELF. BUT I KNOW THE WHOLE WORLD MUST BURN FIRST. PURGE ITSELF OF THE DISEASE AFFLICTING IT...
AND MY LAZARUS DEMON WILL DO WHAT RA'S AL GHUL COULD NEVER ALLOW HIMSELF TO DO.
IF I BEAT YOUR DEMON...

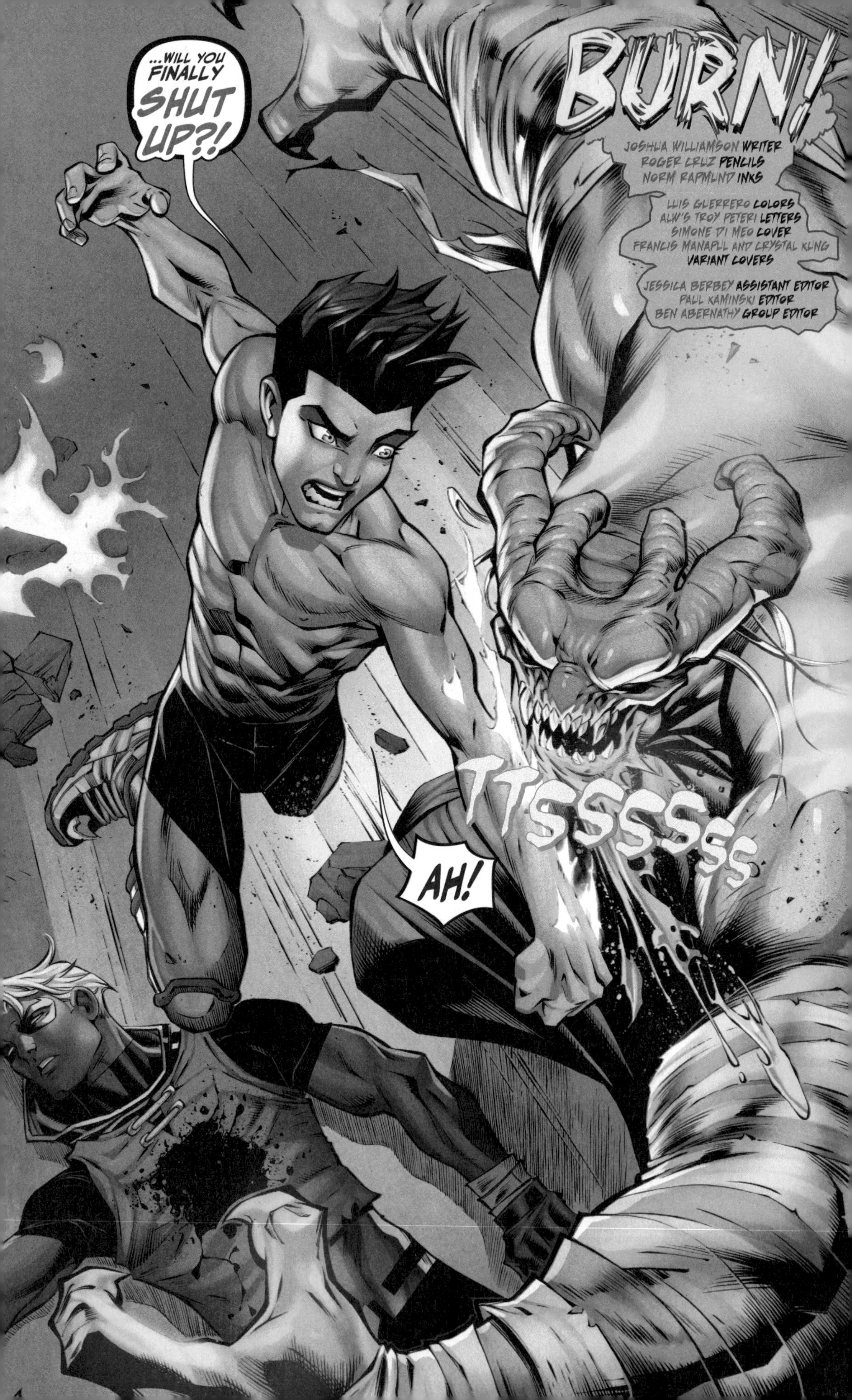
...WILL YOU FINALLY SHUT UP?!
BURN!
JOSHUA WILLIAMSON WRITER
ROGER CRUZ PENCILS
NORM RAPMUND INKS
LUIS GUERRERO COLORS
ALW'S TROY PETERI LETTERS
SIMONE DI MEO COVER
FRANCIS MANAPUL AND CRYSTAL KUNG VARIANT COVERS
JESSICA BERBEY ASSISTANT EDITOR
PAUL KAMINSKI EDITOR
BEN ABERNATHY GROUP EDITOR
TTSSSSSS
AH!

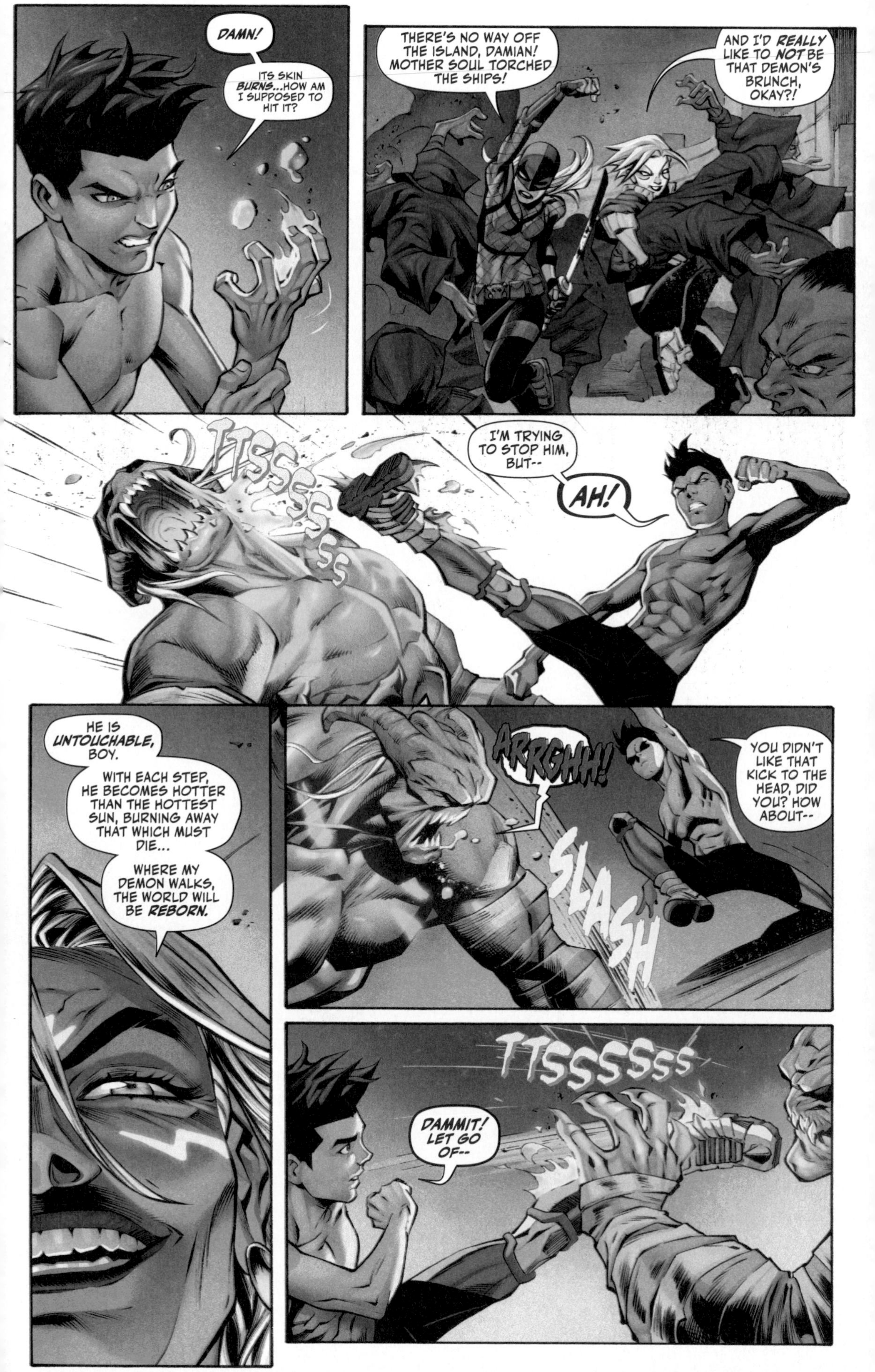

DAMN!
ITS SKIN BURNS...HOW AM I SUPPOSED TO HIT IT?
THERE'S NO WAY OFF THE ISLAND, DAMIAN! MOTHER SOUL TORCHED THE SHIPS!
AND I'D REALLY LIKE TO NOT BE THAT DEMON'S BRUNCH, OKAY?!
TTSSSSSSS
I'M TRYING TO STOP HIM, BUT--
AH!
HE IS UNTOUCHABLE, BOY.
WITH EACH STEP, HE BECOMES HOTTER THAN THE HOTTEST SUN, BURNING AWAY THAT WHICH MUST DIE...
WHERE MY DEMON WALKS, THE WORLD WILL BE REBORN.
ARRGHH!
YOU DIDN'T LIKE THAT KICK TO THE HEAD, DID YOU? HOW ABOUT--
SLASH
TTSSSSSSS
DAMMIT! LET GO OF--

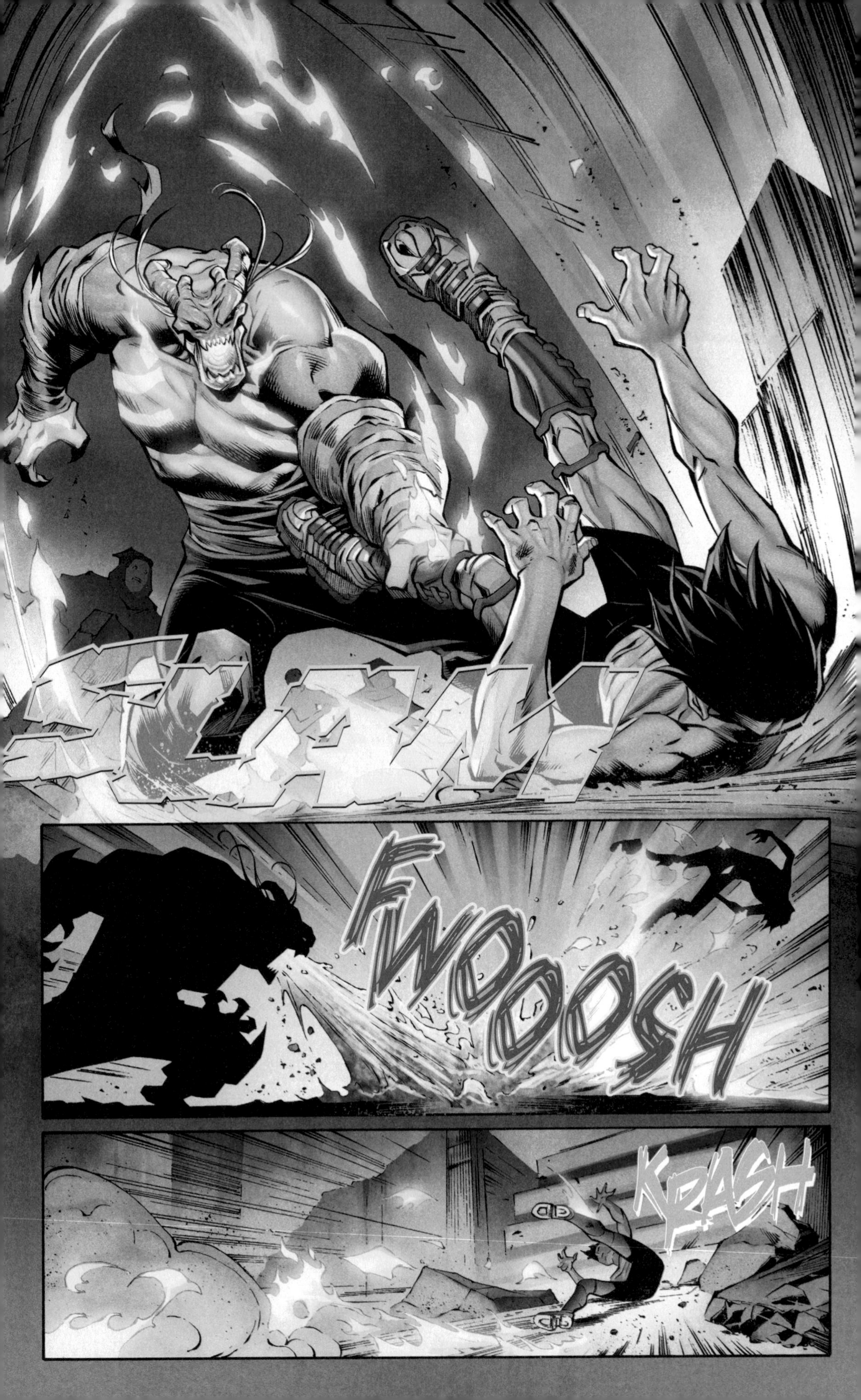
SLAM
FWOOOSH
KRASH

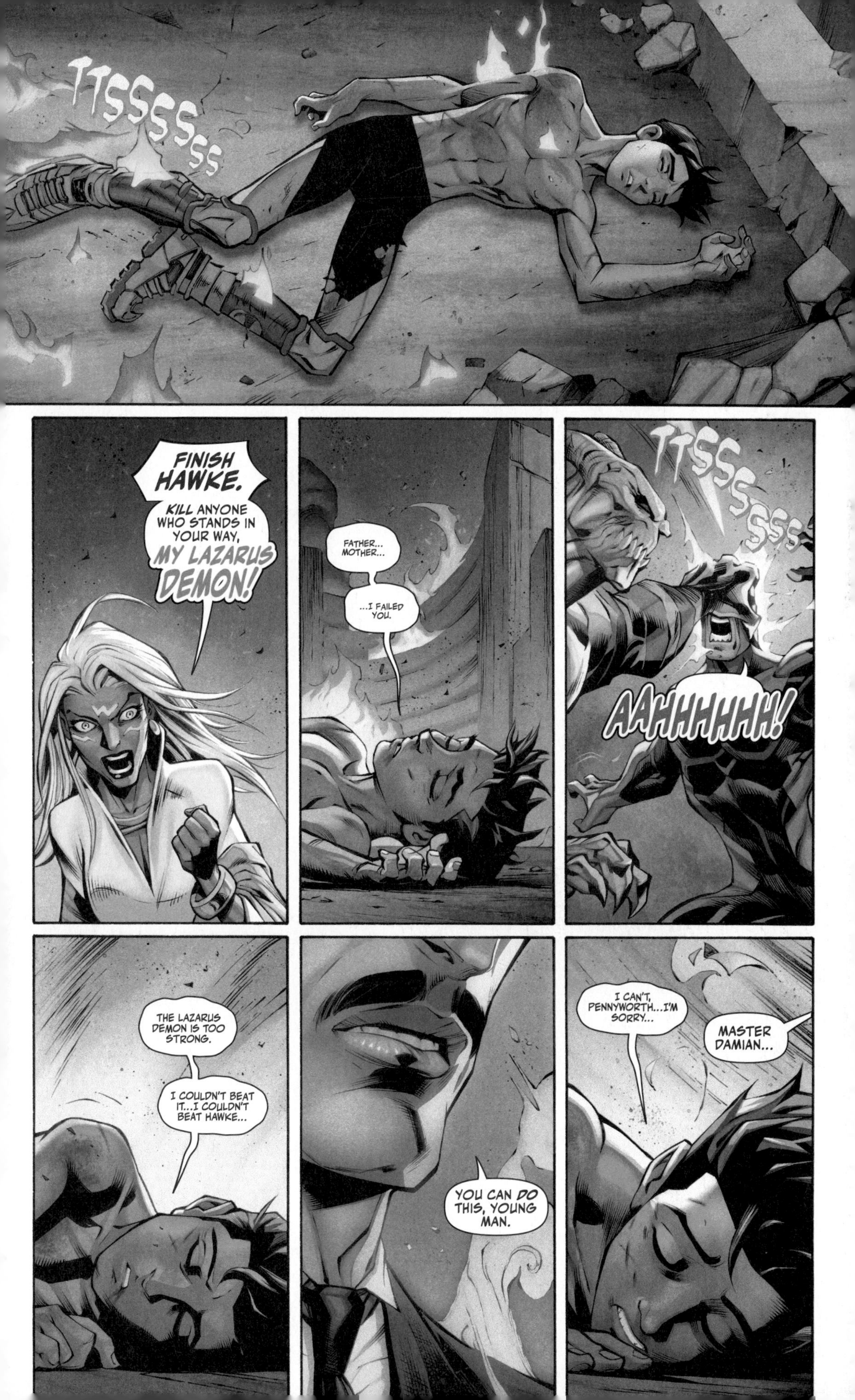
TTSSSSSSS
FINISH HAWKE.
KILL ANYONE WHO STANDS IN YOUR WAY, MY LAZARUS DEMON!
FATHER... MOTHER...
...I FAILED YOU.
TTSSSSSSSS
AAHHHHHH!
THE LAZARUS DEMON IS TOO STRONG.
I COULDN'T BEAT IT...I COULDN'T BEAT HAWKE...
YOU CAN DO THIS, YOUNG MAN.
MASTER DAMIAN...
I CAN'T, PENNYWORTH...I'M SORRY...

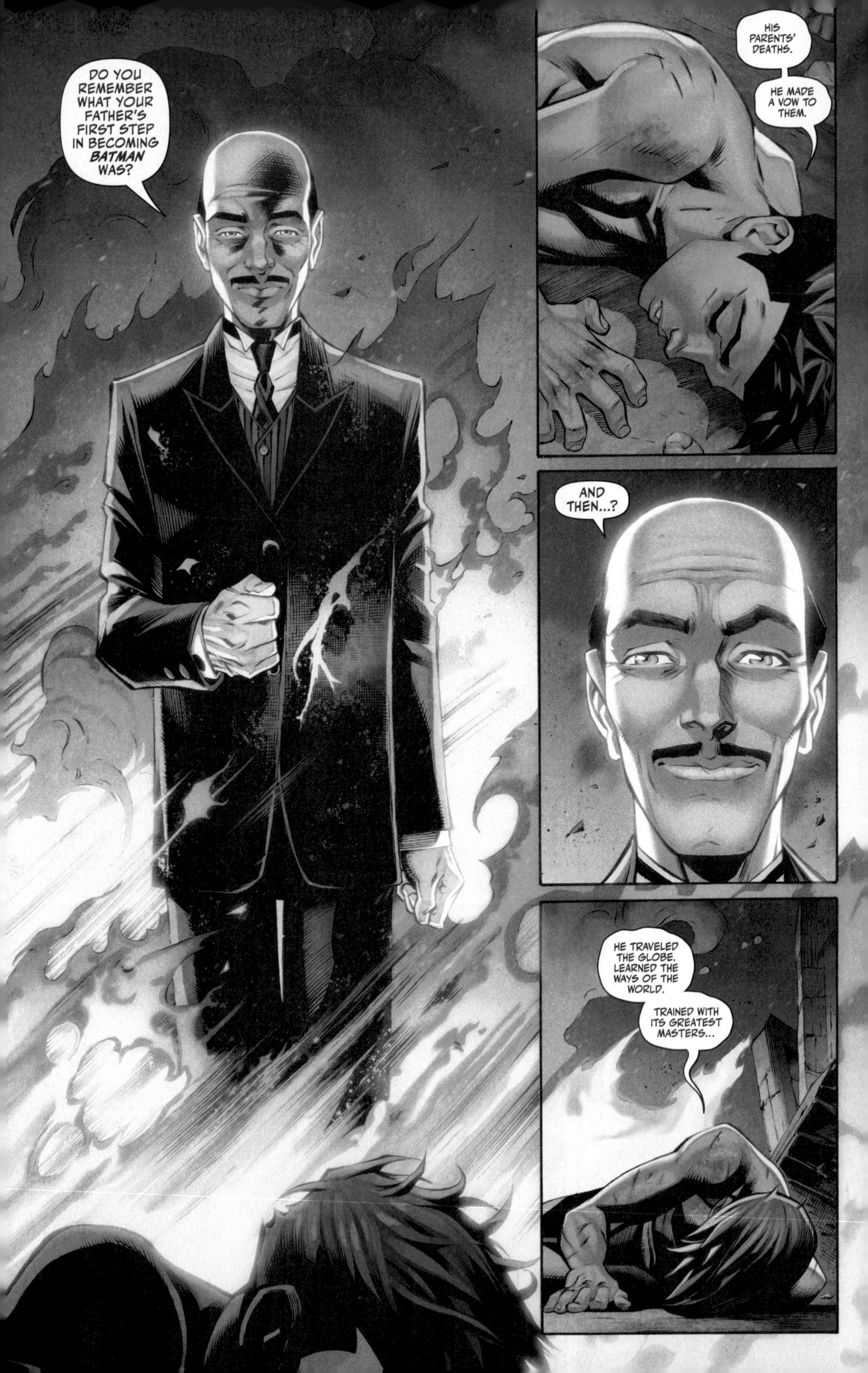
DO YOU REMEMBER WHAT YOUR FATHER'S FIRST STEP IN BECOMING BATMAN WAS?
HIS PARENTS' DEATHS.
HE MADE A VOW TO THEM.
AND THEN...?
HE TRAVELED THE GLOBE. LEARNED THE WAYS OF THE WORLD.
TRAINED WITH ITS GREATEST MASTERS...

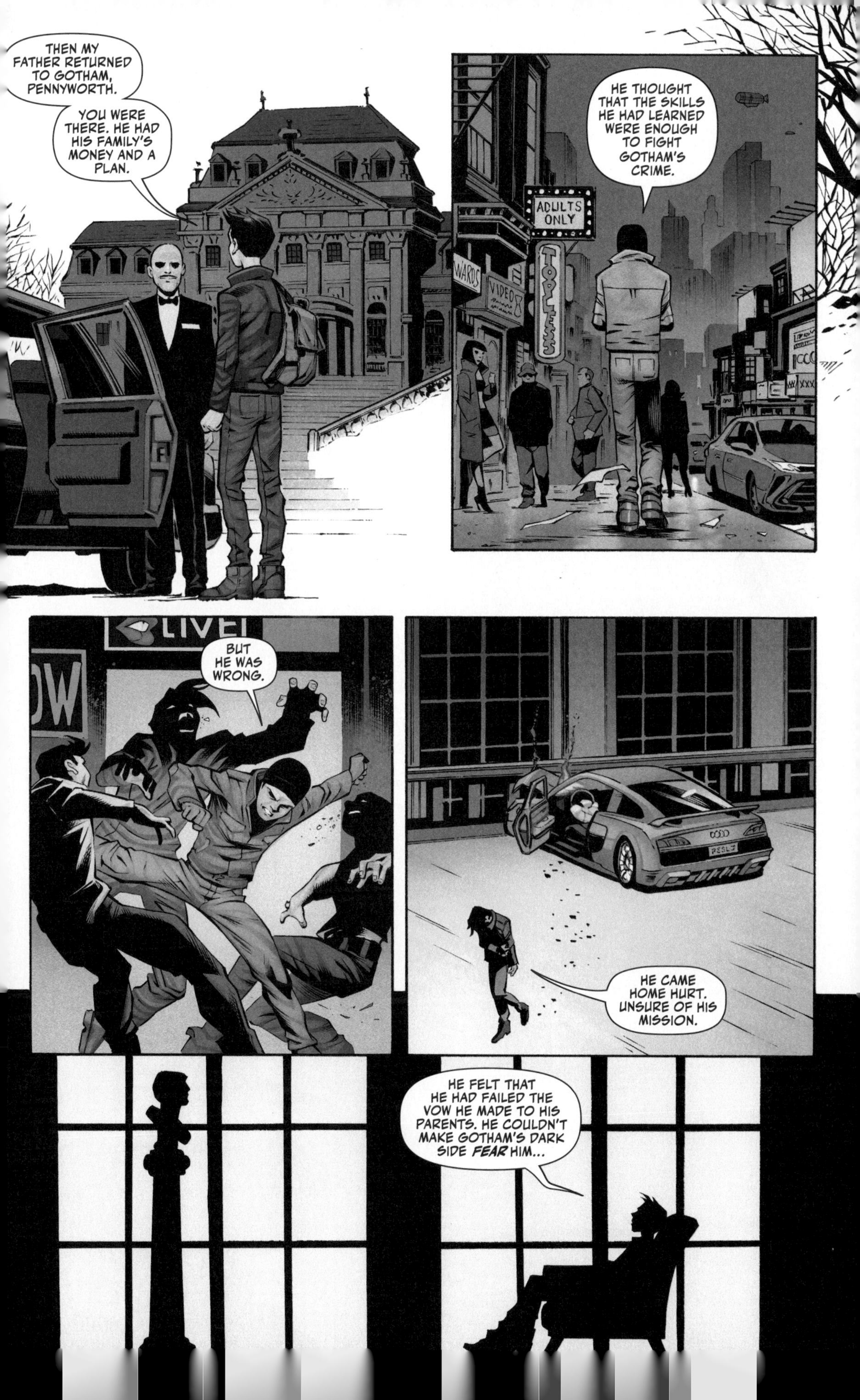
THEN MY FATHER RETURNED TO GOTHAM, PENNYWORTH.
YOU WERE THERE. HE HAD HIS FAMILY'S MONEY AND A PLAN.
HE THOUGHT THAT THE SKILLS HE HAD LEARNED WERE ENOUGH TO FIGHT GOTHAM'S CRIME.
ADULTS ONLY
TOPLESS
VIDEO
WARDS
BUT HE WAS WRONG.
LIVE!
HE CAME HOME HURT. UNSURE OF HIS MISSION.
HE FELT THAT HE HAD FAILED THE VOW HE MADE TO HIS PARENTS. HE COULDN'T MAKE GOTHAM'S DARK SIDE *FEAR* HIM...

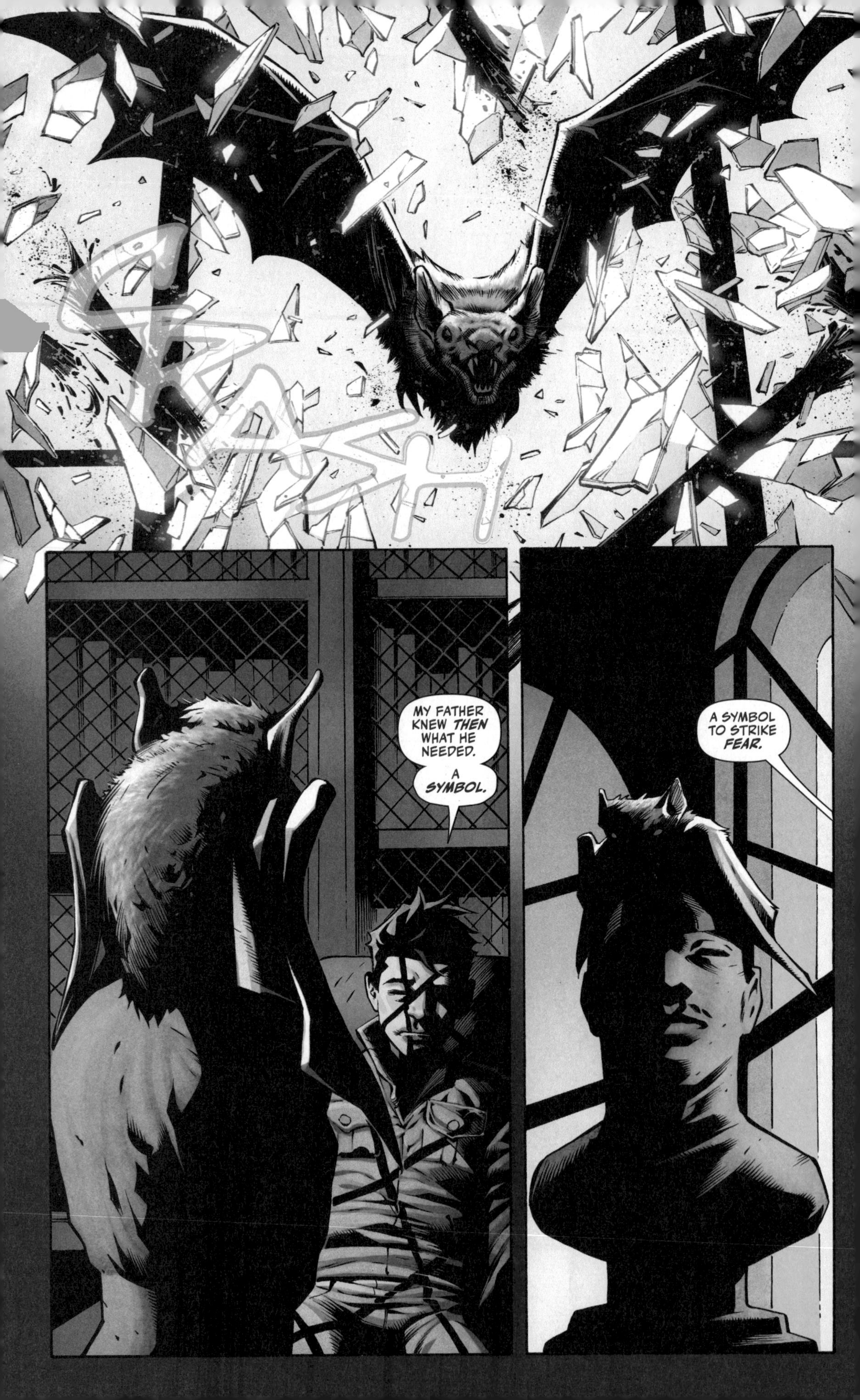
CRASH
MY FATHER KNEW *THEN* WHAT HE NEEDED.
A *SYMBOL.*
A SYMBOL TO STRIKE *FEAR.*

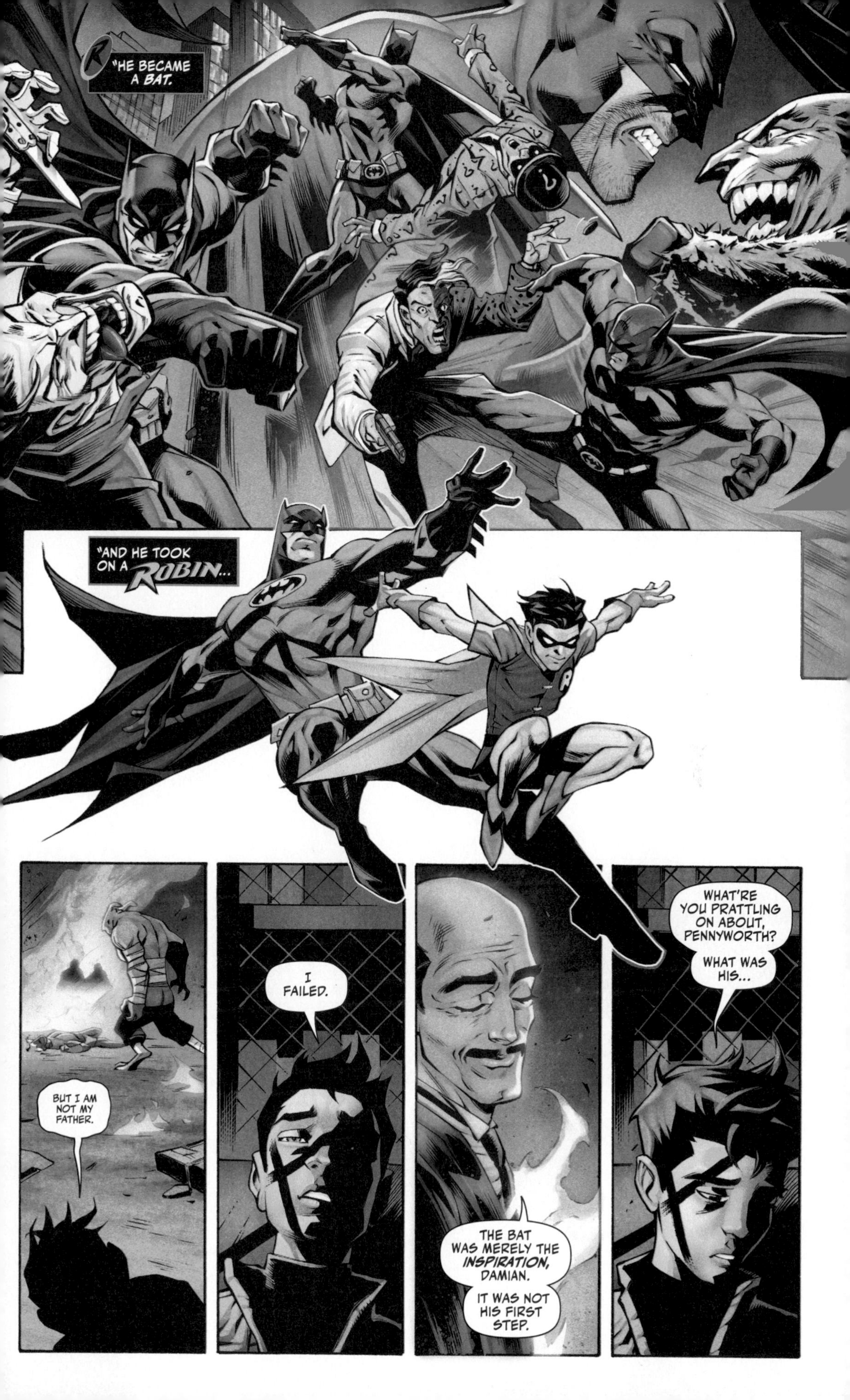
"HE BECAME A BAT.
"AND HE TOOK ON A ROBIN...
BUT I AM NOT MY FATHER.
I FAILED.
THE BAT WAS MERELY THE INSPIRATION, DAMIAN.
IT WAS NOT HIS FIRST STEP.
WHAT'RE YOU PRATTLING ON ABOUT, PENNYWORTH?
WHAT WAS HIS...

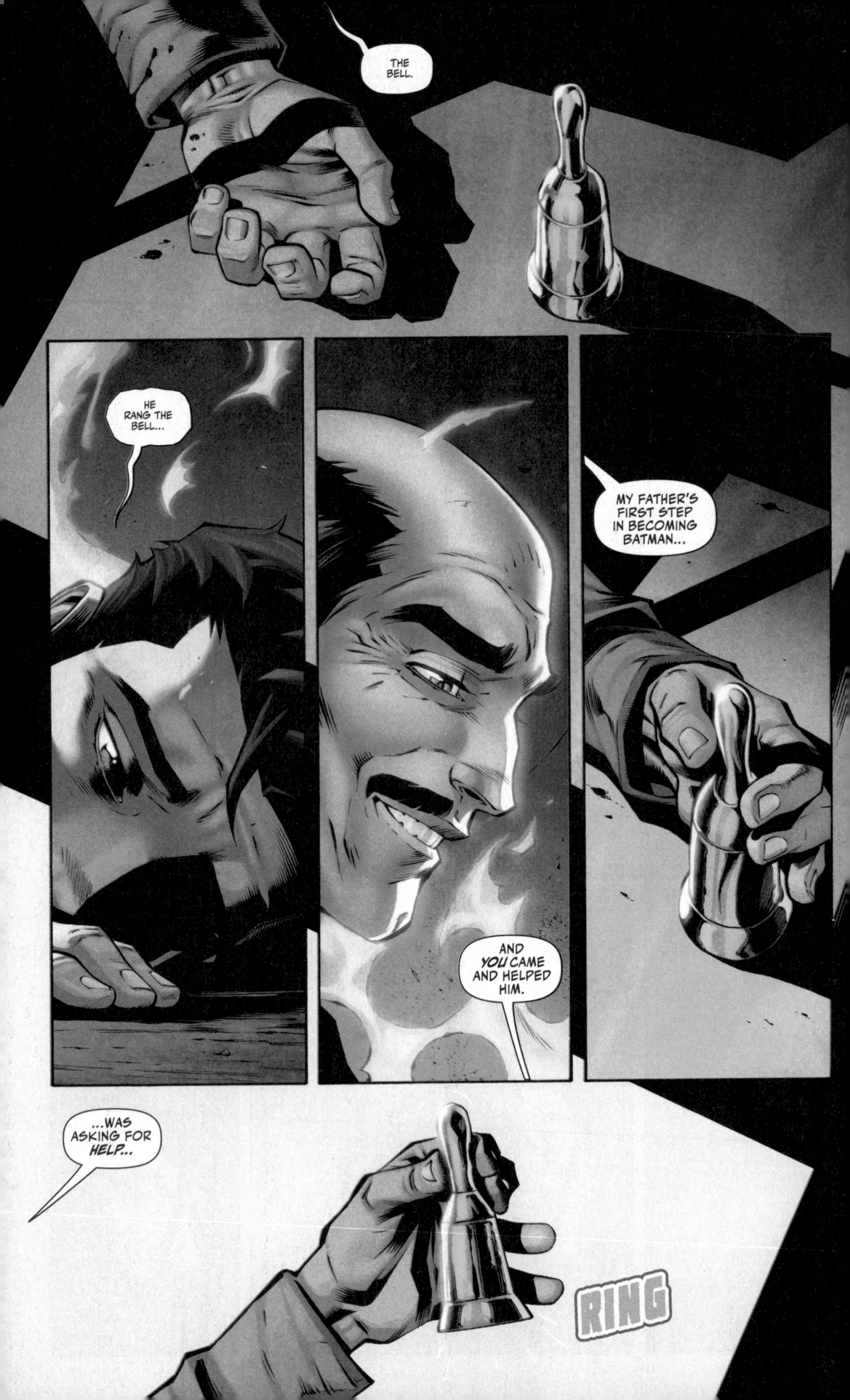
THE BELL.
HE RANG THE BELL...
MY FATHER'S FIRST STEP IN BECOMING BATMAN...
AND YOU CAME AND HELPED HIM.
...WAS ASKING FOR HELP...
RING

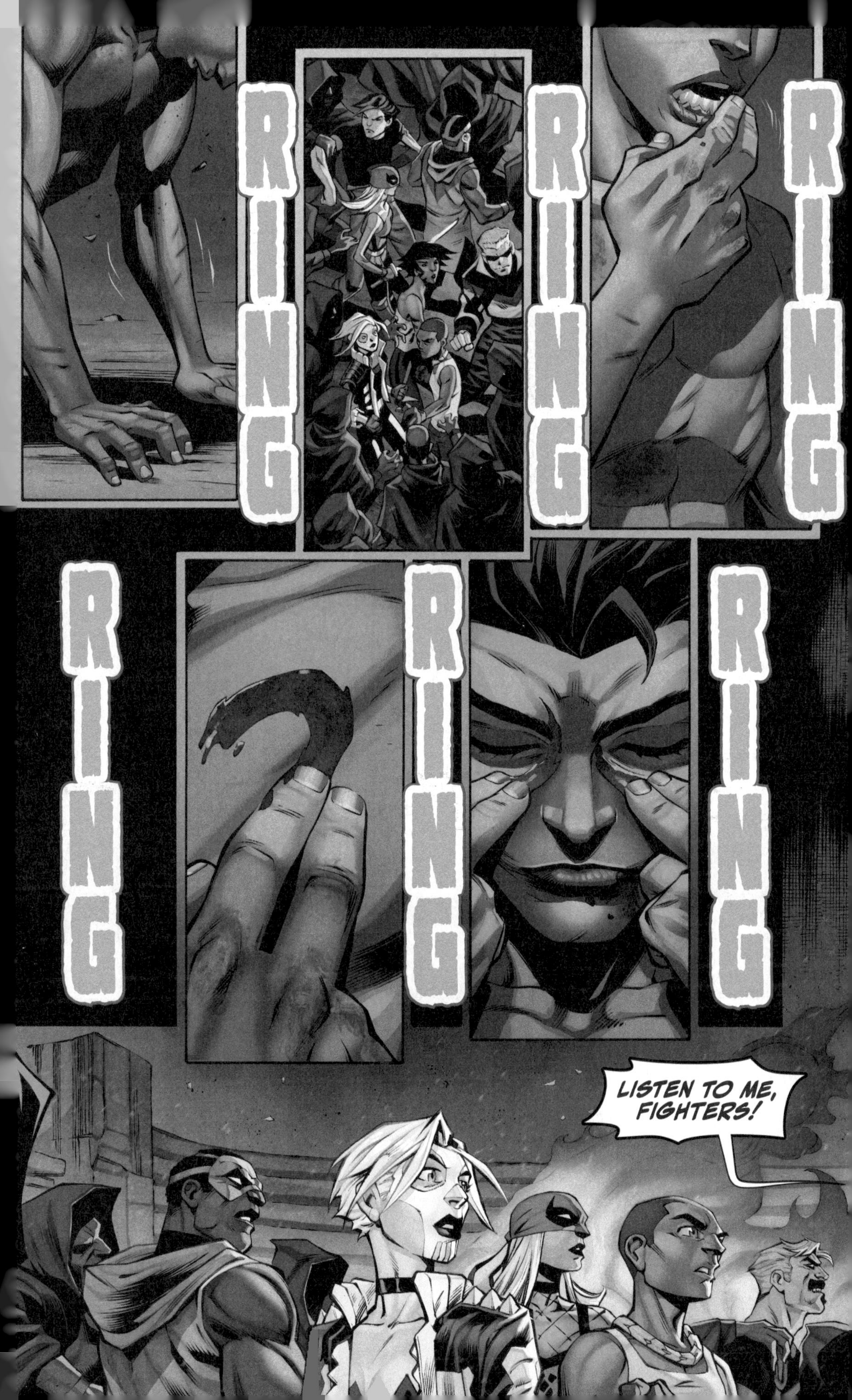
RING
RING
RING
RING
RING
RING
LISTEN TO ME, FIGHTERS!

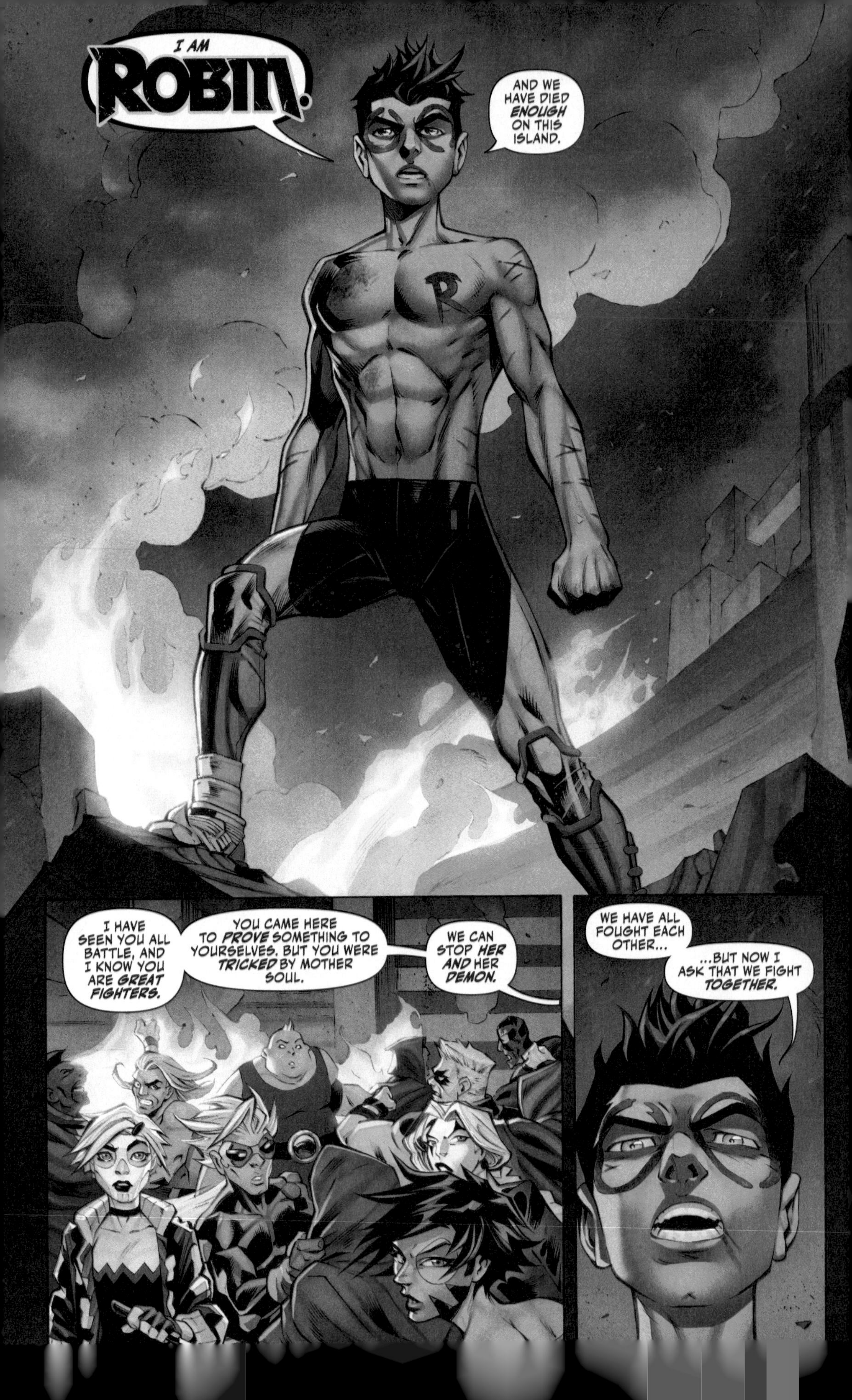
I AM ROBIN.
AND WE HAVE DIED ENOUGH ON THIS ISLAND.
I HAVE SEEN YOU ALL BATTLE, AND I KNOW YOU ARE GREAT FIGHTERS.
YOU CAME HERE TO PROVE SOMETHING TO YOURSELVES. BUT YOU WERE TRICKED BY MOTHER SOUL.
WE CAN STOP HER AND HER DEMON.
WE HAVE ALL FOUGHT EACH OTHER...
...BUT NOW I ASK THAT WE FIGHT TOGETHER.

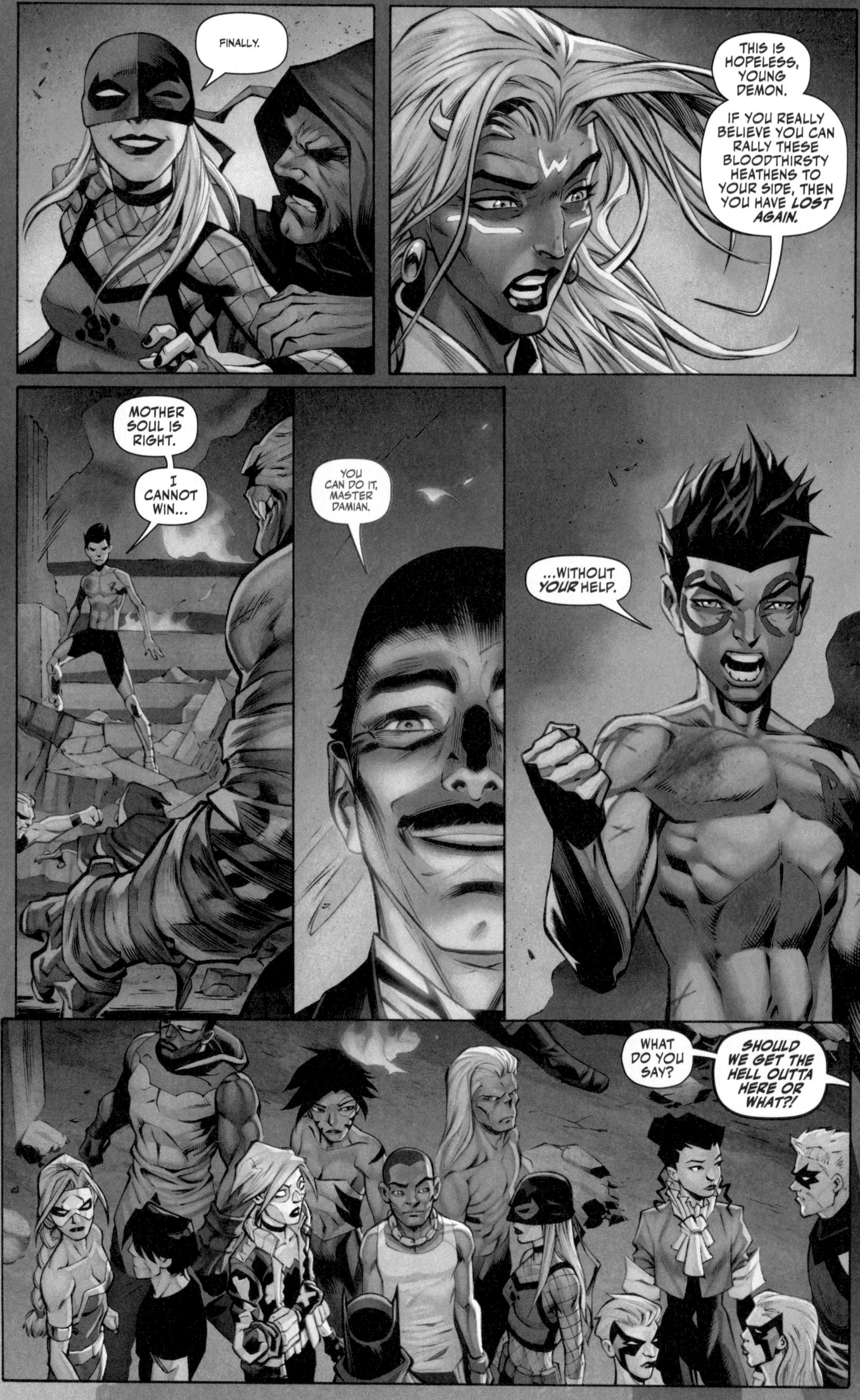
FINALLY.
THIS IS HOPELESS, YOUNG DEMON.
IF YOU REALLY BELIEVE YOU CAN RALLY THESE BLOODTHIRSTY HEATHENS TO YOUR SIDE, THEN YOU HAVE *LOST AGAIN.*
MOTHER SOUL IS RIGHT.
I CANNOT WIN...
YOU CAN DO IT, MASTER DAMIAN.
...WITHOUT *YOUR* HELP.
WHAT DO YOU SAY?
SHOULD WE GET THE HELL OUTTA HERE OR WHAT?!

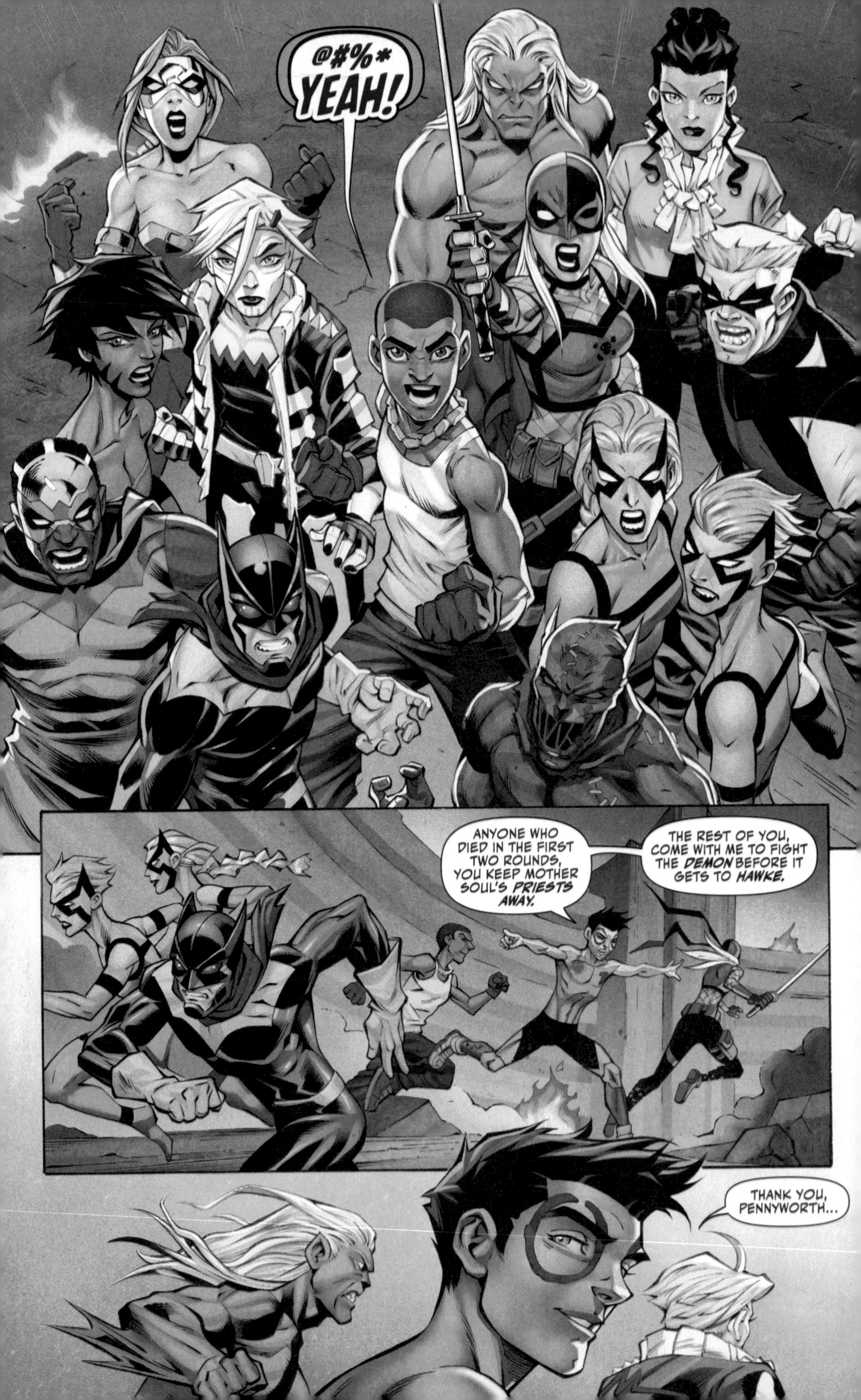
@#%* YEAH!
ANYONE WHO DIED IN THE FIRST TWO ROUNDS, YOU KEEP MOTHER SOUL'S PRIESTS AWAY.
THE REST OF YOU, COME WITH ME TO FIGHT THE DEMON BEFORE IT GETS TO HAWKE.
THANK YOU, PENNYWORTH...

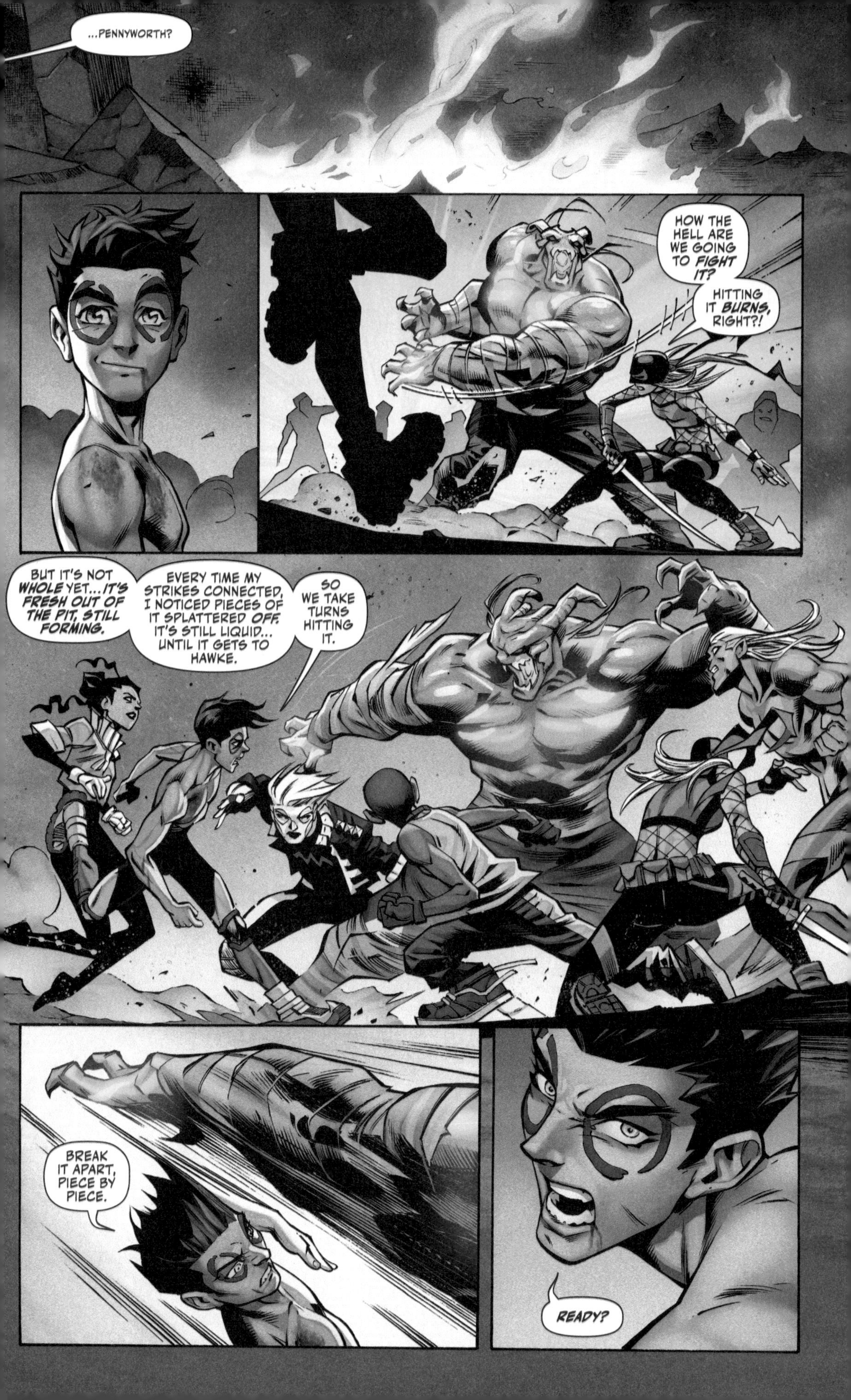
...PENNYWORTH?
HOW THE HELL ARE WE GOING TO *FIGHT* IT?
HITTING IT *BURNS*, RIGHT?!
BUT IT'S NOT *WHOLE* YET...*IT'S FRESH OUT OF THE PIT, STILL FORMING.*
EVERY TIME MY STRIKES CONNECTED, I NOTICED PIECES OF IT SPLATTERED *OFF*. IT'S STILL LIQUID... UNTIL IT GETS TO HAWKE.
SO WE TAKE TURNS HITTING IT.
BREAK IT APART, PIECE BY PIECE.
READY?

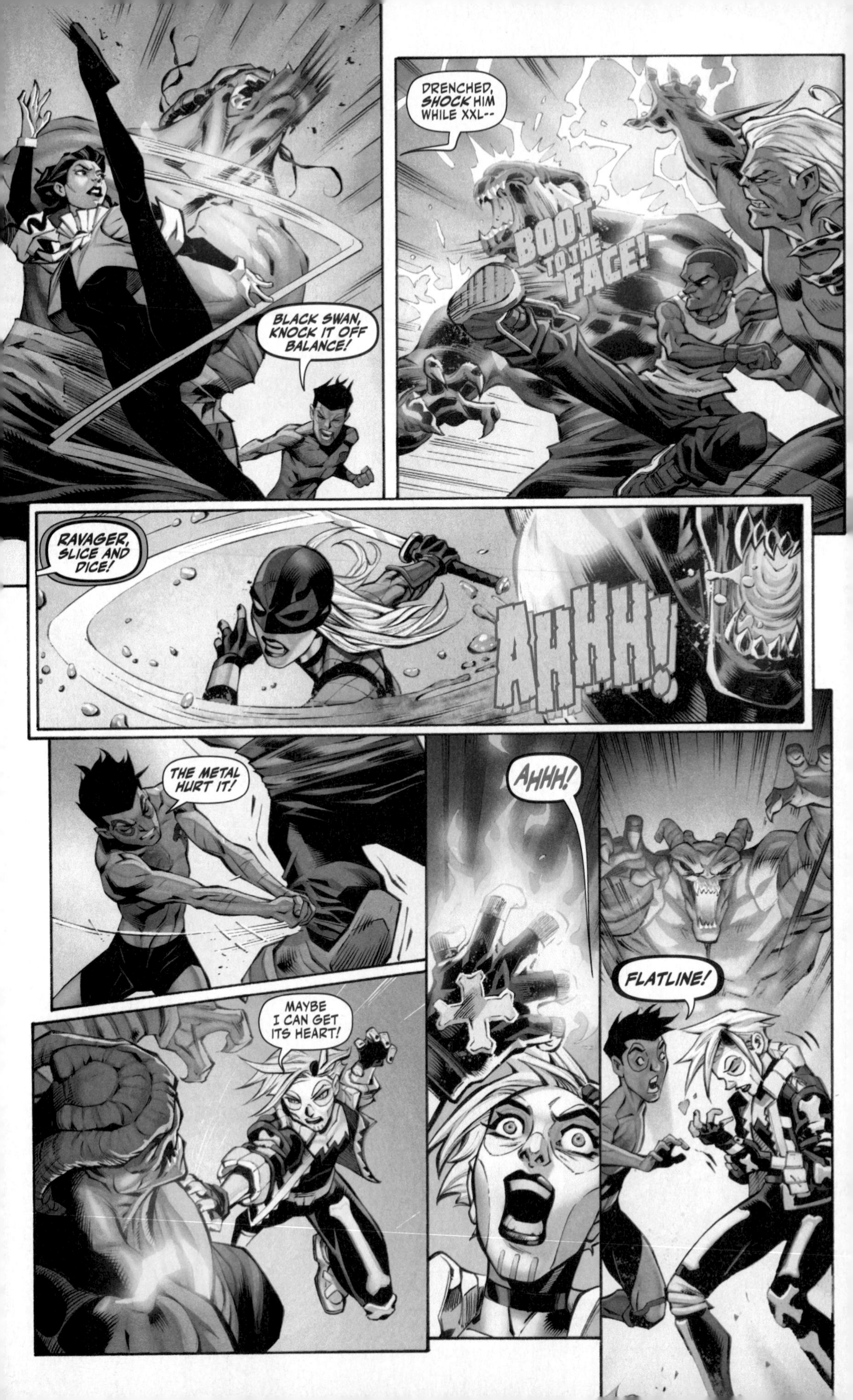
BLACK SWAN, KNOCK IT OFF BALANCE!
DRENCHED, SHOCK HIM WHILE XXL--
BOOT TO THE FACE!
RAVAGER, SLICE AND DICE!
AHHHH!
THE METAL HURT IT!
MAYBE I CAN GET ITS HEART!
AHHH!
FLATLINE!

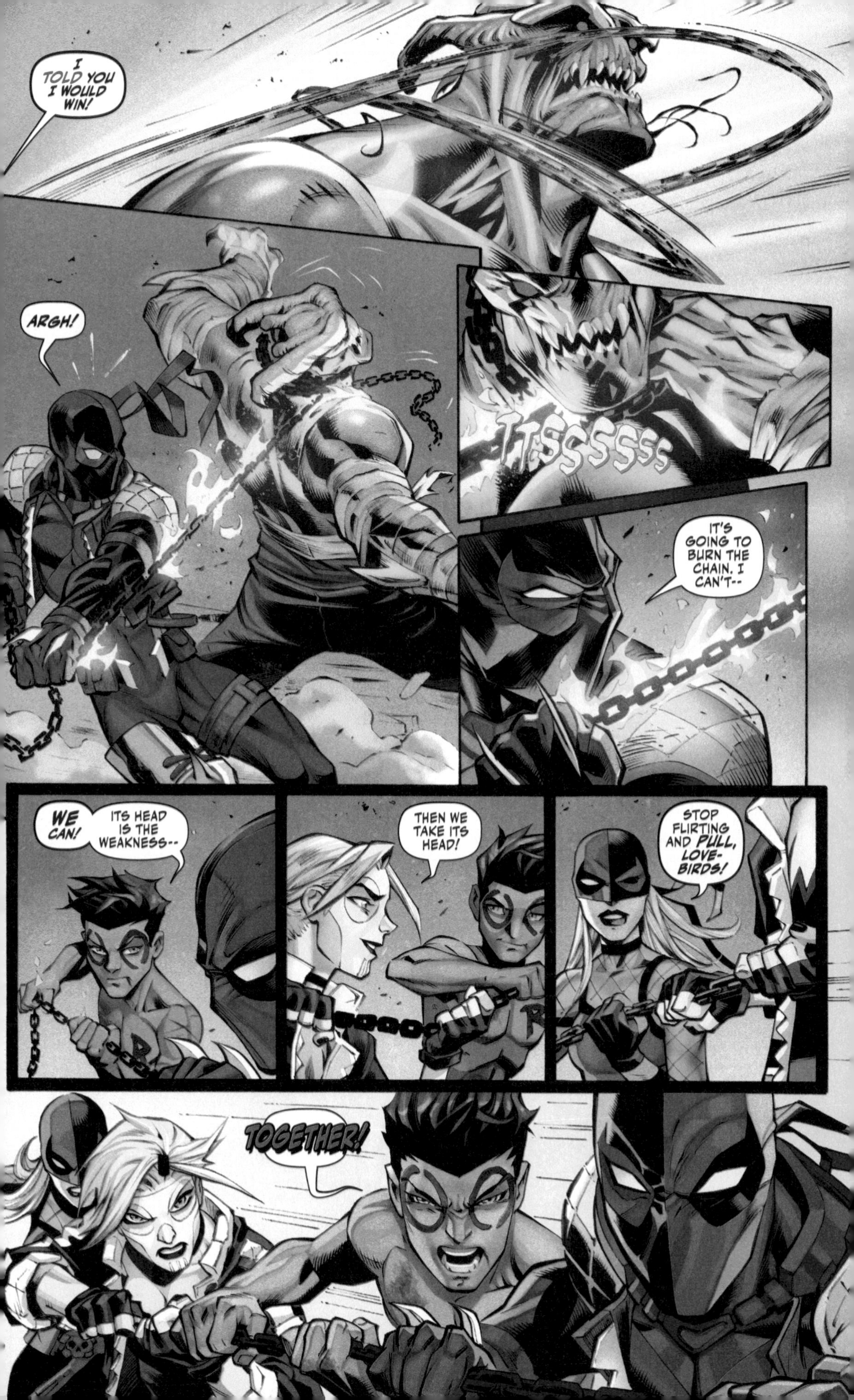
I TOLD YOU I WOULD WIN!
ARGH!
TSSSSSSS
IT'S GOING TO BURN THE CHAIN. I CAN'T--
WE CAN!
ITS HEAD IS THE WEAKNESS--
THEN WE TAKE ITS HEAD!
STOP FLIRTING AND PULL, LOVE-BIRDS!
TOGETHER!

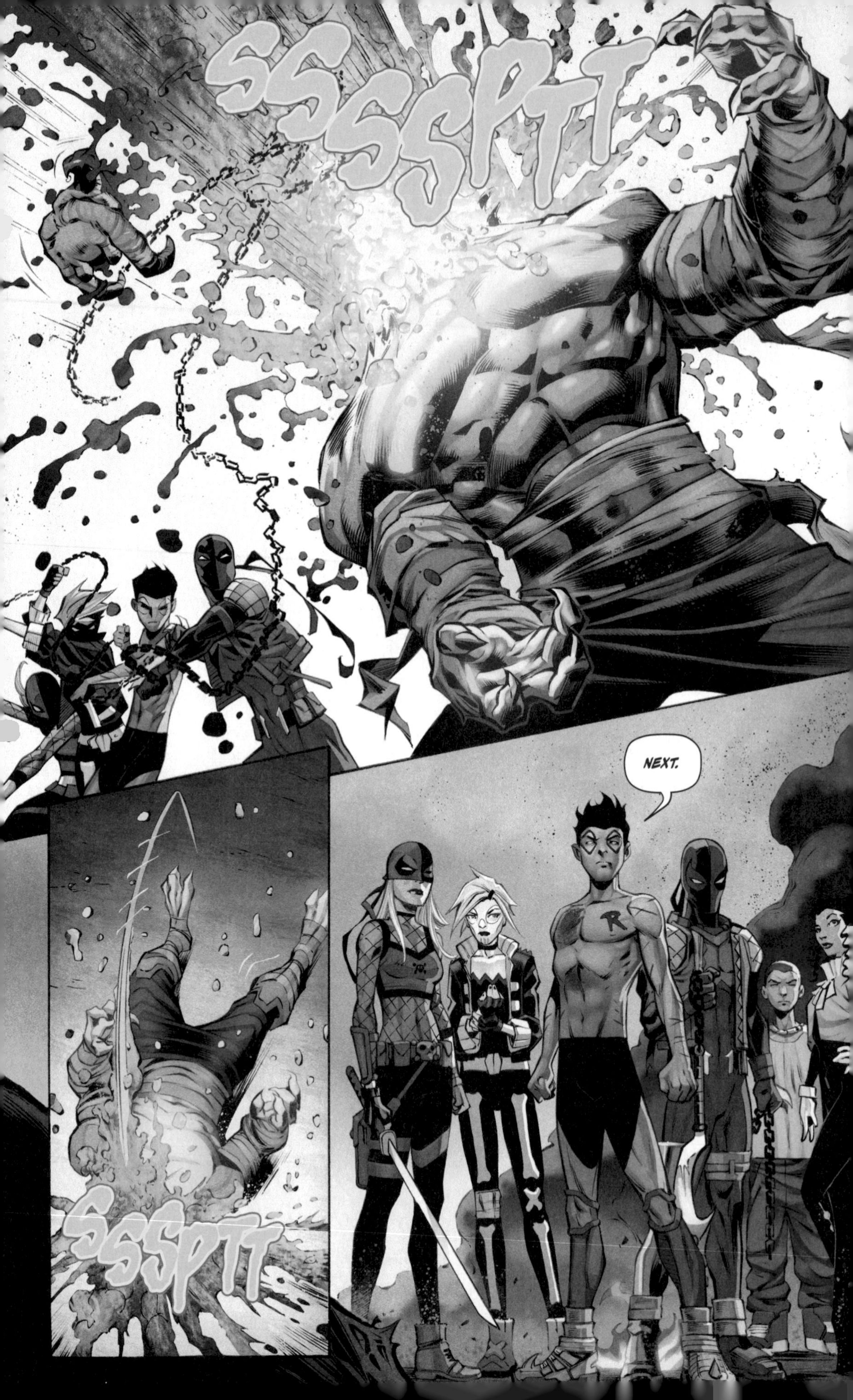
SSSPTT
NEXT.
SSSPTT

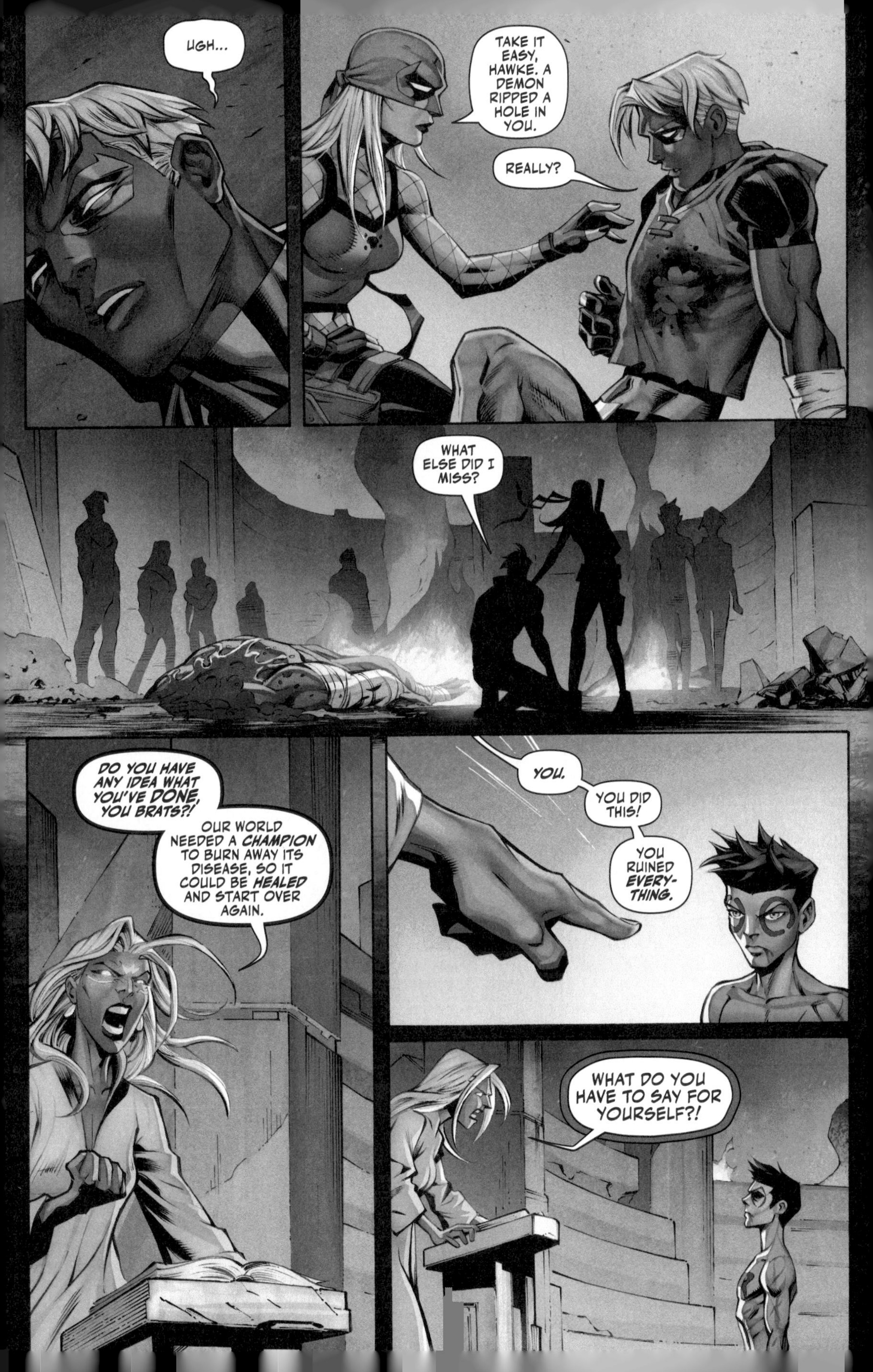
UGH...
TAKE IT EASY, HAWKE. A DEMON RIPPED A HOLE IN YOU.
REALLY?
WHAT ELSE DID I MISS?
DO YOU HAVE ANY IDEA WHAT YOU'VE DONE, YOU BRATS?!
OUR WORLD NEEDED A CHAMPION TO BURN AWAY ITS DISEASE, SO IT COULD BE HEALED AND START OVER AGAIN.
YOU.
YOU DID THIS!
YOU RUINED EVERYTHING.
WHAT DO YOU HAVE TO SAY FOR YOURSELF?!

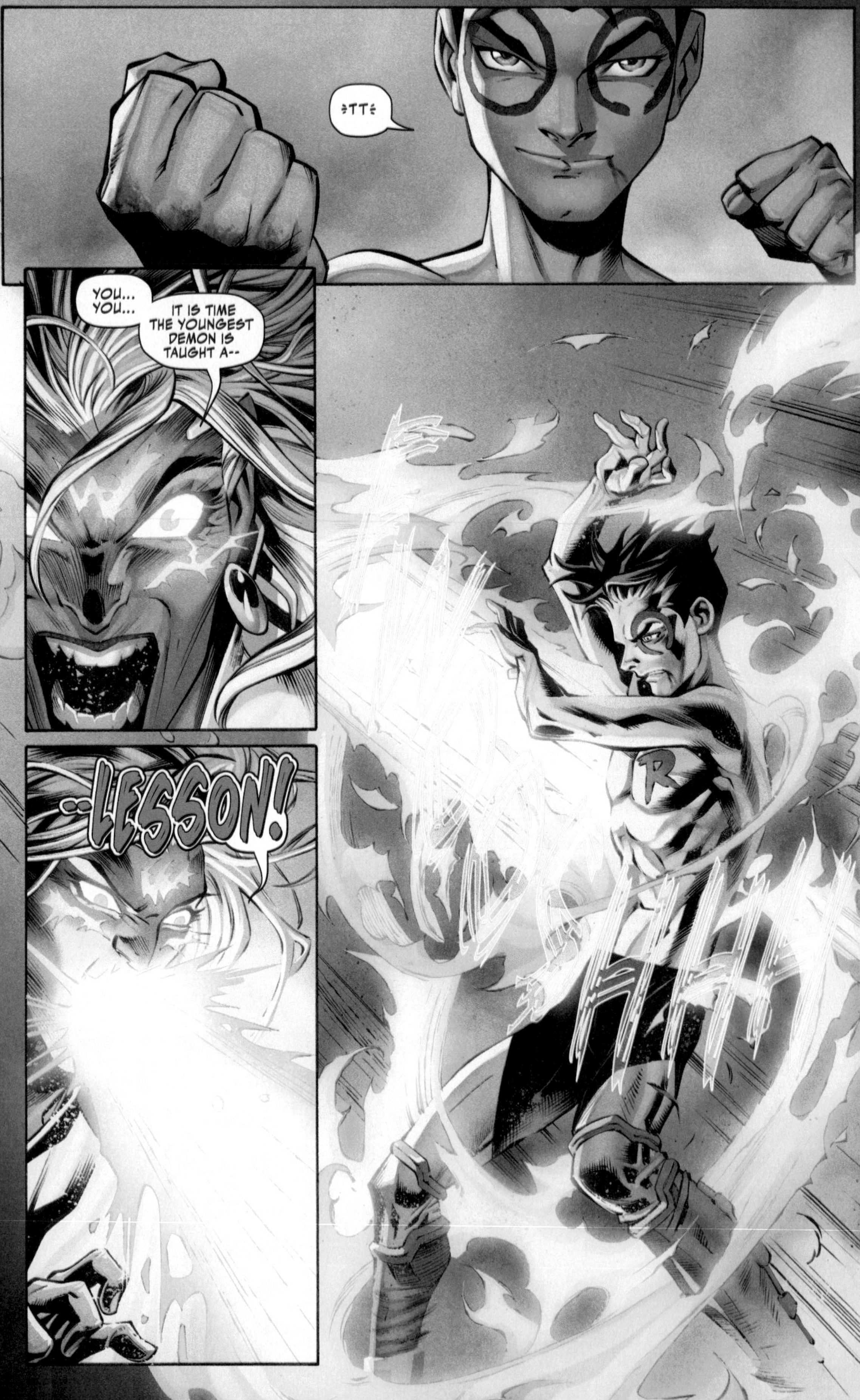
TT
YOU... YOU...
IT IS TIME THE YOUNGEST DEMON IS TAUGHT A--
--LESSON!

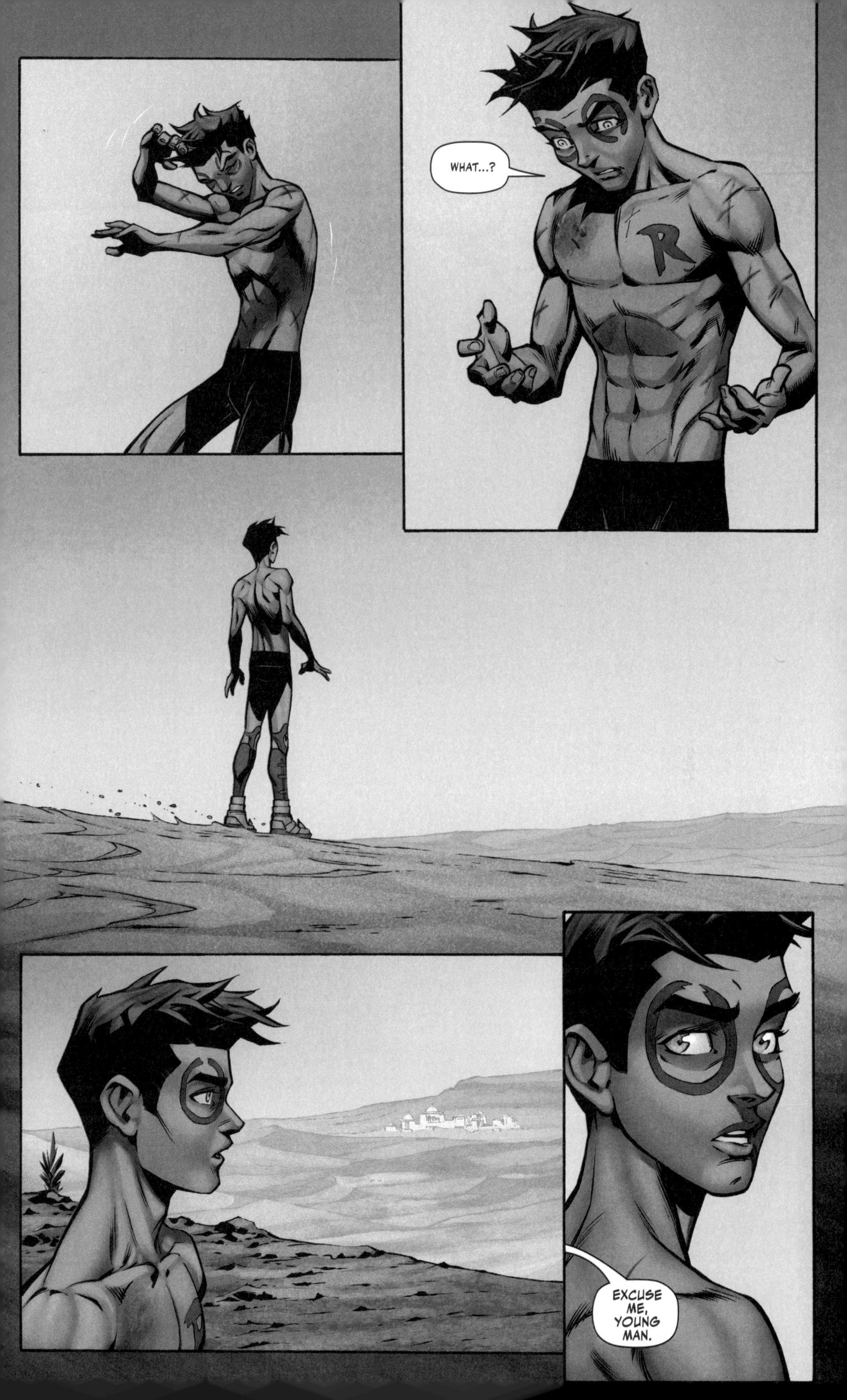
WHAT...?
EXCUSE ME, YOUNG MAN.

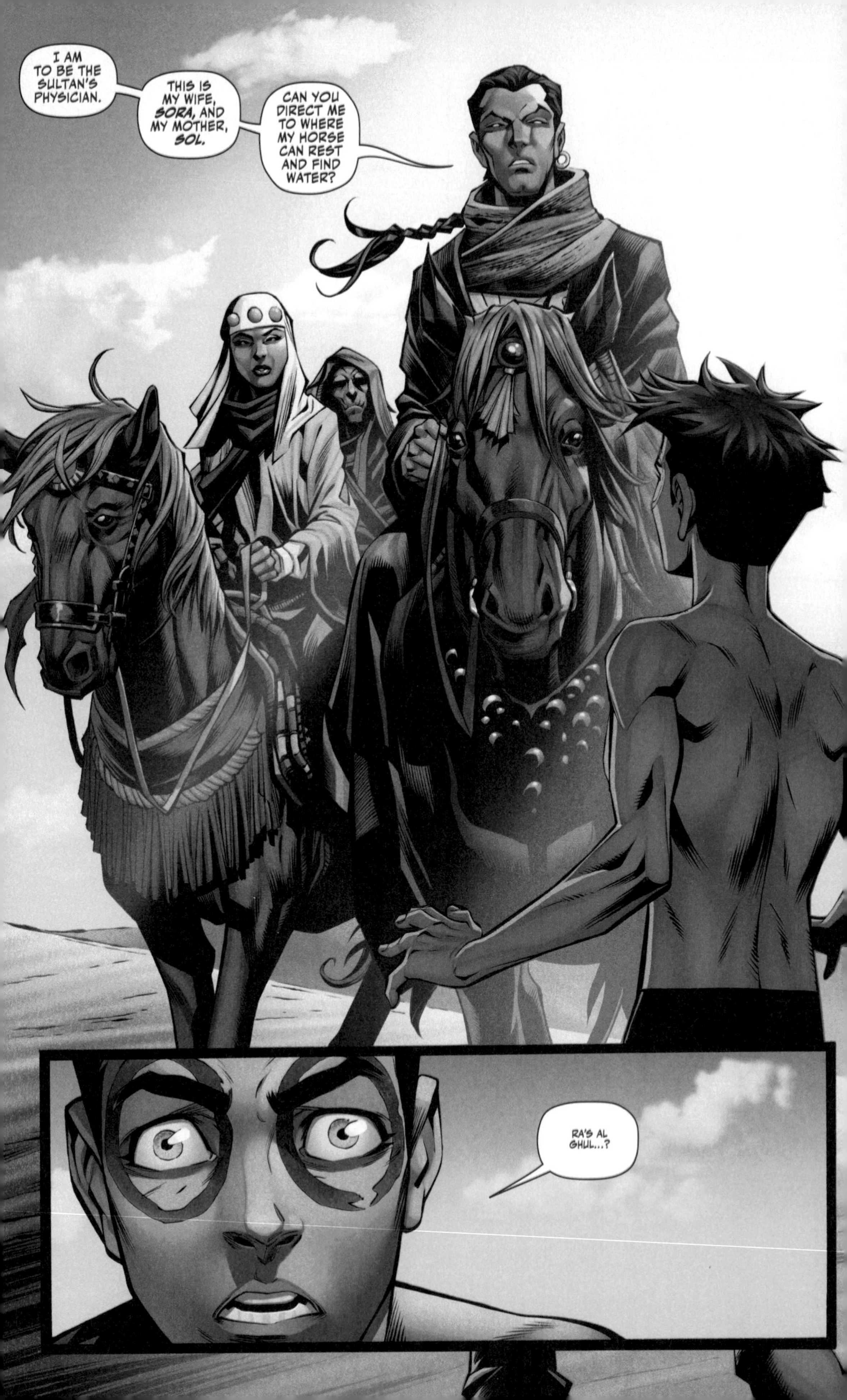
I AM TO BE THE SULTAN'S PHYSICIAN.
THIS IS MY WIFE, SORA, AND MY MOTHER, SOL.
CAN YOU DIRECT ME TO WHERE MY HORSE CAN REST AND FIND WATER?
RA'S AL GHUL...?

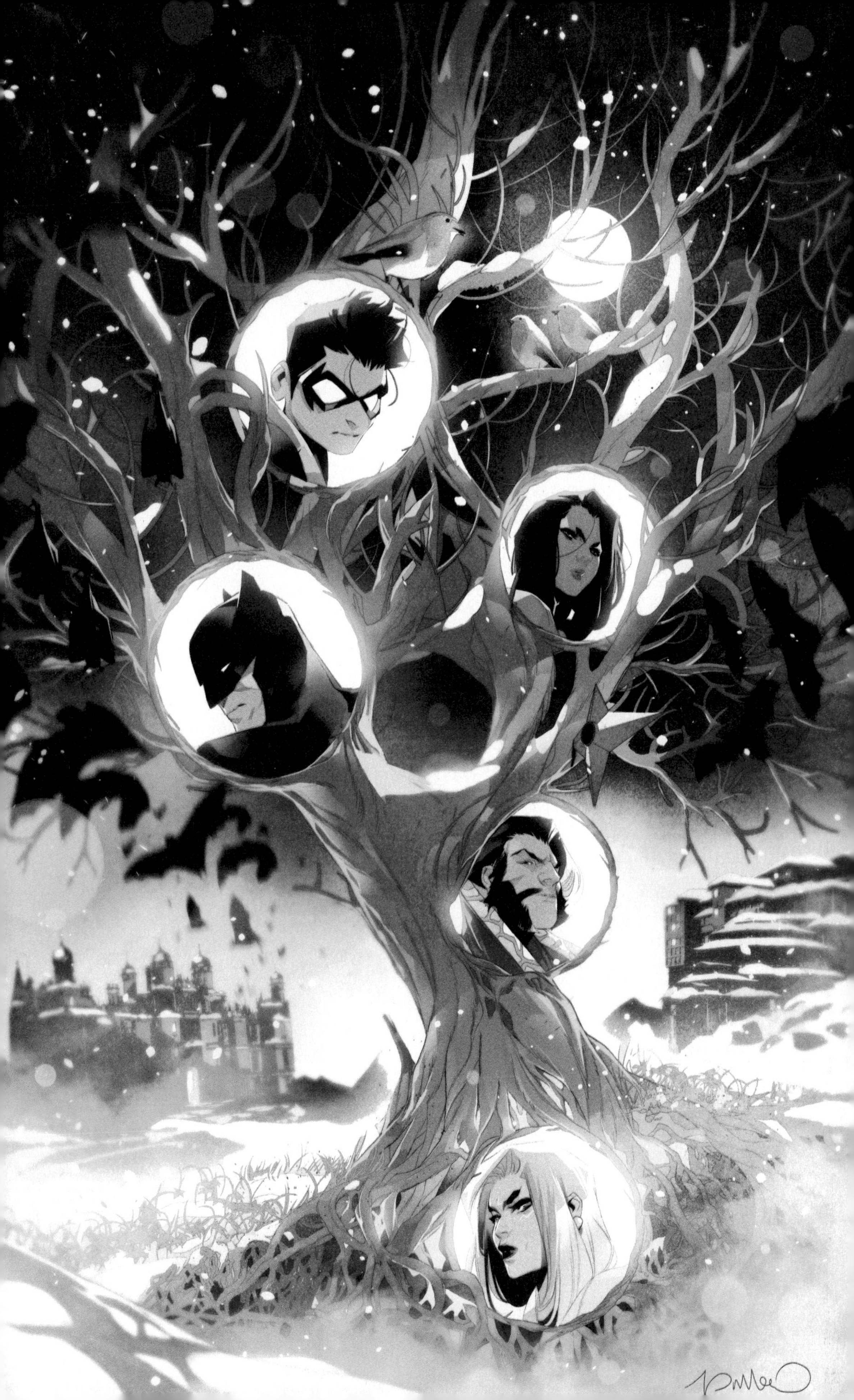

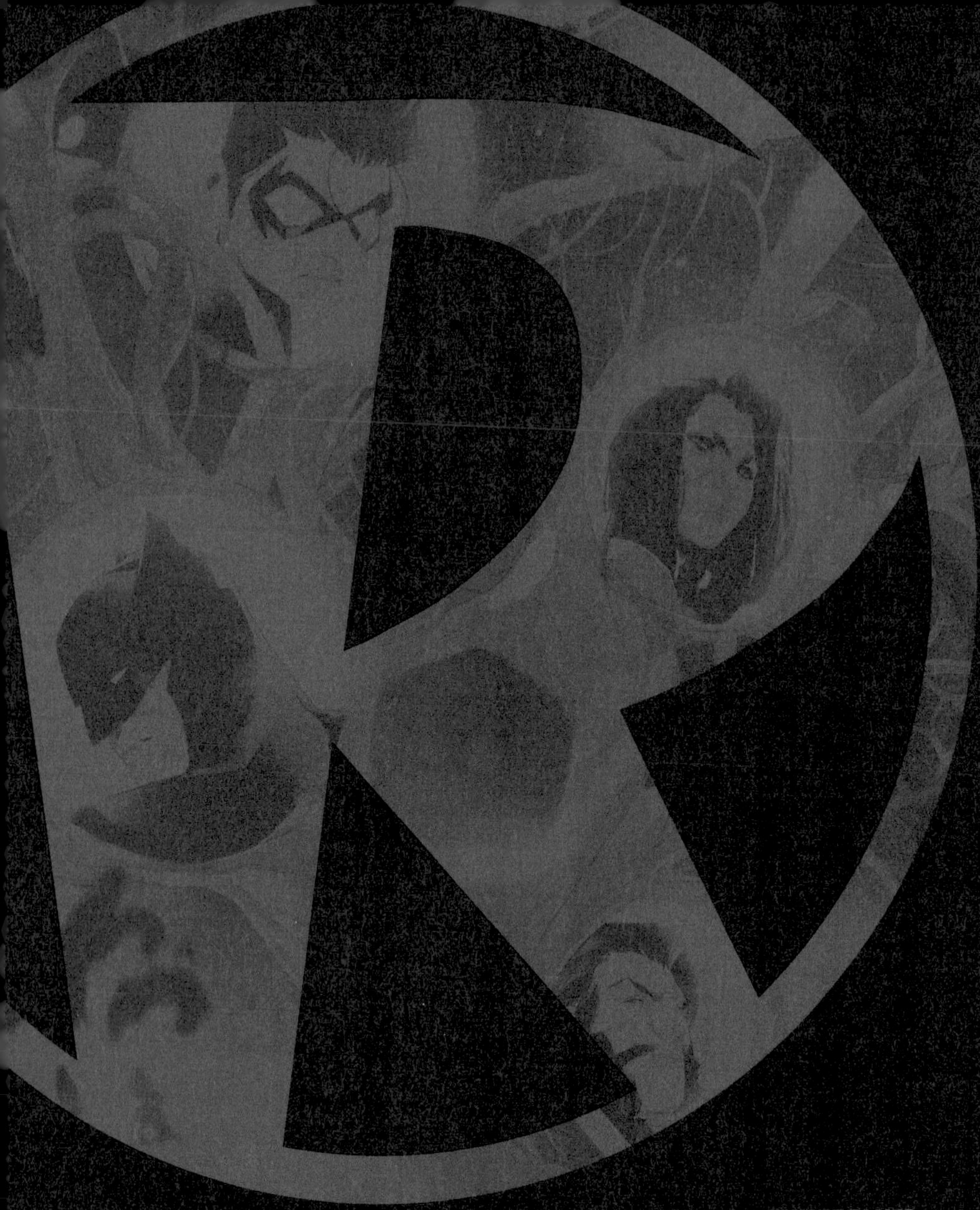

Robin #10 cover by **SIMONE DI MEO**

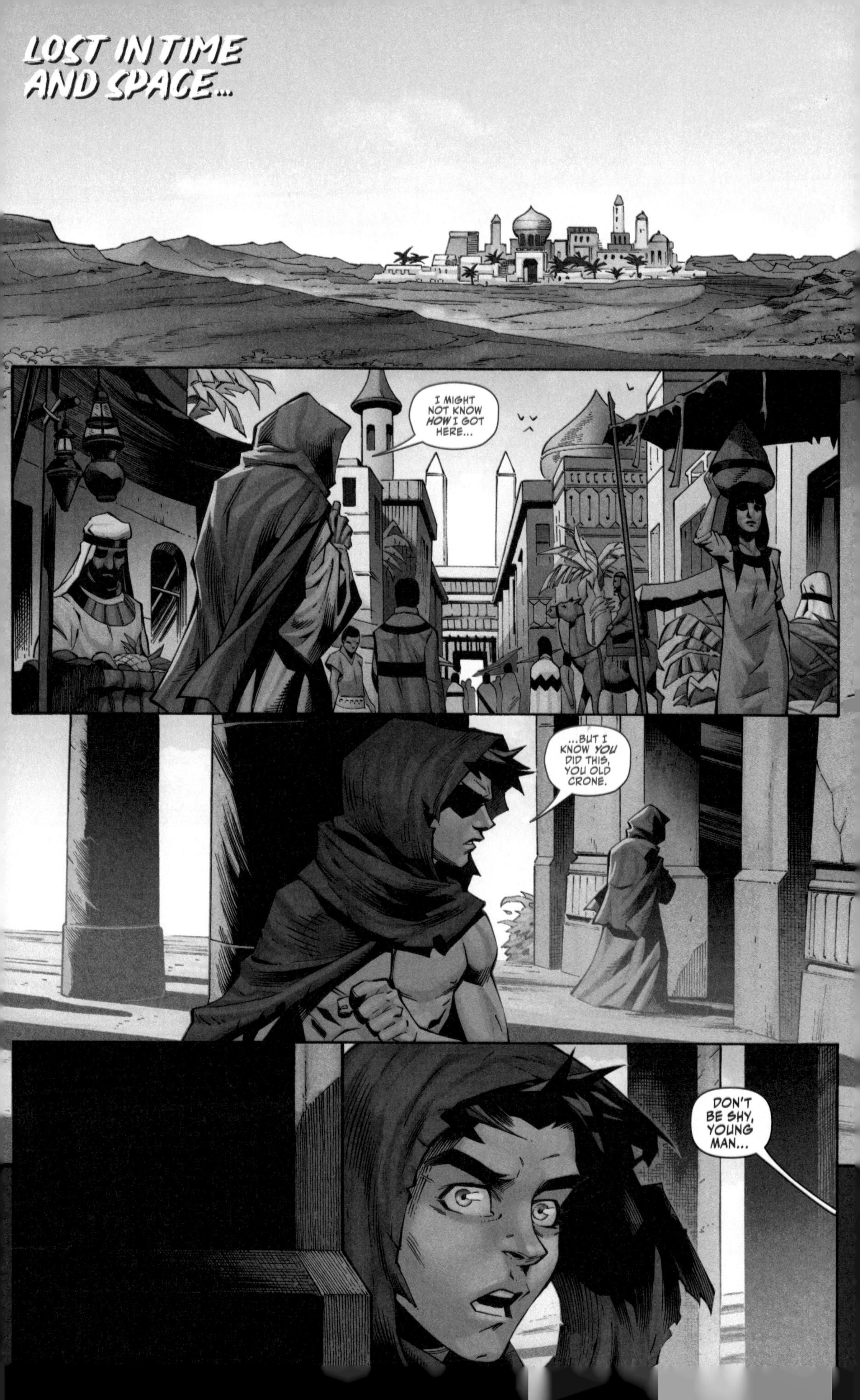
LOST IN TIME AND SPACE...
I MIGHT NOT KNOW HOW I GOT HERE...
...BUT I KNOW YOU DID THIS, YOU OLD CRONE.
DON'T BE SHY, YOUNG MAN...

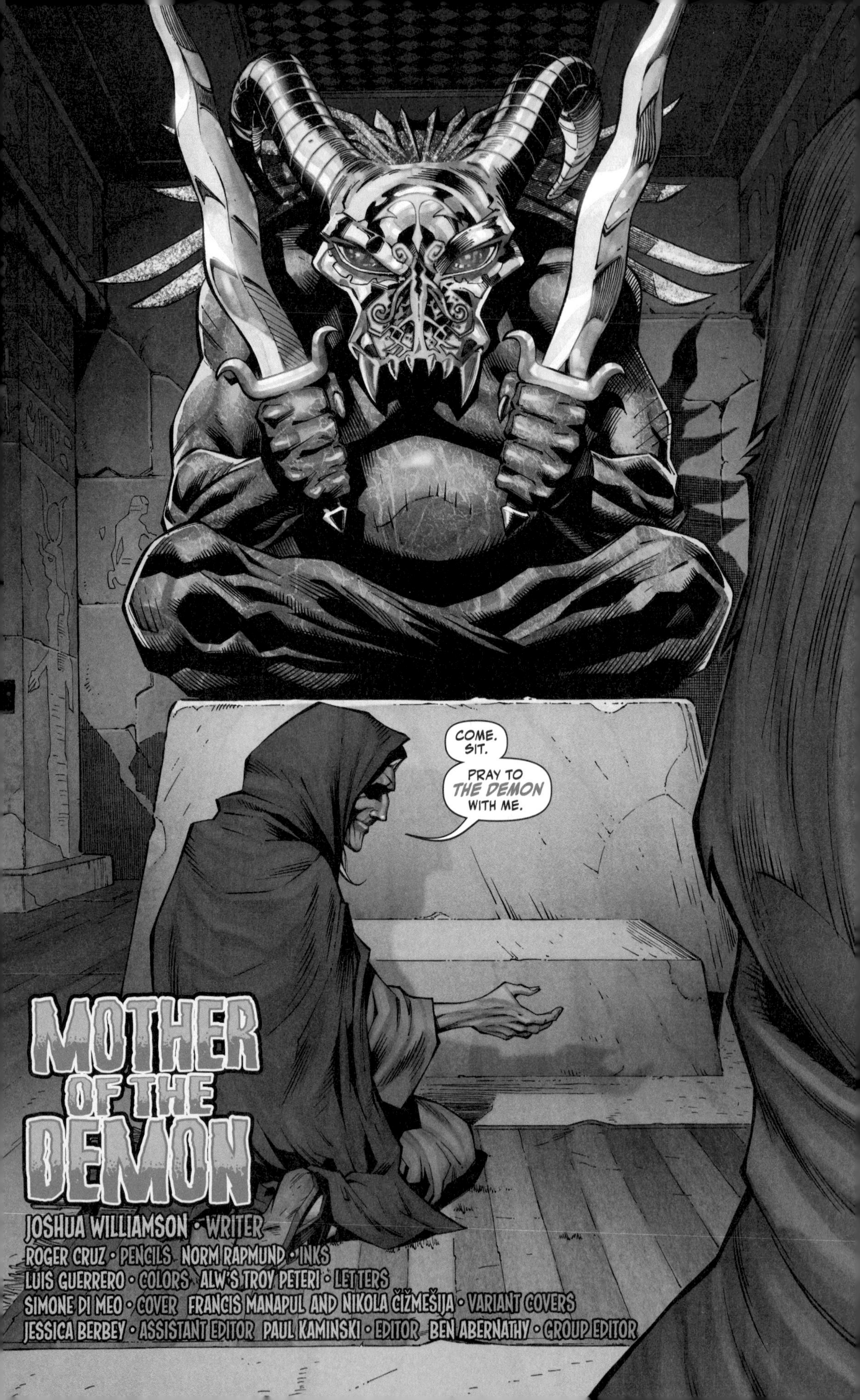
COME. SIT.
PRAY TO THE DEMON WITH ME.
MOTHER OF THE DEMON
JOSHUA WILLIAMSON • WRITER
ROGER CRUZ • PENCILS NORM RAPMUND • INKS
LUIS GUERRERO • COLORS ALW'S TROY PETERI • LETTERS
SIMONE DI MEO • COVER FRANCIS MANAPUL AND NIKOLA ČIŽMEŠIJA • VARIANT COVERS
JESSICA BERBEY • ASSISTANT EDITOR PAUL KAMINSKI • EDITOR BEN ABERNATHY • GROUP EDITOR

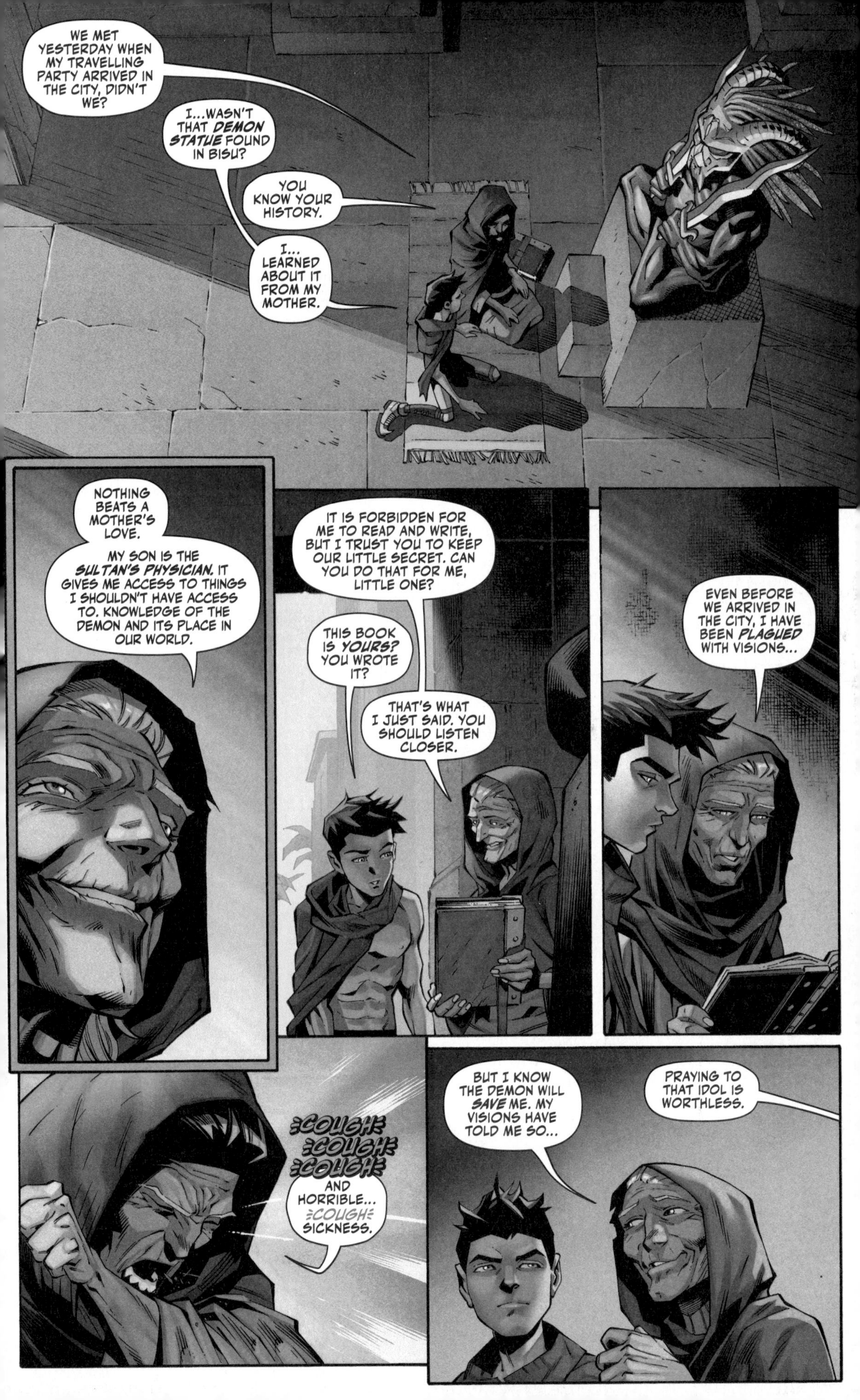
WE MET YESTERDAY WHEN MY TRAVELLING PARTY ARRIVED IN THE CITY, DIDN'T WE?
I...WASN'T THAT DEMON STATUE FOUND IN BISU?
YOU KNOW YOUR HISTORY.
I... LEARNED ABOUT IT FROM MY MOTHER.
NOTHING BEATS A MOTHER'S LOVE.
MY SON IS THE SULTAN'S PHYSICIAN. IT GIVES ME ACCESS TO THINGS I SHOULDN'T HAVE ACCESS TO. KNOWLEDGE OF THE DEMON AND ITS PLACE IN OUR WORLD.
IT IS FORBIDDEN FOR ME TO READ AND WRITE, BUT I TRUST YOU TO KEEP OUR LITTLE SECRET. CAN YOU DO THAT FOR ME, LITTLE ONE?
THIS BOOK IS YOURS? YOU WROTE IT?
THAT'S WHAT I JUST SAID. YOU SHOULD LISTEN CLOSER.
EVEN BEFORE WE ARRIVED IN THE CITY, I HAVE BEEN PLAGUED WITH VISIONS...
COUGH COUGH COUGH
AND HORRIBLE... COUGH SICKNESS.
BUT I KNOW THE DEMON WILL SAVE ME. MY VISIONS HAVE TOLD ME SO...
PRAYING TO THAT IDOL IS WORTHLESS.

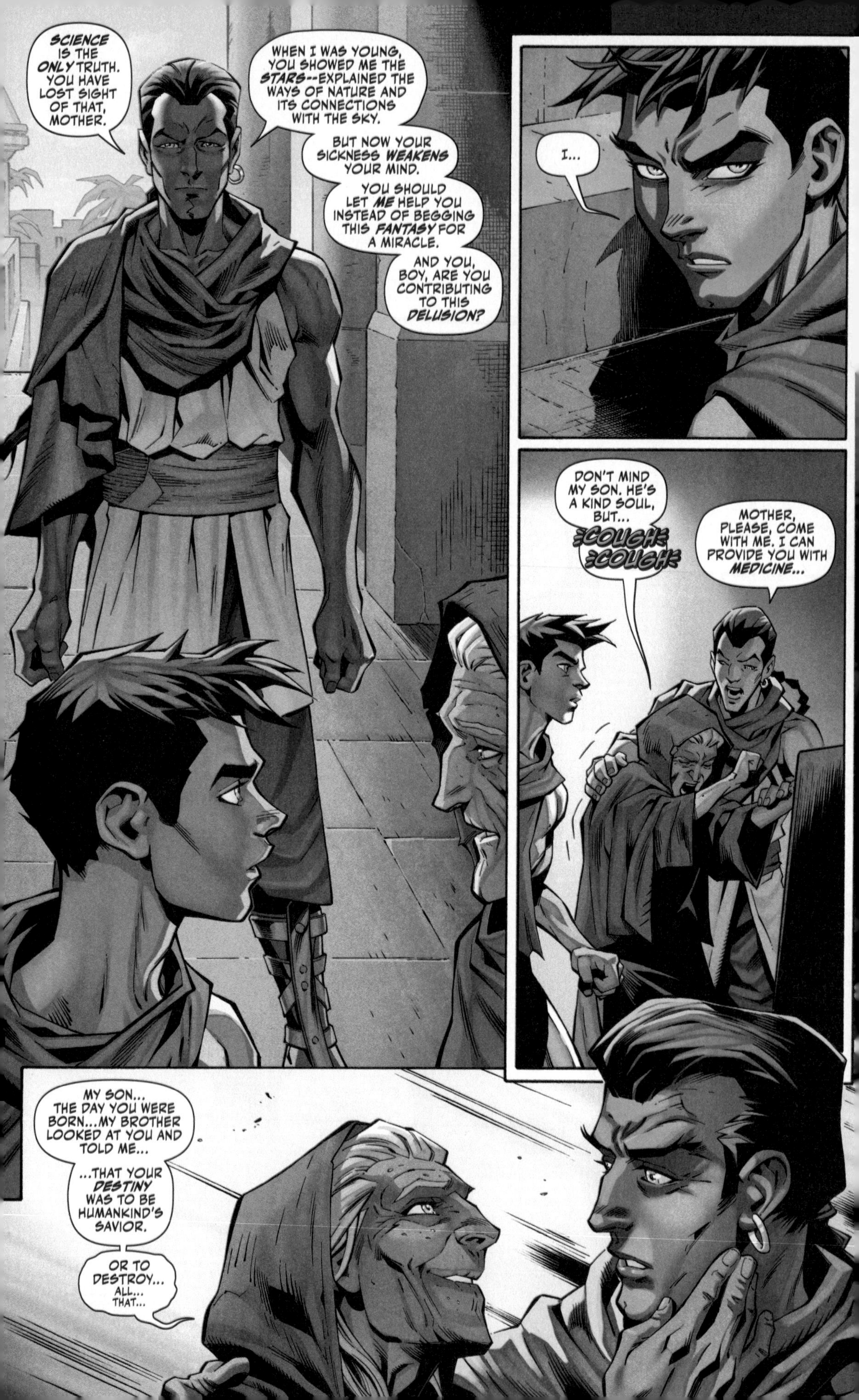
SCIENCE IS THE ONLY TRUTH. YOU HAVE LOST SIGHT OF THAT, MOTHER.
WHEN I WAS YOUNG, YOU SHOWED ME THE STARS--EXPLAINED THE WAYS OF NATURE AND ITS CONNECTIONS WITH THE SKY.
BUT NOW YOUR SICKNESS WEAKENS YOUR MIND.
YOU SHOULD LET ME HELP YOU INSTEAD OF BEGGING THIS FANTASY FOR A MIRACLE.
AND YOU, BOY, ARE YOU CONTRIBUTING TO THIS DELUSION?
I...
DON'T MIND MY SON. HE'S A KIND SOUL, BUT...
COUGH
COUGH
MOTHER, PLEASE, COME WITH ME. I CAN PROVIDE YOU WITH MEDICINE...
MY SON... THE DAY YOU WERE BORN...MY BROTHER LOOKED AT YOU AND TOLD ME...
...THAT YOUR DESTINY WAS TO BE HUMANKIND'S SAVIOR.
OR TO DESTROY... ALL... THAT...

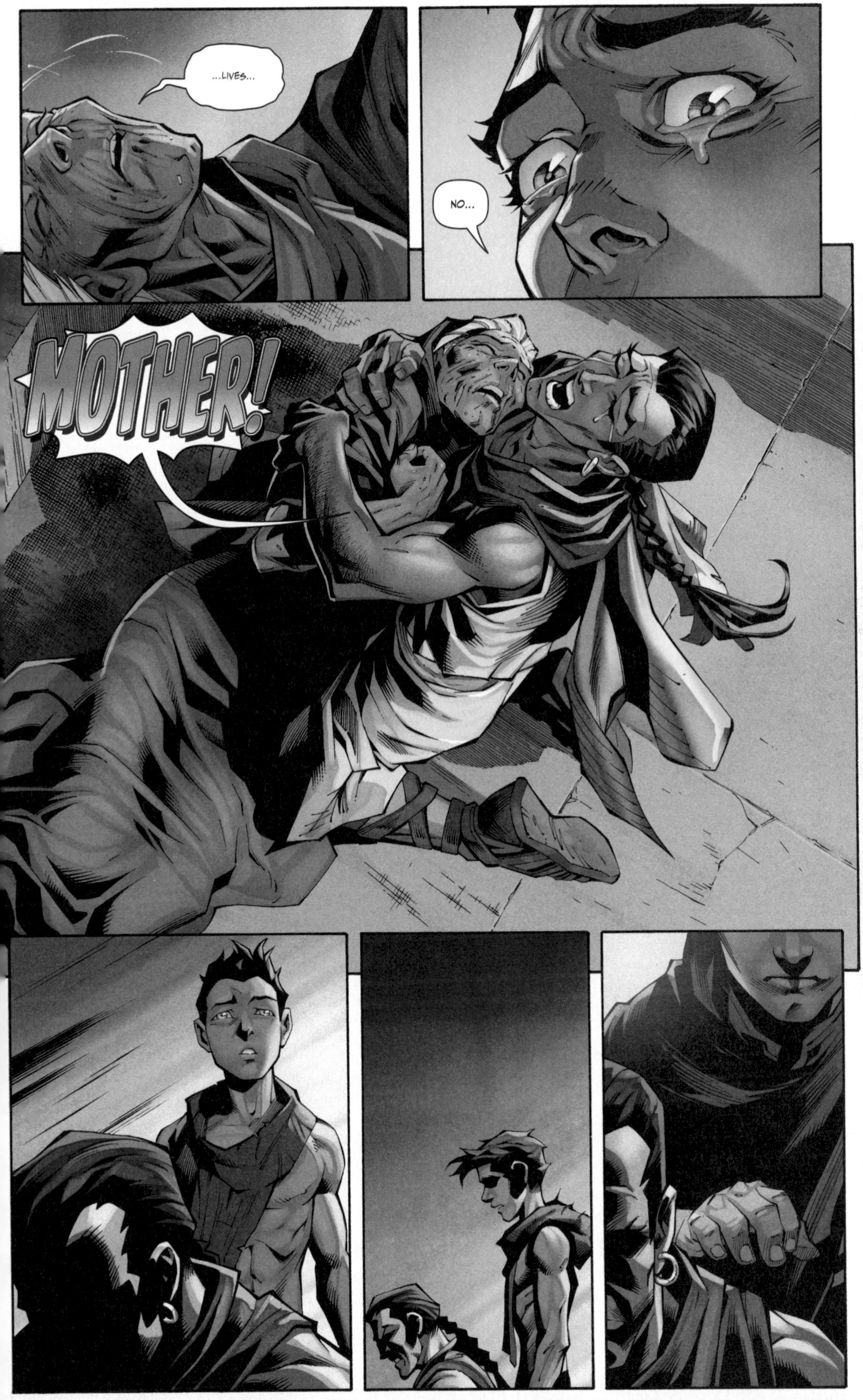
...LIVES...
NO...
MOTHER!

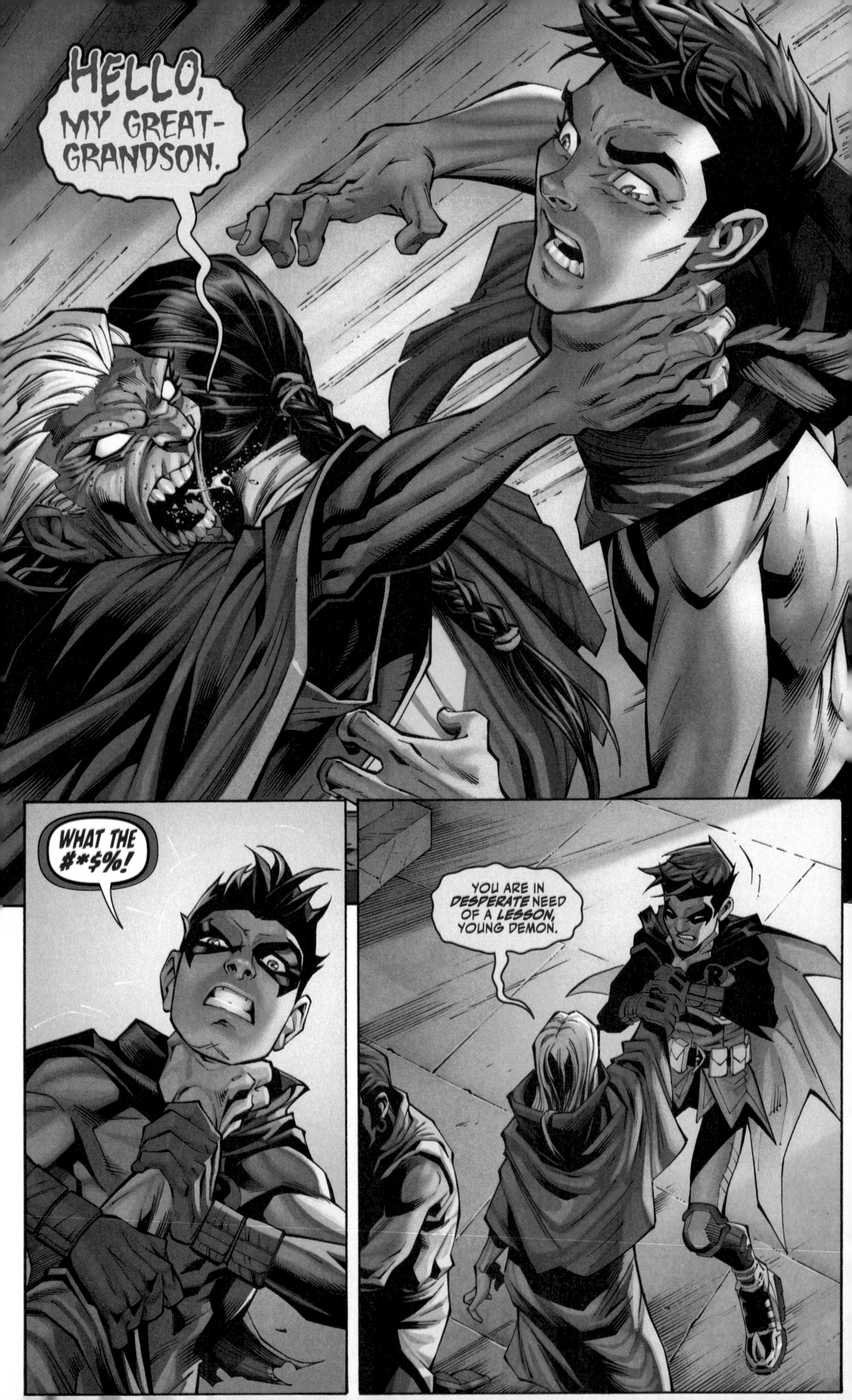
HELLO, MY GREAT-GRANDSON.
WHAT THE #*$%!
YOU ARE IN *DESPERATE* NEED OF A *LESSON*, YOUNG DEMON.

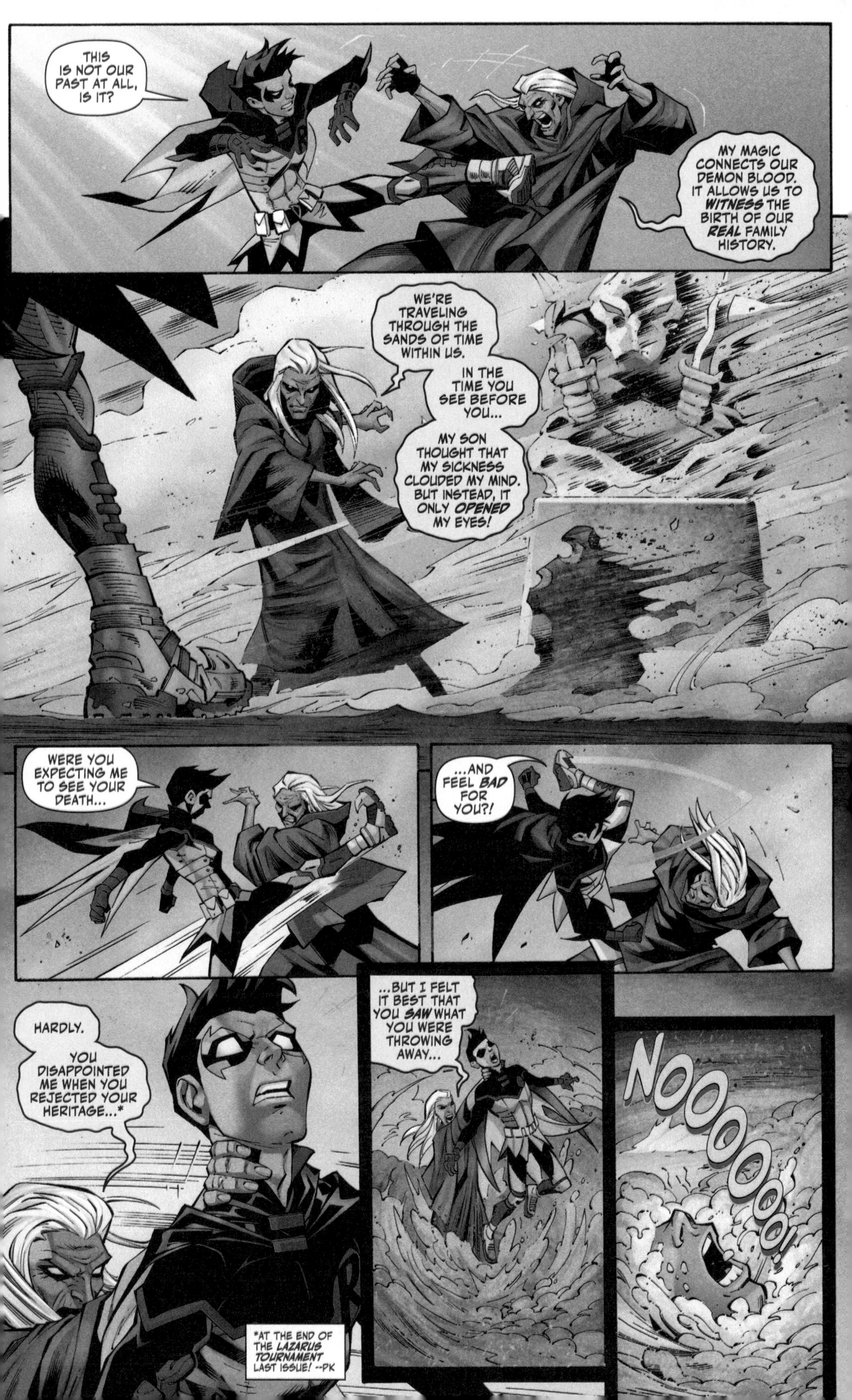
THIS IS NOT OUR PAST AT ALL, IS IT?
MY MAGIC CONNECTS OUR DEMON BLOOD. IT ALLOWS US TO WITNESS THE BIRTH OF OUR REAL FAMILY HISTORY.
WE'RE TRAVELING THROUGH THE SANDS OF TIME WITHIN US.
IN THE TIME YOU SEE BEFORE YOU...
MY SON THOUGHT THAT MY SICKNESS CLOUDED MY MIND. BUT INSTEAD, IT ONLY OPENED MY EYES!
WERE YOU EXPECTING ME TO SEE YOUR DEATH...
...AND FEEL BAD FOR YOU?!
HARDLY.
YOU DISAPPOINTED ME WHEN YOU REJECTED YOUR HERITAGE...*
*AT THE END OF THE LAZARUS TOURNAMENT LAST ISSUE! --PK
...BUT I FELT IT BEST THAT YOU SAW WHAT YOU WERE THROWING AWAY...
NOOOOOOO!

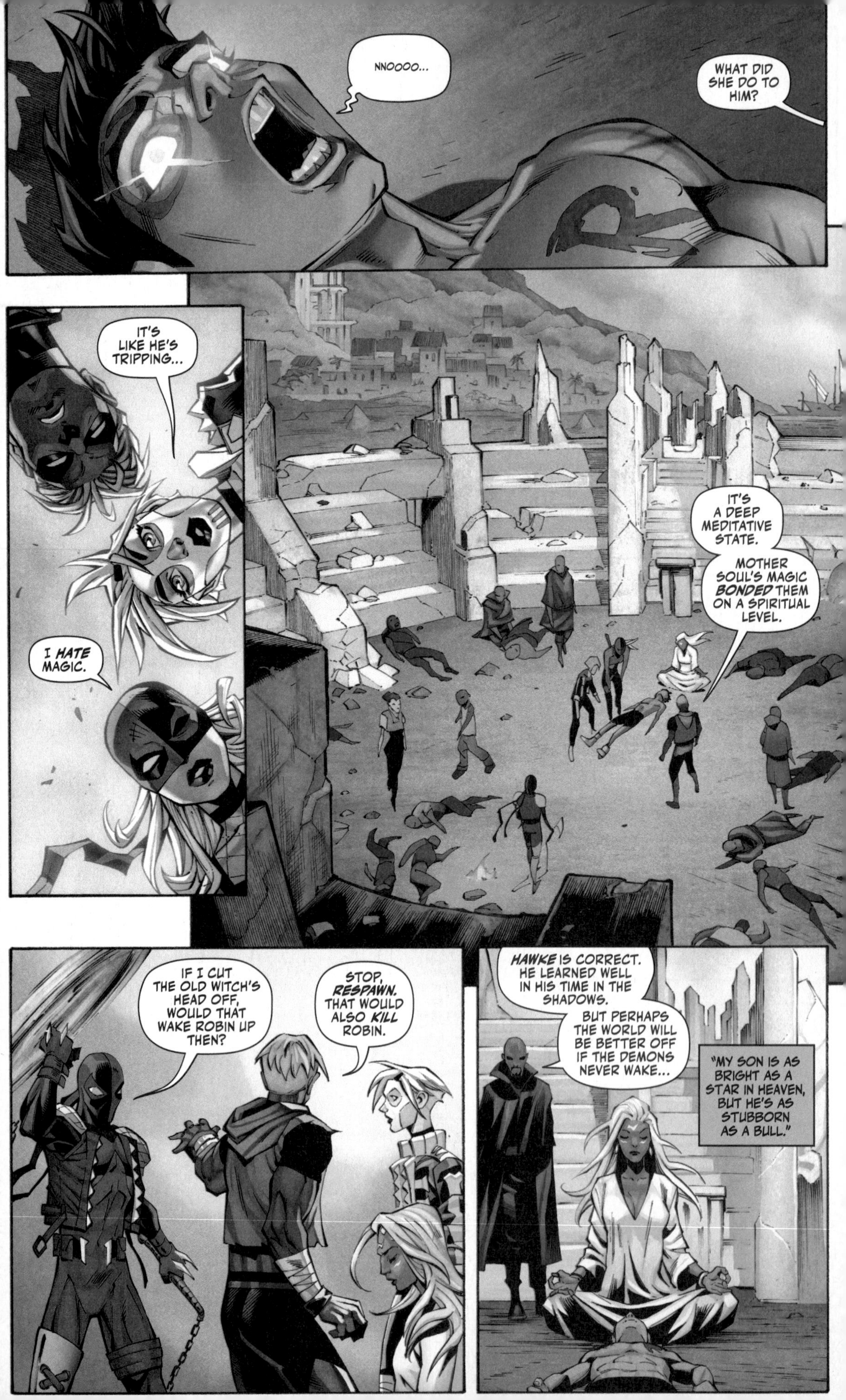
NNOOOO...
WHAT DID SHE DO TO HIM?
IT'S LIKE HE'S TRIPPING...
I HATE MAGIC.
IT'S A DEEP MEDITATIVE STATE.
MOTHER SOUL'S MAGIC BONDED THEM ON A SPIRITUAL LEVEL.
IF I CUT THE OLD WITCH'S HEAD OFF, WOULD THAT WAKE ROBIN UP THEN?
STOP, RESPAWN. THAT WOULD ALSO KILL ROBIN.
HAWKE IS CORRECT. HE LEARNED WELL IN HIS TIME IN THE SHADOWS.
BUT PERHAPS THE WORLD WILL BE BETTER OFF IF THE DEMONS NEVER WAKE...
"MY SON IS AS BRIGHT AS A STAR IN HEAVEN, BUT HE'S AS STUBBORN AS A BULL."

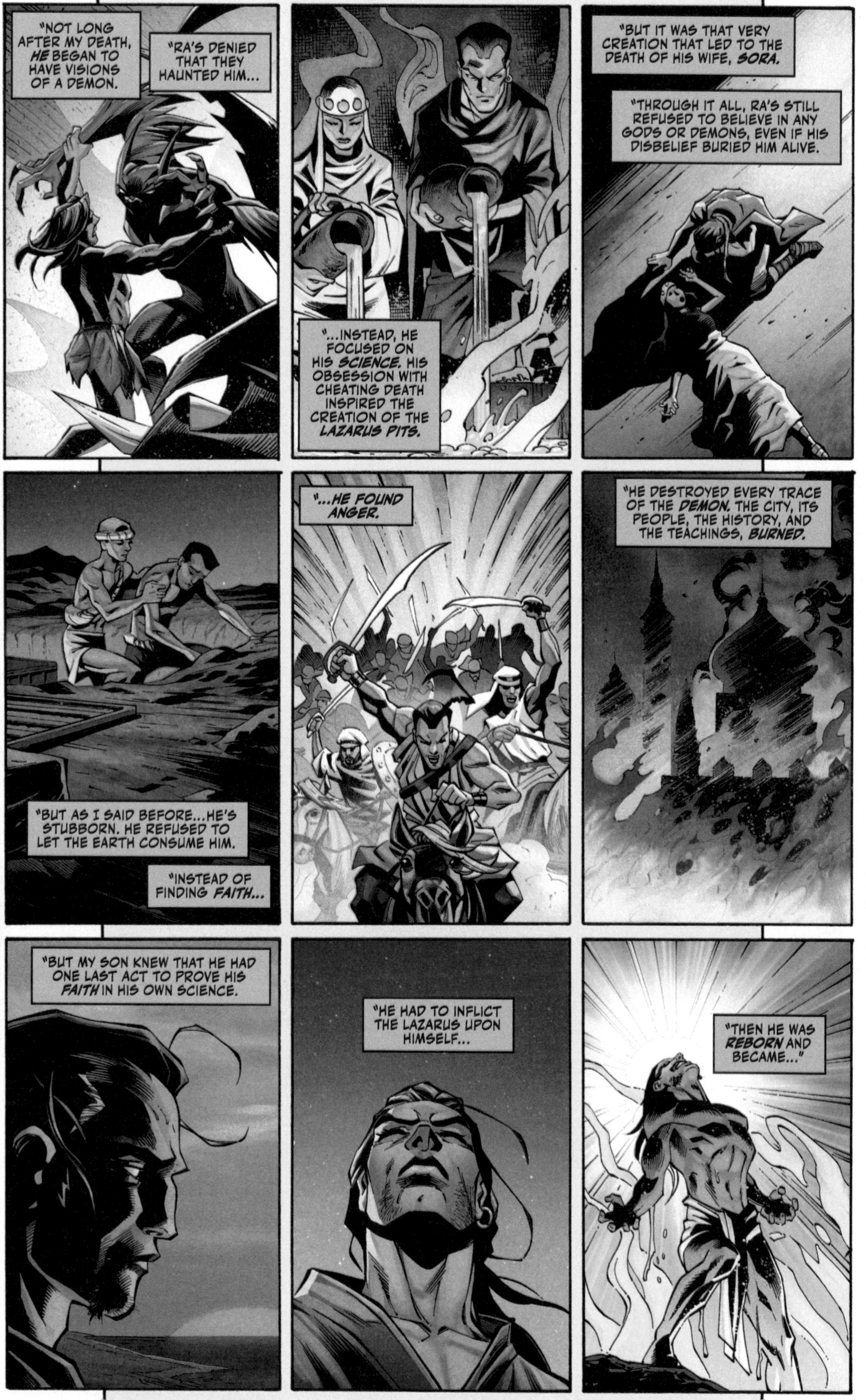
"NOT LONG AFTER MY DEATH, HE BEGAN TO HAVE VISIONS OF A DEMON.
"RA'S DENIED THAT THEY HAUNTED HIM...
"...INSTEAD, HE FOCUSED ON HIS SCIENCE. HIS OBSESSION WITH CHEATING DEATH INSPIRED THE CREATION OF THE LAZARUS PITS.
"BUT IT WAS THAT VERY CREATION THAT LED TO THE DEATH OF HIS WIFE, SORA.
"THROUGH IT ALL, RA'S STILL REFUSED TO BELIEVE IN ANY GODS OR DEMONS, EVEN IF HIS DISBELIEF BURIED HIM ALIVE.
"BUT AS I SAID BEFORE...HE'S STUBBORN. HE REFUSED TO LET THE EARTH CONSUME HIM.
"INSTEAD OF FINDING FAITH...
"...HE FOUND ANGER.
"HE DESTROYED EVERY TRACE OF THE DEMON. THE CITY, ITS PEOPLE, THE HISTORY, AND THE TEACHINGS, BURNED.
"BUT MY SON KNEW THAT HE HAD ONE LAST ACT TO PROVE HIS FAITH IN HIS OWN SCIENCE.
"HE HAD TO INFLICT THE LAZARUS UPON HIMSELF...
"THEN HE WAS REBORN AND BECAME..."

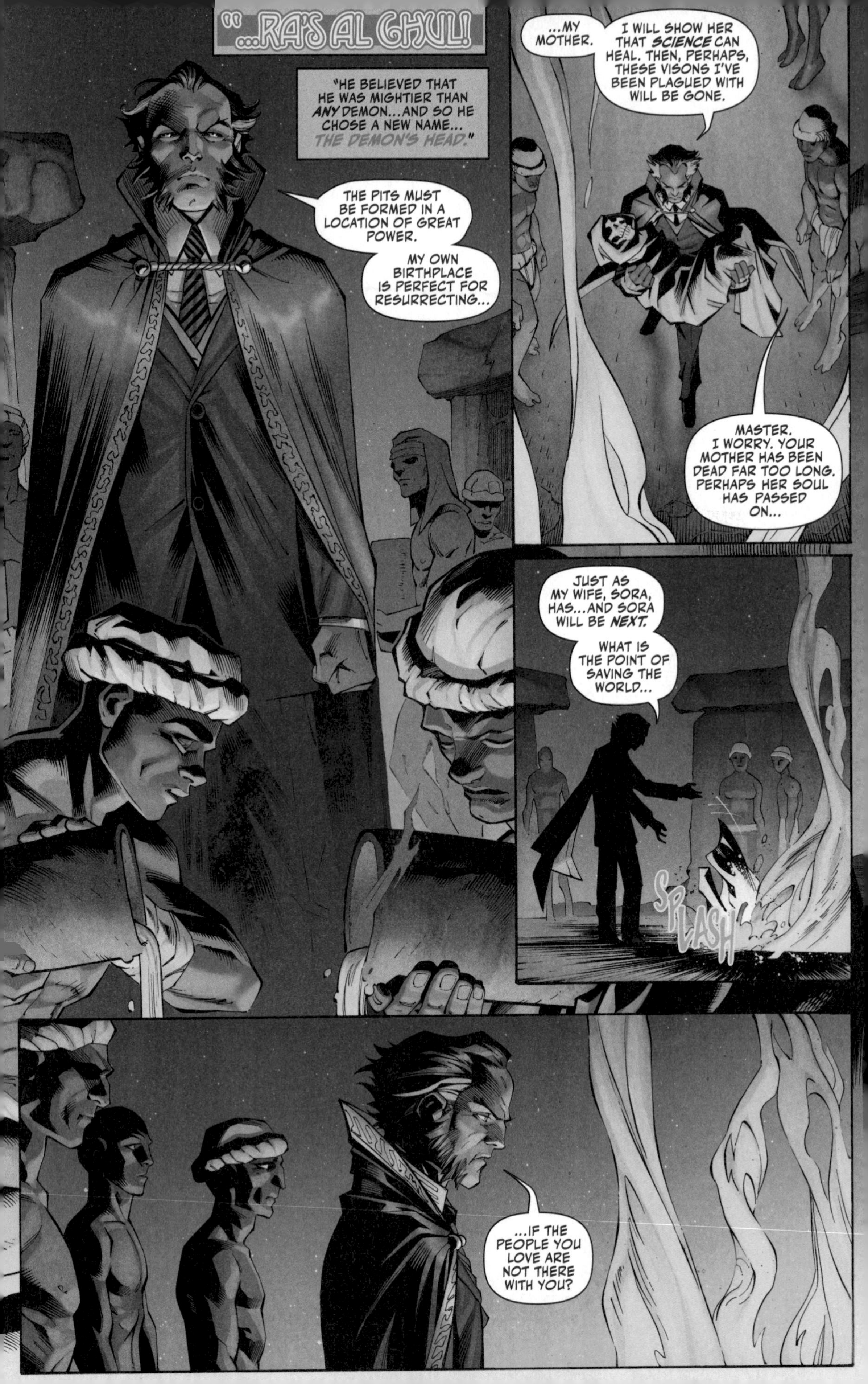
"...RA'S AL GHUL!
"HE BELIEVED THAT HE WAS MIGHTIER THAN ANY DEMON...AND SO HE CHOSE A NEW NAME... THE DEMON'S HEAD."
THE PITS MUST BE FORMED IN A LOCATION OF GREAT POWER.
MY OWN BIRTHPLACE IS PERFECT FOR RESURRECTING...
...MY MOTHER.
I WILL SHOW HER THAT SCIENCE CAN HEAL. THEN, PERHAPS, THESE VISONS I'VE BEEN PLAGUED WITH WILL BE GONE.
MASTER. I WORRY. YOUR MOTHER HAS BEEN DEAD FAR TOO LONG. PERHAPS HER SOUL HAS PASSED ON...
JUST AS MY WIFE, SORA, HAS...AND SORA WILL BE NEXT.
WHAT IS THE POINT OF SAVING THE WORLD...
SPLASH
...IF THE PEOPLE YOU LOVE ARE NOT THERE WITH YOU?

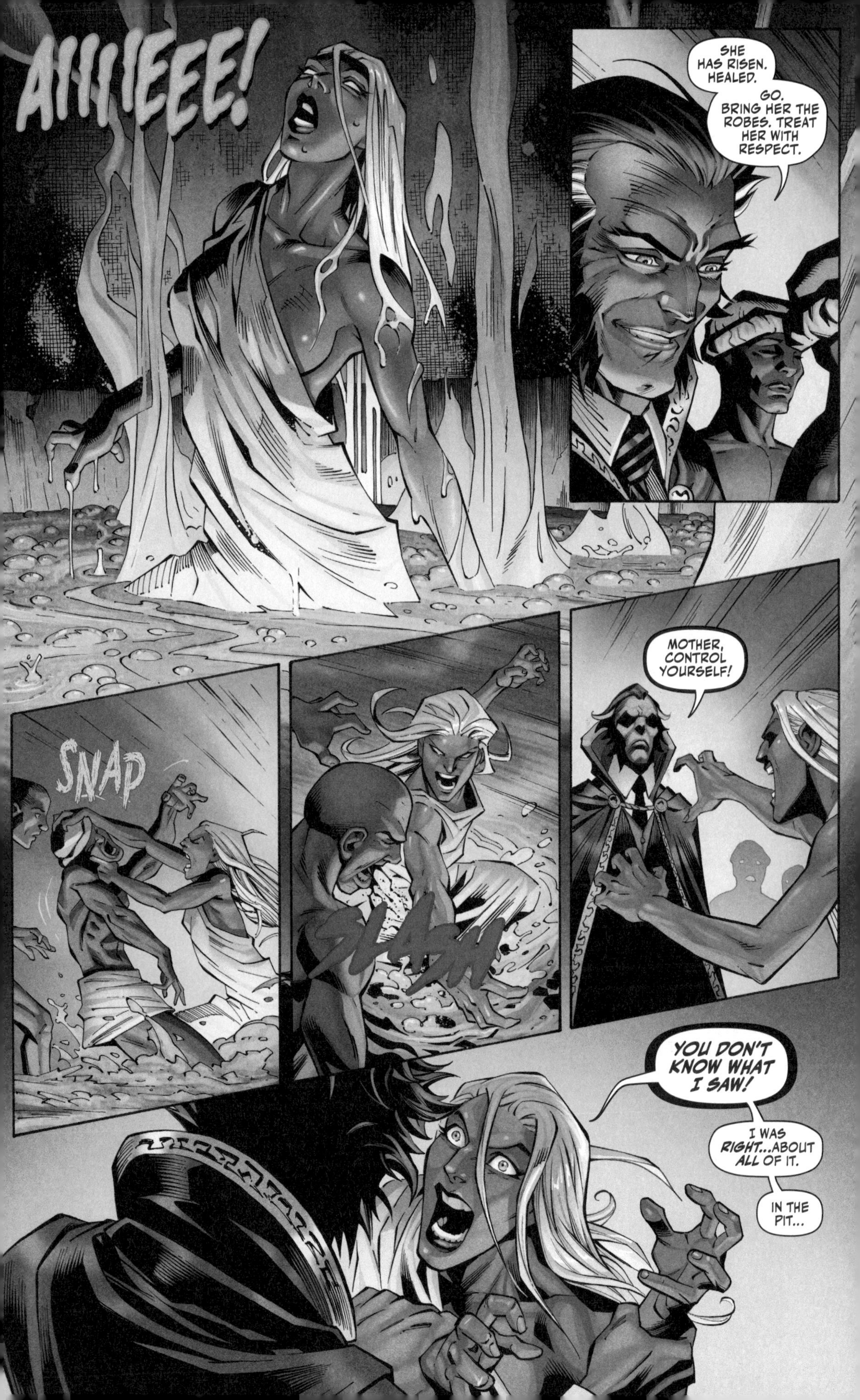
AIIIIEEE!
SHE HAS RISEN. HEALED.
GO. BRING HER THE ROBES. TREAT HER WITH RESPECT.
SNAP
SLASH
MOTHER, CONTROL YOURSELF!
YOU DON'T KNOW WHAT I SAW!
I WAS RIGHT...ABOUT ALL OF IT.
IN THE PIT...

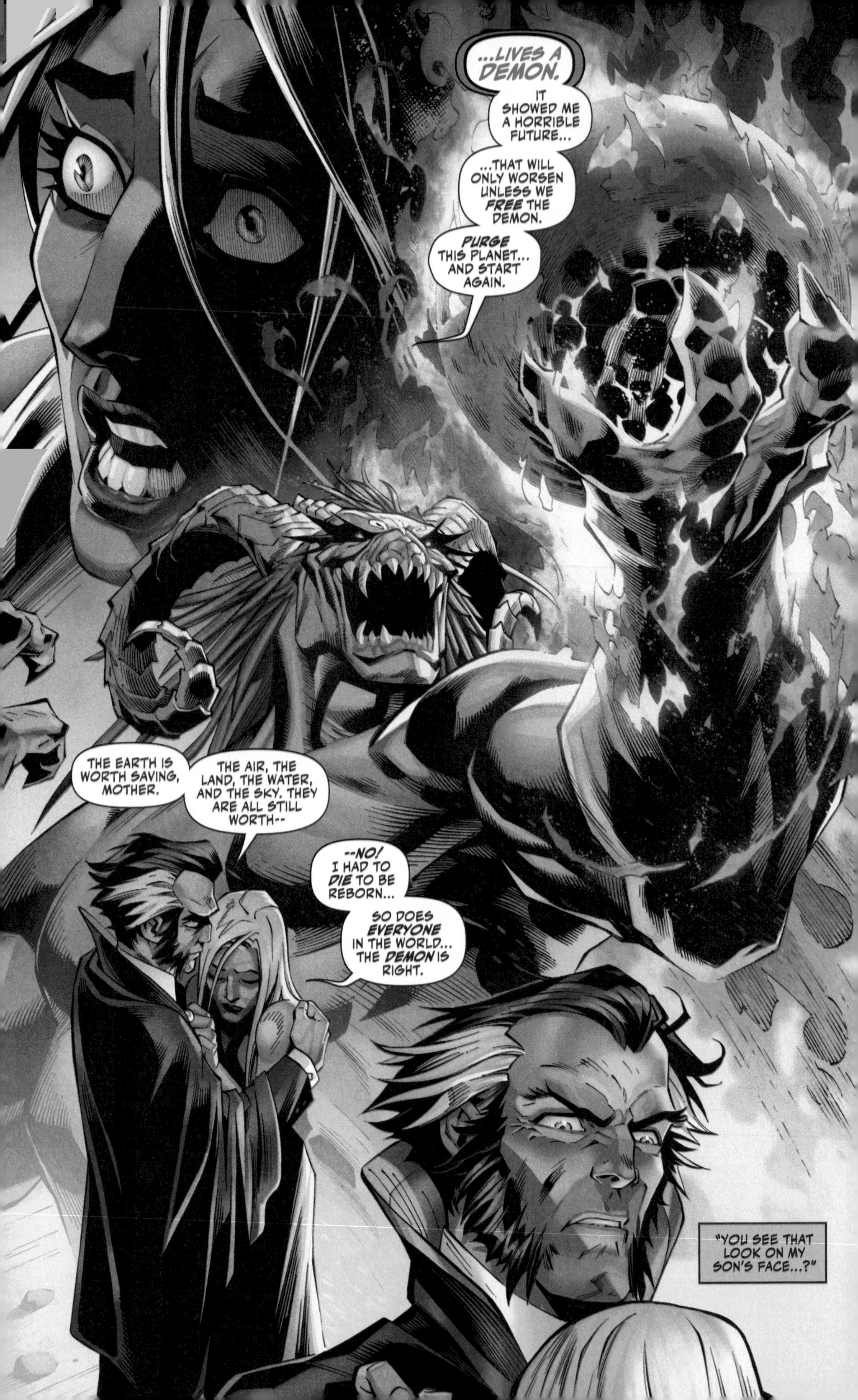
...LIVES A DEMON.
IT SHOWED ME A HORRIBLE FUTURE...
...THAT WILL ONLY WORSEN UNLESS WE FREE THE DEMON.
PURGE THIS PLANET... AND START AGAIN.
THE EARTH IS WORTH SAVING, MOTHER.
THE AIR, THE LAND, THE WATER, AND THE SKY. THEY ARE ALL STILL WORTH--
--NO! I HAD TO DIE TO BE REBORN...
SO DOES EVERYONE IN THE WORLD... THE DEMON IS RIGHT.
"YOU SEE THAT LOOK ON MY SON'S FACE...?"

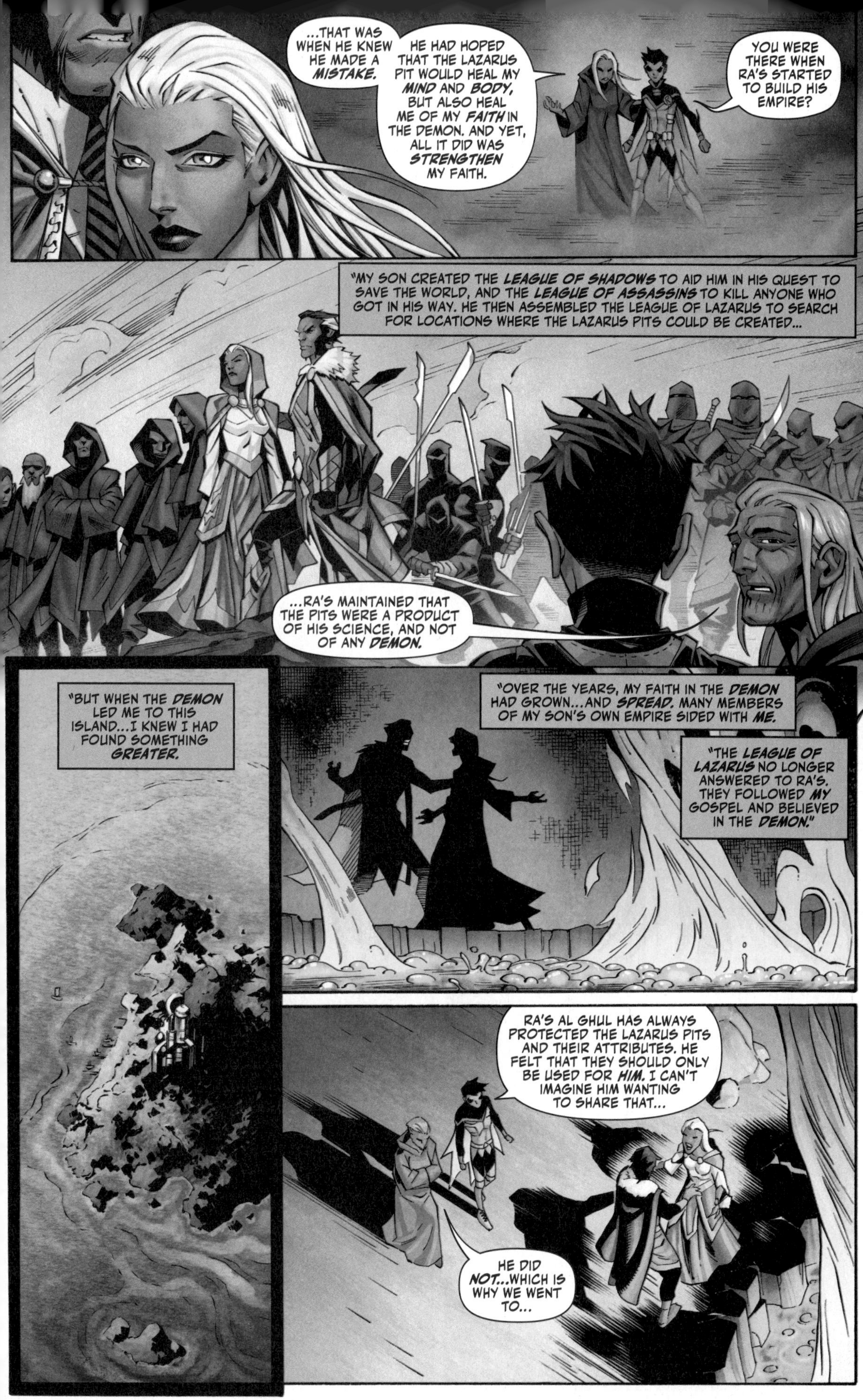

...THAT WAS WHEN HE KNEW HE MADE A MISTAKE.
HE HAD HOPED THAT THE LAZARUS PIT WOULD HEAL MY MIND AND BODY, BUT ALSO HEAL ME OF MY FAITH IN THE DEMON. AND YET, ALL IT DID WAS STRENGTHEN MY FAITH.
YOU WERE THERE WHEN RA'S STARTED TO BUILD HIS EMPIRE?
"MY SON CREATED THE LEAGUE OF SHADOWS TO AID HIM IN HIS QUEST TO SAVE THE WORLD, AND THE LEAGUE OF ASSASSINS TO KILL ANYONE WHO GOT IN HIS WAY. HE THEN ASSEMBLED THE LEAGUE OF LAZARUS TO SEARCH FOR LOCATIONS WHERE THE LAZARUS PITS COULD BE CREATED...
...RA'S MAINTAINED THAT THE PITS WERE A PRODUCT OF HIS SCIENCE, AND NOT OF ANY DEMON.
"BUT WHEN THE DEMON LED ME TO THIS ISLAND...I KNEW I HAD FOUND SOMETHING GREATER.
"OVER THE YEARS, MY FAITH IN THE DEMON HAD GROWN...AND SPREAD. MANY MEMBERS OF MY SON'S OWN EMPIRE SIDED WITH ME.
"THE LEAGUE OF LAZARUS NO LONGER ANSWERED TO RA'S. THEY FOLLOWED MY GOSPEL AND BELIEVED IN THE DEMON."
RA'S AL GHUL HAS ALWAYS PROTECTED THE LAZARUS PITS AND THEIR ATTRIBUTES. HE FELT THAT THEY SHOULD ONLY BE USED FOR HIM. I CAN'T IMAGINE HIM WANTING TO SHARE THAT...
HE DID NOT...WHICH IS WHY WE WENT TO...

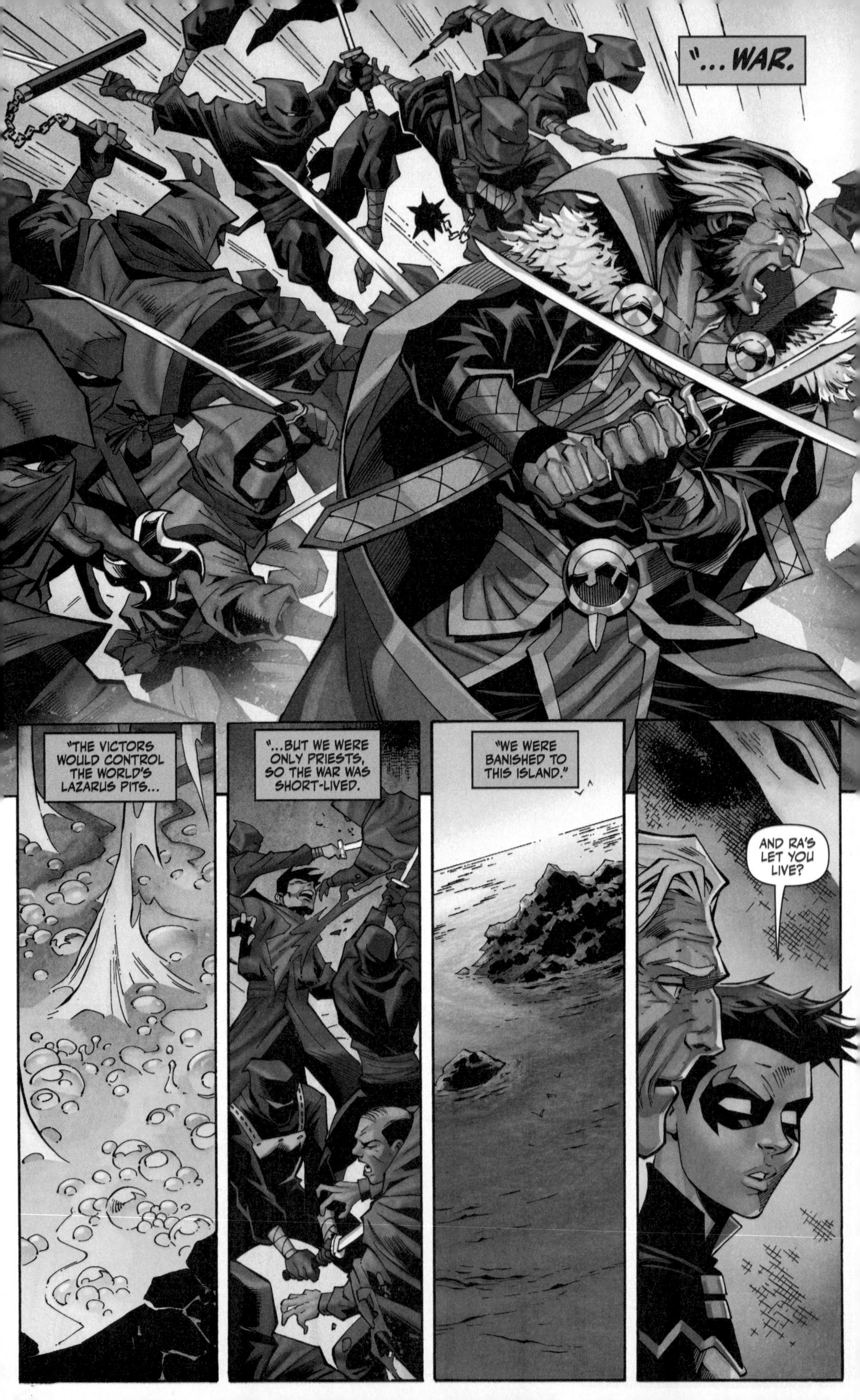
"...WAR.
"THE VICTORS WOULD CONTROL THE WORLD'S LAZARUS PITS...
"...BUT WE WERE ONLY PRIESTS, SO THE WAR WAS SHORT-LIVED.
"WE WERE BANISHED TO THIS ISLAND."
AND RA'S LET YOU LIVE?

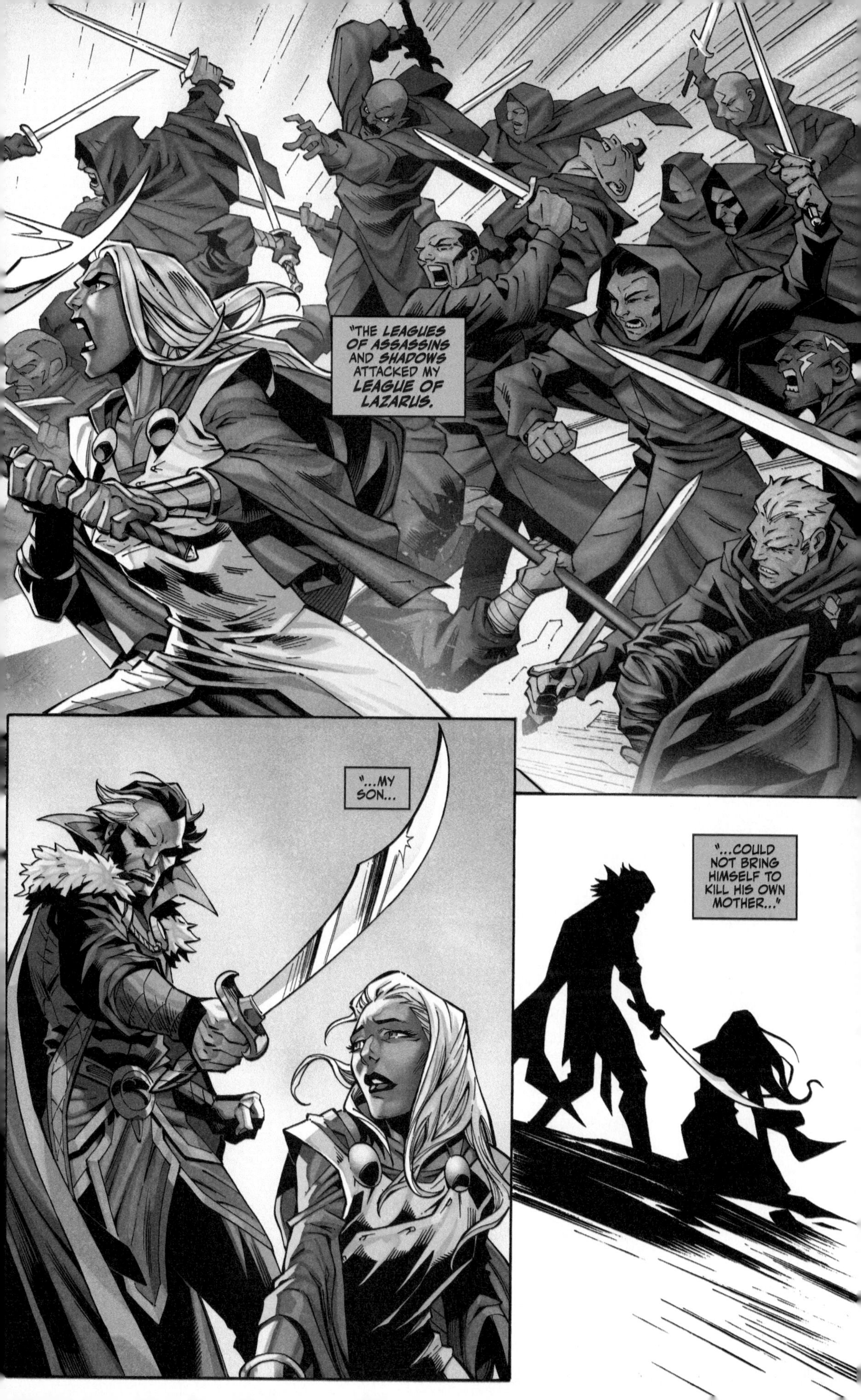
"THE LEAGUES OF ASSASSINS AND SHADOWS ATTACKED MY LEAGUE OF LAZARUS.
"...MY SON...
"...COULD NOT BRING HIMSELF TO KILL HIS OWN MOTHER..."

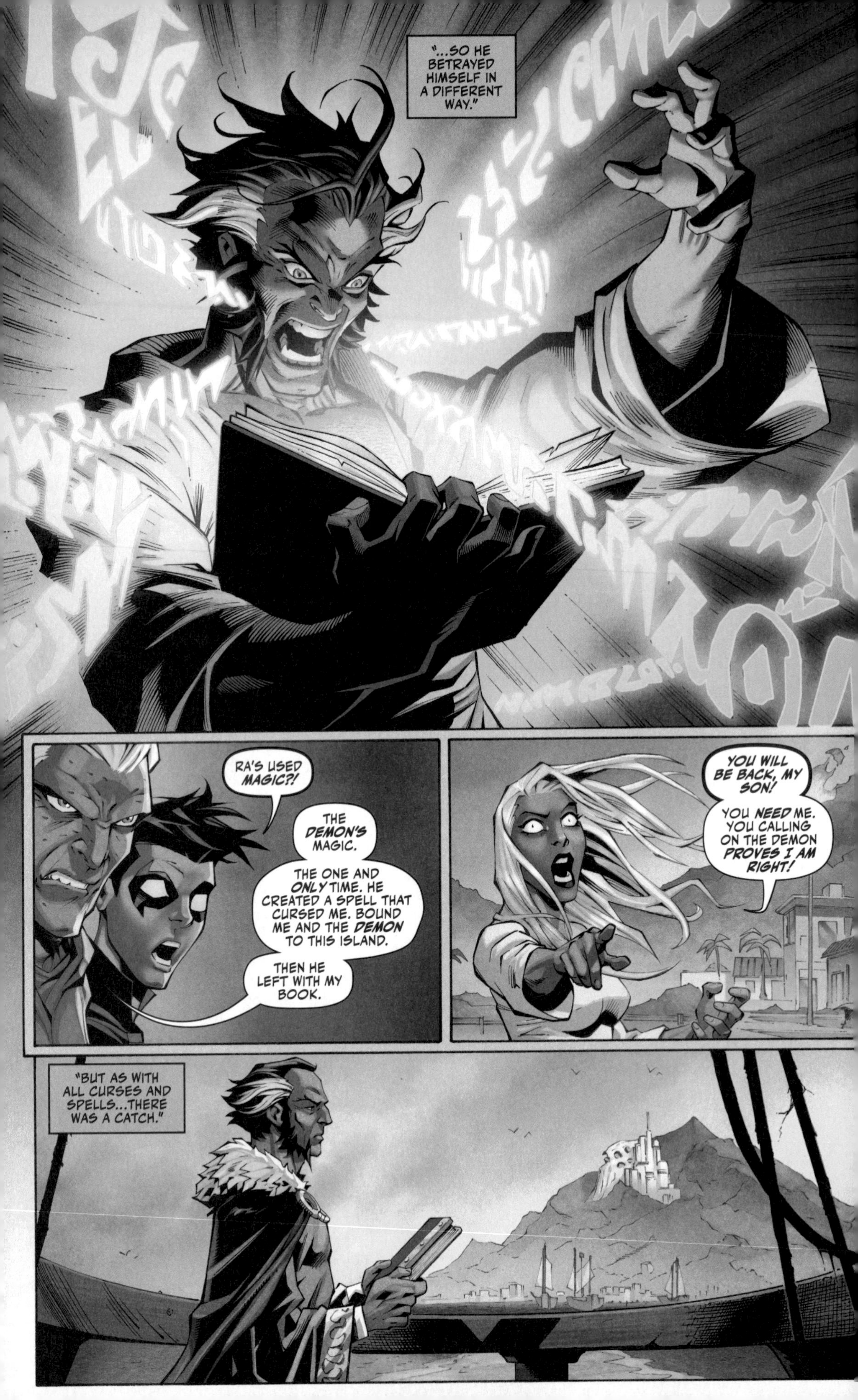
"...SO HE BETRAYED HIMSELF IN A DIFFERENT WAY."
RA'S USED MAGIC?!
THE DEMON'S MAGIC.
THE ONE AND ONLY TIME. HE CREATED A SPELL THAT CURSED ME. BOUND ME AND THE DEMON TO THIS ISLAND.
THEN HE LEFT WITH MY BOOK.
YOU WILL BE BACK, MY SON!
YOU NEED ME. YOU CALLING ON THE DEMON PROVES I AM RIGHT!
"BUT AS WITH ALL CURSES AND SPELLS...THERE WAS A CATCH."

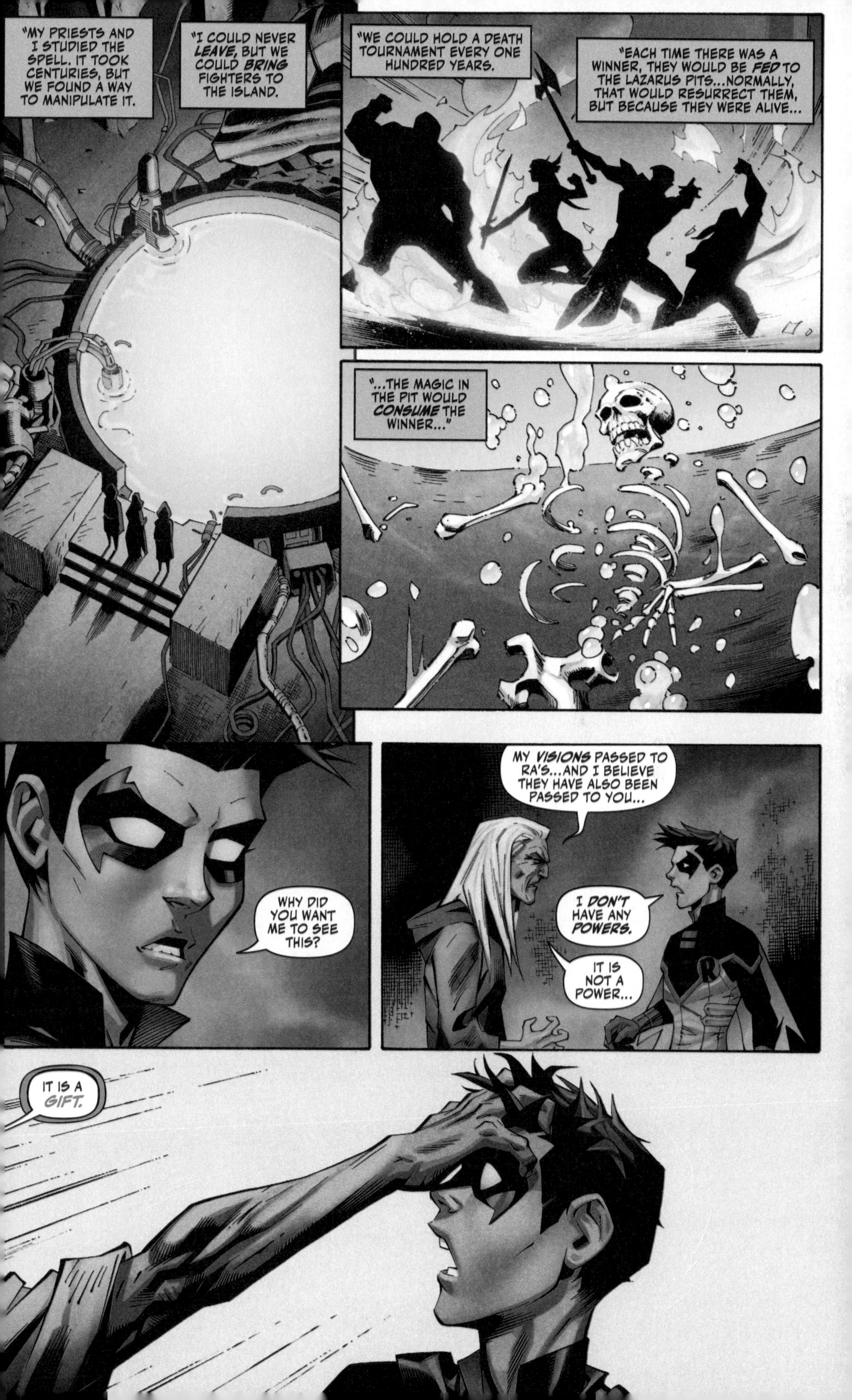
"MY PRIESTS AND I STUDIED THE SPELL. IT TOOK CENTURIES, BUT WE FOUND A WAY TO MANIPULATE IT.
"I COULD NEVER LEAVE, BUT WE COULD BRING FIGHTERS TO THE ISLAND.
"WE COULD HOLD A DEATH TOURNAMENT EVERY ONE HUNDRED YEARS.
"EACH TIME THERE WAS A WINNER, THEY WOULD BE FED TO THE LAZARUS PITS...NORMALLY, THAT WOULD RESURRECT THEM, BUT BECAUSE THEY WERE ALIVE...
"...THE MAGIC IN THE PIT WOULD CONSUME THE WINNER..."
WHY DID YOU WANT ME TO SEE THIS?
MY VISIONS PASSED TO RA'S...AND I BELIEVE THEY HAVE ALSO BEEN PASSED TO YOU...
I DON'T HAVE ANY POWERS.
IT IS NOT A POWER...
IT IS A GIFT.

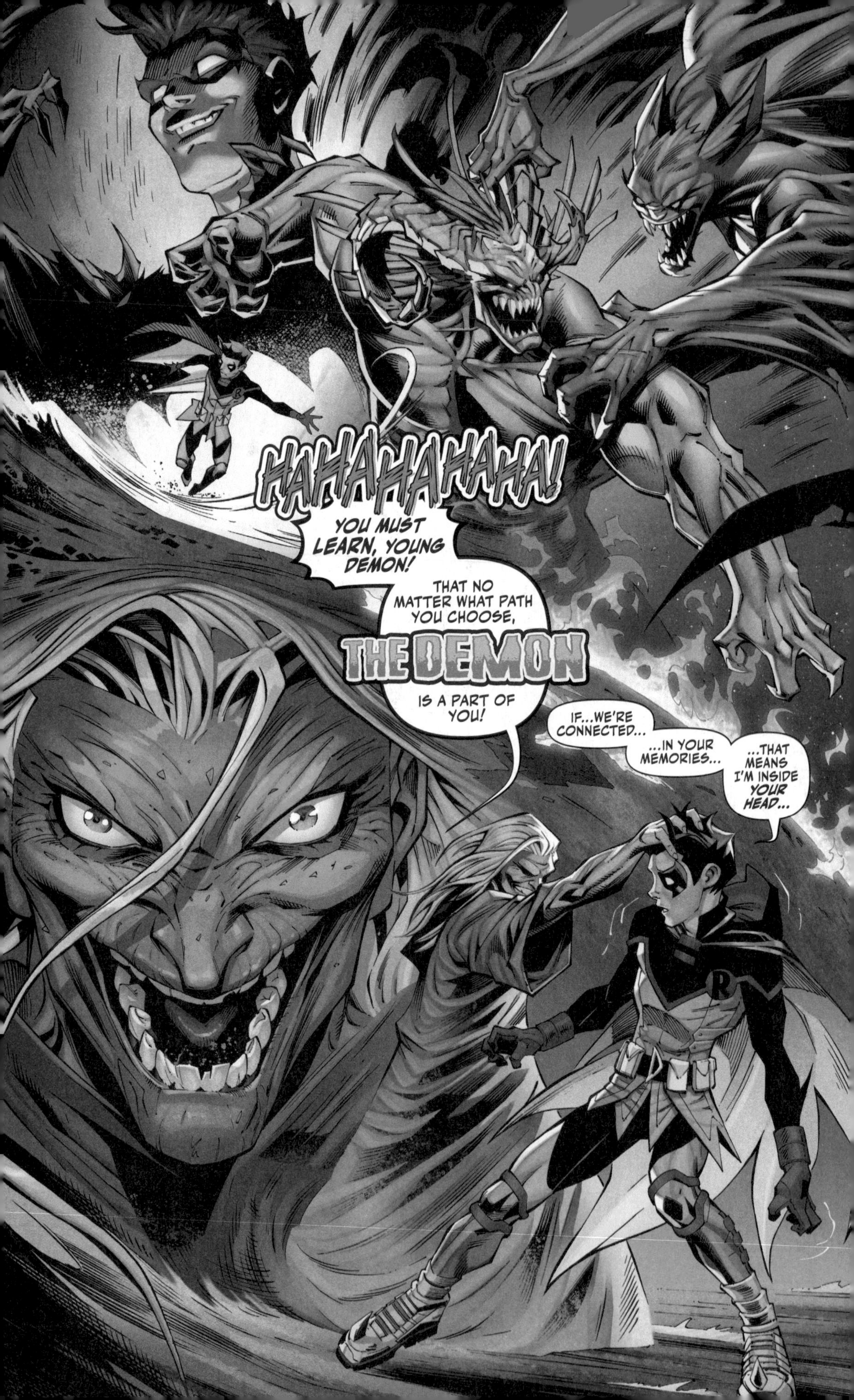
HAHAHAHAHAHA!
YOU MUST LEARN, YOUNG DEMON!
THAT NO MATTER WHAT PATH YOU CHOOSE,
THE DEMON
IS A PART OF YOU!
IF...WE'RE CONNECTED...
...IN YOUR MEMORIES...
...THAT MEANS I'M INSIDE YOUR HEAD...

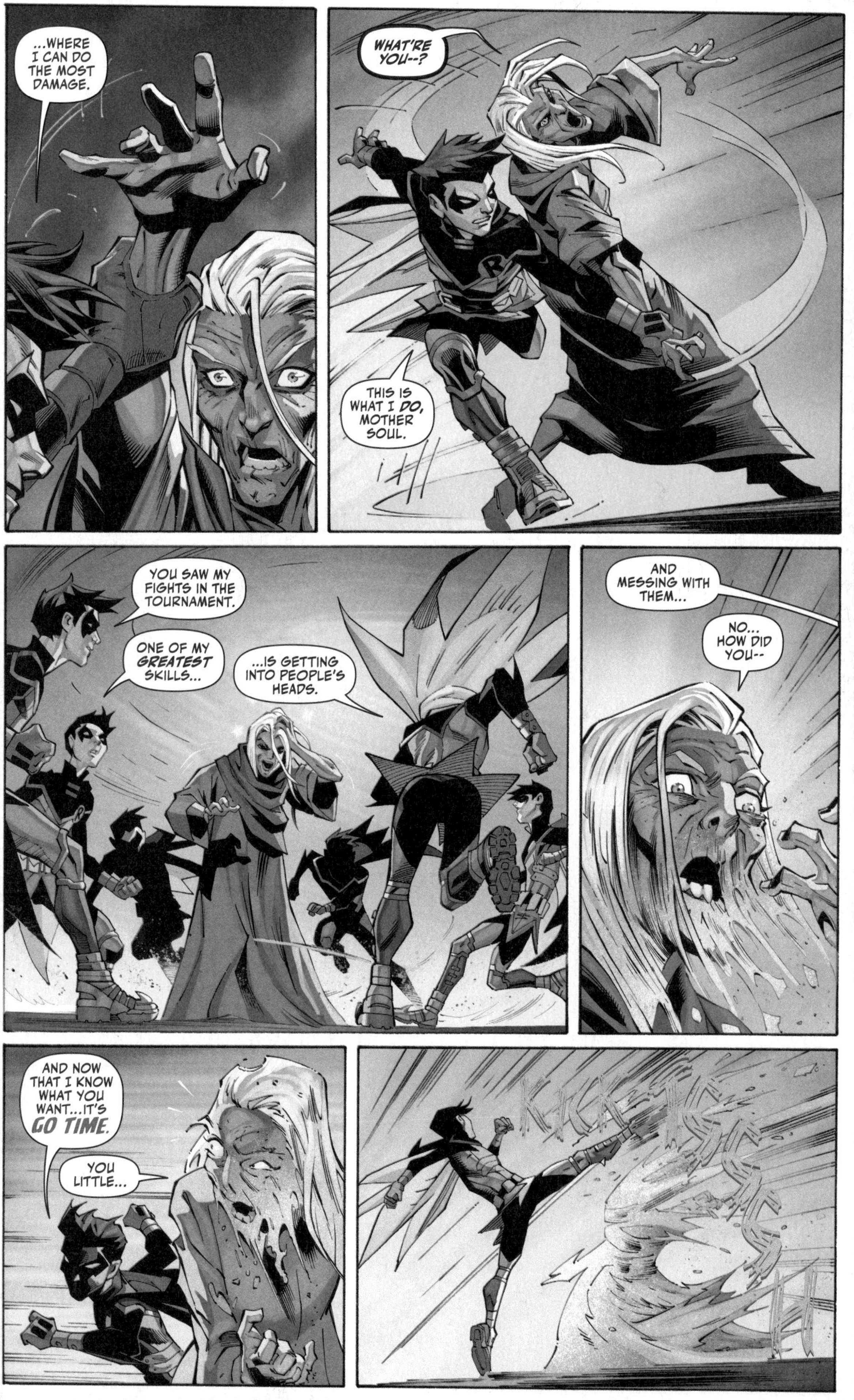
...WHERE I CAN DO THE MOST DAMAGE.
WHAT'RE YOU--?
THIS IS WHAT I DO, MOTHER SOUL.
YOU SAW MY FIGHTS IN THE TOURNAMENT.
ONE OF MY GREATEST SKILLS...
...IS GETTING INTO PEOPLE'S HEADS.
AND MESSING WITH THEM...
NO... HOW DID YOU--
AND NOW THAT I KNOW WHAT YOU WANT...IT'S GO TIME.
YOU LITTLE...

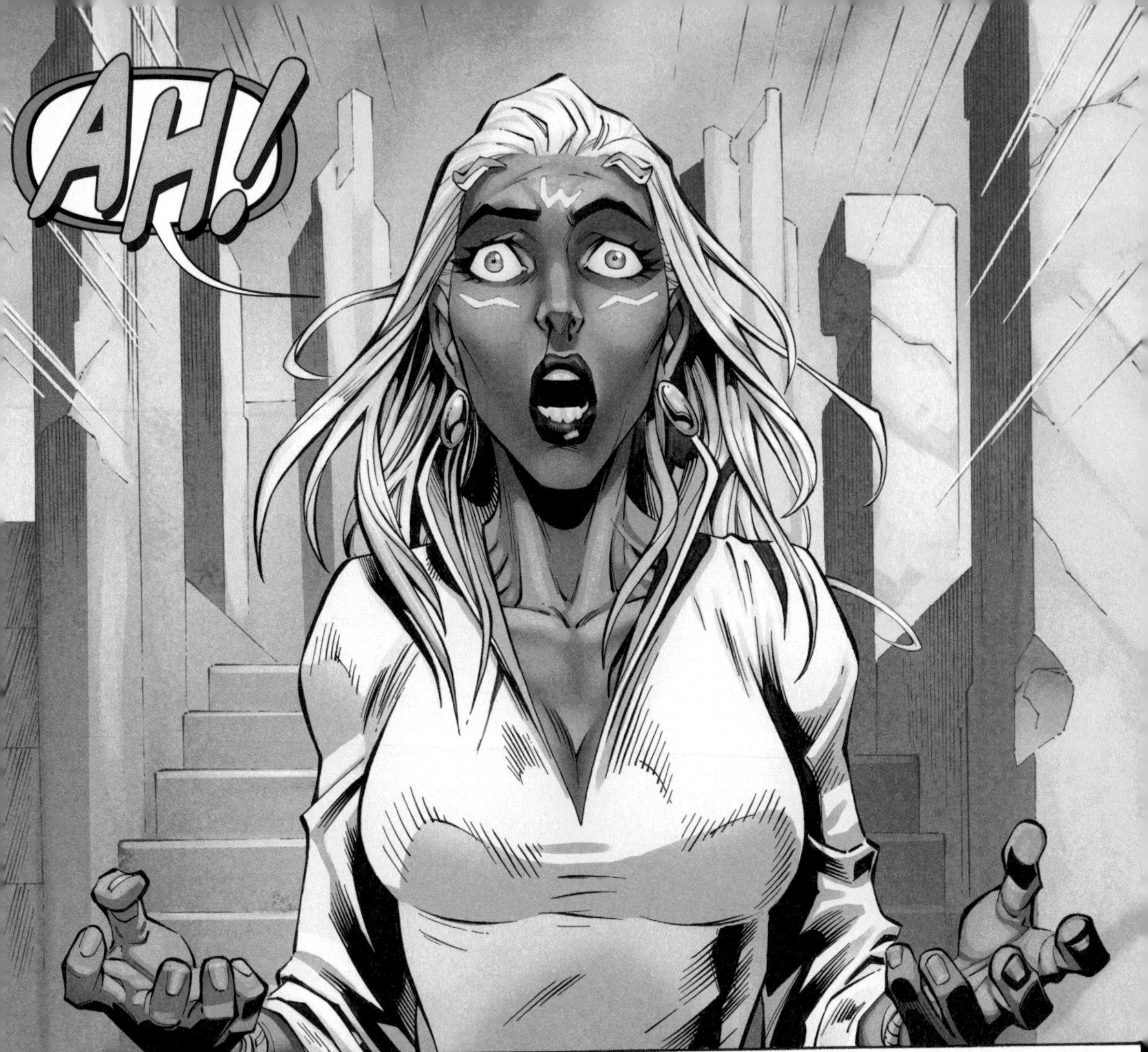
AH!

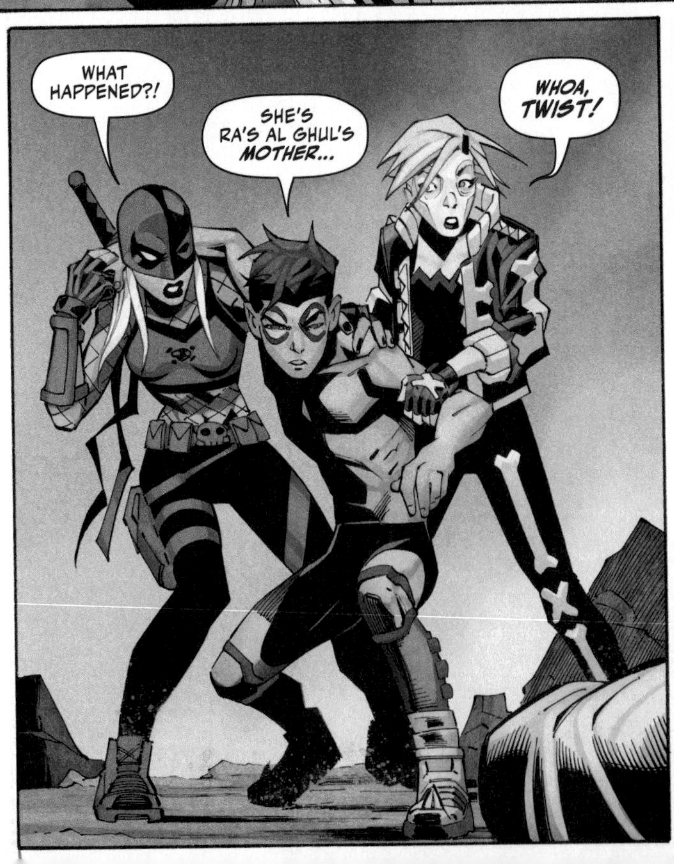
WHAT HAPPENED?!
SHE'S RA'S AL GHUL'S *MOTHER*...
WHOA, TWIST!

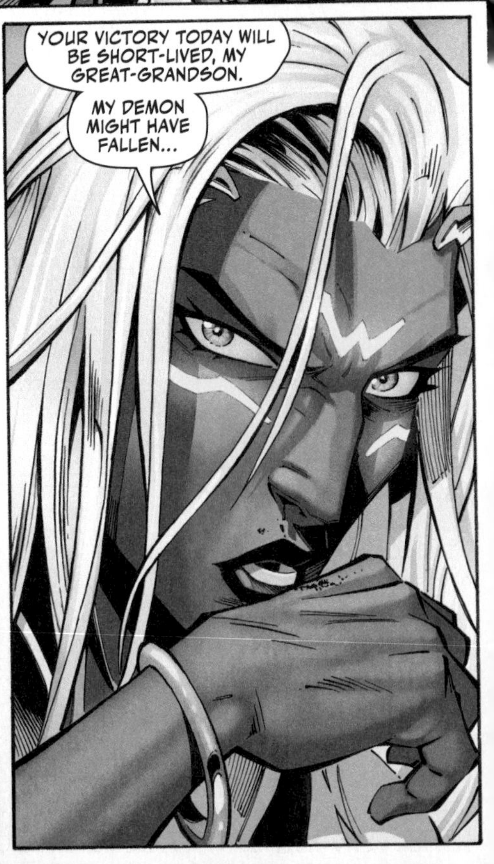
YOUR VICTORY TODAY WILL BE SHORT-LIVED, MY GREAT-GRANDSON.
MY DEMON MIGHT HAVE FALLEN...

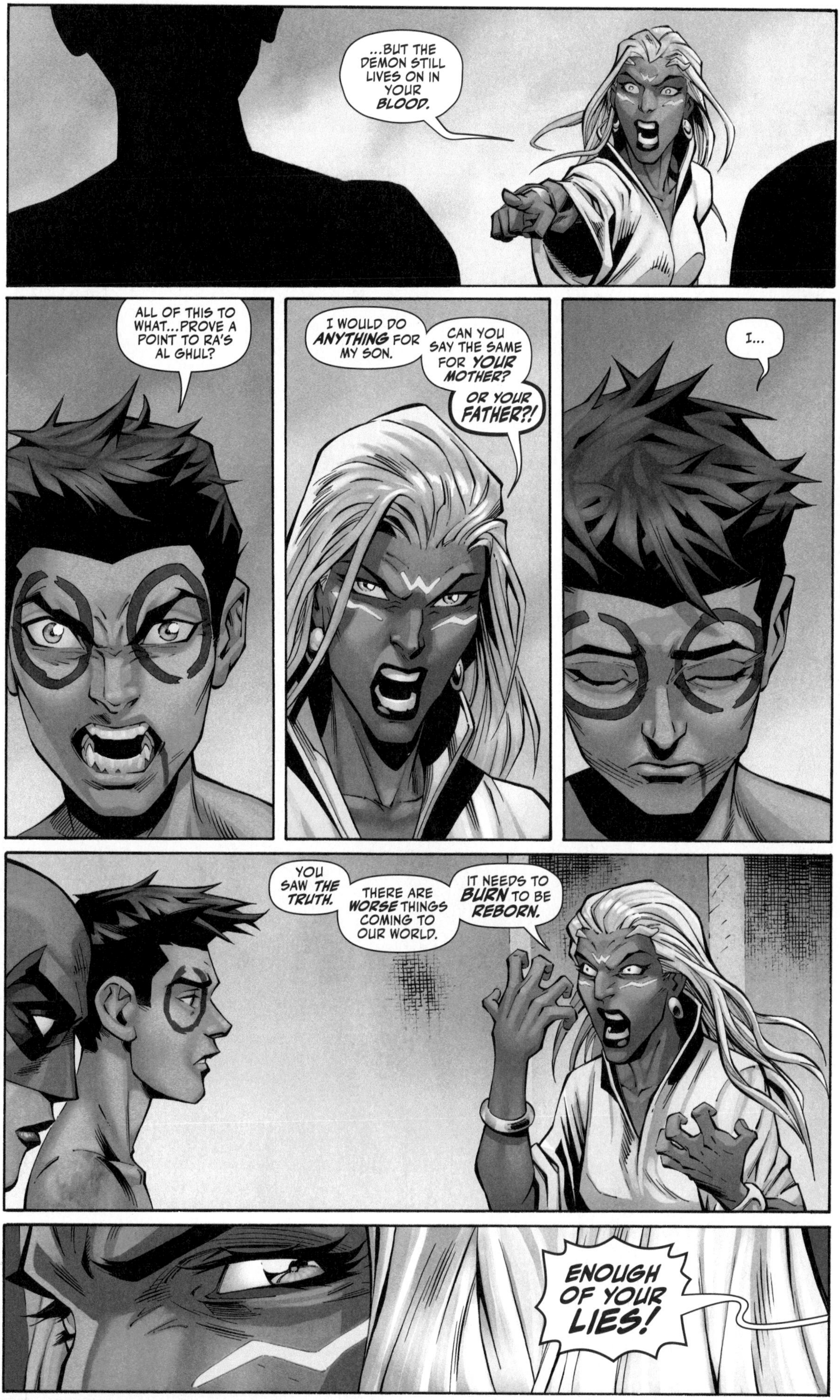
...BUT THE DEMON STILL LIVES ON IN YOUR BLOOD.
ALL OF THIS TO WHAT...PROVE A POINT TO RA'S AL GHUL?
I WOULD DO ANYTHING FOR MY SON.
CAN YOU SAY THE SAME FOR YOUR MOTHER?
OR YOUR FATHER?!
I...
YOU SAW THE TRUTH.
THERE ARE WORSE THINGS COMING TO OUR WORLD.
IT NEEDS TO BURN TO BE REBORN.
ENOUGH OF YOUR LIES!

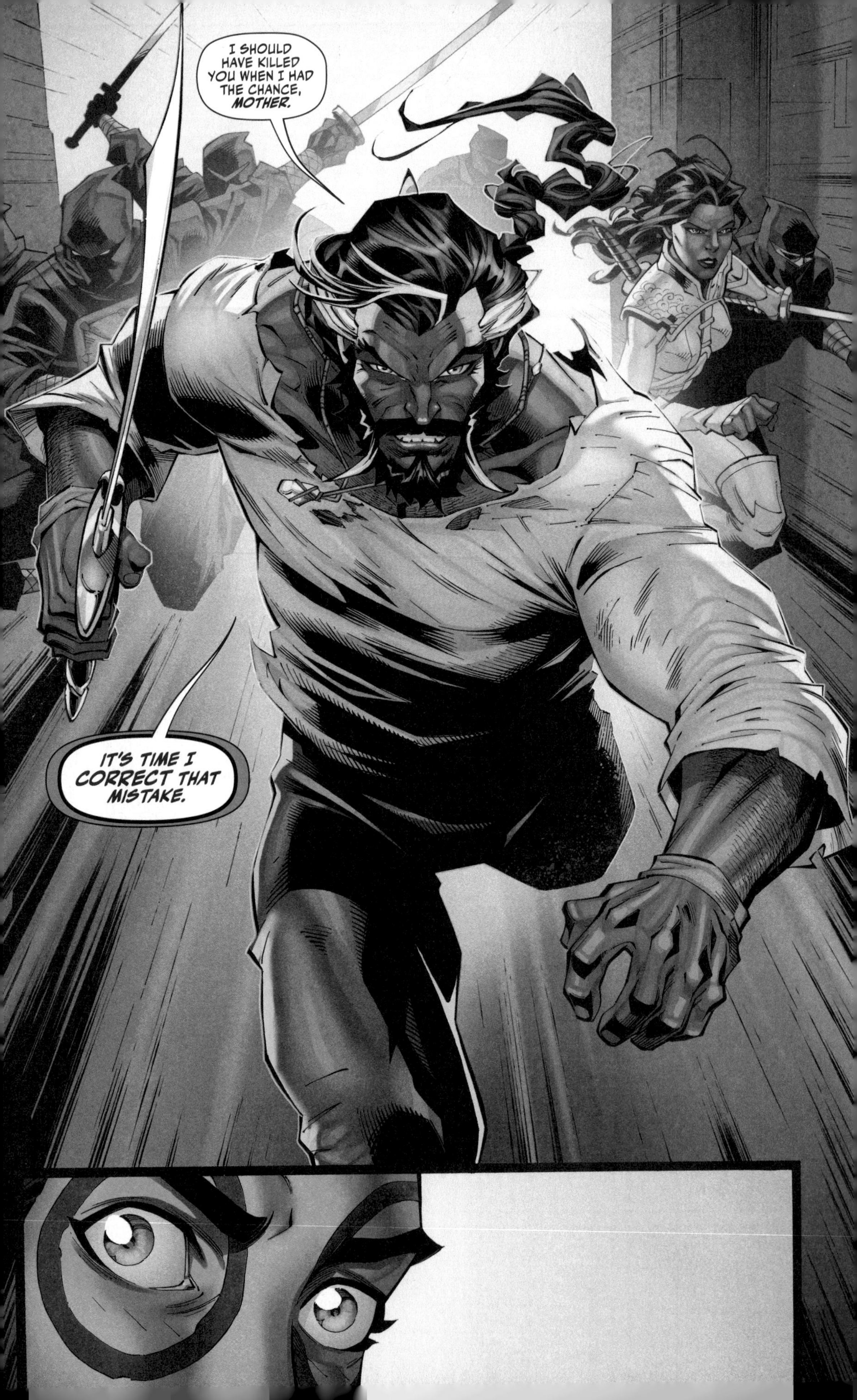
I SHOULD HAVE KILLED YOU WHEN I HAD THE CHANCE, *MOTHER.*
IT'S TIME I CORRECT THAT MISTAKE.

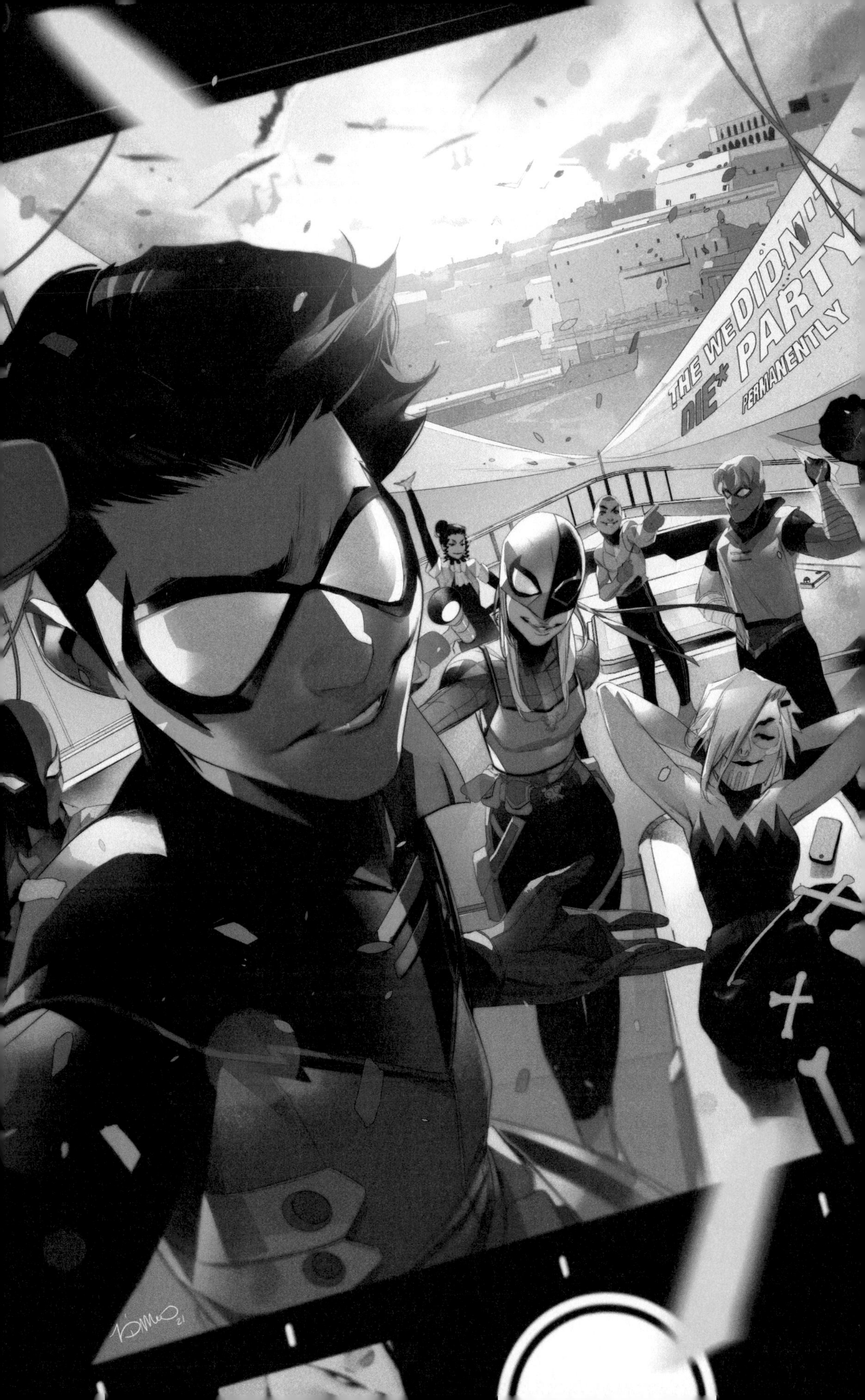
THE WE DIDN'T DIE* PARTY
*PERMANENTLY

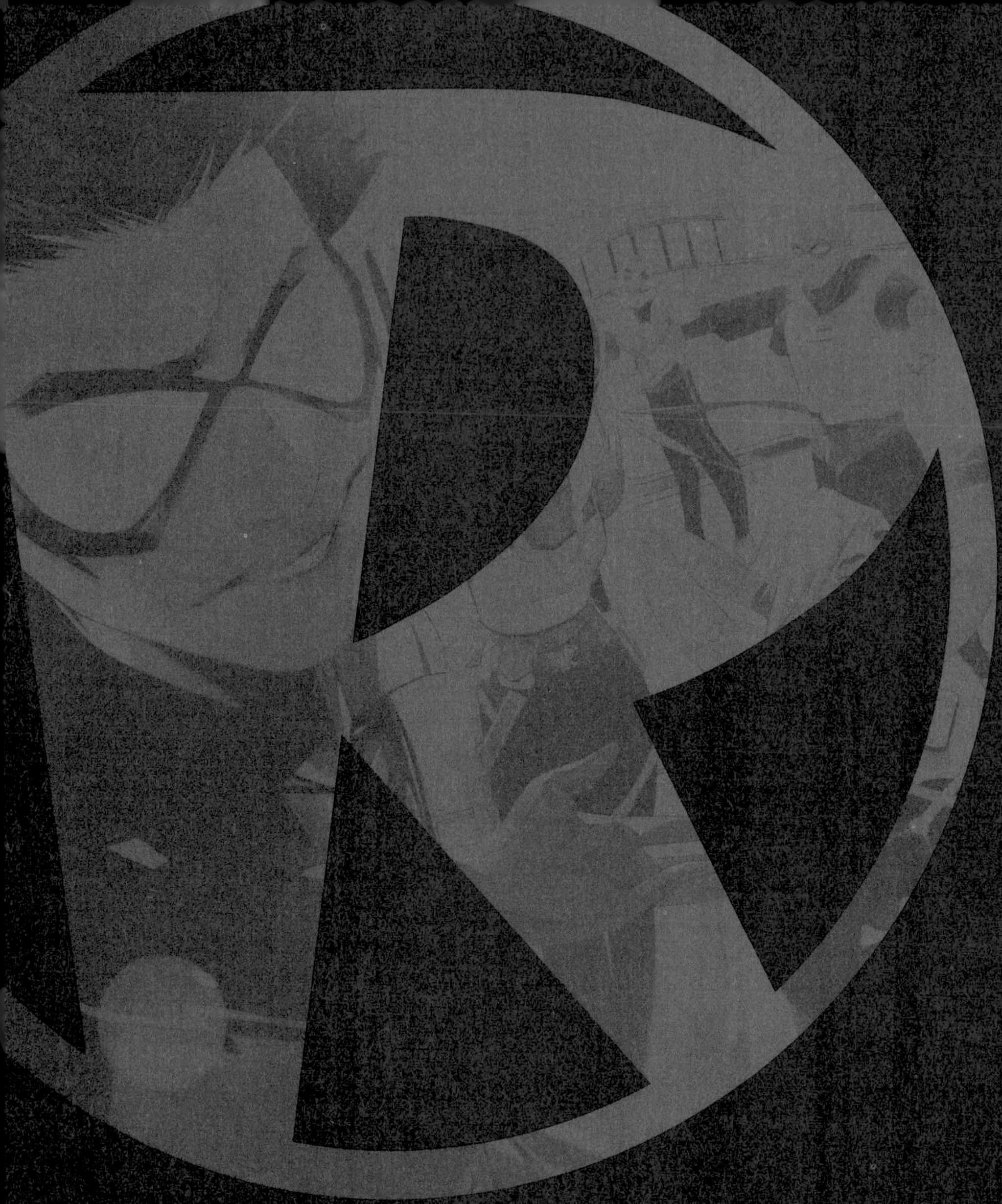

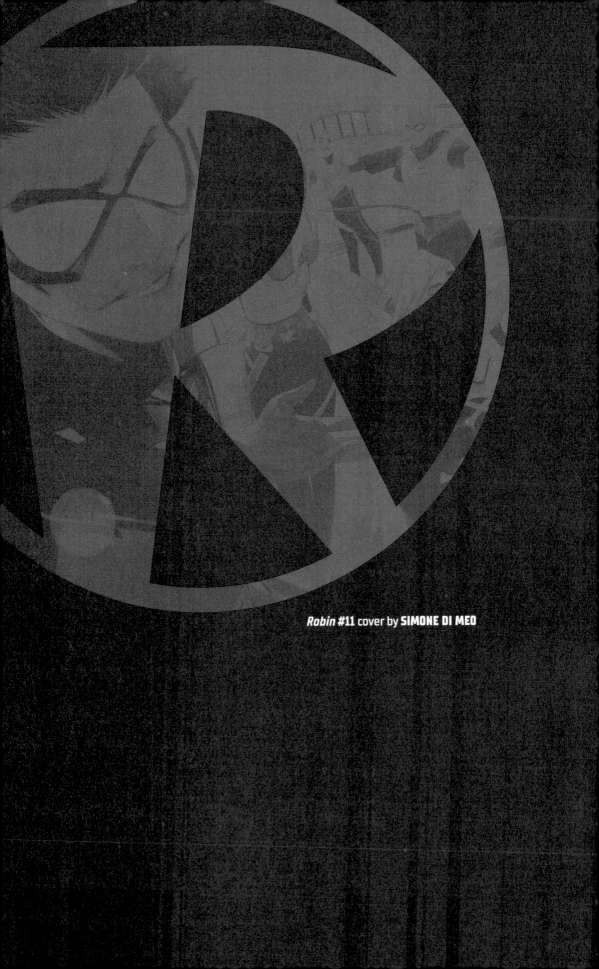

Robin **#11** cover by **SIMONE DI MEO**

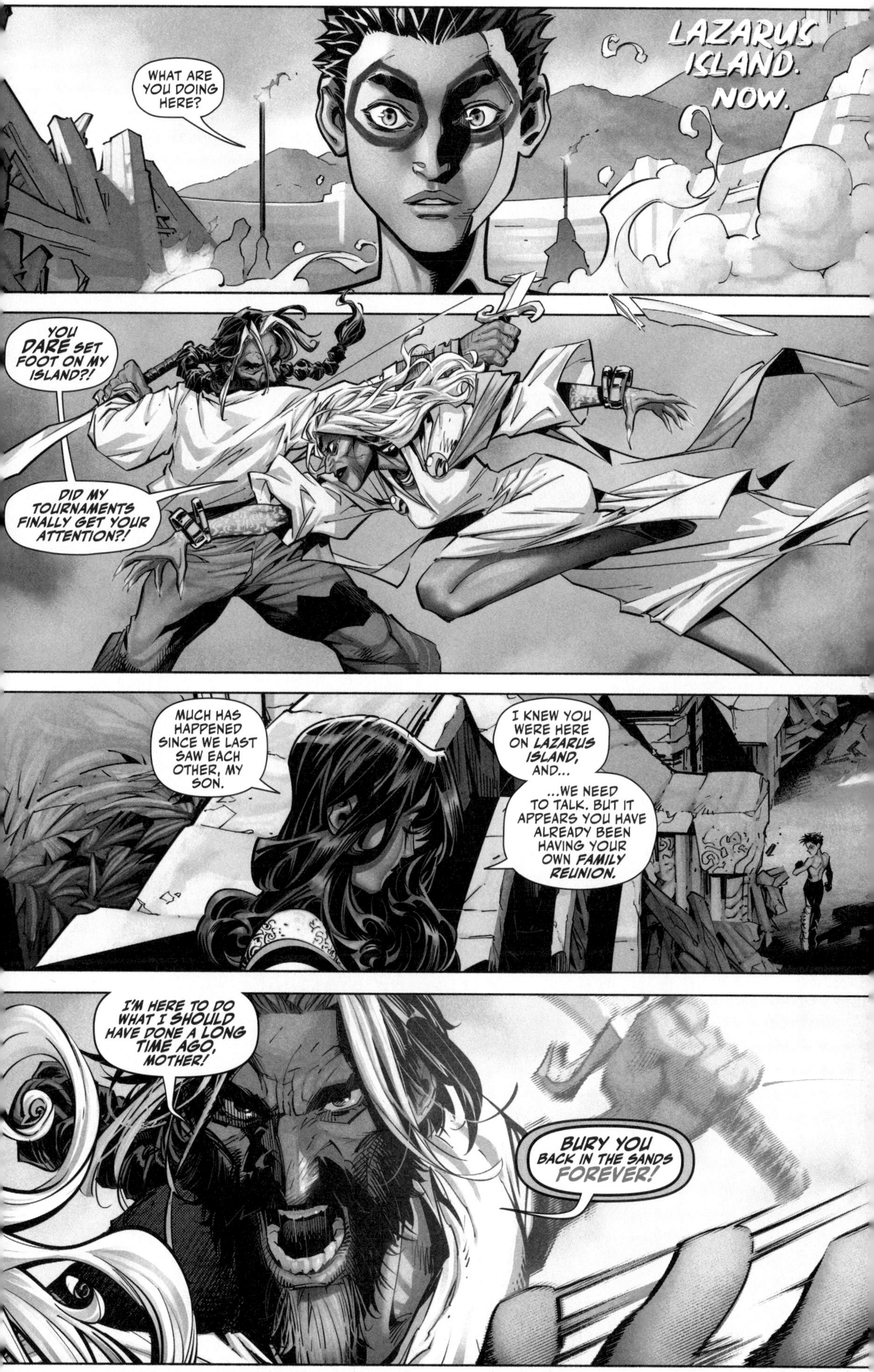
LAZARUS ISLAND. NOW.
WHAT ARE YOU DOING HERE?
YOU DARE SET FOOT ON MY ISLAND?!
DID MY TOURNAMENTS FINALLY GET YOUR ATTENTION?!
MUCH HAS HAPPENED SINCE WE LAST SAW EACH OTHER, MY SON.
I KNEW YOU WERE HERE ON LAZARUS ISLAND, AND...
...WE NEED TO TALK. BUT IT APPEARS YOU HAVE ALREADY BEEN HAVING YOUR OWN FAMILY REUNION.
I'M HERE TO DO WHAT I SHOULD HAVE DONE A LONG TIME AGO, MOTHER!
BURY YOU BACK IN THE SANDS FOREVER!

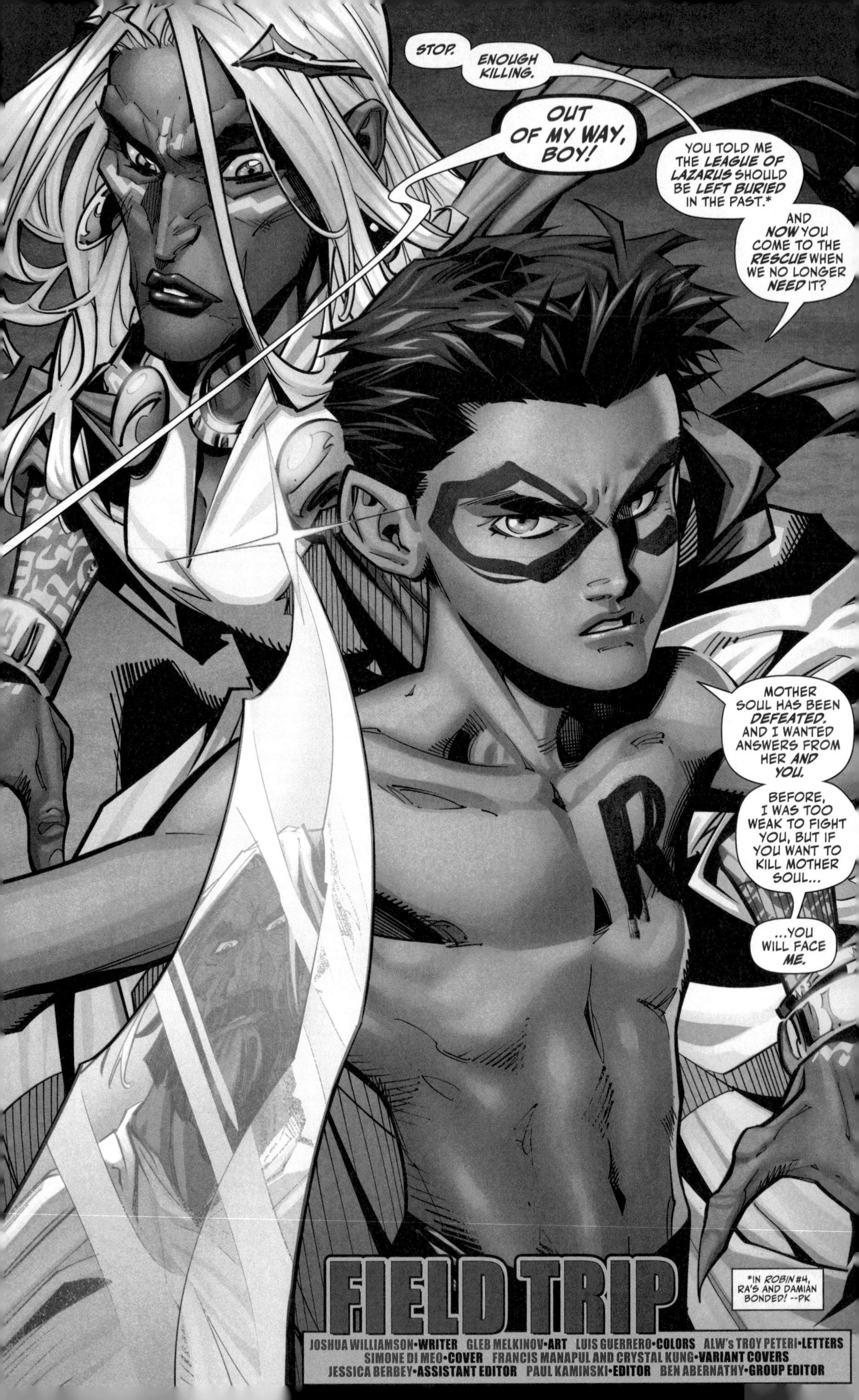
STOP.
ENOUGH KILLING.
OUT OF MY WAY, BOY!
YOU TOLD ME THE LEAGUE OF LAZARUS SHOULD BE LEFT BURIED IN THE PAST.*
AND NOW YOU COME TO THE RESCUE WHEN WE NO LONGER NEED IT?
MOTHER SOUL HAS BEEN DEFEATED. AND I WANTED ANSWERS FROM HER AND YOU.
BEFORE, I WAS TOO WEAK TO FIGHT YOU, BUT IF YOU WANT TO KILL MOTHER SOUL...
...YOU WILL FACE ME.
FIELD TRIP
*IN ROBIN #4, RA'S AND DAMIAN BONDED! --PK
JOSHUA WILLIAMSON•WRITER GLEB MELKINOV•ART LUIS GUERRERO•COLORS ALW's TROY PETERI•LETTERS
SIMONE DI MEO•COVER FRANCIS MANAPUL AND CRYSTAL KUNG•VARIANT COVERS
JESSICA BERBEY•ASSISTANT EDITOR PAUL KAMINSKI•EDITOR BEN ABERNATHY•GROUP EDITOR

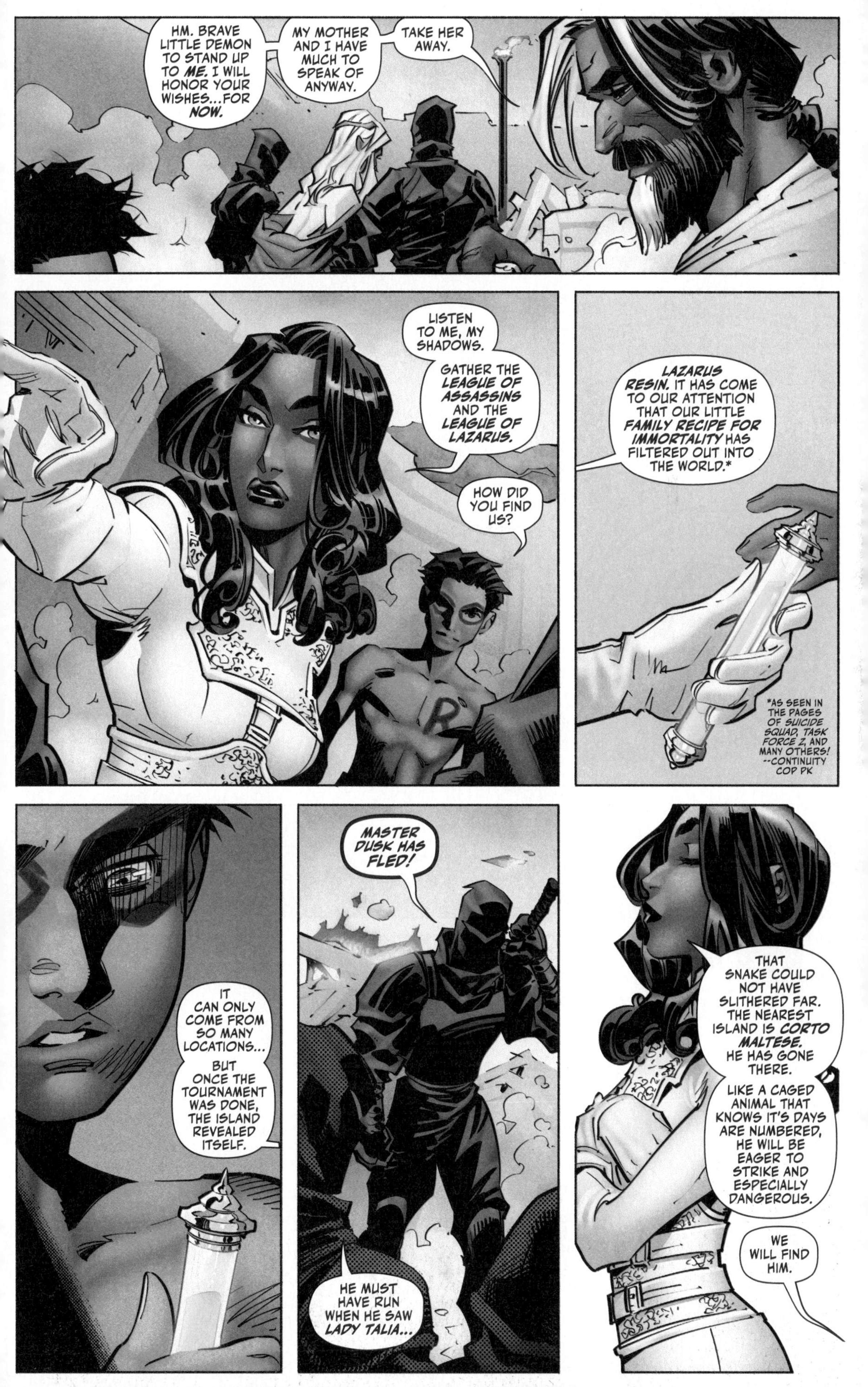
HM. BRAVE LITTLE DEMON TO STAND UP TO *ME*. I WILL HONOR YOUR WISHES...FOR *NOW*.
MY MOTHER AND I HAVE MUCH TO SPEAK OF ANYWAY.
TAKE HER AWAY.
LISTEN TO ME, MY SHADOWS.
GATHER THE *LEAGUE OF ASSASSINS* AND THE *LEAGUE OF LAZARUS*.
HOW DID YOU FIND US?
LAZARUS RESIN. IT HAS COME TO OUR ATTENTION THAT OUR LITTLE *FAMILY RECIPE FOR IMMORTALITY* HAS FILTERED OUT INTO THE WORLD.*
*AS SEEN IN THE PAGES OF *SUICIDE SQUAD, TASK FORCE Z*, AND MANY OTHERS! --CONTINUITY COP PK
IT CAN ONLY COME FROM SO MANY LOCATIONS...
BUT ONCE THE TOURNAMENT WAS DONE, THE ISLAND REVEALED ITSELF.
MASTER DUSK HAS FLED!
HE MUST HAVE RUN WHEN HE SAW *LADY TALIA*...
THAT SNAKE COULD NOT HAVE SLITHERED FAR. THE NEAREST ISLAND IS *CORTO MALTESE*. HE HAS GONE THERE.
LIKE A CAGED ANIMAL THAT KNOWS IT'S DAYS ARE NUMBERED, HE WILL BE EAGER TO STRIKE AND ESPECIALLY DANGEROUS.
WE WILL FIND HIM.

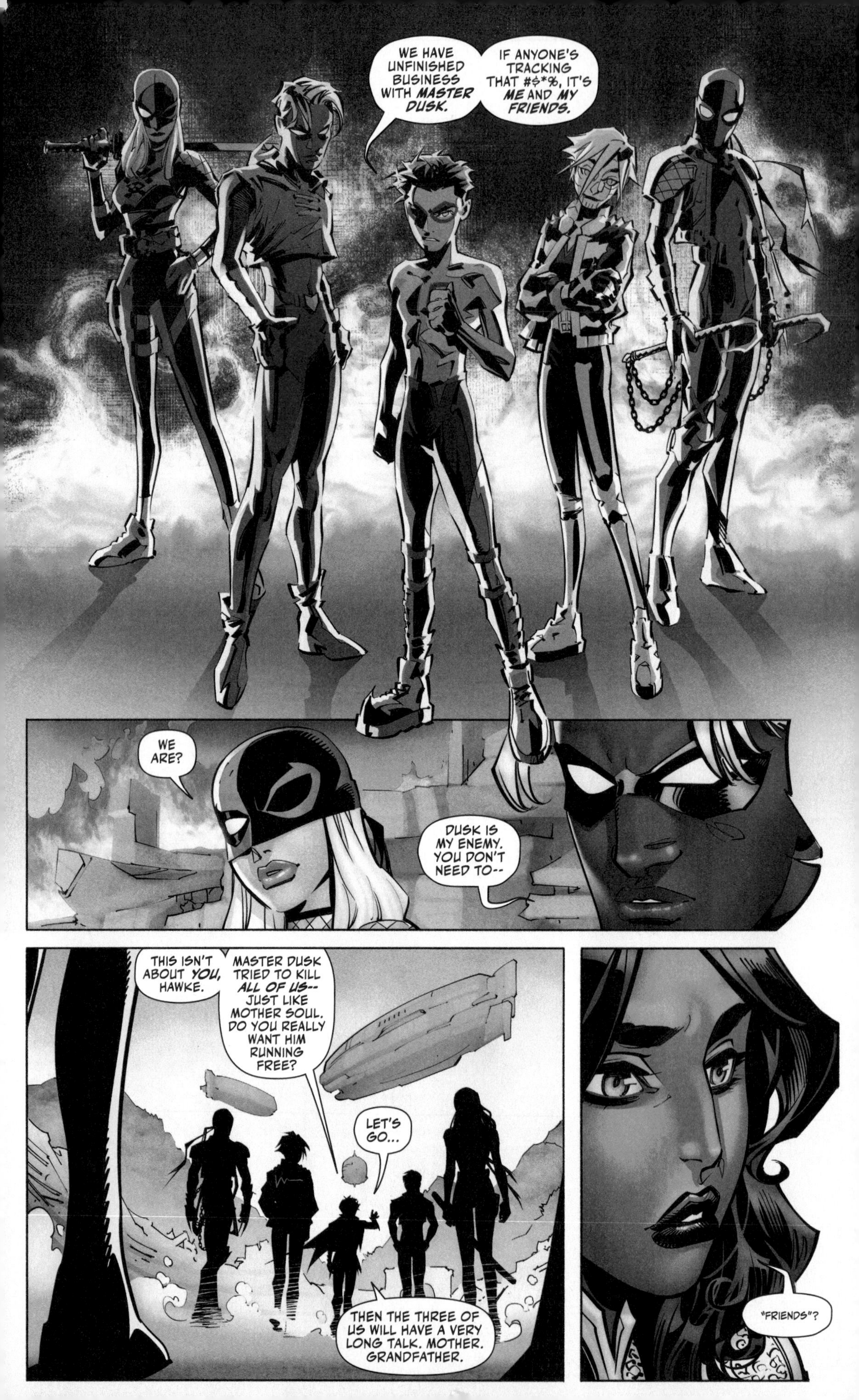
WE HAVE UNFINISHED BUSINESS WITH MASTER DUSK.
IF ANYONE'S TRACKING THAT #$*%, IT'S ME AND MY FRIENDS.
WE ARE?
DUSK IS MY ENEMY. YOU DON'T NEED TO--
THIS ISN'T ABOUT YOU, HAWKE.
MASTER DUSK TRIED TO KILL ALL OF US-- JUST LIKE MOTHER SOUL. DO YOU REALLY WANT HIM RUNNING FREE?
LET'S GO...
THEN THE THREE OF US WILL HAVE A VERY LONG TALK. MOTHER. GRANDFATHER.
"FRIENDS"?

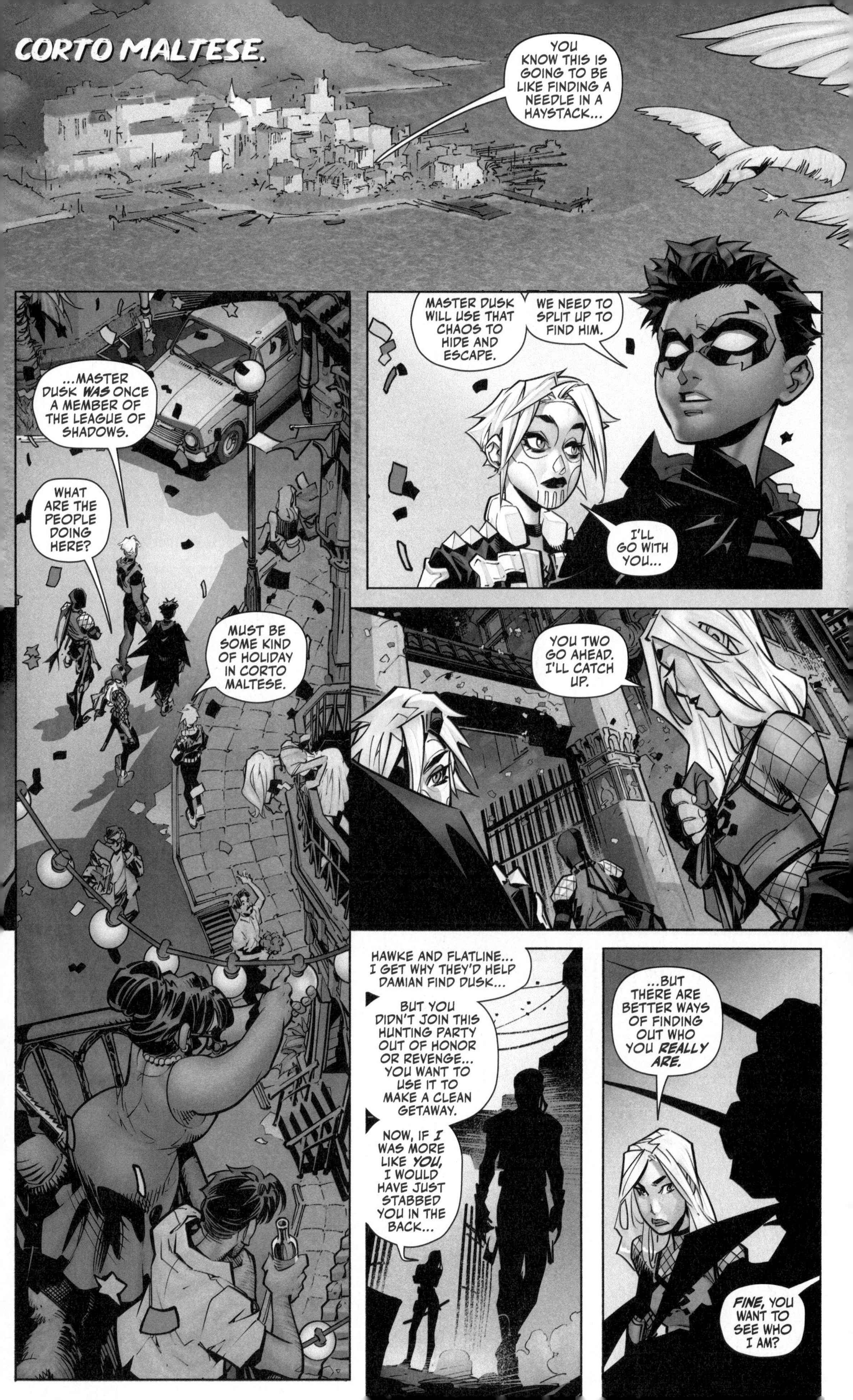
CORTO MALTESE.
YOU KNOW THIS IS GOING TO BE LIKE FINDING A NEEDLE IN A HAYSTACK...
...MASTER DUSK WAS ONCE A MEMBER OF THE LEAGUE OF SHADOWS.
WHAT ARE THE PEOPLE DOING HERE?
MUST BE SOME KIND OF HOLIDAY IN CORTO MALTESE.
MASTER DUSK WILL USE THAT CHAOS TO HIDE AND ESCAPE.
WE NEED TO SPLIT UP TO FIND HIM.
I'LL GO WITH YOU...
YOU TWO GO AHEAD. I'LL CATCH UP.
HAWKE AND FLATLINE... I GET WHY THEY'D HELP DAMIAN FIND DUSK...
BUT YOU DIDN'T JOIN THIS HUNTING PARTY OUT OF HONOR OR REVENGE... YOU WANT TO USE IT TO MAKE A CLEAN GETAWAY.
NOW, IF I WAS MORE LIKE YOU, I WOULD HAVE JUST STABBED YOU IN THE BACK...
...BUT THERE ARE BETTER WAYS OF FINDING OUT WHO YOU REALLY ARE.
FINE, YOU WANT TO SEE WHO I AM?

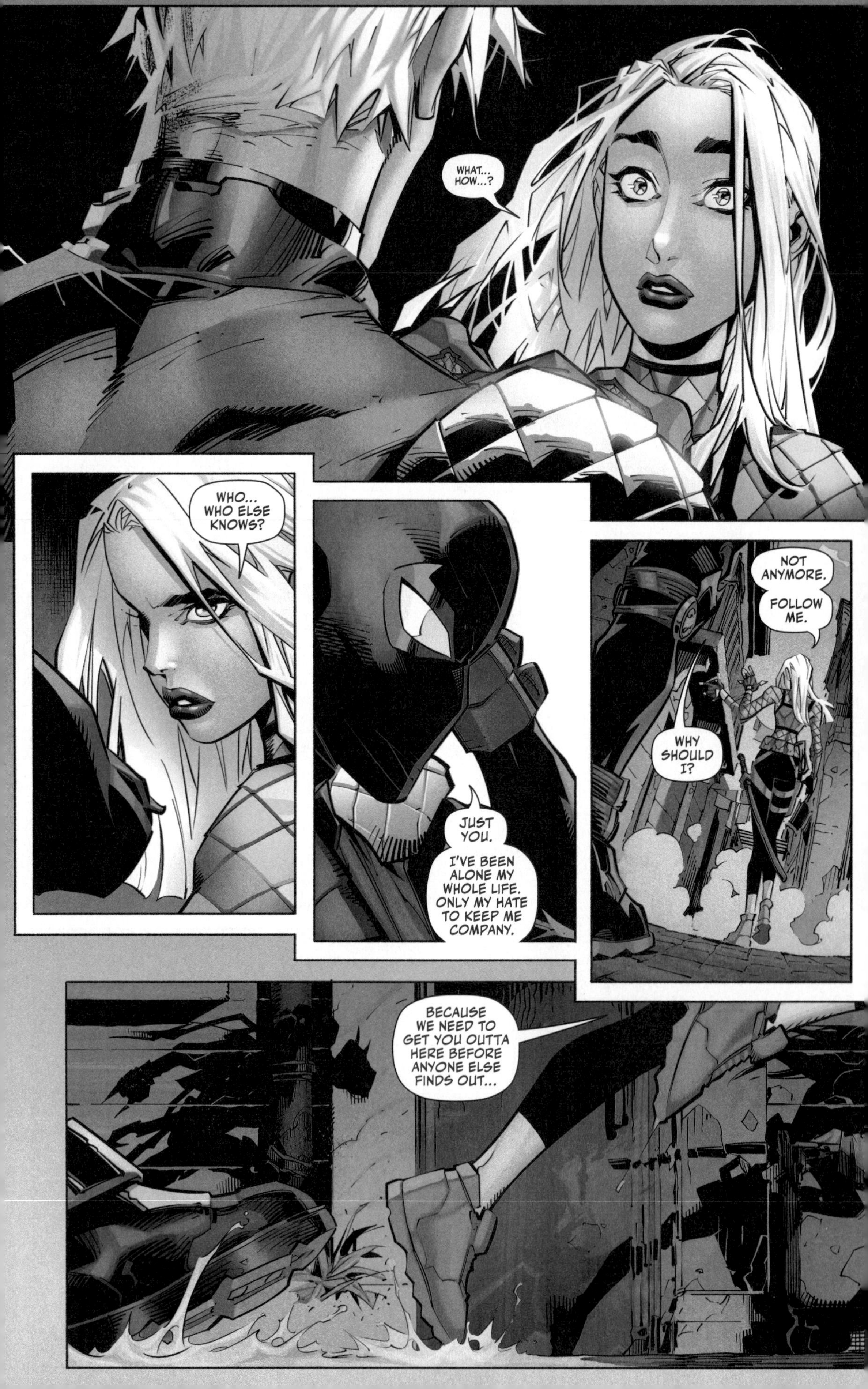
WHAT... HOW...?
WHO... WHO ELSE KNOWS?
JUST YOU.
I'VE BEEN ALONE MY WHOLE LIFE. ONLY MY HATE TO KEEP ME COMPANY.
NOT ANYMORE.
FOLLOW ME.
WHY SHOULD I?
BECAUSE WE NEED TO GET YOU OUTTA HERE BEFORE ANYONE ELSE FINDS OUT...

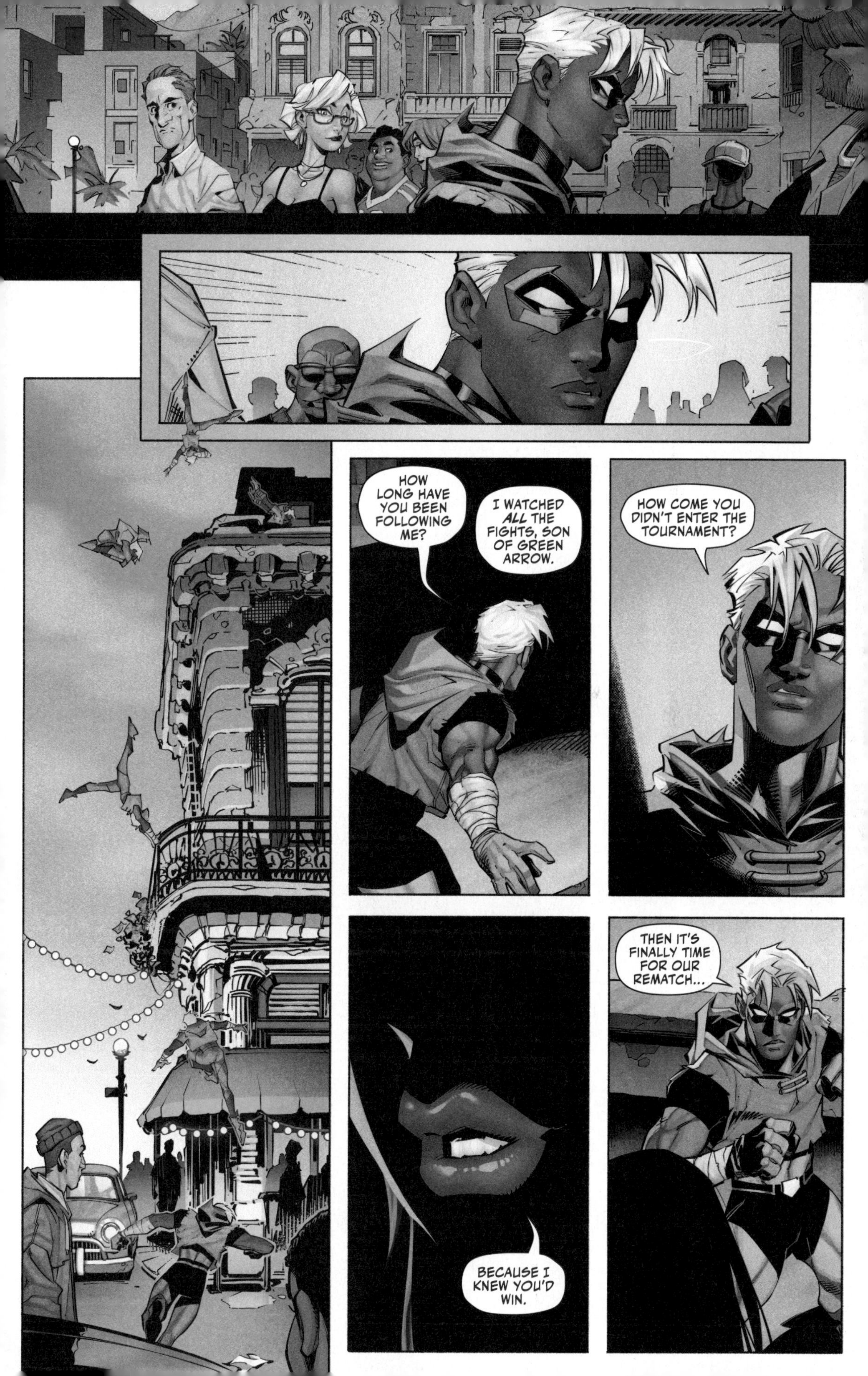

HOW LONG HAVE YOU BEEN FOLLOWING ME?
I WATCHED ALL THE FIGHTS, SON OF GREEN ARROW.
HOW COME YOU DIDN'T ENTER THE TOURNAMENT?
BECAUSE I KNEW YOU'D WIN.
THEN IT'S FINALLY TIME FOR OUR REMATCH...

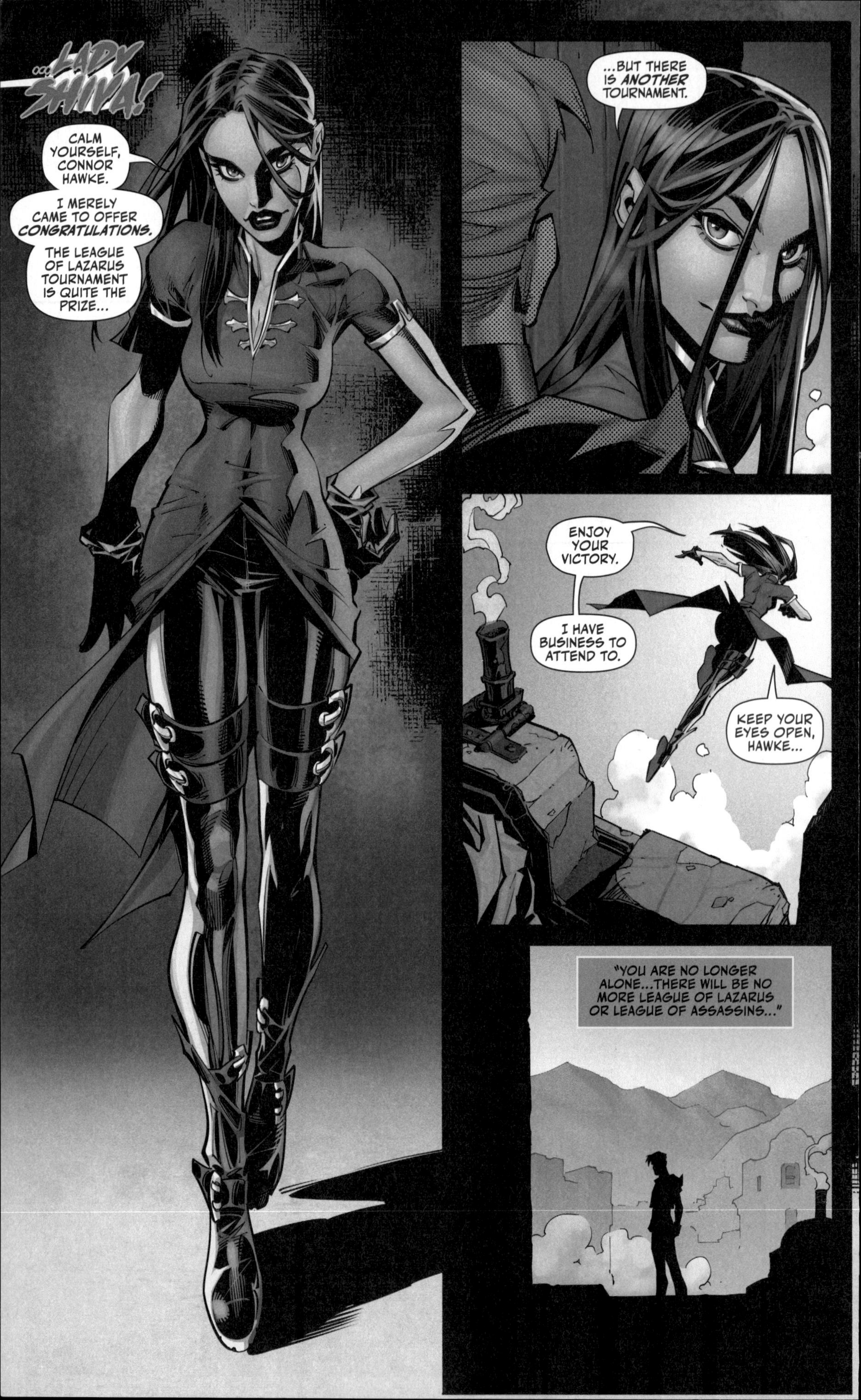
...LADY SHIVA!
CALM YOURSELF, CONNOR HAWKE.
I MERELY CAME TO OFFER CONGRATULATIONS.
THE LEAGUE OF LAZARUS TOURNAMENT IS QUITE THE PRIZE...
...BUT THERE IS ANOTHER TOURNAMENT.
ENJOY YOUR VICTORY.
I HAVE BUSINESS TO ATTEND TO.
KEEP YOUR EYES OPEN, HAWKE...
"YOU ARE NO LONGER ALONE...THERE WILL BE NO MORE LEAGUE OF LAZARUS OR LEAGUE OF ASSASSINS..."

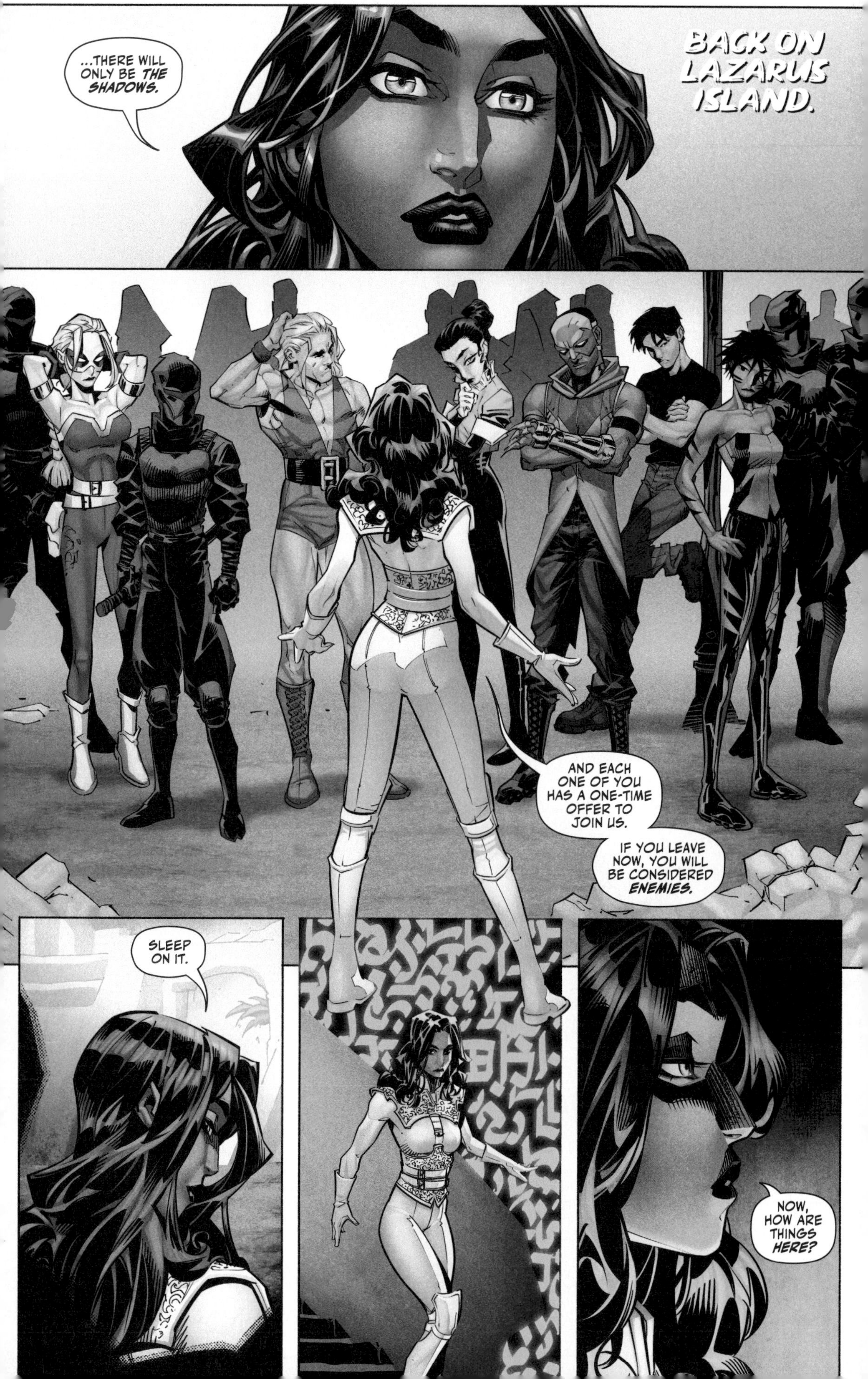
...THERE WILL ONLY BE THE SHADOWS.
BACK ON LAZARUS ISLAND.
AND EACH ONE OF YOU HAS A ONE-TIME OFFER TO JOIN US.
IF YOU LEAVE NOW, YOU WILL BE CONSIDERED ENEMIES.
SLEEP ON IT.
NOW, HOW ARE THINGS HERE?

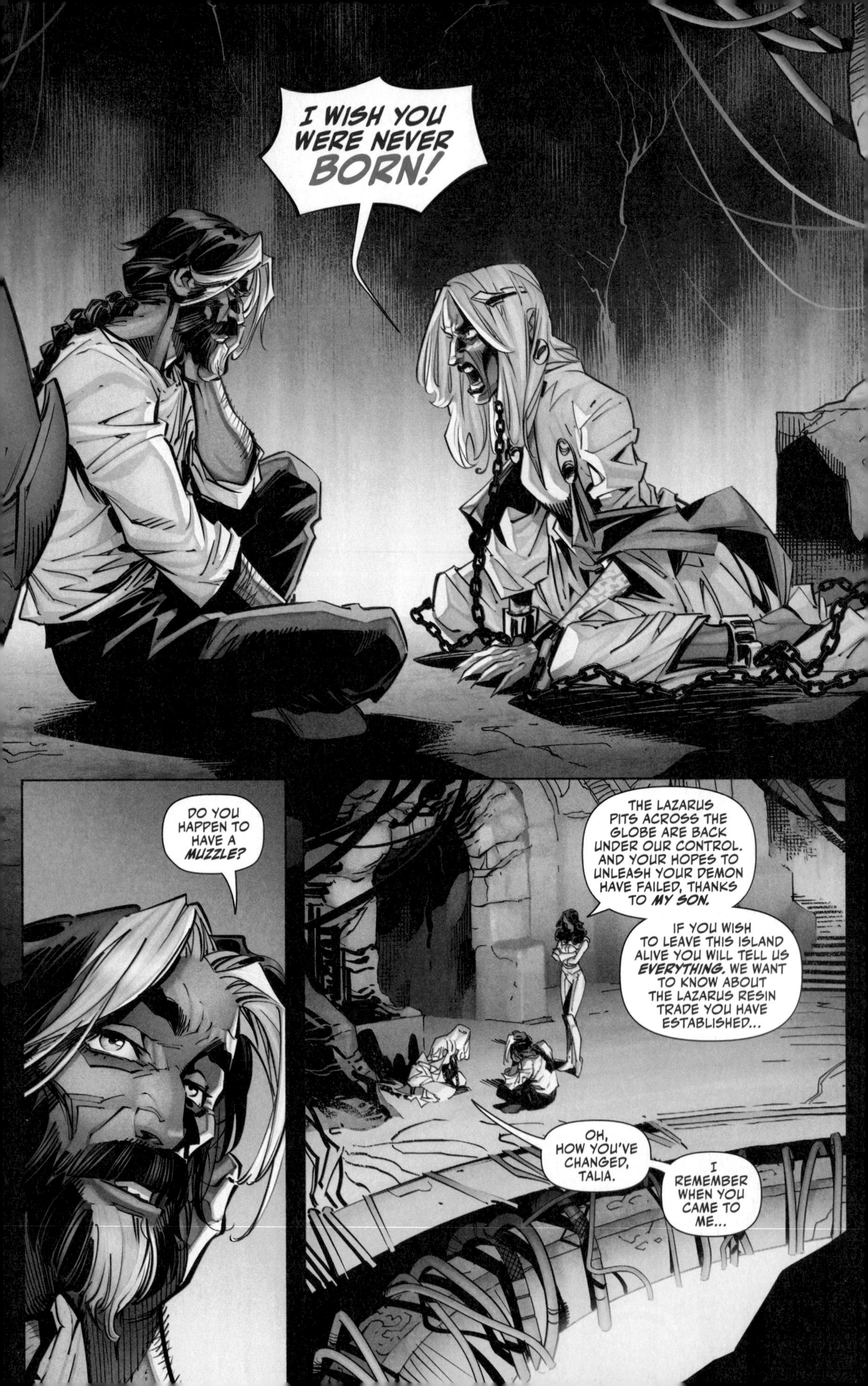
I WISH YOU WERE NEVER BORN!
DO YOU HAPPEN TO HAVE A MUZZLE?
THE LAZARUS PITS ACROSS THE GLOBE ARE BACK UNDER OUR CONTROL. AND YOUR HOPES TO UNLEASH YOUR DEMON HAVE FAILED, THANKS TO MY SON.
IF YOU WISH TO LEAVE THIS ISLAND ALIVE YOU WILL TELL US EVERYTHING. WE WANT TO KNOW ABOUT THE LAZARUS RESIN TRADE YOU HAVE ESTABLISHED...
OH, HOW YOU'VE CHANGED, TALIA.
I REMEMBER WHEN YOU CAME TO ME...

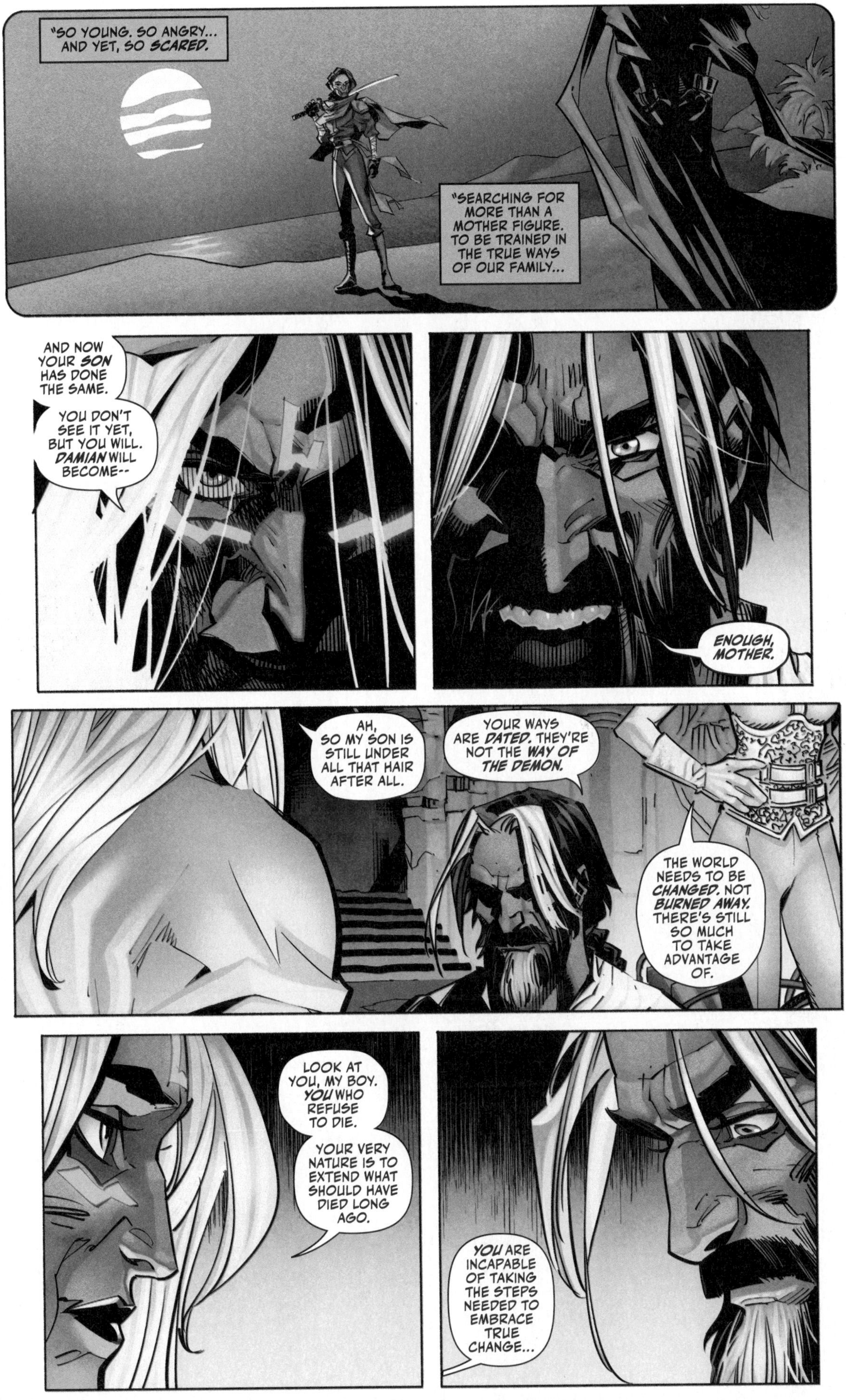
"SO YOUNG. SO ANGRY... AND YET, SO SCARED.
"SEARCHING FOR MORE THAN A MOTHER FIGURE. TO BE TRAINED IN THE TRUE WAYS OF OUR FAMILY...
AND NOW YOUR SON HAS DONE THE SAME.
YOU DON'T SEE IT YET, BUT YOU WILL. DAMIAN WILL BECOME--
ENOUGH, MOTHER.
AH, SO MY SON IS STILL UNDER ALL THAT HAIR AFTER ALL.
YOUR WAYS ARE DATED. THEY'RE NOT THE WAY OF THE DEMON.
THE WORLD NEEDS TO BE CHANGED. NOT BURNED AWAY. THERE'S STILL SO MUCH TO TAKE ADVANTAGE OF.
LOOK AT YOU, MY BOY. YOU WHO REFUSE TO DIE.
YOUR VERY NATURE IS TO EXTEND WHAT SHOULD HAVE DIED LONG AGO.
YOU ARE INCAPABLE OF TAKING THE STEPS NEEDED TO EMBRACE TRUE CHANGE...

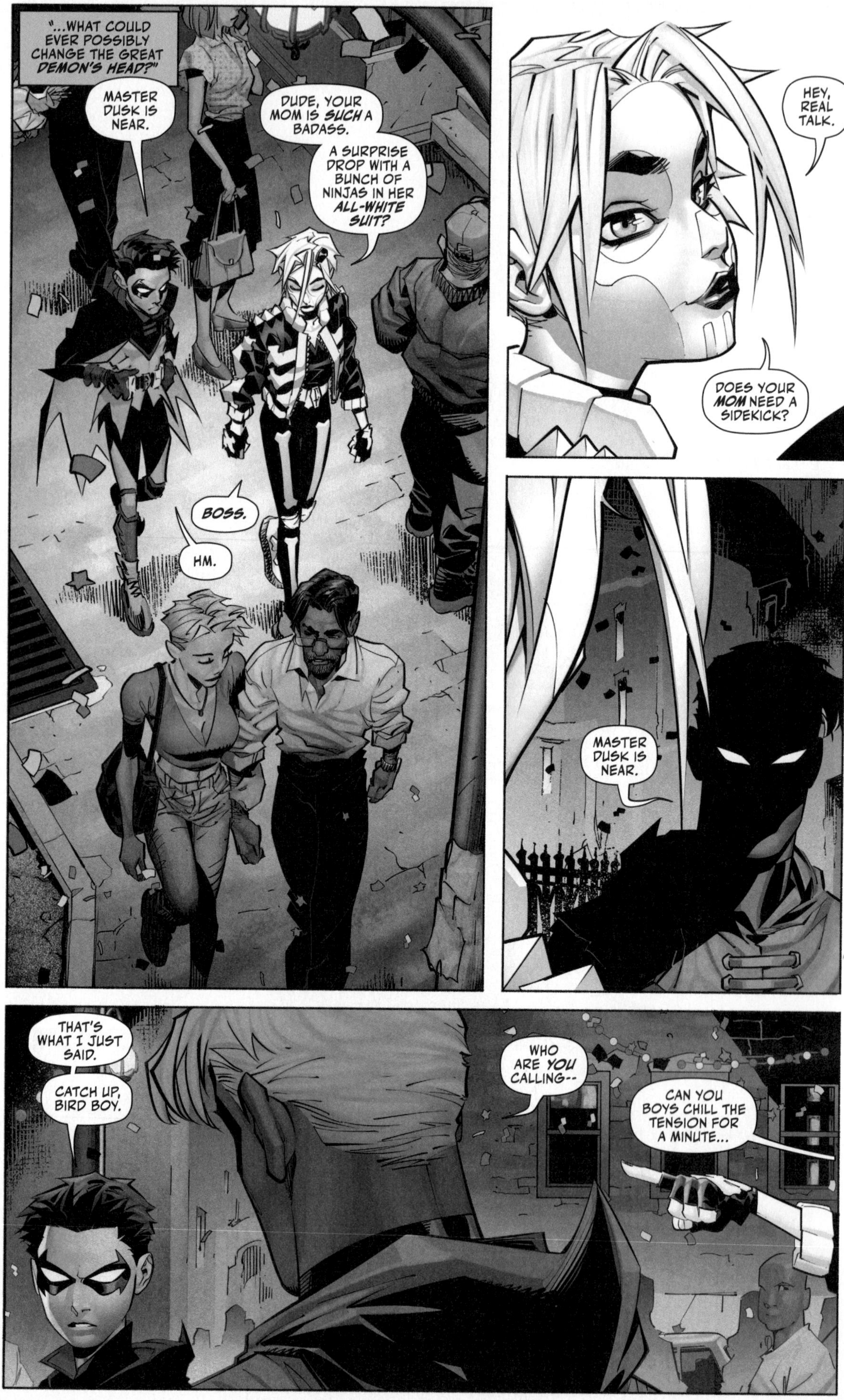
"...WHAT COULD EVER POSSIBLY CHANGE THE GREAT DEMON'S HEAD?"
MASTER DUSK IS NEAR.
DUDE, YOUR MOM IS SUCH A BADASS.
A SURPRISE DROP WITH A BUNCH OF NINJAS IN HER ALL-WHITE SUIT?
BOSS.
HM.
HEY, REAL TALK.
DOES YOUR MOM NEED A SIDEKICK?
MASTER DUSK IS NEAR.
THAT'S WHAT I JUST SAID.
CATCH UP, BIRD BOY.
WHO ARE YOU CALLING--
CAN YOU BOYS CHILL THE TENSION FOR A MINUTE...

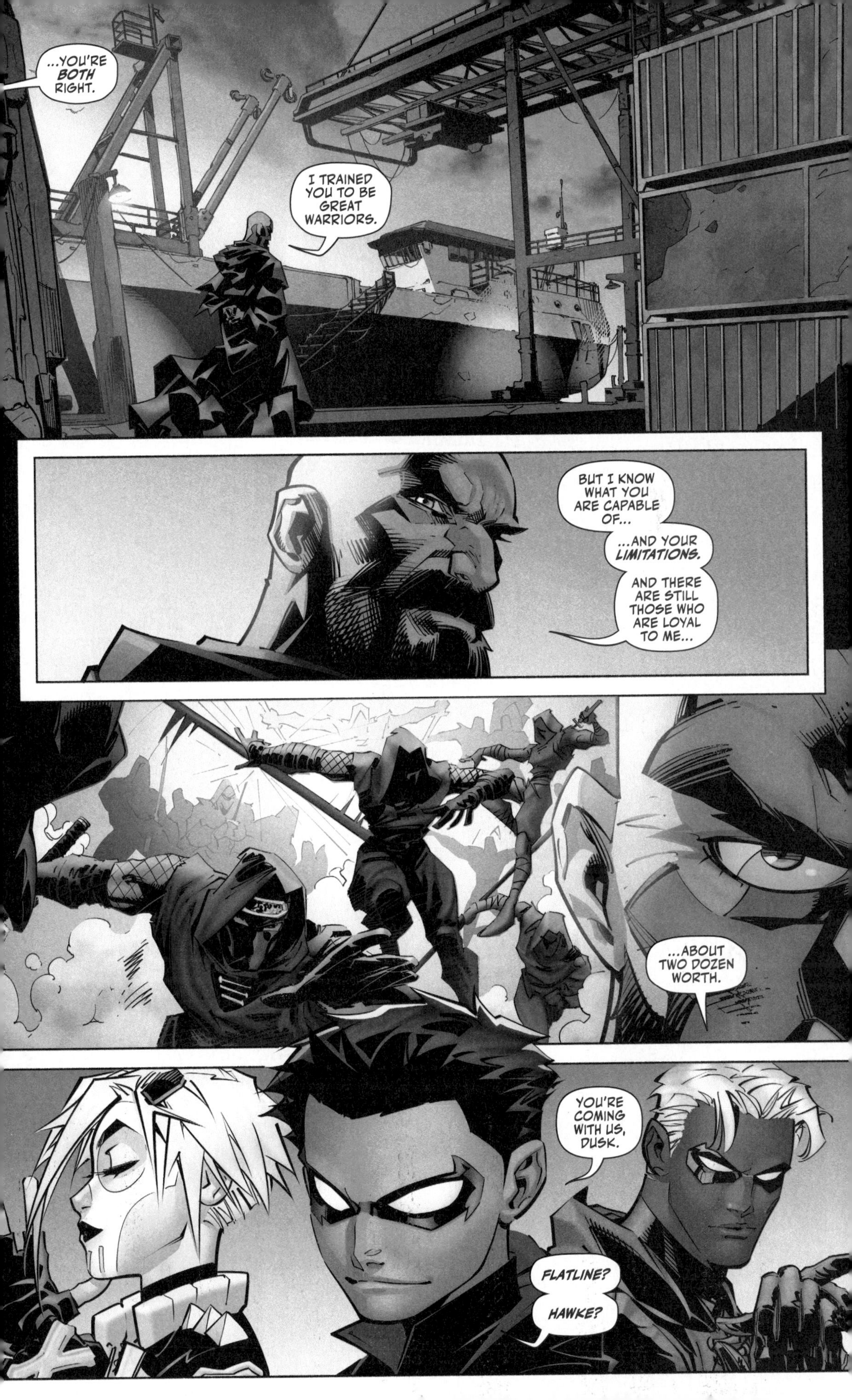
...YOU'RE *BOTH* RIGHT.
I TRAINED YOU TO BE GREAT WARRIORS.
BUT I KNOW WHAT YOU ARE CAPABLE OF...
...AND YOUR *LIMITATIONS.*
AND THERE ARE STILL THOSE WHO ARE LOYAL TO ME...
...ABOUT TWO DOZEN WORTH.
YOU'RE COMING WITH US, DUSK.
FLATLINE?
HAWKE?

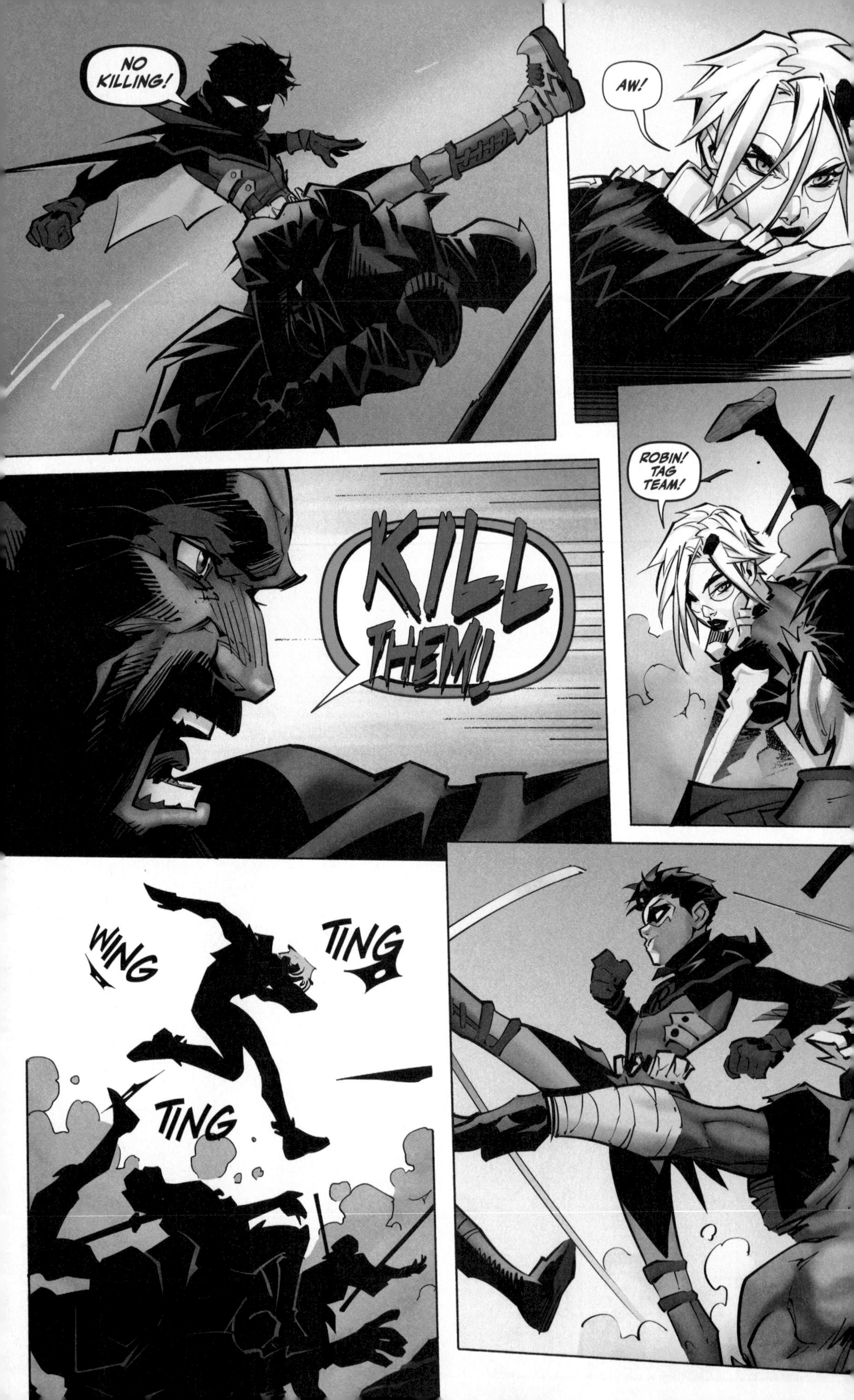
NO KILLING!
AW!
KILL THEM!
ROBIN! TAG TEAM!
WING
TING
TING

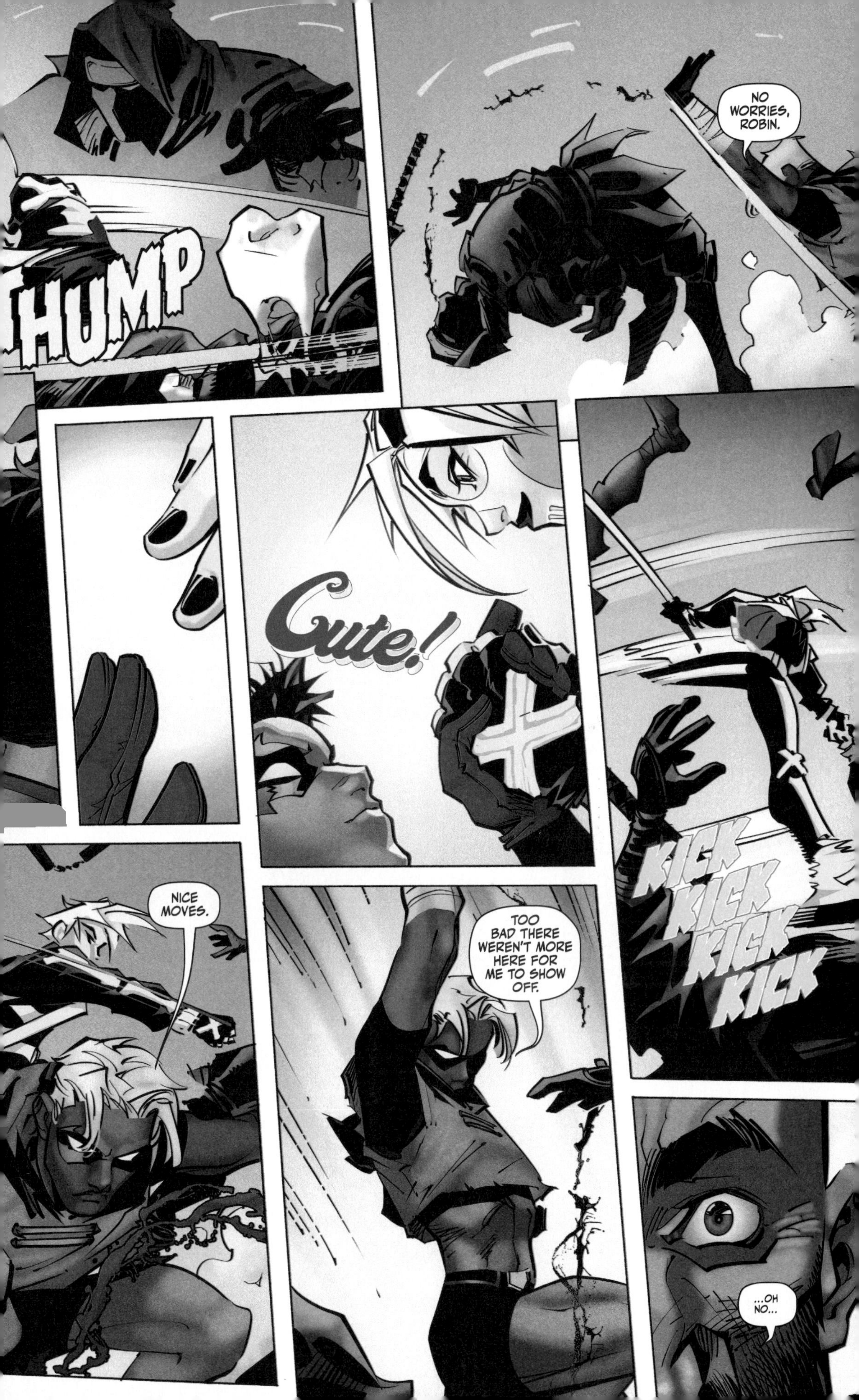
HUMP
NO WORRIES, ROBIN.
Cute!
KICK KICK KICK KICK
NICE MOVES.
TOO BAD THERE WEREN'T MORE HERE FOR ME TO SHOW OFF.
...OH NO...

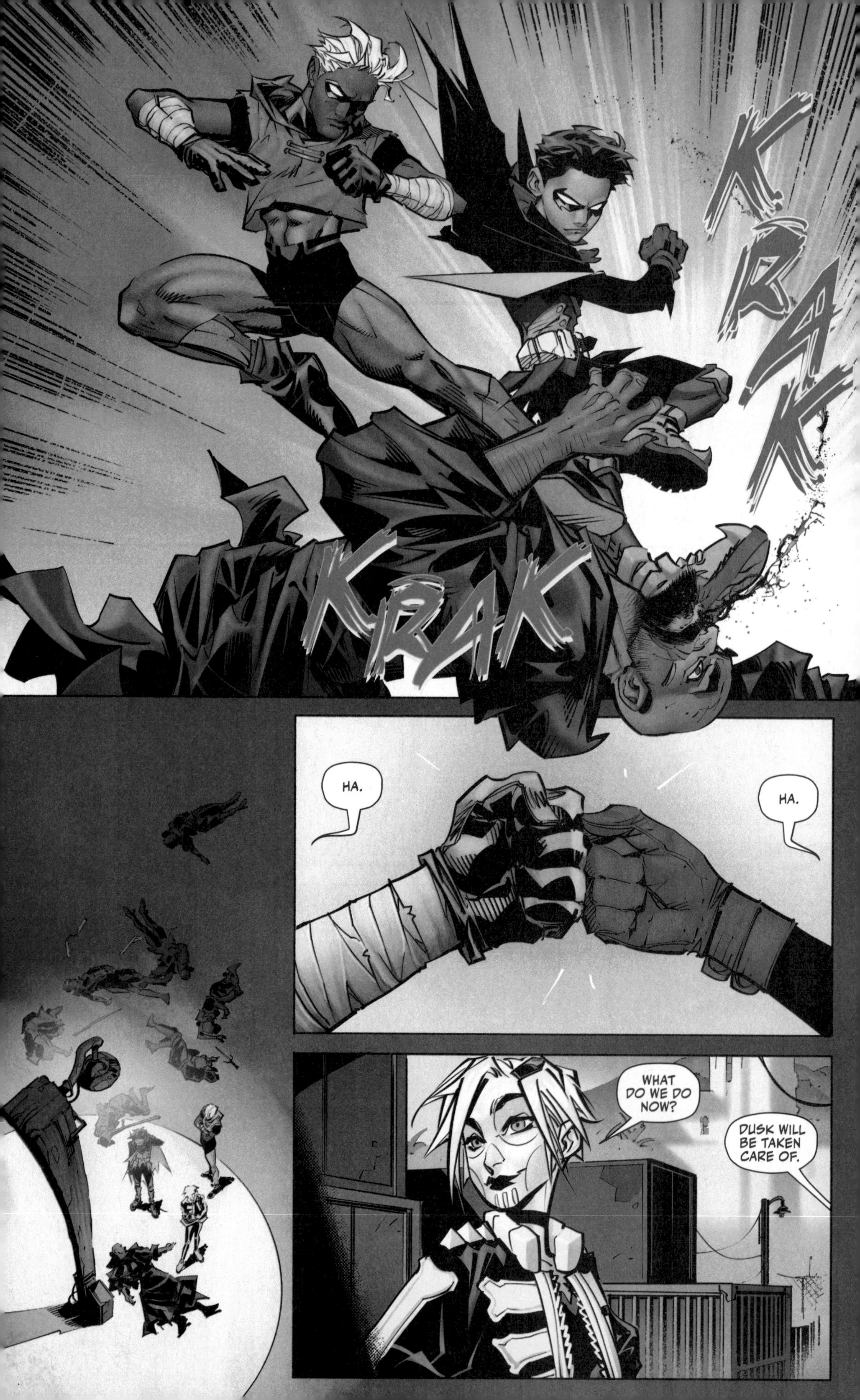
KRAK
KRAK
HA.
HA.
WHAT DO WE DO NOW?
DUSK WILL BE TAKEN CARE OF.

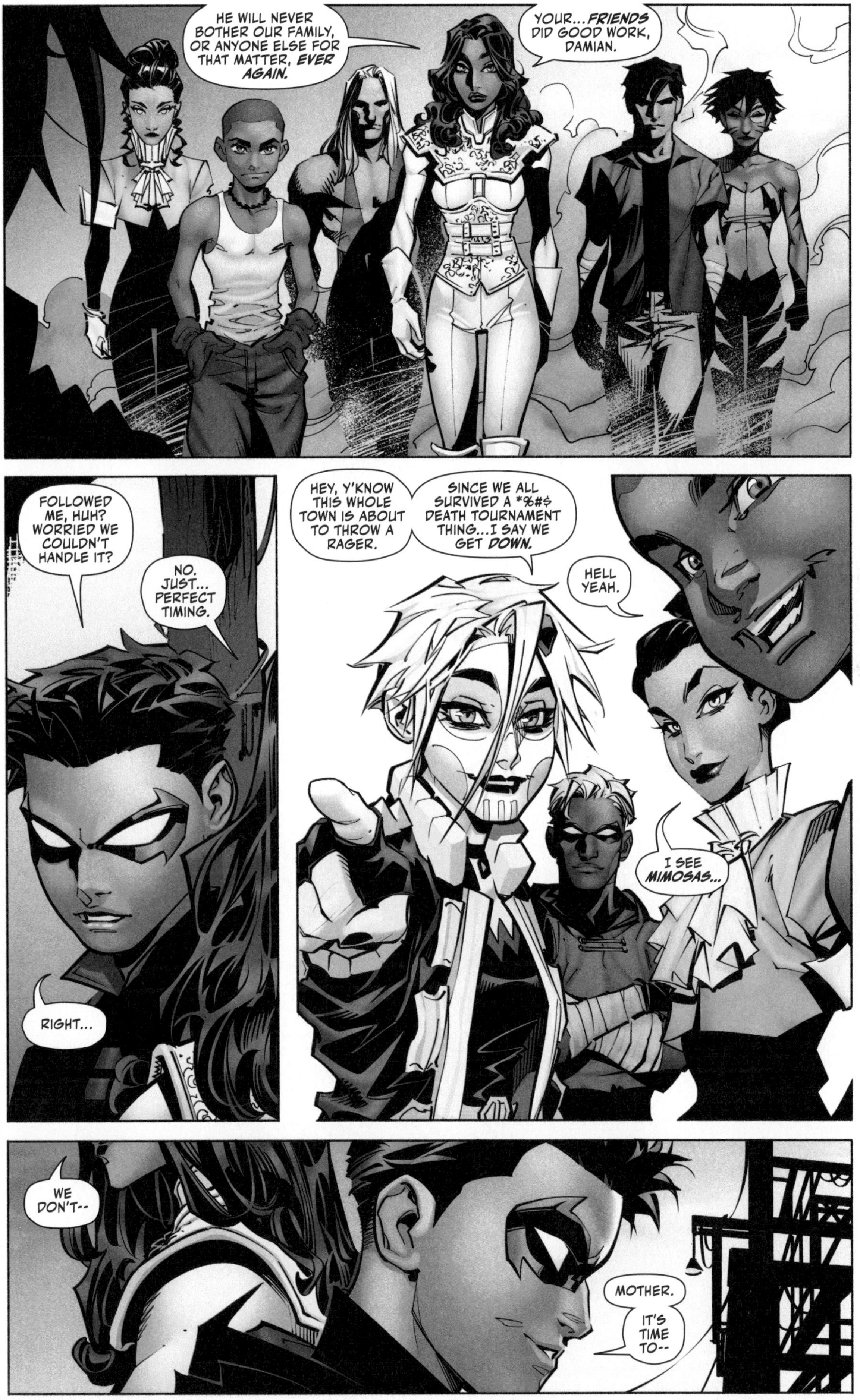
HE WILL NEVER BOTHER OUR FAMILY, OR ANYONE ELSE FOR THAT MATTER, EVER AGAIN.
YOUR...FRIENDS DID GOOD WORK, DAMIAN.
FOLLOWED ME, HUH? WORRIED WE COULDN'T HANDLE IT?
NO. JUST... PERFECT TIMING.
RIGHT...
HEY, Y'KNOW THIS WHOLE TOWN IS ABOUT TO THROW A RAGER.
SINCE WE ALL SURVIVED A *%#$ DEATH TOURNAMENT THING...I SAY WE GET DOWN.
HELL YEAH.
I SEE MIMOSAS...
WE DON'T--
MOTHER.
IT'S TIME TO--

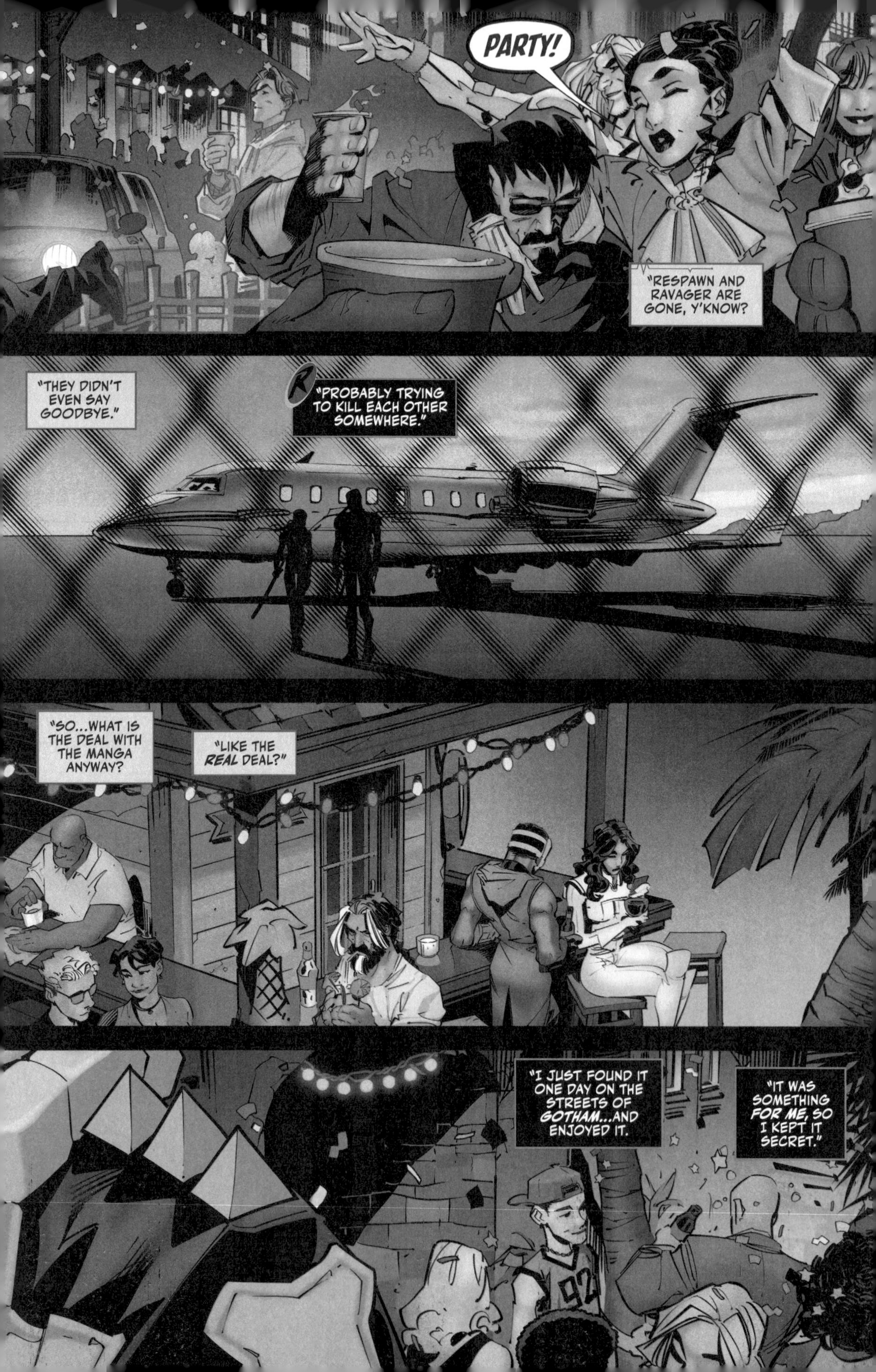
PARTY!
"RESPAWN AND RAVAGER ARE GONE, Y'KNOW?
"THEY DIDN'T EVEN SAY GOODBYE."
"PROBABLY TRYING TO KILL EACH OTHER SOMEWHERE."
"SO...WHAT IS THE DEAL WITH THE MANGA ANYWAY?
"LIKE THE REAL DEAL?"
"I JUST FOUND IT ONE DAY ON THE STREETS OF GOTHAM...AND ENJOYED IT.
"IT WAS SOMETHING FOR ME, SO I KEPT IT SECRET."

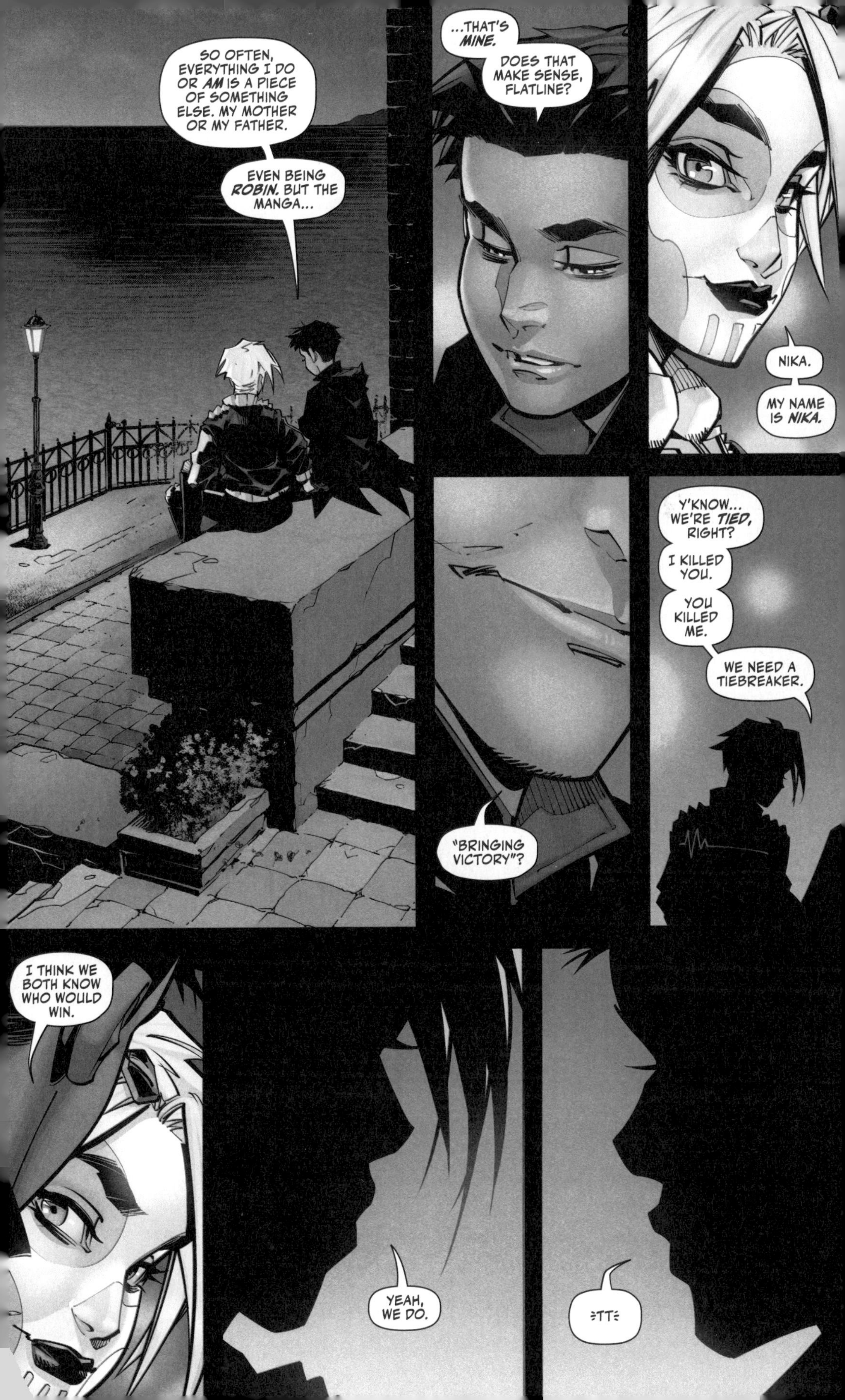
SO OFTEN, EVERYTHING I DO OR AM IS A PIECE OF SOMETHING ELSE. MY MOTHER OR MY FATHER.
EVEN BEING ROBIN. BUT THE MANGA...
...THAT'S MINE.
DOES THAT MAKE SENSE, FLATLINE?
NIKA.
MY NAME IS NIKA.
"BRINGING VICTORY"?
Y'KNOW... WE'RE TIED, RIGHT?
I KILLED YOU.
YOU KILLED ME.
WE NEED A TIEBREAKER.
I THINK WE BOTH KNOW WHO WOULD WIN.
YEAH, WE DO.
TT

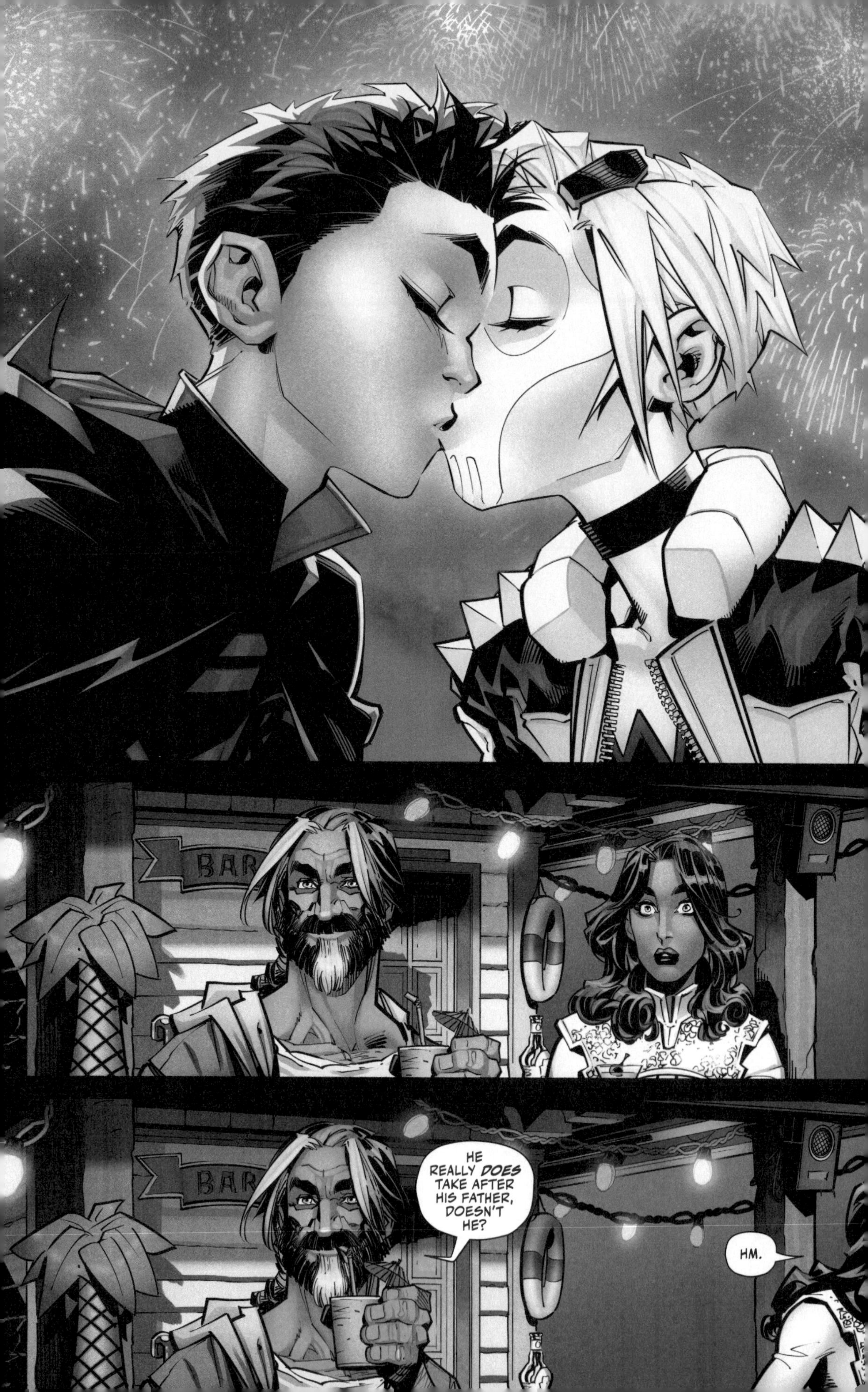
BAR
BAR
HE REALLY DOES TAKE AFTER HIS FATHER, DOESN'T HE?
HM.

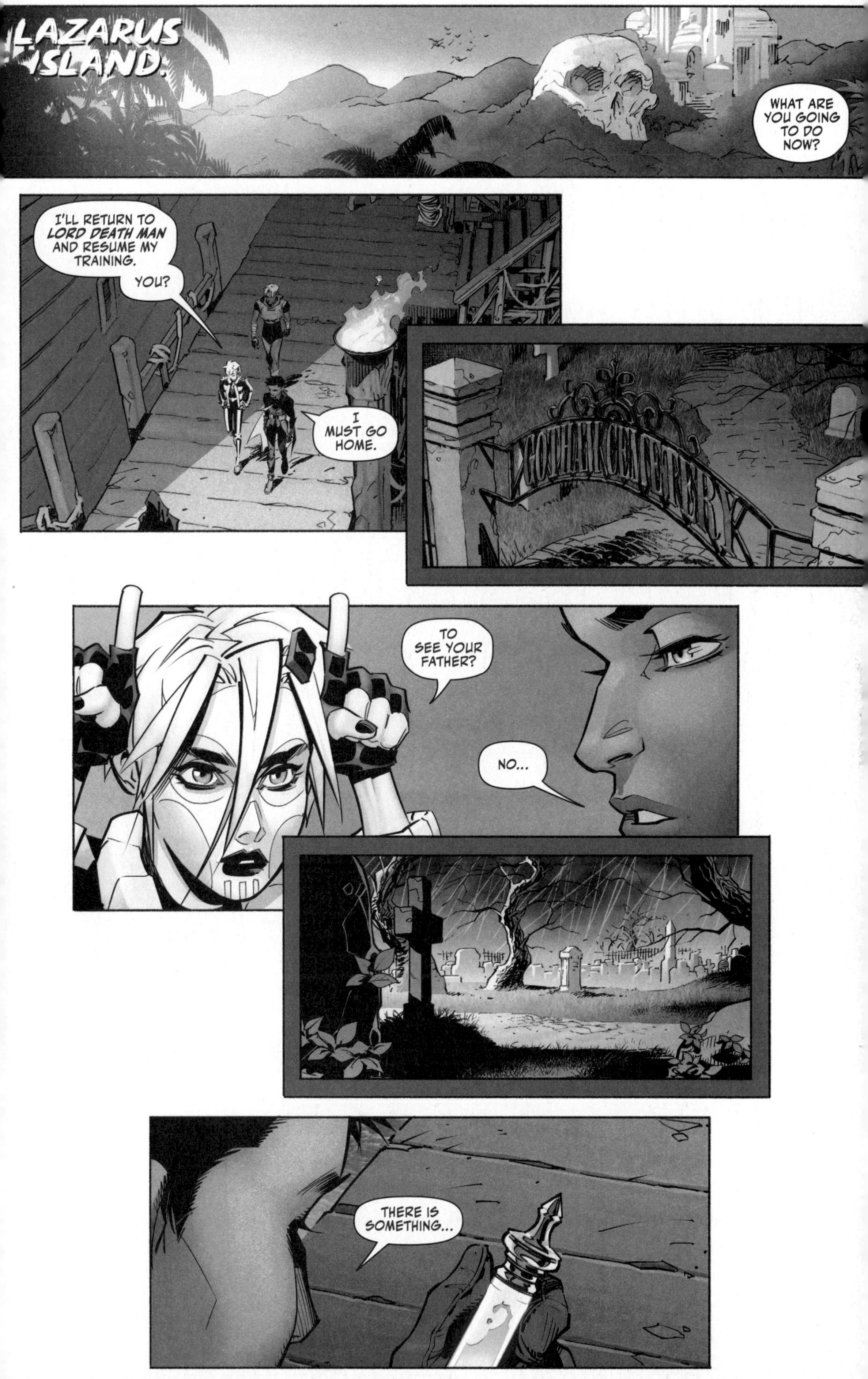
LAZARUS ISLAND.
WHAT ARE YOU GOING TO DO NOW?
I'LL RETURN TO LORD DEATH MAN AND RESUME MY TRAINING.
YOU?
I MUST GO HOME.
GOTHAM CEMETERY
TO SEE YOUR FATHER?
NO...
THERE IS SOMETHING...

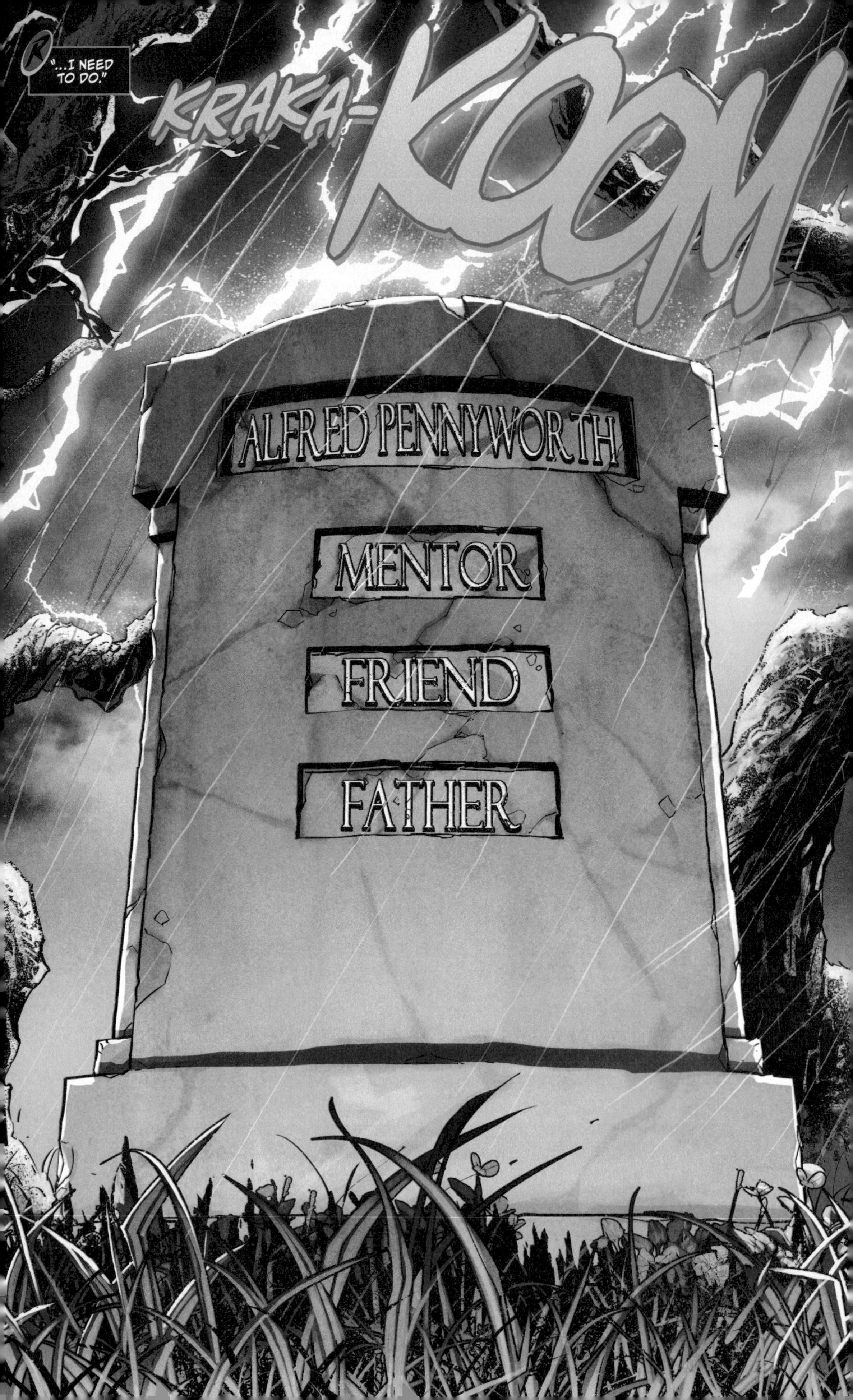
"...I NEED TO DO."
KRAKA-KOOM
ALFRED PENNYWORTH
MENTOR
FRIEND
FATHER

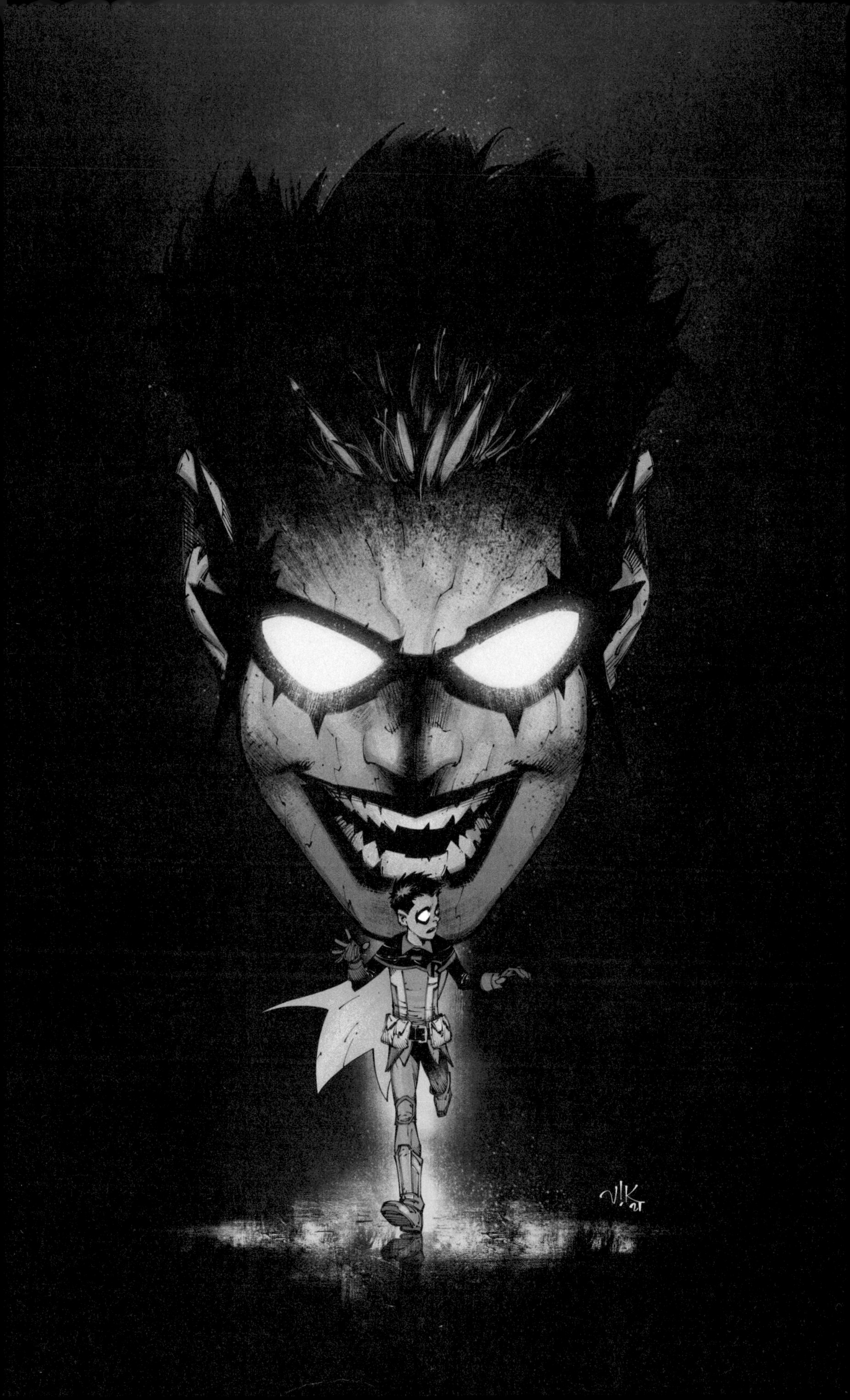

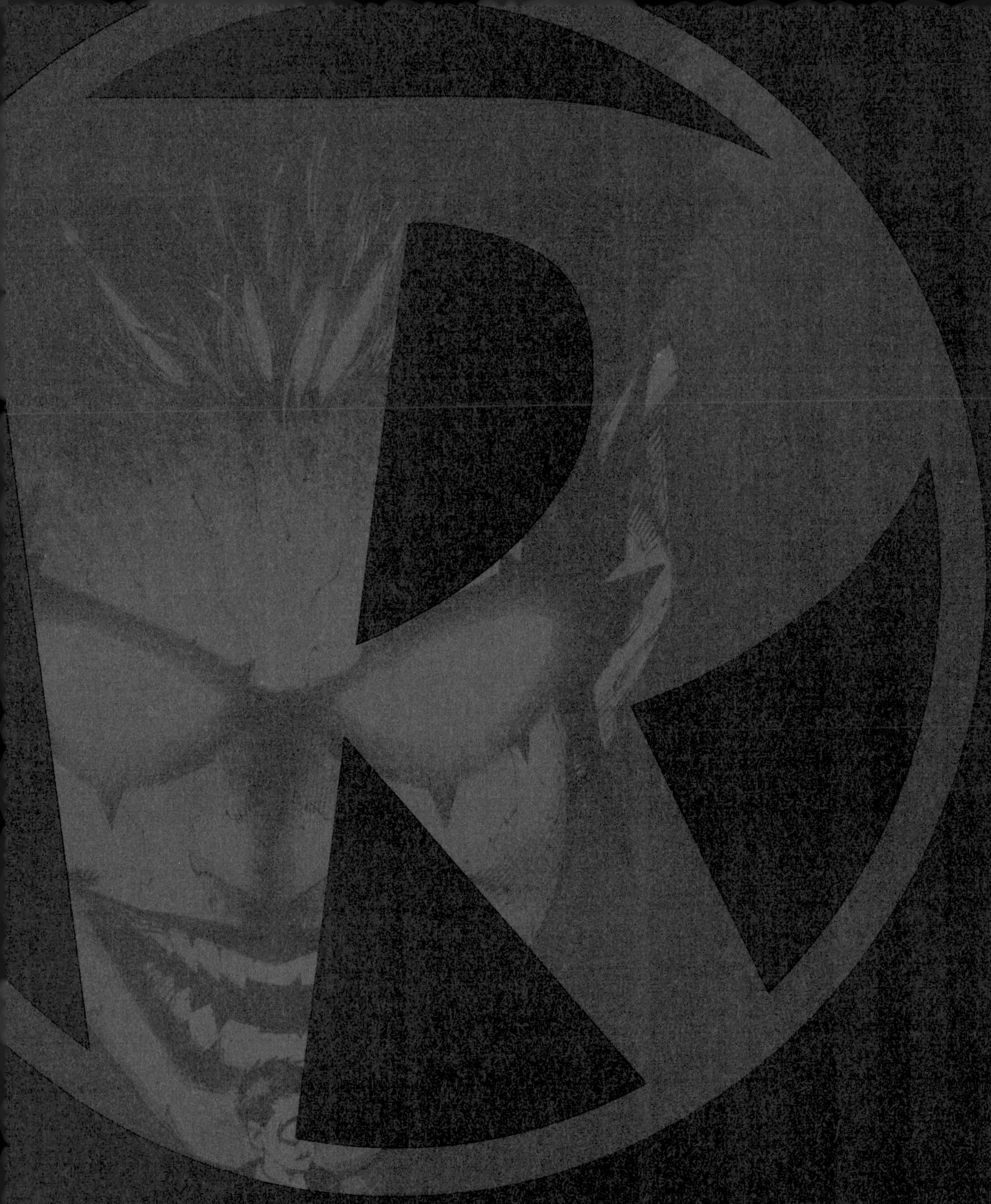

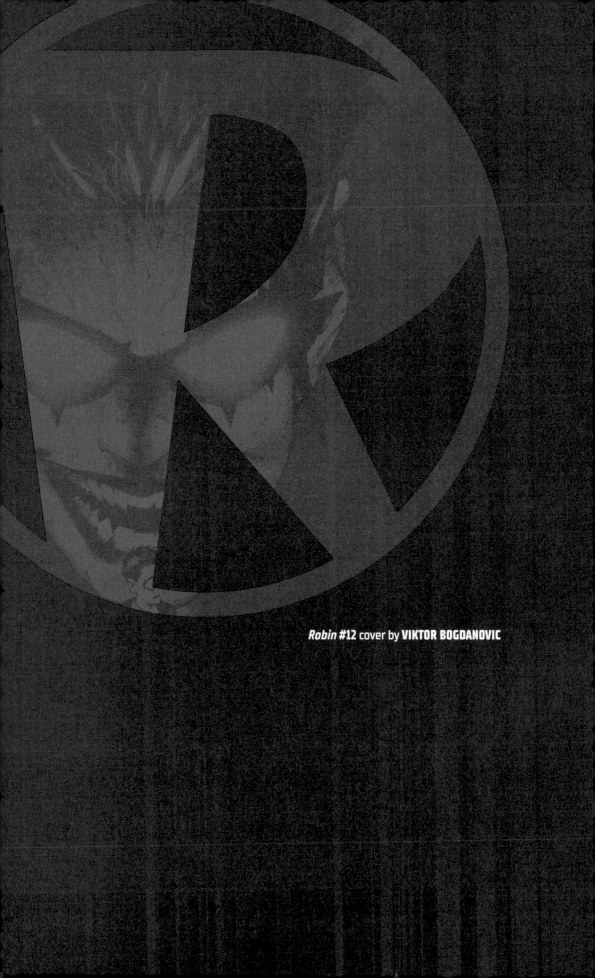

Robin #12 cover by **VIKTOR BOGDANOVIC**

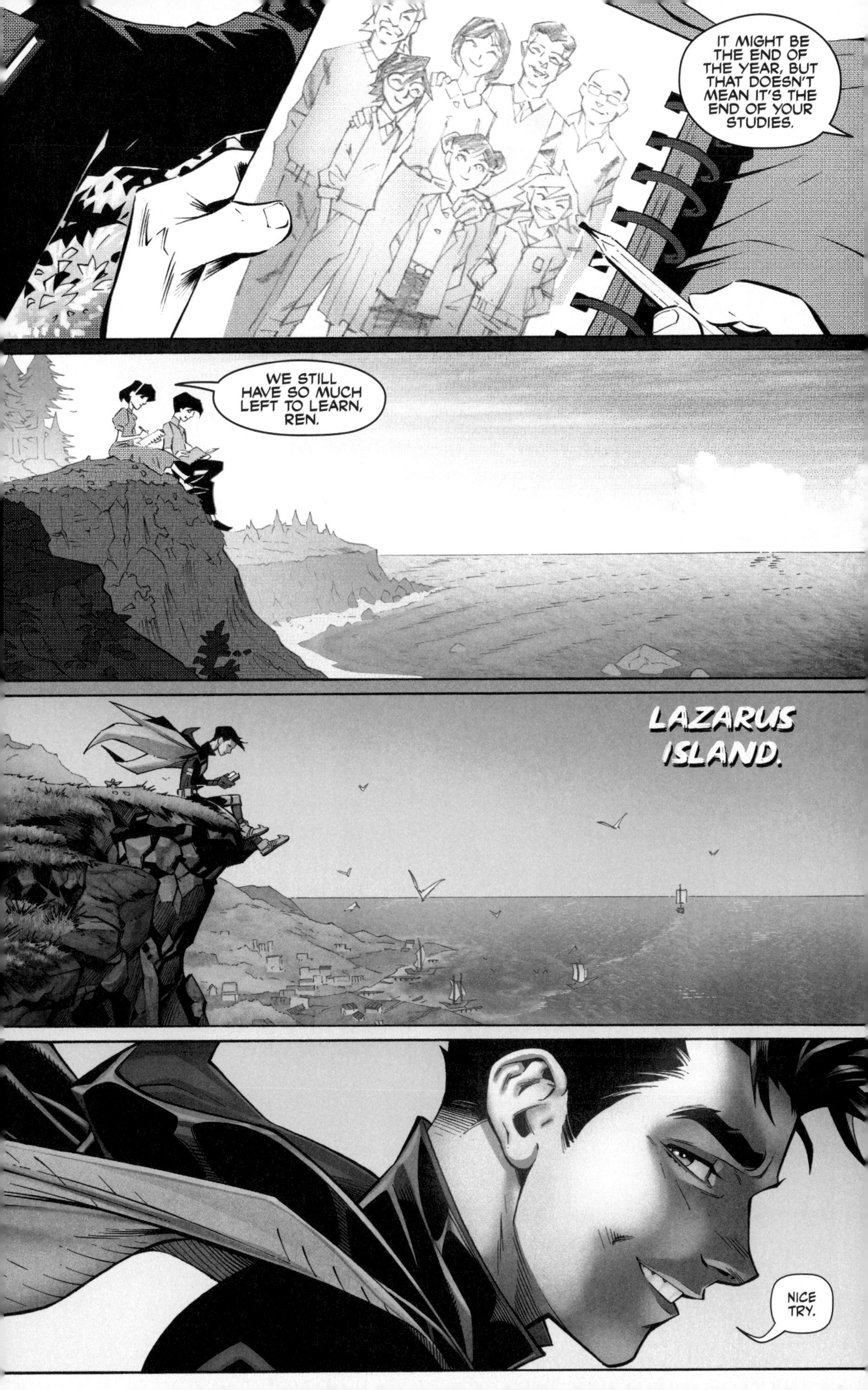
IT MIGHT BE THE END OF THE YEAR, BUT THAT DOESN'T MEAN IT'S THE END OF YOUR STUDIES.
WE STILL HAVE SO MUCH LEFT TO LEARN, REN.
LAZARUS ISLAND.
NICE TRY.

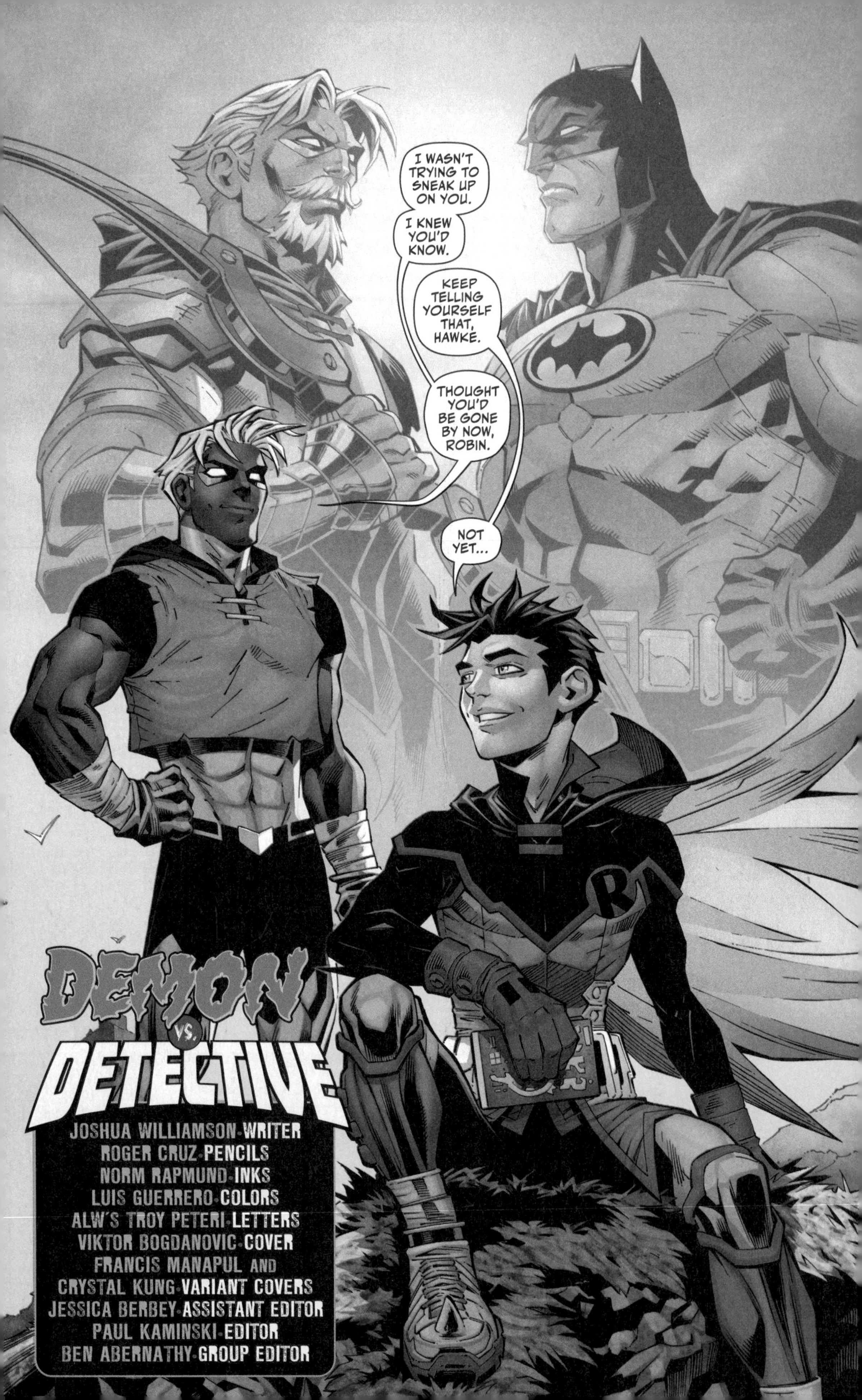
I WASN'T TRYING TO SNEAK UP ON YOU.
I KNEW YOU'D KNOW.
KEEP TELLING YOURSELF THAT, HAWKE.
THOUGHT YOU'D BE GONE BY NOW, ROBIN.
NOT YET...
DEMON VS. DETECTIVE
JOSHUA WILLIAMSON·WRITER
ROGER CRUZ·PENCILS
NORM RAPMUND·INKS
LUIS GUERRERO·COLORS
ALW'S TROY PETERI·LETTERS
VIKTOR BOGDANOVIC·COVER
FRANCIS MANAPUL AND
CRYSTAL KUNG·VARIANT COVERS
JESSICA BERBEY·ASSISTANT EDITOR
PAUL KAMINSKI·EDITOR
BEN ABERNATHY·GROUP EDITOR

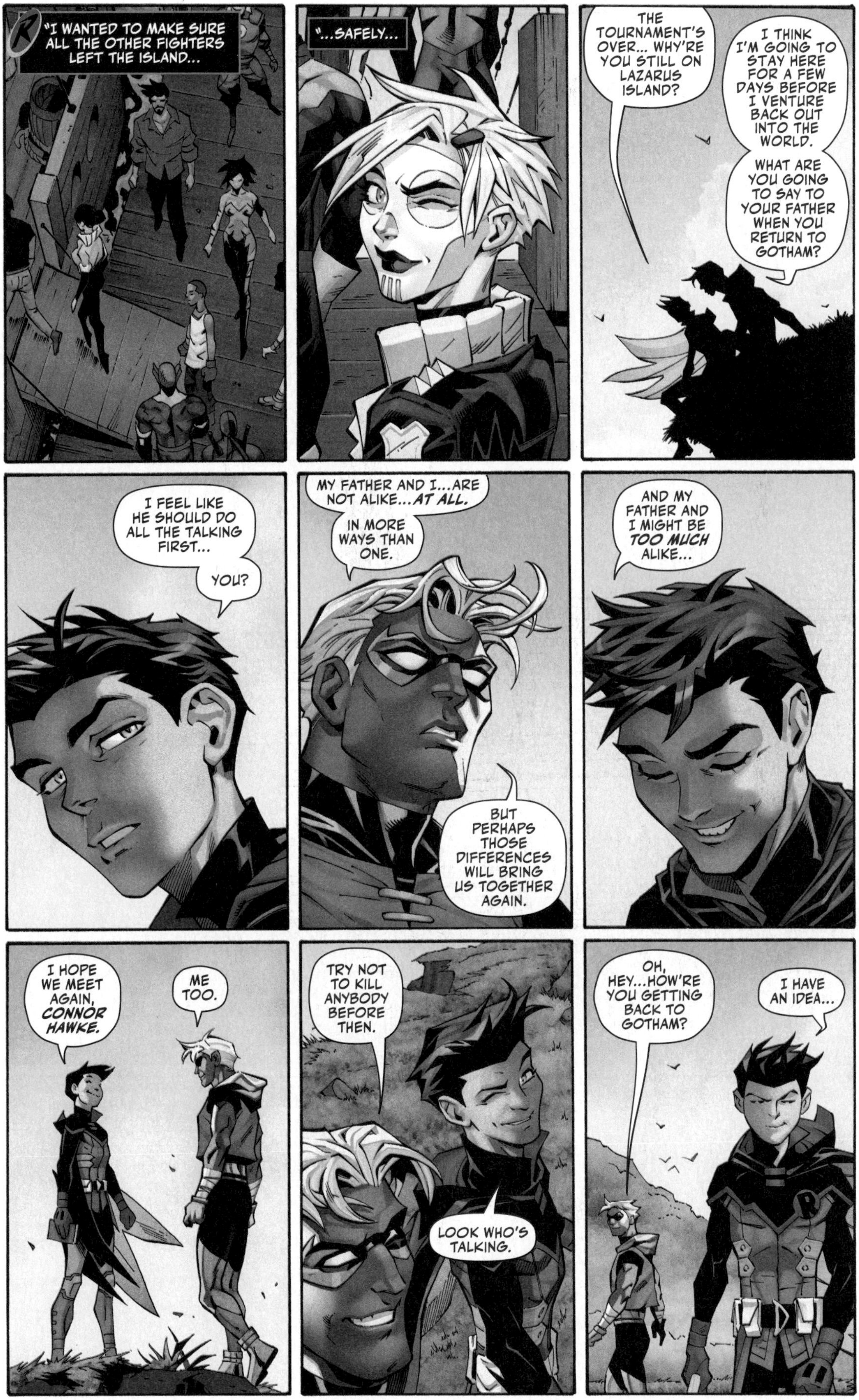
"I WANTED TO MAKE SURE ALL THE OTHER FIGHTERS LEFT THE ISLAND...
"...SAFELY...
THE TOURNAMENT'S OVER... WHY'RE YOU STILL ON LAZARUS ISLAND?
I THINK I'M GOING TO STAY HERE FOR A FEW DAYS BEFORE I VENTURE BACK OUT INTO THE WORLD.
WHAT ARE YOU GOING TO SAY TO YOUR FATHER WHEN YOU RETURN TO GOTHAM?
I FEEL LIKE HE SHOULD DO ALL THE TALKING FIRST...
YOU?
MY FATHER AND I...ARE NOT ALIKE...AT ALL.
IN MORE WAYS THAN ONE.
BUT PERHAPS THOSE DIFFERENCES WILL BRING US TOGETHER AGAIN.
AND MY FATHER AND I MIGHT BE TOO MUCH ALIKE...
I HOPE WE MEET AGAIN, CONNOR HAWKE.
ME TOO.
TRY NOT TO KILL ANYBODY BEFORE THEN.
LOOK WHO'S TALKING.
OH, HEY...HOW'RE YOU GETTING BACK TO GOTHAM?
I HAVE AN IDEA...

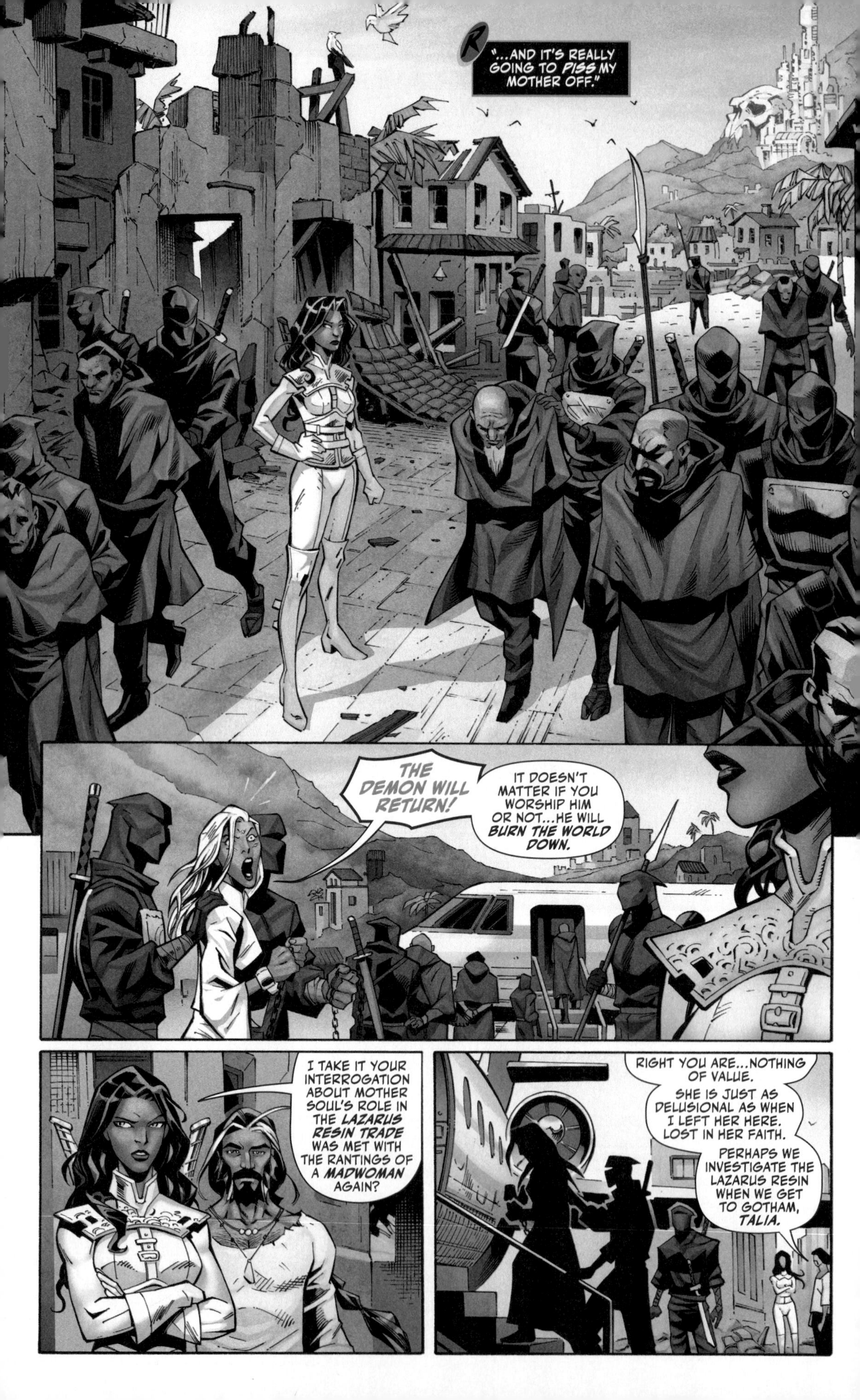
"...AND IT'S REALLY GOING TO PISS MY MOTHER OFF."
THE DEMON WILL RETURN!
IT DOESN'T MATTER IF YOU WORSHIP HIM OR NOT...HE WILL BURN THE WORLD DOWN.
I TAKE IT YOUR INTERROGATION ABOUT MOTHER SOUL'S ROLE IN THE LAZARUS RESIN TRADE WAS MET WITH THE RANTINGS OF A MADWOMAN AGAIN?
RIGHT YOU ARE...NOTHING OF VALUE.
SHE IS JUST AS DELUSIONAL AS WHEN I LEFT HER HERE. LOST IN HER FAITH.
PERHAPS WE INVESTIGATE THE LAZARUS RESIN WHEN WE GET TO GOTHAM, TALIA.

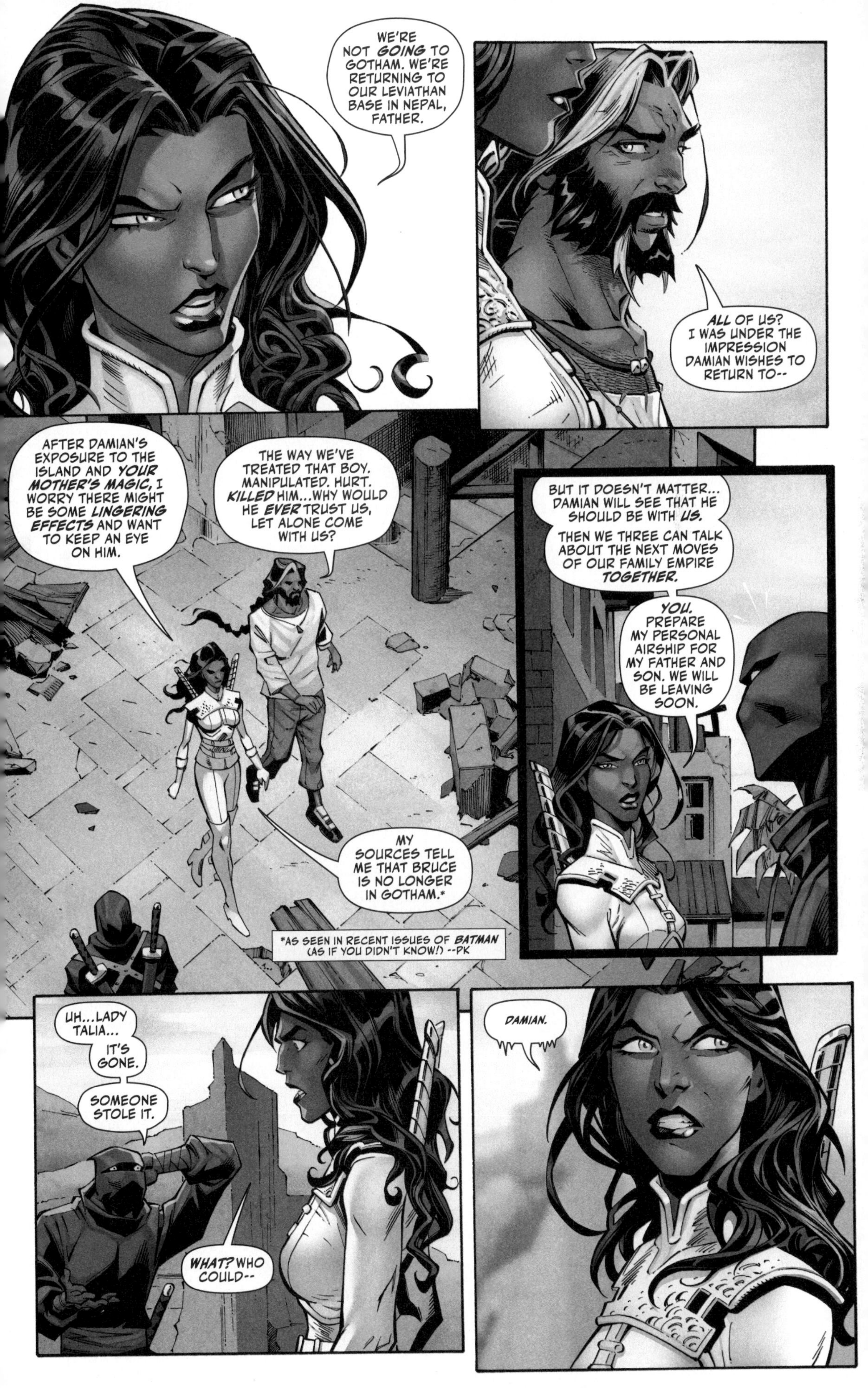
WE'RE NOT GOING TO GOTHAM. WE'RE RETURNING TO OUR LEVIATHAN BASE IN NEPAL, FATHER.
ALL OF US? I WAS UNDER THE IMPRESSION DAMIAN WISHES TO RETURN TO--
AFTER DAMIAN'S EXPOSURE TO THE ISLAND AND YOUR MOTHER'S MAGIC, I WORRY THERE MIGHT BE SOME LINGERING EFFECTS AND WANT TO KEEP AN EYE ON HIM.
THE WAY WE'VE TREATED THAT BOY. MANIPULATED. HURT. KILLED HIM...WHY WOULD HE EVER TRUST US, LET ALONE COME WITH US?
MY SOURCES TELL ME THAT BRUCE IS NO LONGER IN GOTHAM.*
*AS SEEN IN RECENT ISSUES OF BATMAN (AS IF YOU DIDN'T KNOW!) --PK
BUT IT DOESN'T MATTER... DAMIAN WILL SEE THAT HE SHOULD BE WITH US.
THEN WE THREE CAN TALK ABOUT THE NEXT MOVES OF OUR FAMILY EMPIRE TOGETHER.
YOU. PREPARE MY PERSONAL AIRSHIP FOR MY FATHER AND SON. WE WILL BE LEAVING SOON.
UH...LADY TALIA...
IT'S GONE.
SOMEONE STOLE IT.
WHAT? WHO COULD--
DAMIAN.

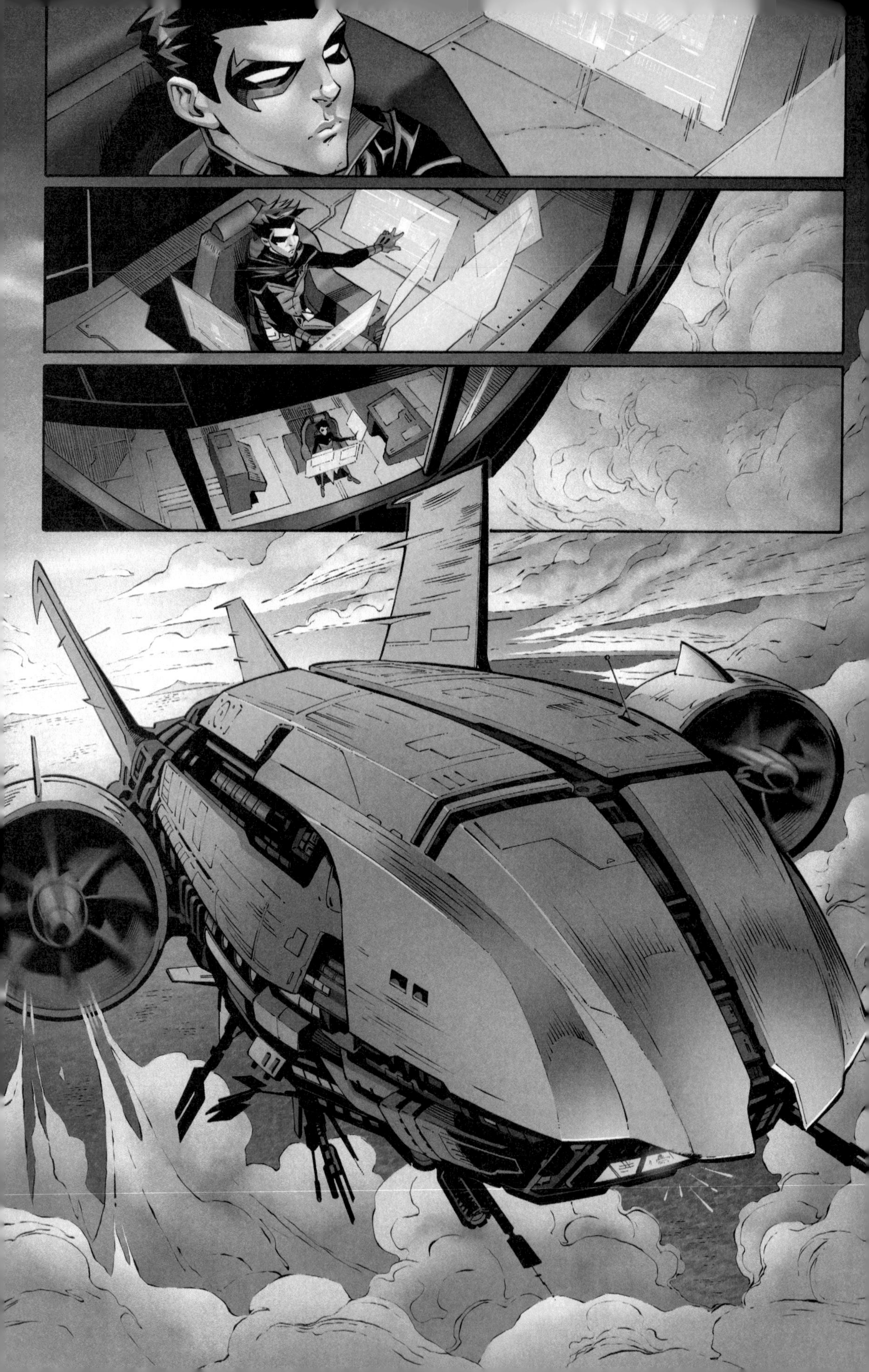

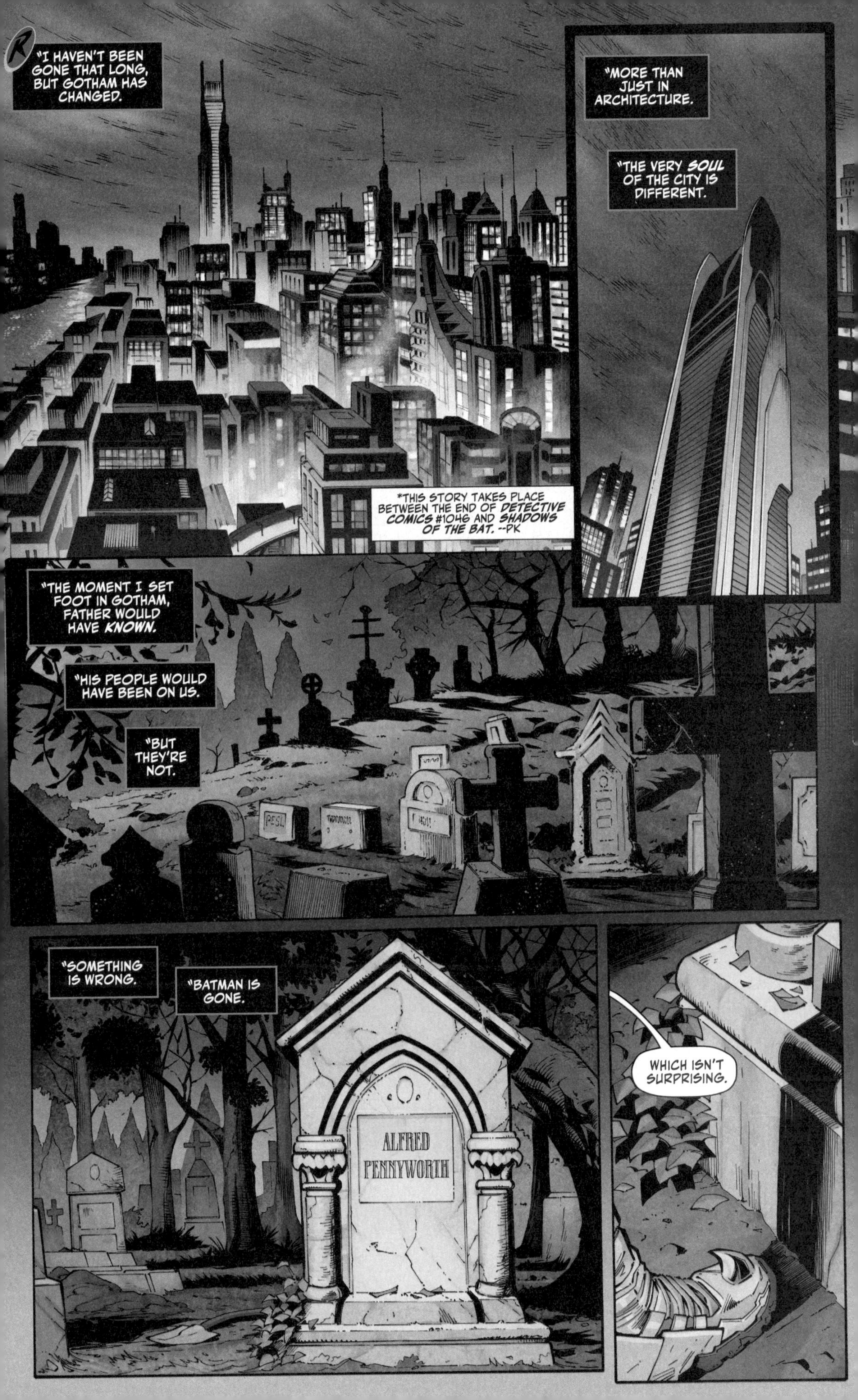
"I HAVEN'T BEEN GONE THAT LONG, BUT GOTHAM HAS CHANGED.
"MORE THAN JUST IN ARCHITECTURE.
"THE VERY SOUL OF THE CITY IS DIFFERENT.
*THIS STORY TAKES PLACE BETWEEN THE END OF DETECTIVE COMICS #1046 AND SHADOWS OF THE BAT. --PK
"THE MOMENT I SET FOOT IN GOTHAM, FATHER WOULD HAVE KNOWN.
"HIS PEOPLE WOULD HAVE BEEN ON US.
"BUT THEY'RE NOT.
"SOMETHING IS WRONG.
"BATMAN IS GONE.
ALFRED PENNYWORTH
WHICH ISN'T SURPRISING.

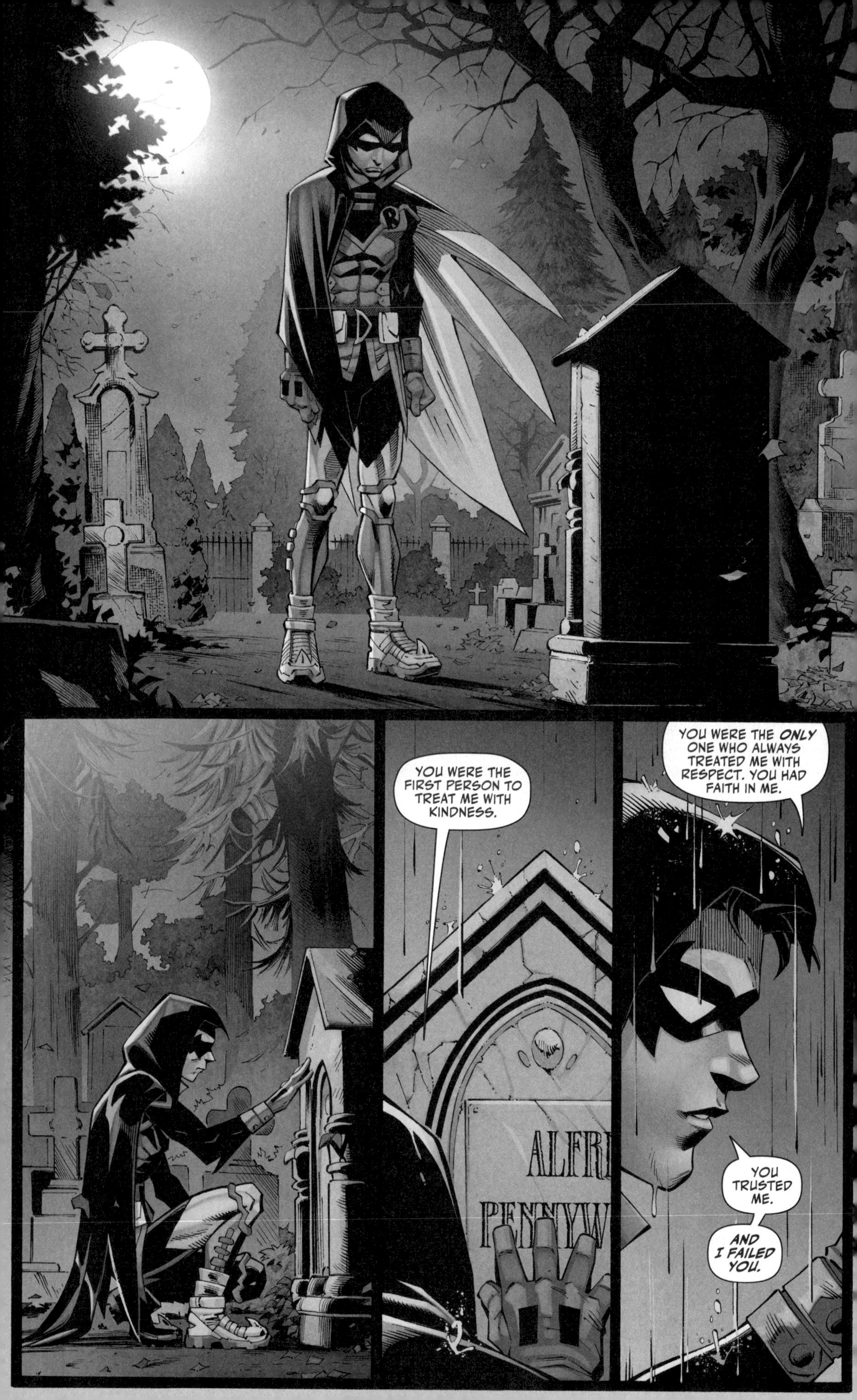
YOU WERE THE FIRST PERSON TO TREAT ME WITH KINDNESS.
YOU WERE THE ONLY ONE WHO ALWAYS TREATED ME WITH RESPECT. YOU HAD FAITH IN ME.
YOU TRUSTED ME.
AND I FAILED YOU.
ALFRE
PENNYW

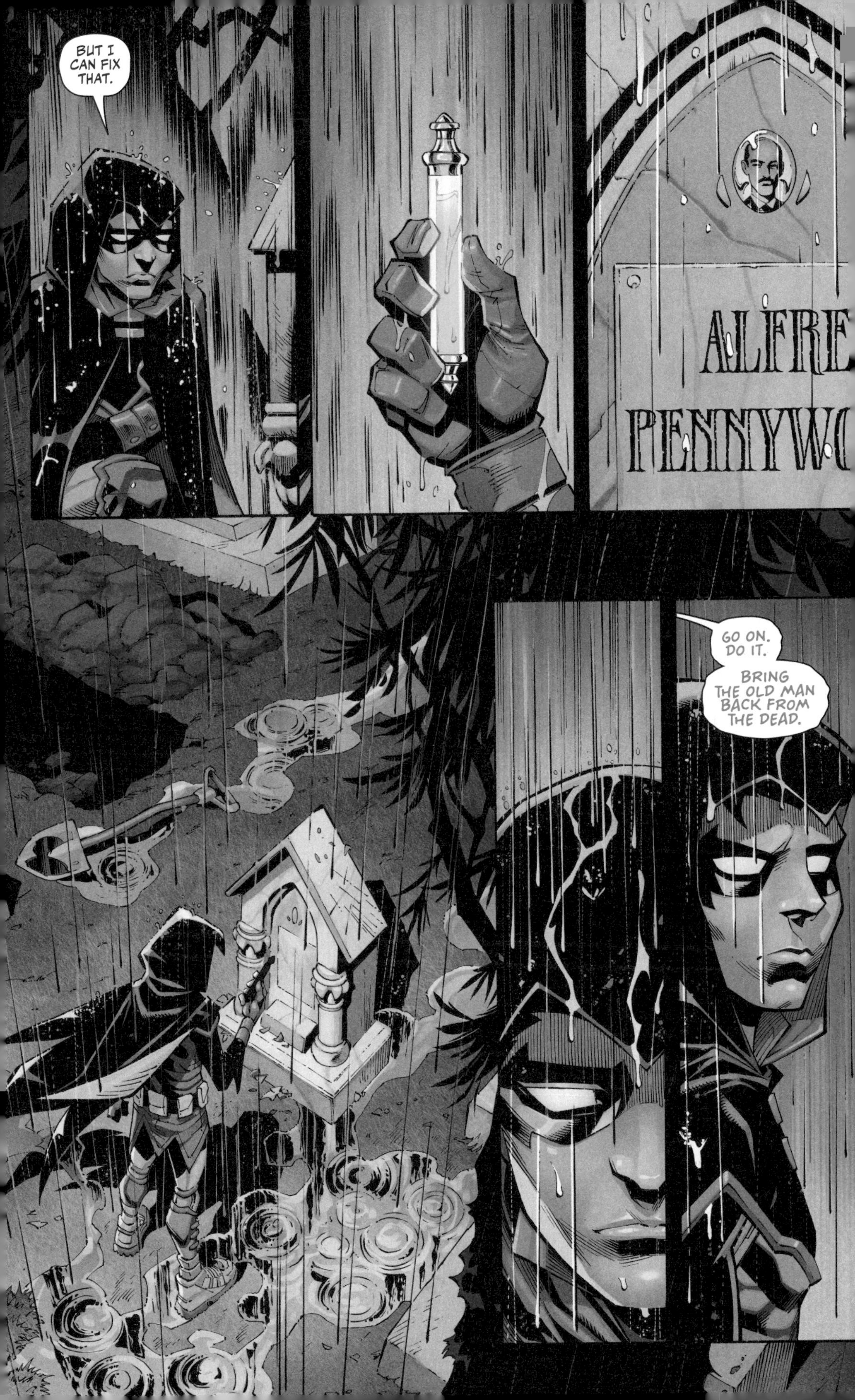
BUT I CAN FIX THAT.
ALFRE
PENNYWO
GO ON. DO IT.
BRING THE OLD MAN BACK FROM THE DEAD.

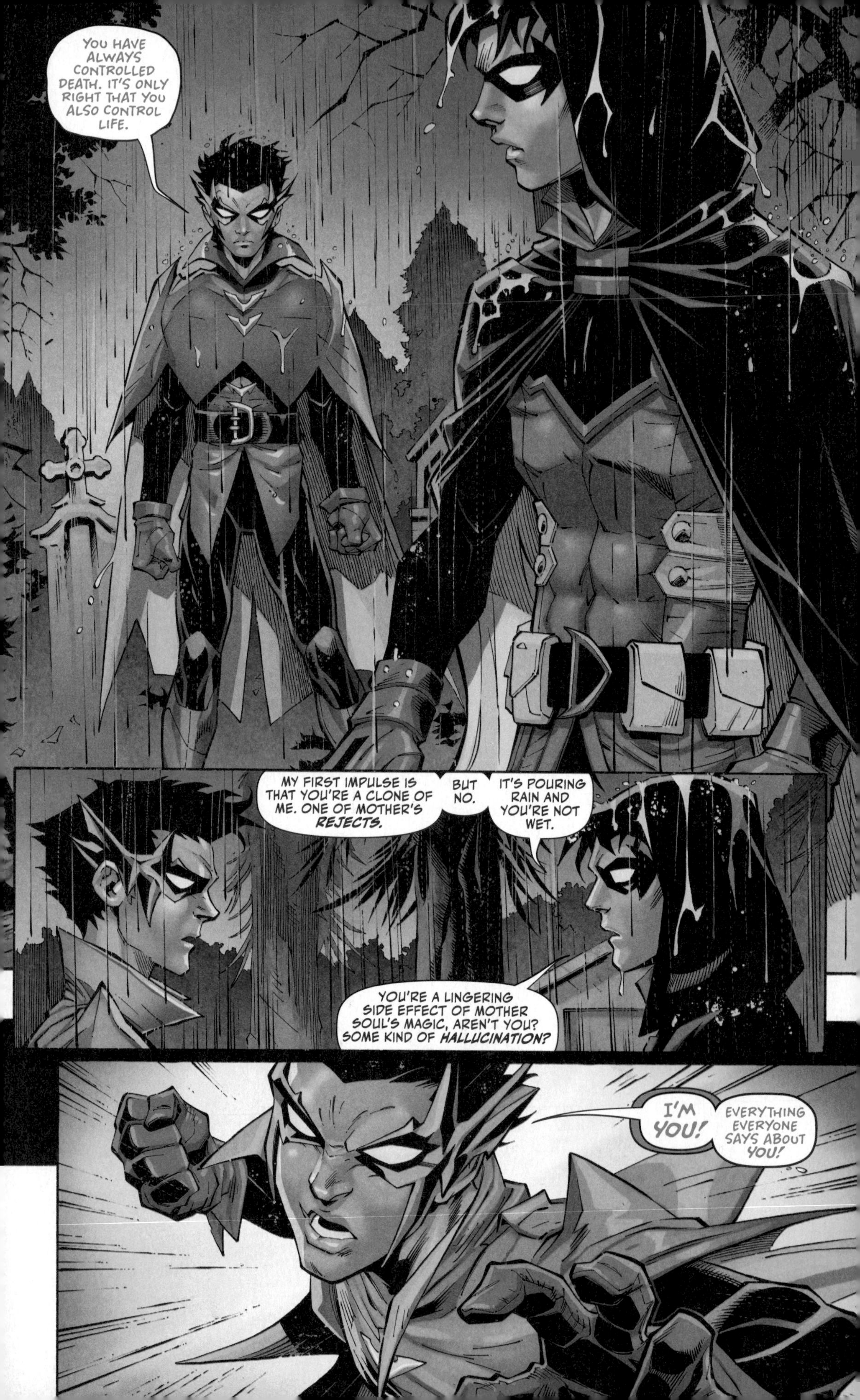
YOU HAVE ALWAYS CONTROLLED DEATH. IT'S ONLY RIGHT THAT YOU ALSO CONTROL LIFE.
MY FIRST IMPULSE IS THAT YOU'RE A CLONE OF ME. ONE OF MOTHER'S *REJECTS.*
BUT NO.
IT'S POURING RAIN AND YOU'RE NOT WET.
YOU'RE A LINGERING SIDE EFFECT OF MOTHER SOUL'S MAGIC, AREN'T YOU? SOME KIND OF *HALLUCINATION?*
I'M *YOU!*
EVERYTHING EVERYONE SAYS ABOUT *YOU!*

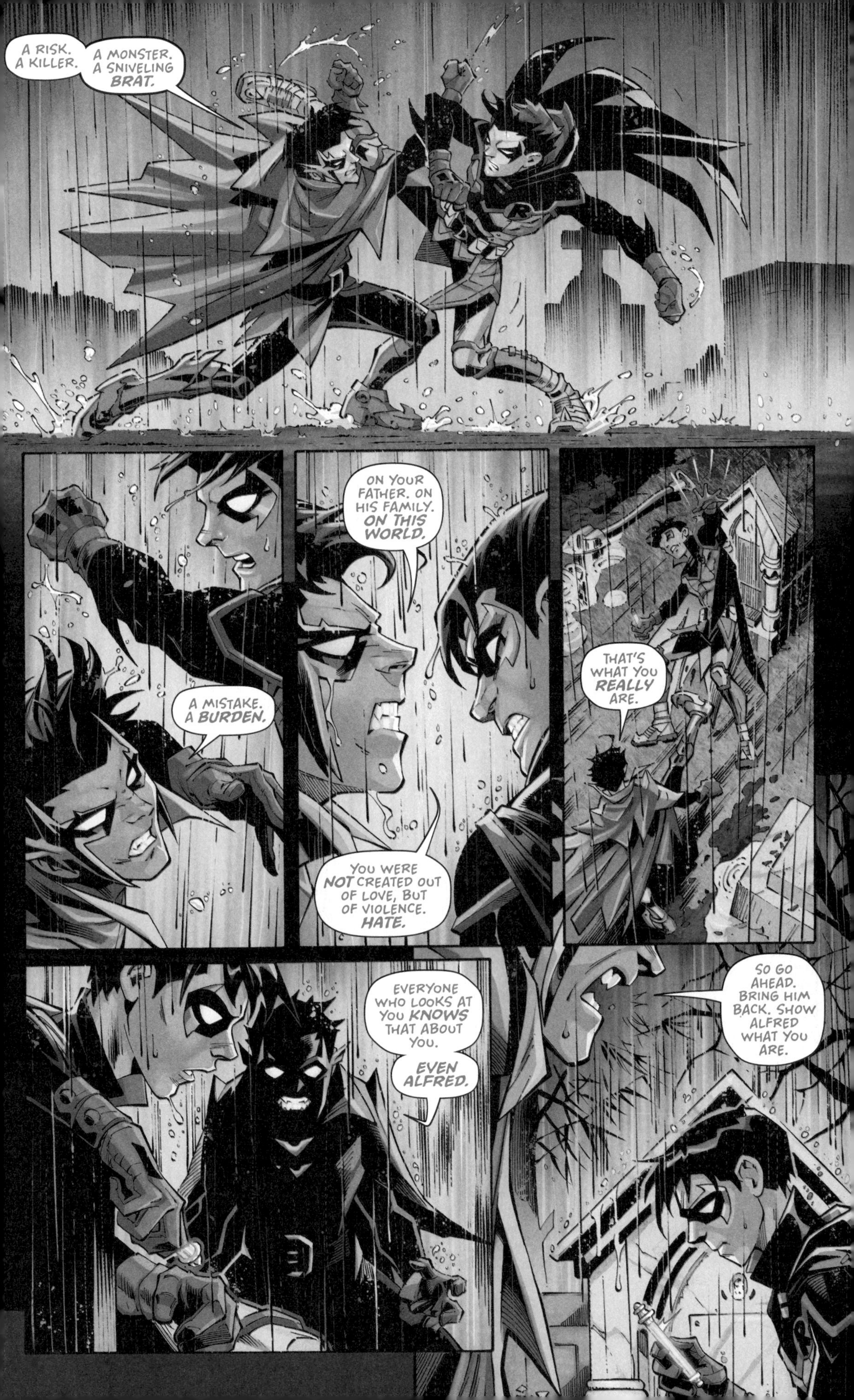
A RISK. A KILLER.
A MONSTER. A SNIVELING BRAT.
A MISTAKE. A BURDEN.
ON YOUR FATHER. ON HIS FAMILY. ON THIS WORLD.
YOU WERE NOT CREATED OUT OF LOVE, BUT OF VIOLENCE. HATE.
THAT'S WHAT YOU REALLY ARE.
EVERYONE WHO LOOKS AT YOU KNOWS THAT ABOUT YOU.
EVEN ALFRED.
SO GO AHEAD. BRING HIM BACK. SHOW ALFRED WHAT YOU ARE.

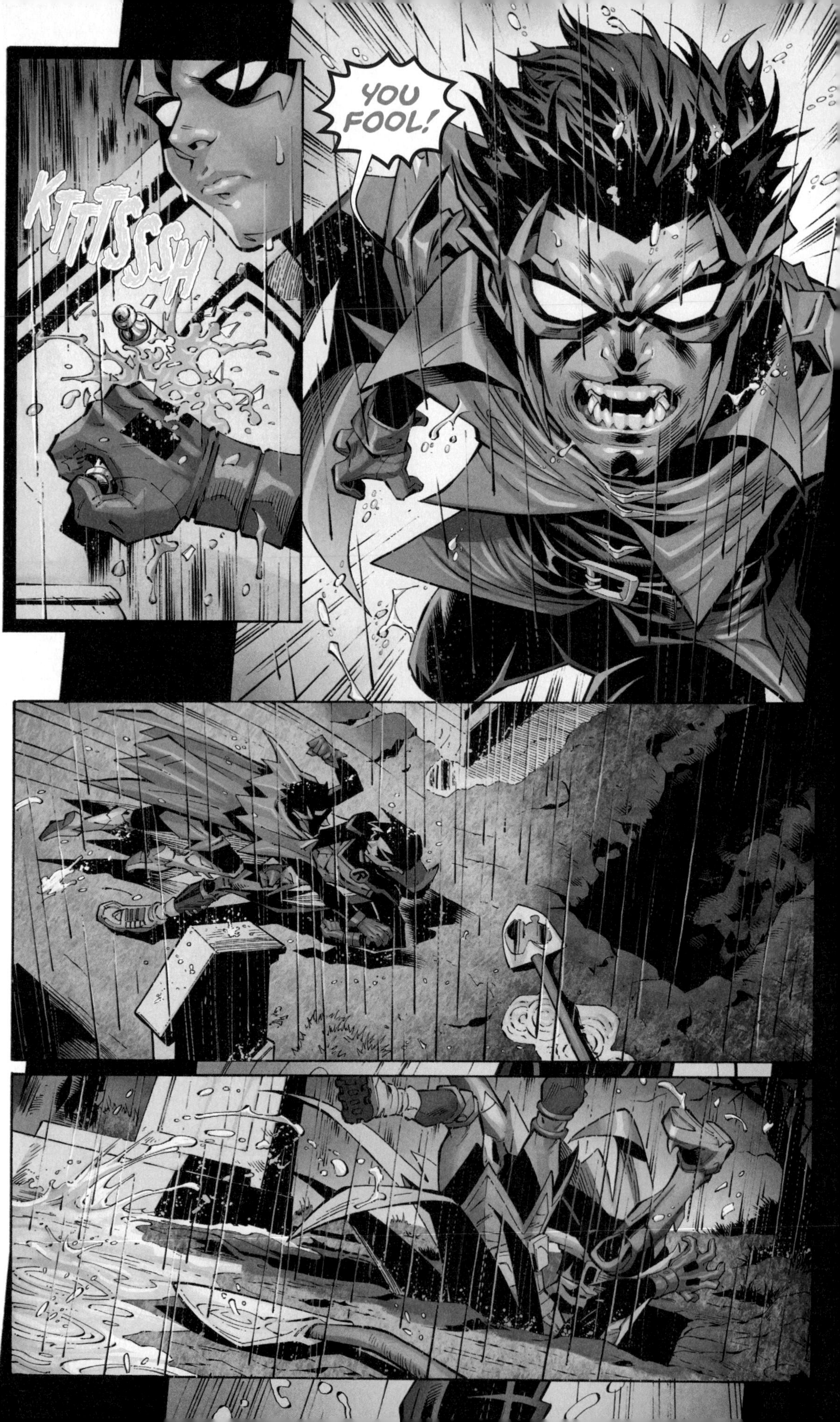
YOU FOOL!
KTTTSSSH

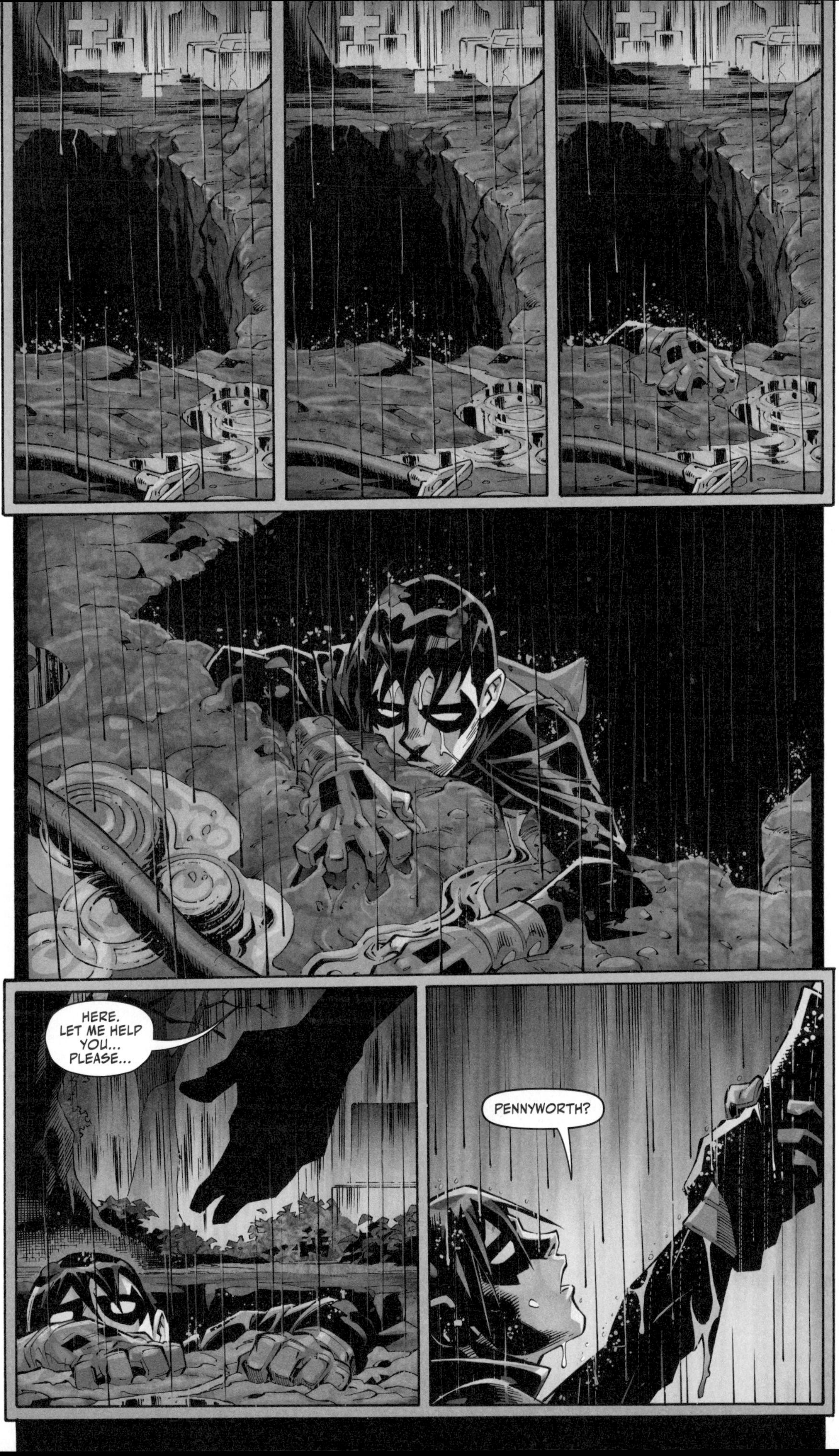
HERE. LET ME HELP YOU... PLEASE...
PENNYWORTH?

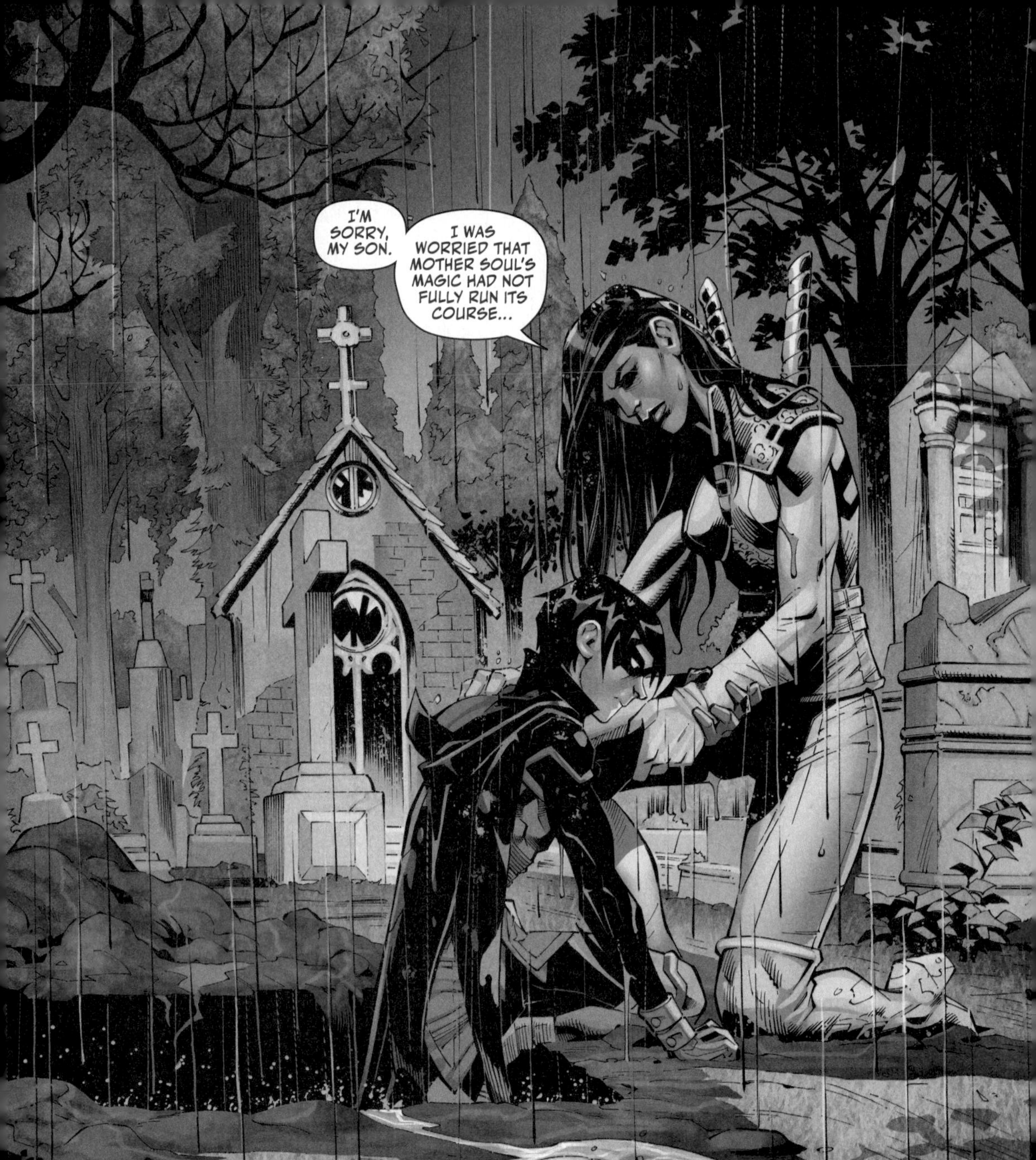
I'M SORRY, MY SON.
I WAS WORRIED THAT MOTHER SOUL'S MAGIC HAD NOT FULLY RUN ITS COURSE...

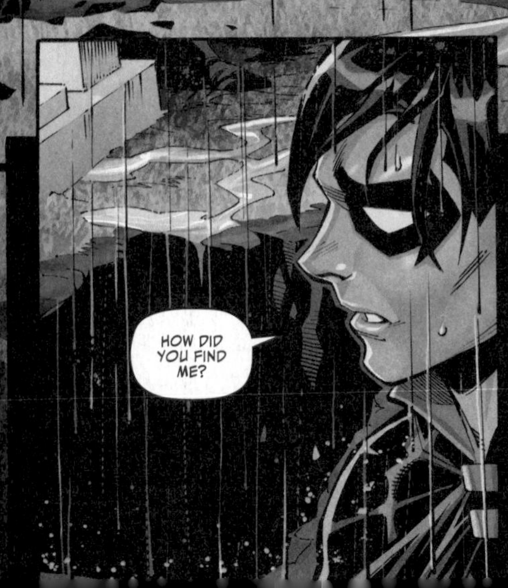
HOW DID YOU FIND ME?

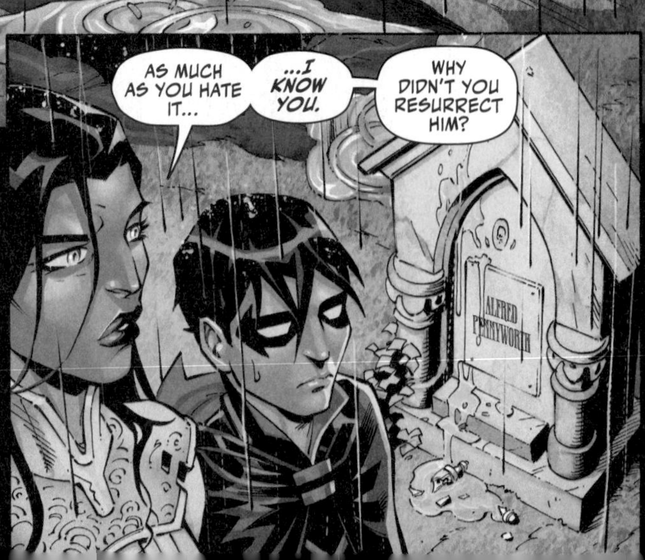
AS MUCH AS YOU HATE IT...
...*I KNOW YOU.*
WHY DIDN'T YOU RESURRECT HIM?
ALFRED PENNYWORTH

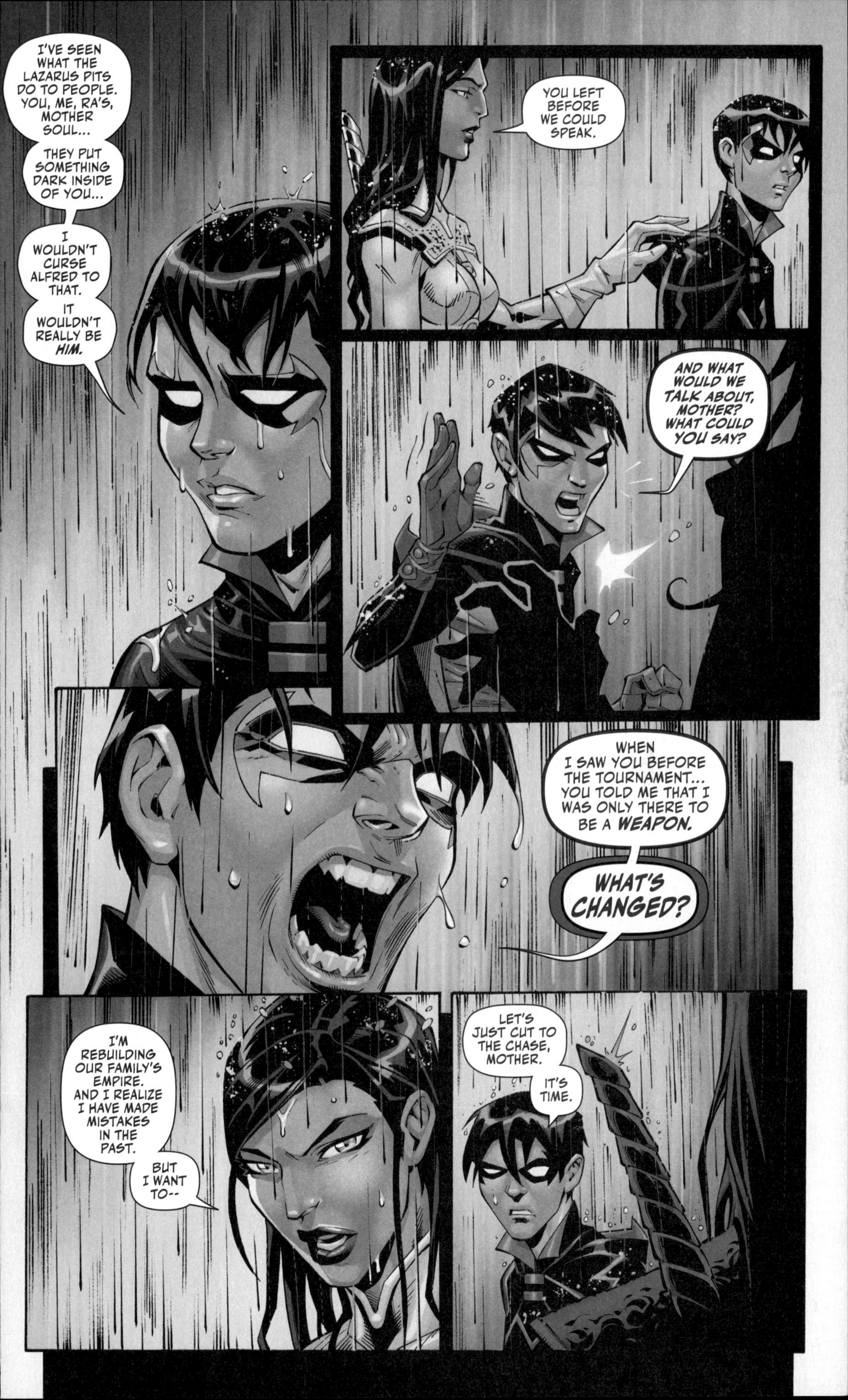
I'VE SEEN WHAT THE LAZARUS PITS DO TO PEOPLE. YOU, ME, RA'S, MOTHER SOUL...
THEY PUT SOMETHING DARK INSIDE OF YOU...
I WOULDN'T CURSE ALFRED TO THAT.
IT WOULDN'T REALLY BE *HIM.*
YOU LEFT BEFORE WE COULD SPEAK.
AND WHAT WOULD WE TALK ABOUT, MOTHER? WHAT COULD *YOU* SAY?
WHEN I SAW YOU BEFORE THE TOURNAMENT... YOU TOLD ME THAT I WAS ONLY THERE TO BE A *WEAPON.*
WHAT'S CHANGED?
I'M REBUILDING OUR FAMILY'S EMPIRE. AND I REALIZE I HAVE MADE MISTAKES IN THE PAST.
BUT I WANT TO--
LET'S JUST CUT TO THE CHASE, MOTHER.
IT'S TIME.

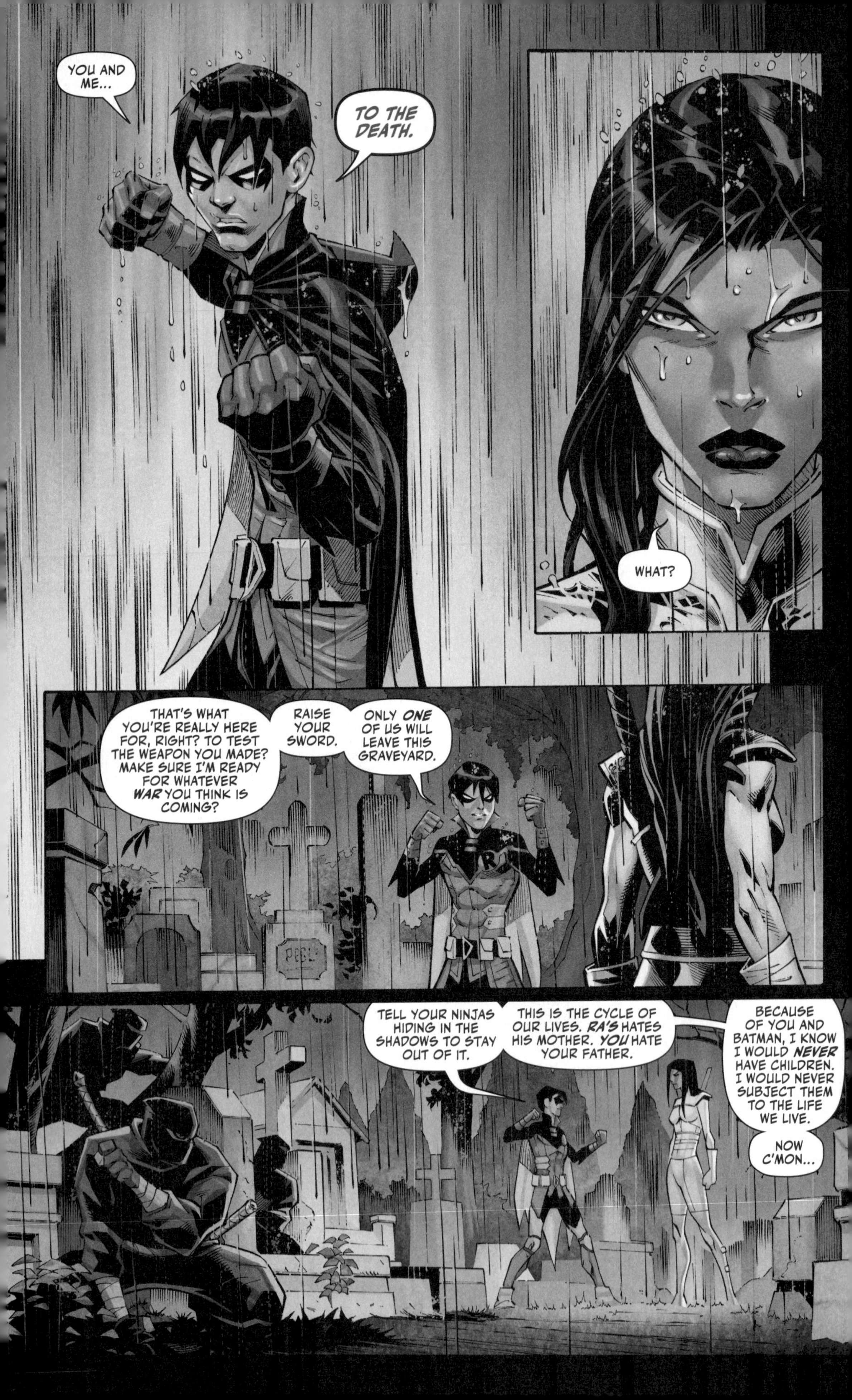
YOU AND ME...
TO THE DEATH.
WHAT?
THAT'S WHAT YOU'RE REALLY HERE FOR, RIGHT? TO TEST THE WEAPON YOU MADE? MAKE SURE I'M READY FOR WHATEVER WAR YOU THINK IS COMING?
RAISE YOUR SWORD.
ONLY ONE OF US WILL LEAVE THIS GRAVEYARD.
TELL YOUR NINJAS HIDING IN THE SHADOWS TO STAY OUT OF IT.
THIS IS THE CYCLE OF OUR LIVES. RA'S HATES HIS MOTHER. YOU HATE YOUR FATHER.
BECAUSE OF YOU AND BATMAN, I KNOW I WOULD NEVER HAVE CHILDREN. I WOULD NEVER SUBJECT THEM TO THE LIFE WE LIVE.
NOW C'MON...

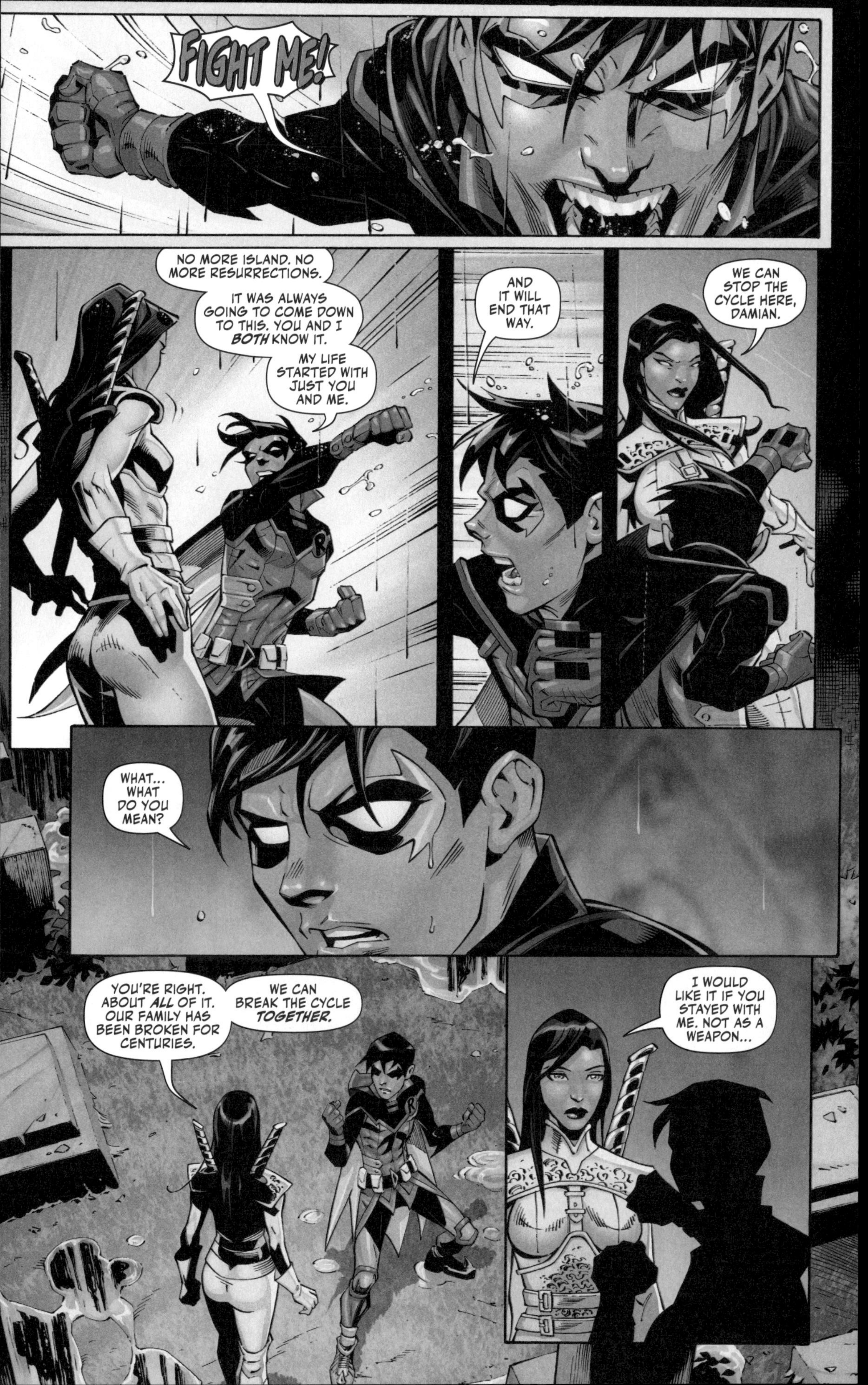
FIGHT ME!
NO MORE ISLAND. NO MORE RESURRECTIONS.
IT WAS ALWAYS GOING TO COME DOWN TO THIS. YOU AND I BOTH KNOW IT.
MY LIFE STARTED WITH JUST YOU AND ME.
AND IT WILL END THAT WAY.
WE CAN STOP THE CYCLE HERE, DAMIAN.
WHAT... WHAT DO YOU MEAN?
YOU'RE RIGHT. ABOUT ALL OF IT. OUR FAMILY HAS BEEN BROKEN FOR CENTURIES.
WE CAN BREAK THE CYCLE TOGETHER.
I WOULD LIKE IT IF YOU STAYED WITH ME. NOT AS A WEAPON...

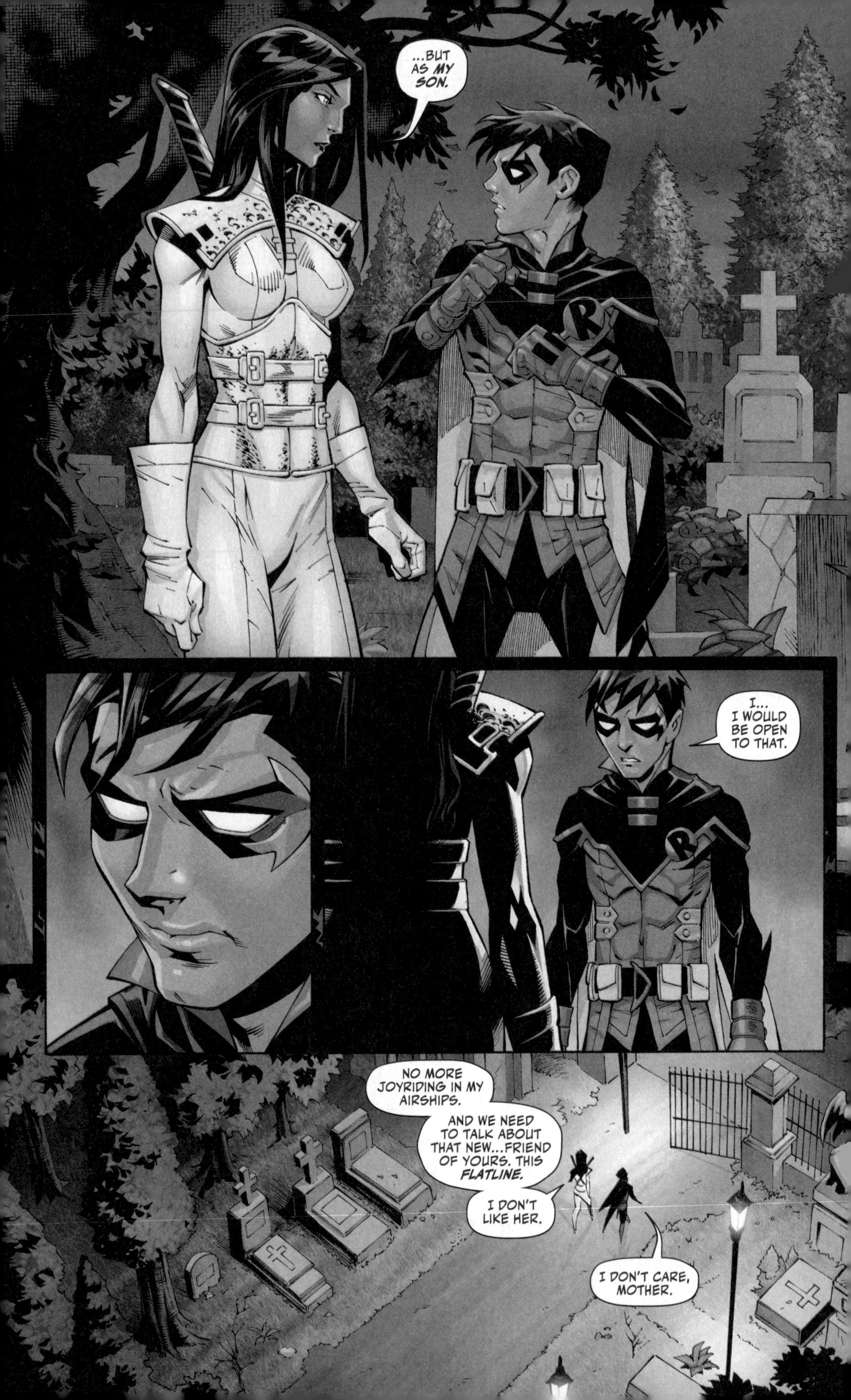
...BUT AS MY SON.
I... I WOULD BE OPEN TO THAT.
NO MORE JOYRIDING IN MY AIRSHIPS.
AND WE NEED TO TALK ABOUT THAT NEW...FRIEND OF YOURS. THIS FLATLINE.
I DON'T LIKE HER.
I DON'T CARE, MOTHER.

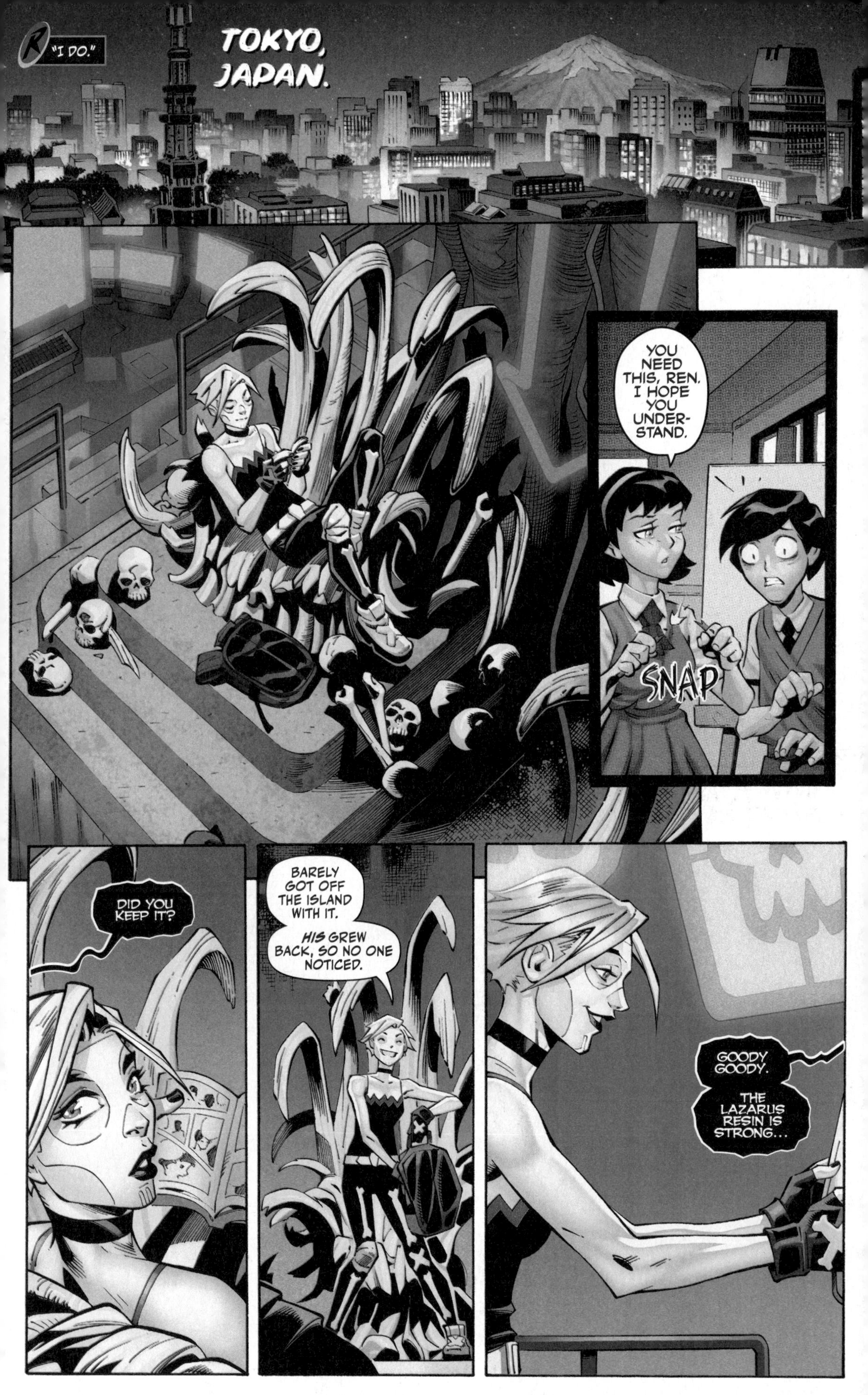
"I DO."
TOKYO, JAPAN.
YOU NEED THIS, REN. I HOPE YOU UNDER-STAND.
SNAP
DID YOU KEEP IT?
BARELY GOT OFF THE ISLAND WITH IT.
HIS GREW BACK, SO NO ONE NOTICED.
GOODY GOODY.
THE LAZARUS RESIN IS STRONG...

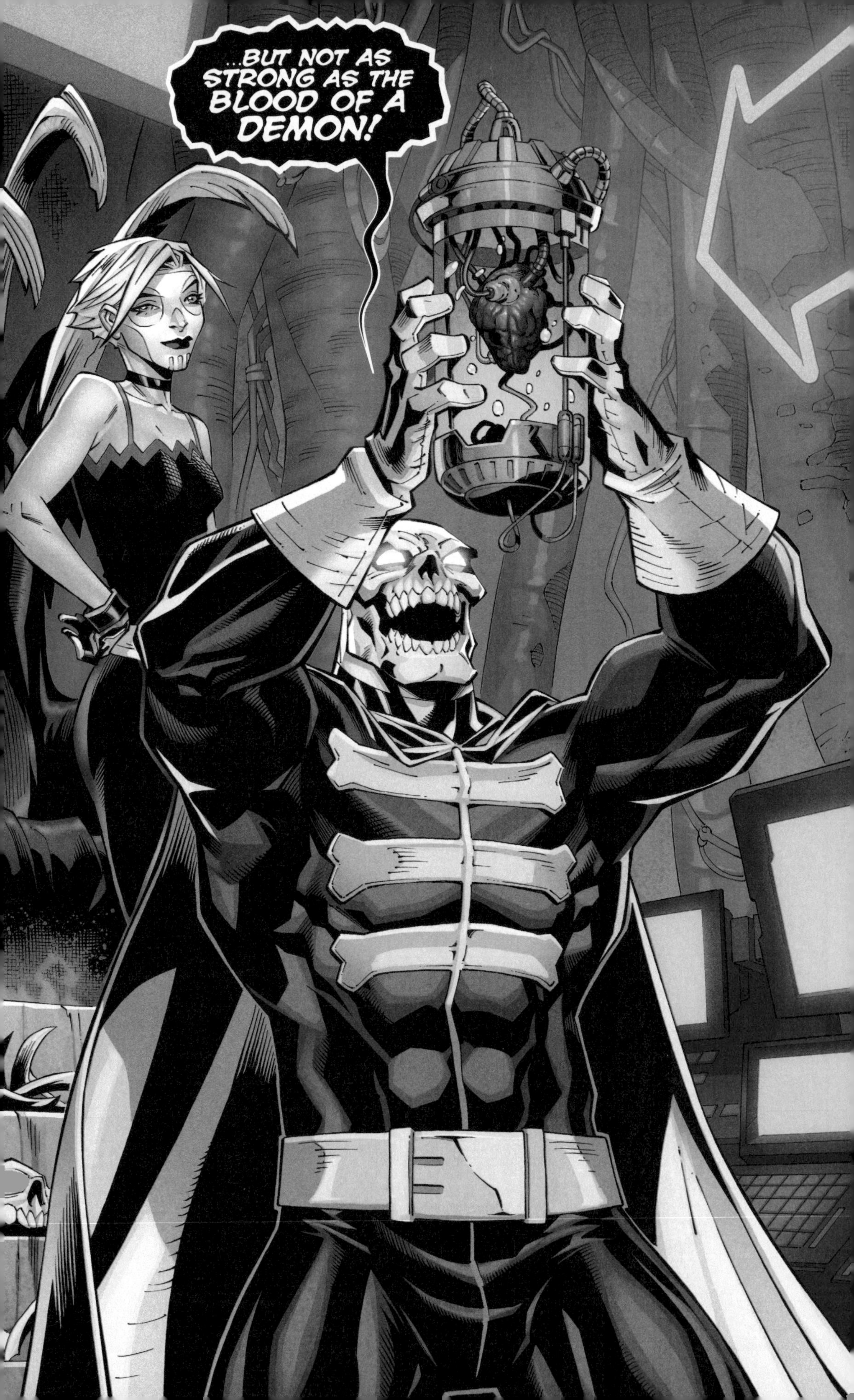
...BUT NOT AS STRONG AS THE BLOOD OF A DEMON!

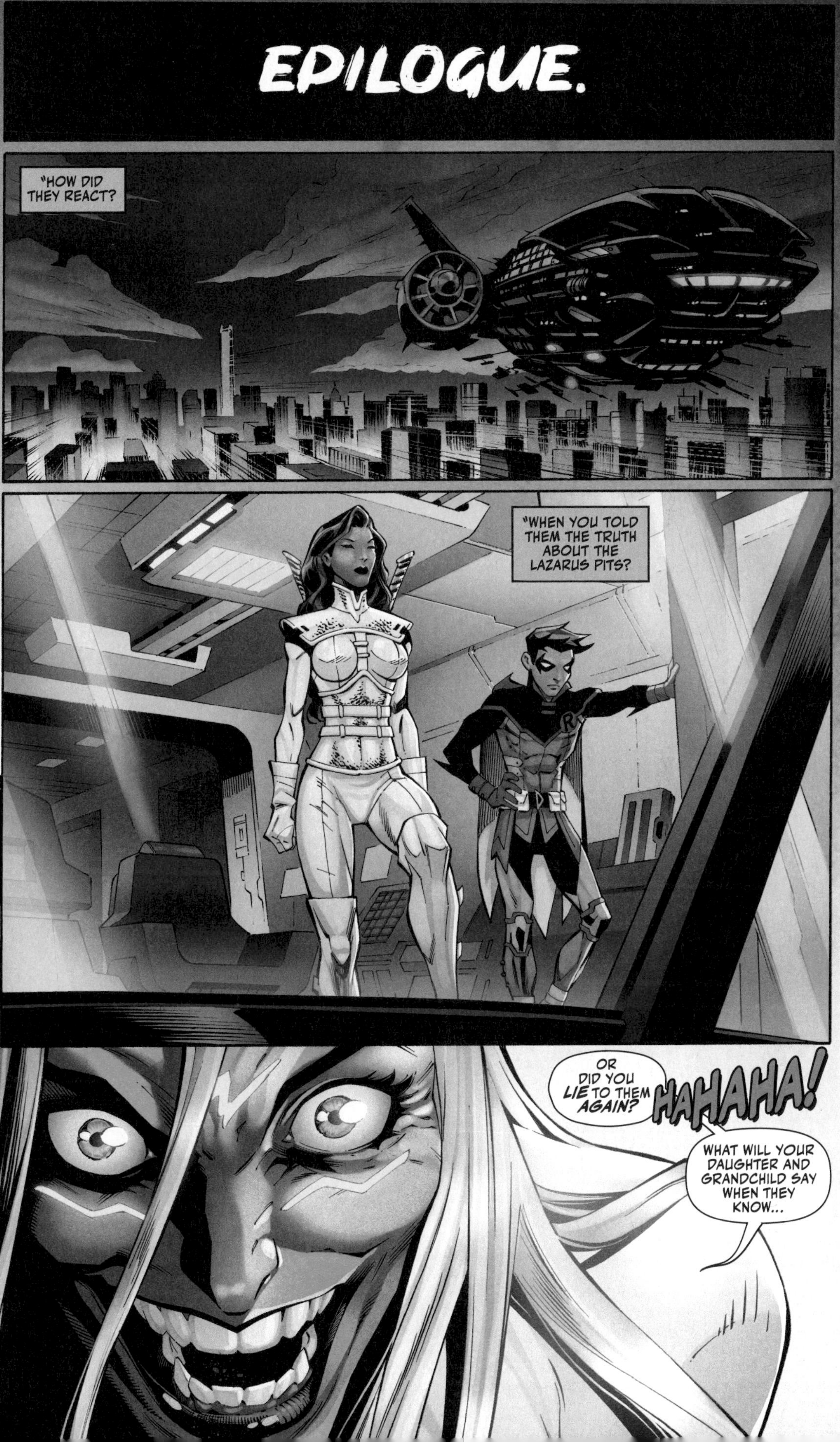
EPILOGUE.
"HOW DID THEY REACT?
"WHEN YOU TOLD THEM THE TRUTH ABOUT THE LAZARUS PITS?
OR DID YOU LIE TO THEM AGAIN?
HAHAHA!
WHAT WILL YOUR DAUGHTER AND GRANDCHILD SAY WHEN THEY KNOW...

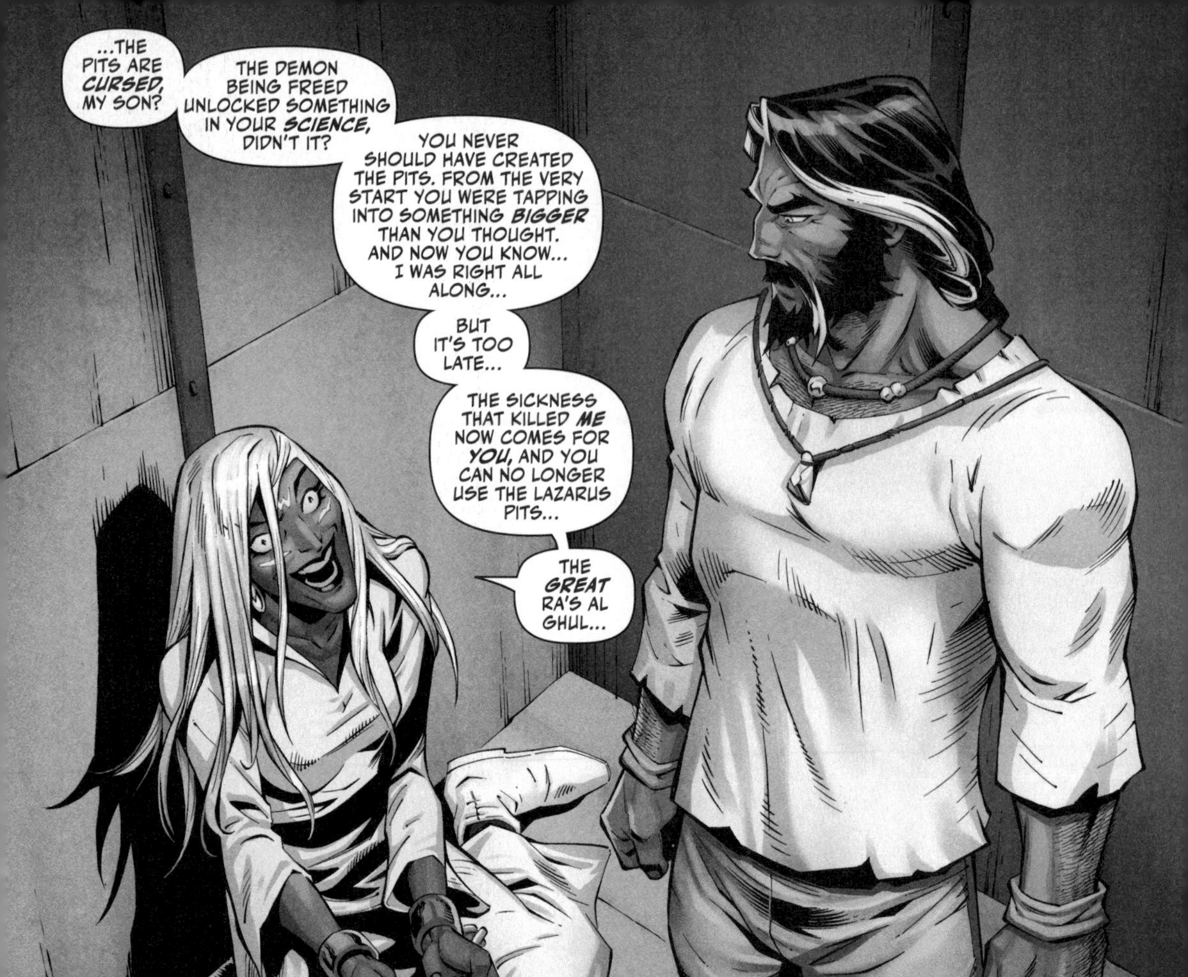
...THE PITS ARE CURSED, MY SON?
THE DEMON BEING FREED UNLOCKED SOMETHING IN YOUR SCIENCE, DIDN'T IT?
YOU NEVER SHOULD HAVE CREATED THE PITS. FROM THE VERY START YOU WERE TAPPING INTO SOMETHING BIGGER THAN YOU THOUGHT. AND NOW YOU KNOW... I WAS RIGHT ALL ALONG...
BUT IT'S TOO LATE...
THE SICKNESS THAT KILLED ME NOW COMES FOR YOU, AND YOU CAN NO LONGER USE THE LAZARUS PITS...
THE GREAT RA'S AL GHUL...

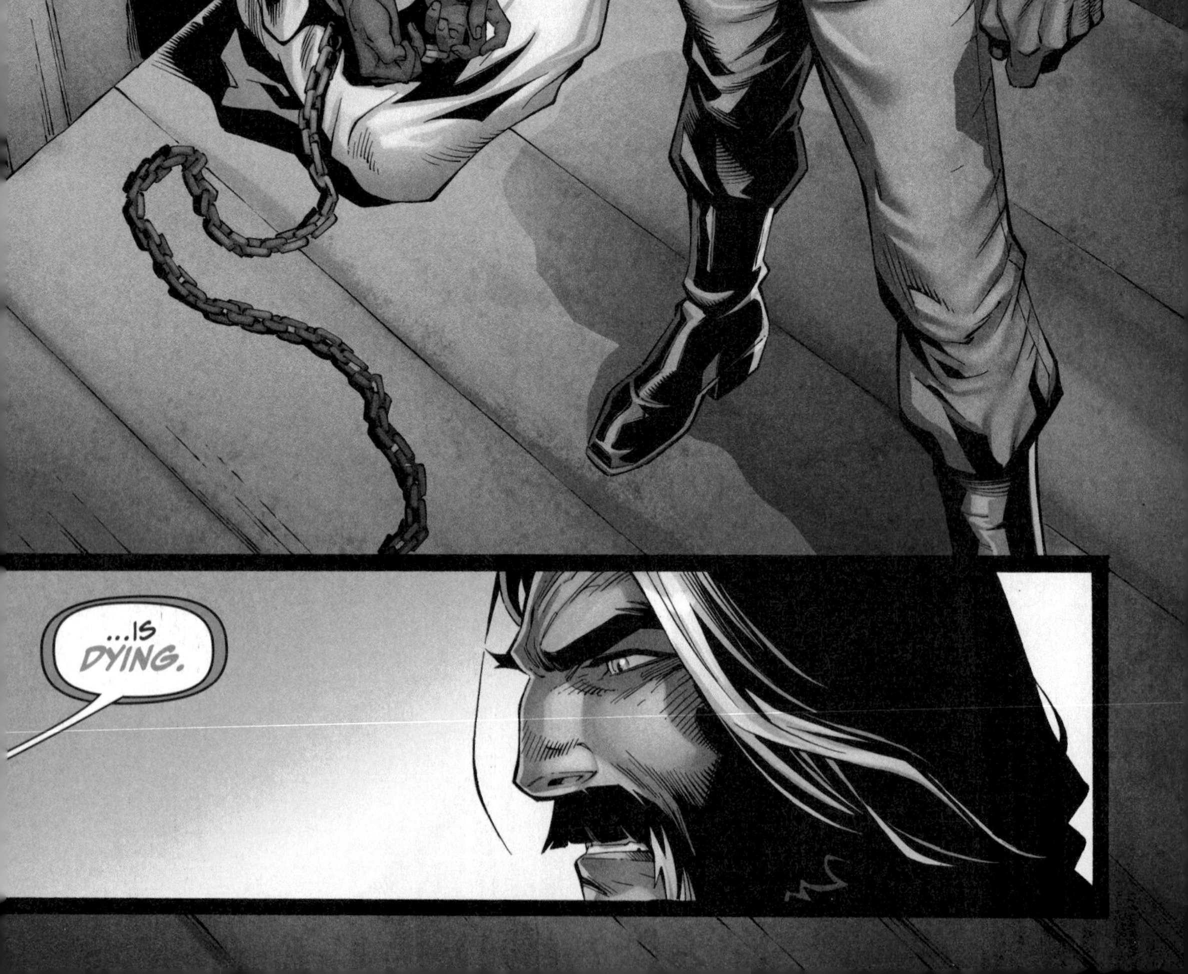
...IS DYING.

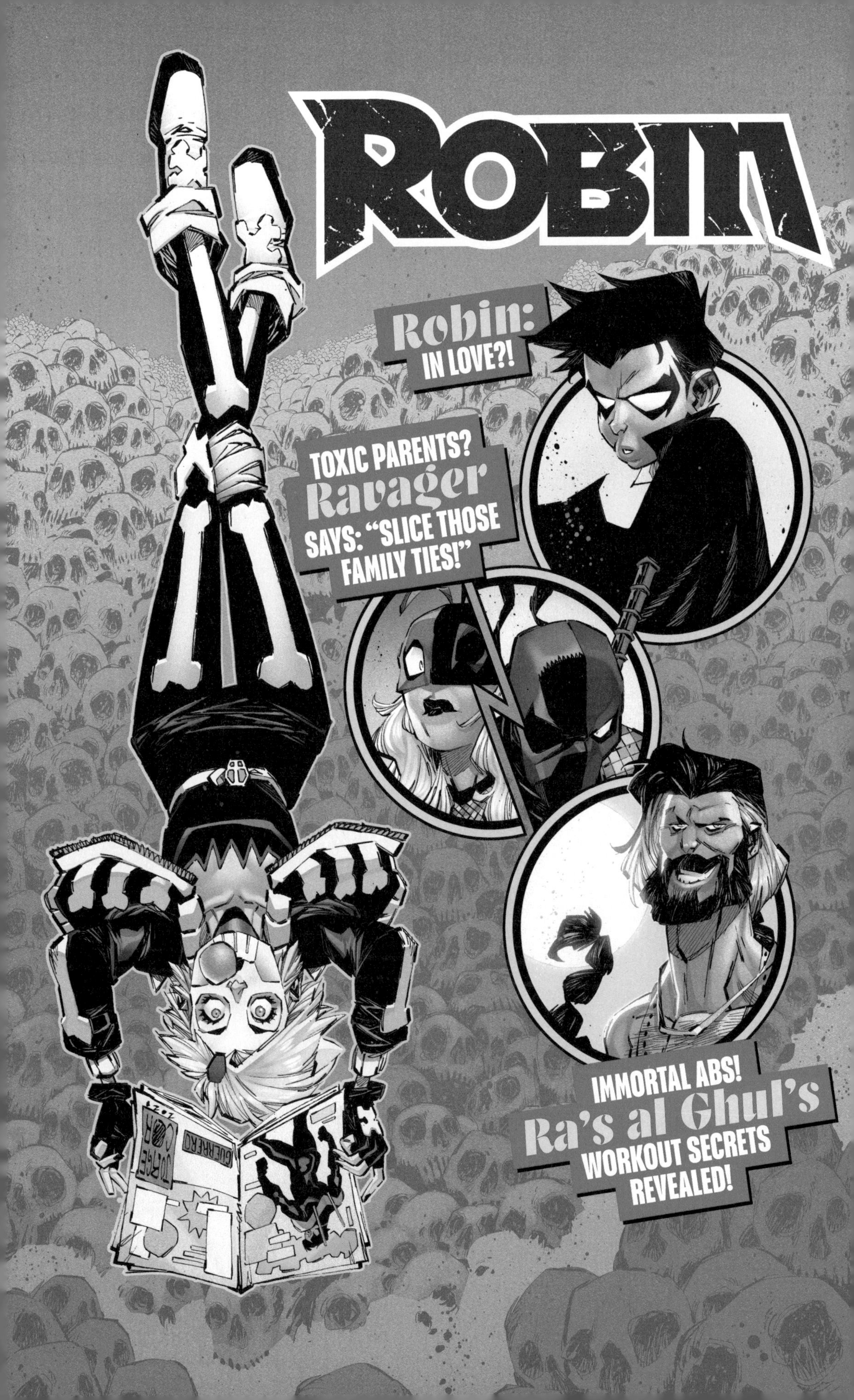
ROBIN
Robin: IN LOVE?!
TOXIC PARENTS? Ravager SAYS: "SLICE THOSE FAMILY TIES!"
IMMORTAL ABS! Ra's al Ghul's WORKOUT SECRETS REVEALED!

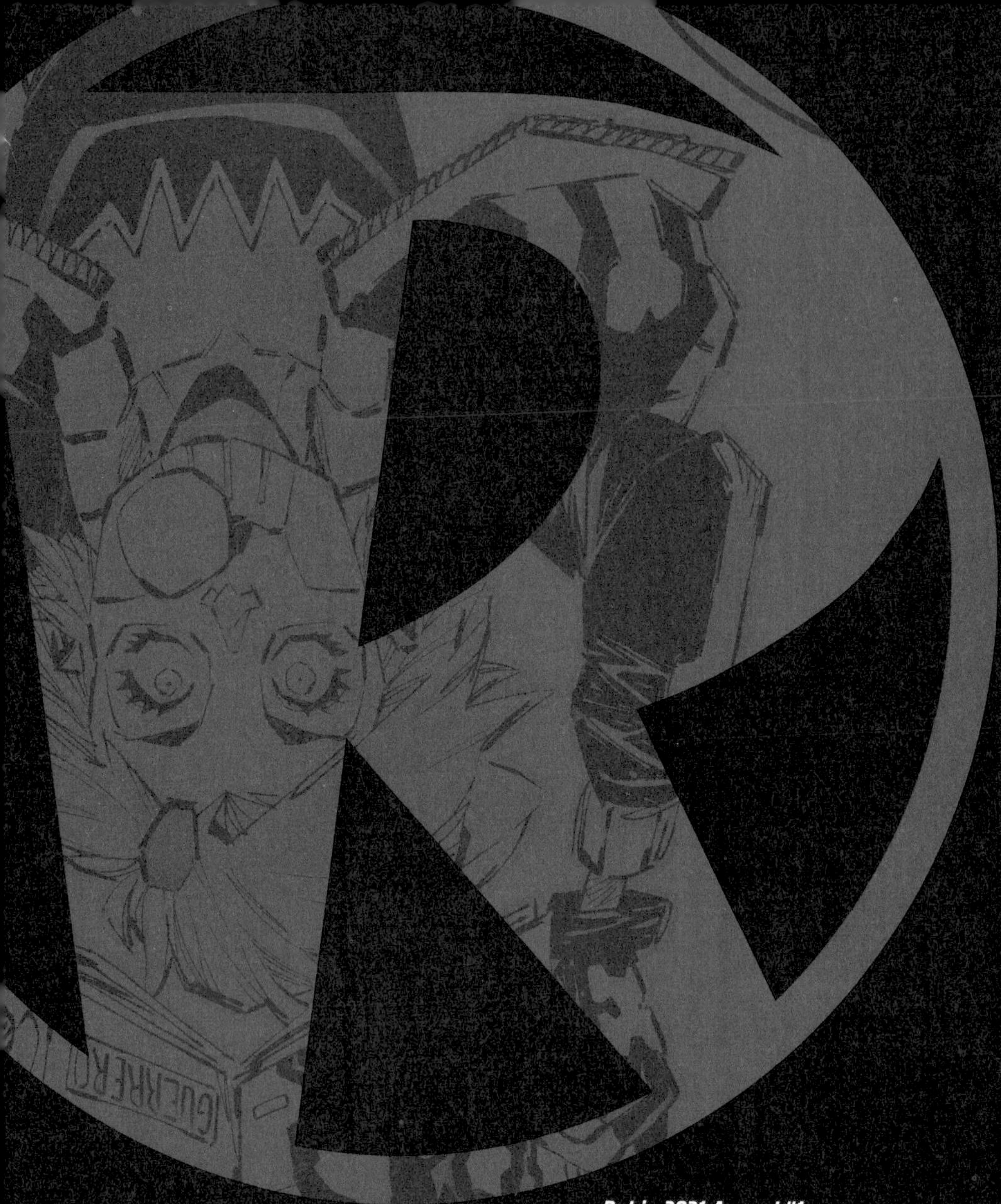

Robin 2021 Annual #1
cover by **JORGE CORONA** and **LUIS GUERRERO**

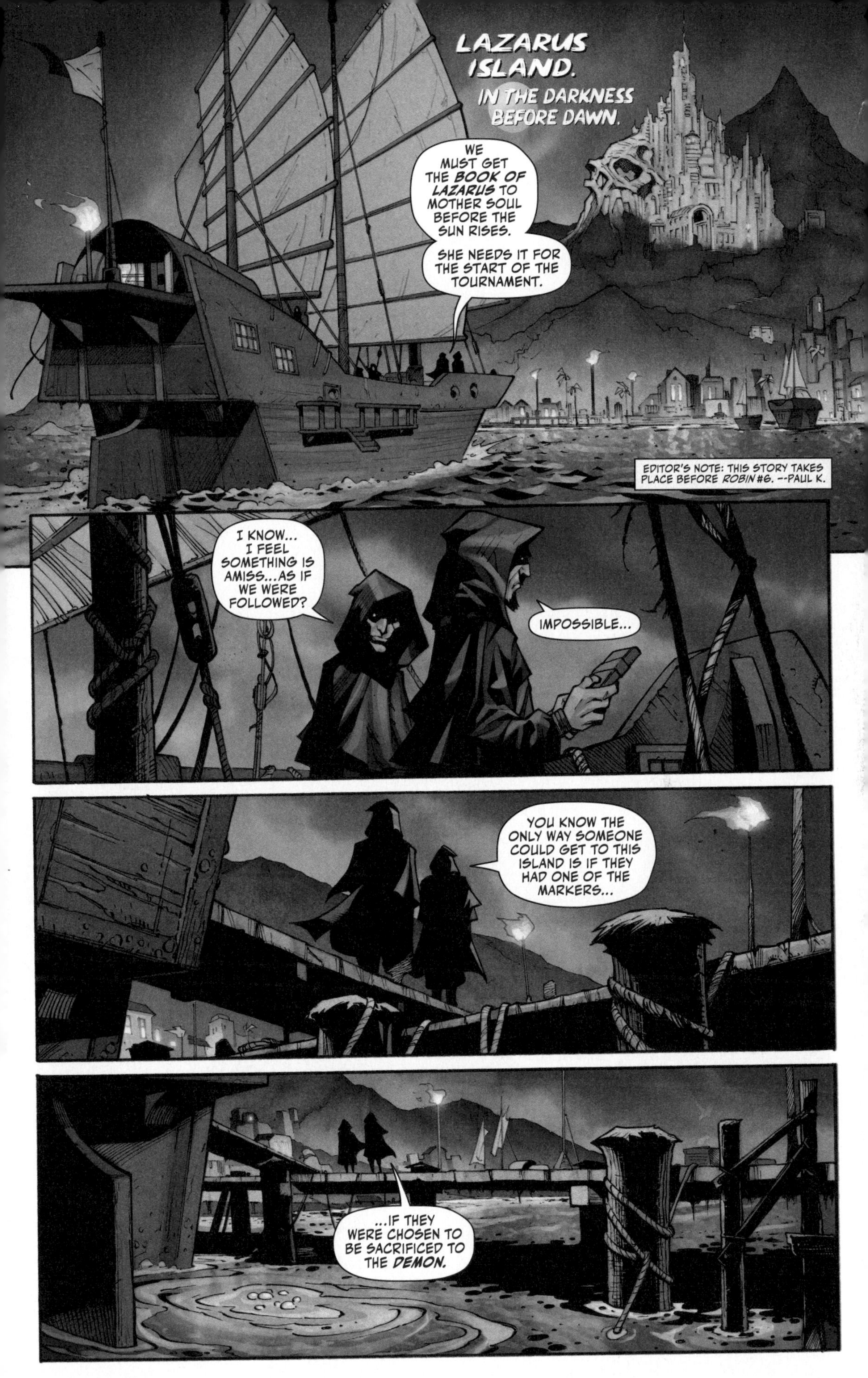
LAZARUS ISLAND.
IN THE DARKNESS BEFORE DAWN.
WE MUST GET THE BOOK OF LAZARUS TO MOTHER SOUL BEFORE THE SUN RISES.
SHE NEEDS IT FOR THE START OF THE TOURNAMENT.
EDITOR'S NOTE: THIS STORY TAKES PLACE BEFORE ROBIN #6. --PAUL K.
I KNOW... I FEEL SOMETHING IS AMISS...AS IF WE WERE FOLLOWED?
IMPOSSIBLE...
YOU KNOW THE ONLY WAY SOMEONE COULD GET TO THIS ISLAND IS IF THEY HAD ONE OF THE MARKERS...
...IF THEY WERE CHOSEN TO BE SACRIFICED TO THE DEMON.

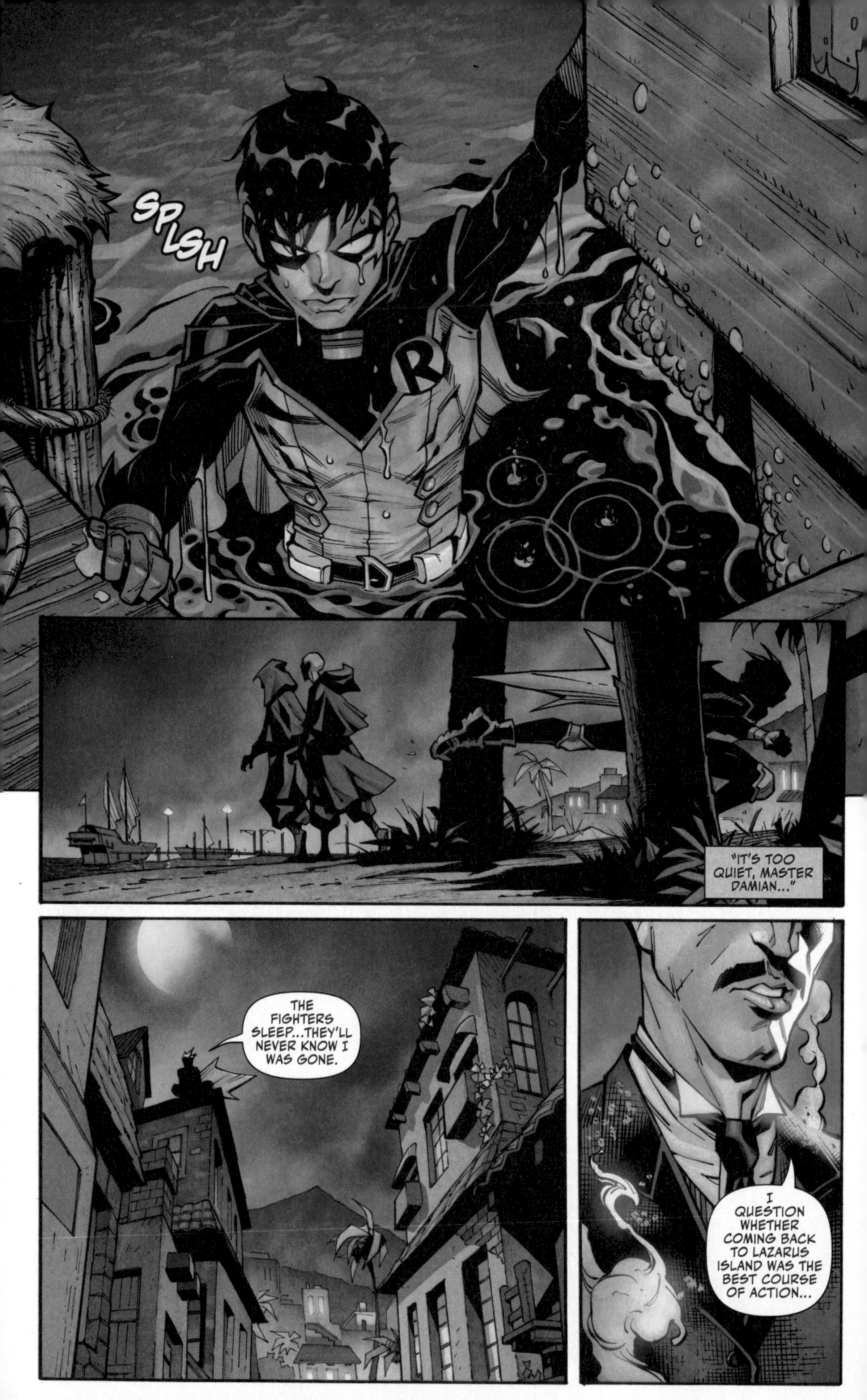
SPLSH
"IT'S TOO QUIET, MASTER DAMIAN..."
THE FIGHTERS SLEEP...THEY'LL NEVER KNOW I WAS GONE.
I QUESTION WHETHER COMING BACK TO LAZARUS ISLAND WAS THE BEST COURSE OF ACTION...

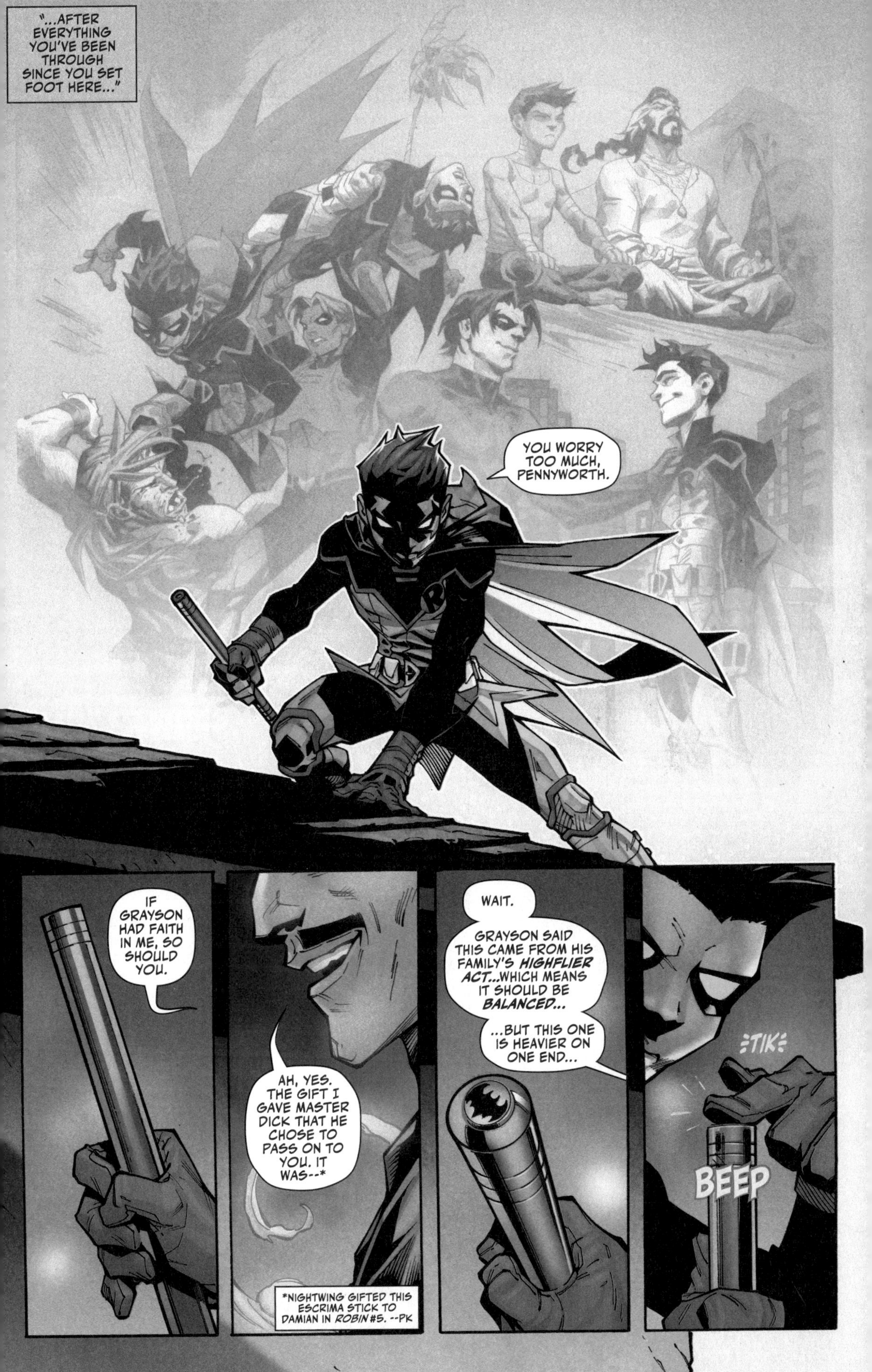
"...AFTER EVERYTHING YOU'VE BEEN THROUGH SINCE YOU SET FOOT HERE..."
YOU WORRY TOO MUCH, PENNYWORTH.
IF GRAYSON HAD FAITH IN ME, SO SHOULD YOU.
AH, YES. THE GIFT I GAVE MASTER DICK THAT HE CHOSE TO PASS ON TO YOU. IT WAS--*
*NIGHTWING GIFTED THIS ESCRIMA STICK TO DAMIAN IN ROBIN #5. --PK
WAIT.
GRAYSON SAID THIS CAME FROM HIS FAMILY'S HIGHFLIER ACT...WHICH MEANS IT SHOULD BE BALANCED...
...BUT THIS ONE IS HEAVIER ON ONE END...
TIK
BEEP

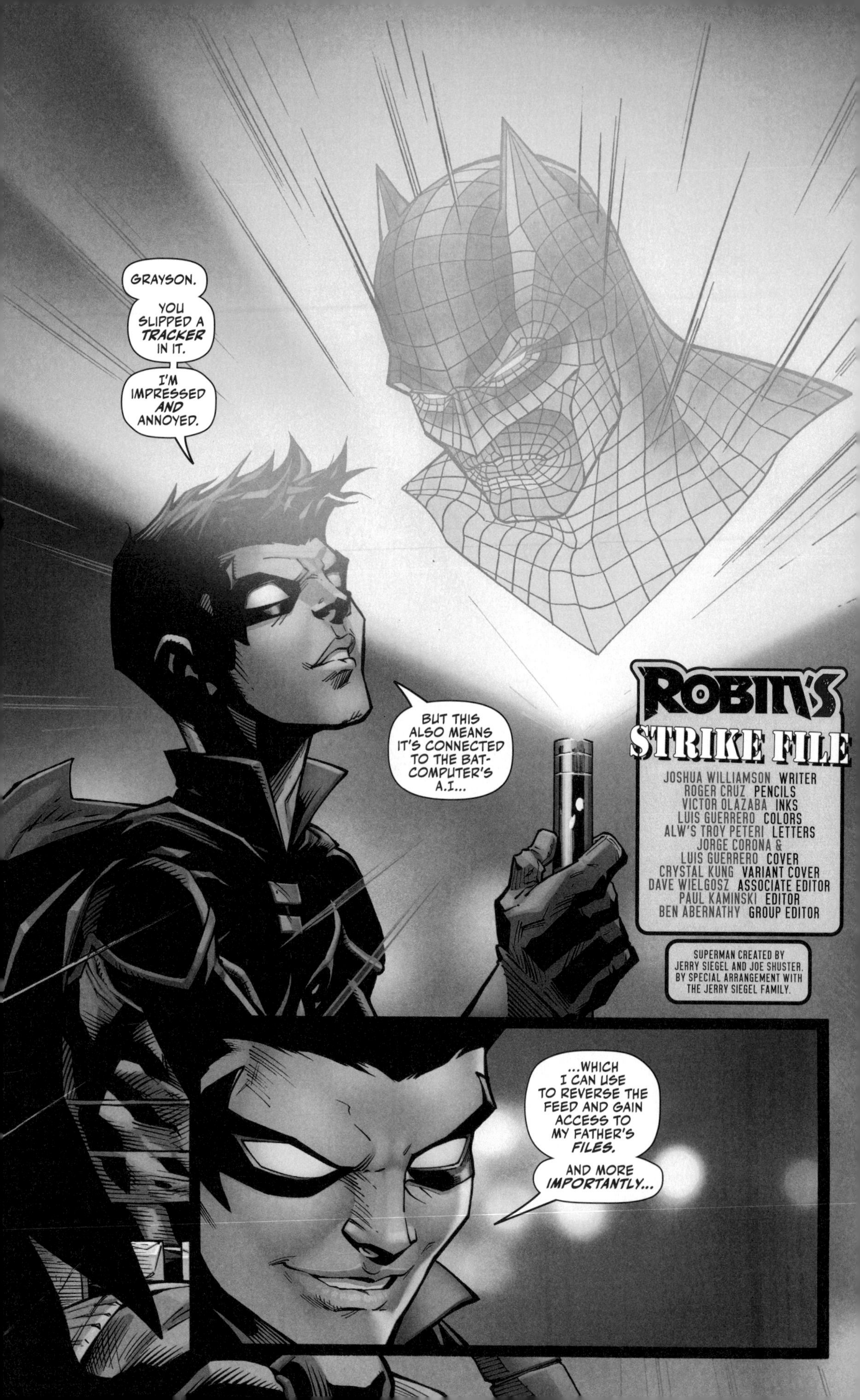
GRAYSON.
YOU SLIPPED A *TRACKER* IN IT.
I'M IMPRESSED *AND* ANNOYED.
BUT THIS ALSO MEANS IT'S CONNECTED TO THE BAT-COMPUTER'S A.I...
ROBIN'S STRIKE FILE
JOSHUA WILLIAMSON WRITER
ROGER CRUZ PENCILS
VICTOR OLAZABA INKS
LUIS GUERRERO COLORS
ALW'S TROY PETERI LETTERS
JORGE CORONA & LUIS GUERRERO COVER
CRYSTAL KUNG VARIANT COVER
DAVE WIELGOSZ ASSOCIATE EDITOR
PAUL KAMINSKI EDITOR
BEN ABERNATHY GROUP EDITOR
SUPERMAN CREATED BY JERRY SIEGEL AND JOE SHUSTER. BY SPECIAL ARRANGEMENT WITH THE JERRY SIEGEL FAMILY.
...WHICH I CAN USE TO REVERSE THE FEED AND GAIN ACCESS TO MY FATHER'S *FILES.*
AND MORE *IMPORTANTLY...*

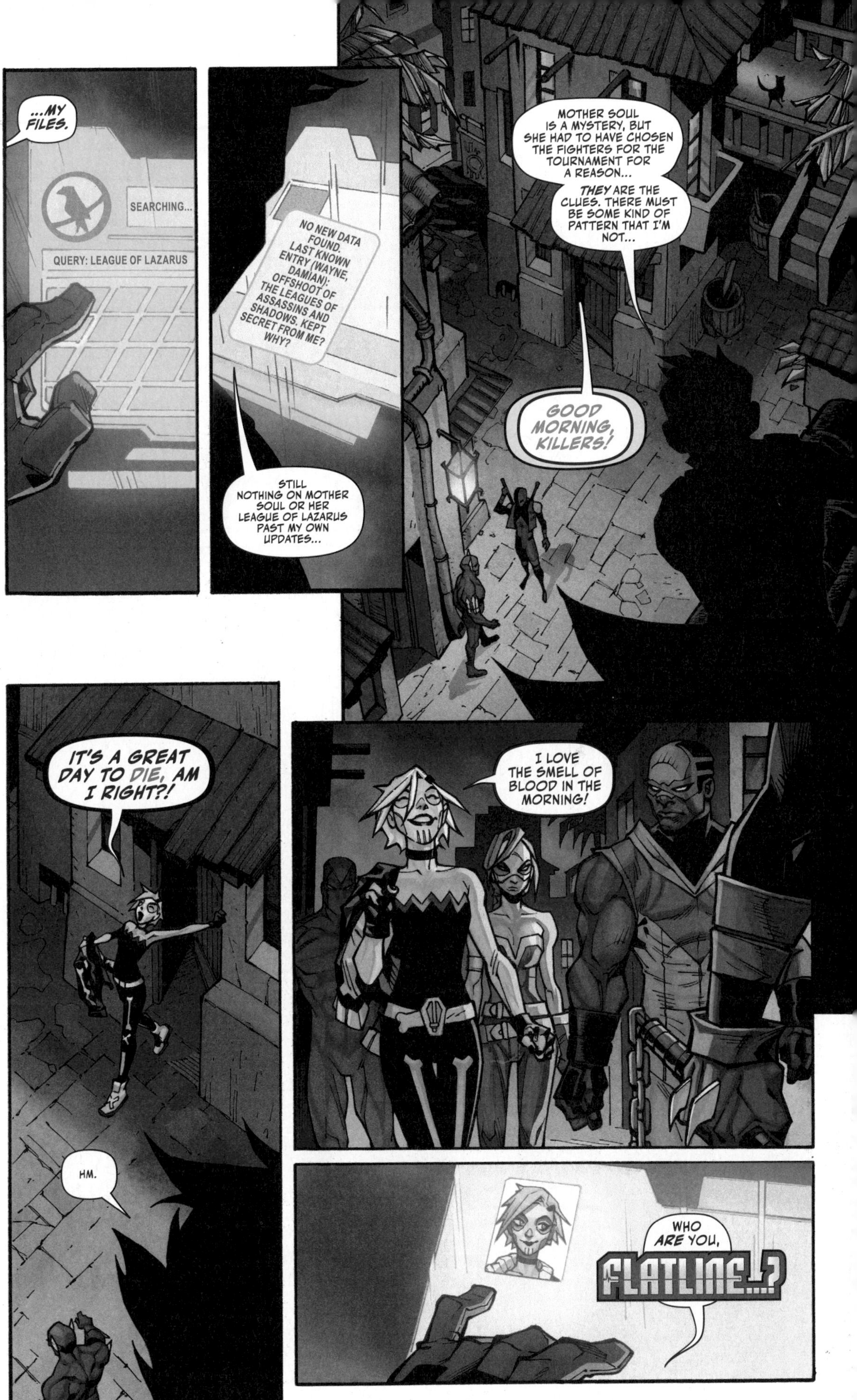
...MY FILES.
SEARCHING...
QUERY: LEAGUE OF LAZARUS
NO NEW DATA FOUND. LAST KNOWN ENTRY (WAYNE, DAMIAN): OFFSHOOT OF THE LEAGUES OF ASSASSINS AND SHADOWS. KEPT SECRET FROM ME? WHY?
STILL NOTHING ON MOTHER SOUL OR HER LEAGUE OF LAZARUS PAST MY OWN UPDATES...
MOTHER SOUL IS A MYSTERY, BUT SHE HAD TO HAVE CHOSEN THE FIGHTERS FOR THE TOURNAMENT FOR A REASON...
THEY ARE THE CLUES. THERE MUST BE SOME KIND OF PATTERN THAT I'M NOT...
GOOD MORNING, KILLERS!
IT'S A GREAT DAY TO DIE, AM I RIGHT?!
I LOVE THE SMELL OF BLOOD IN THE MORNING!
HM.
WHO ARE YOU, FLATLINE...?

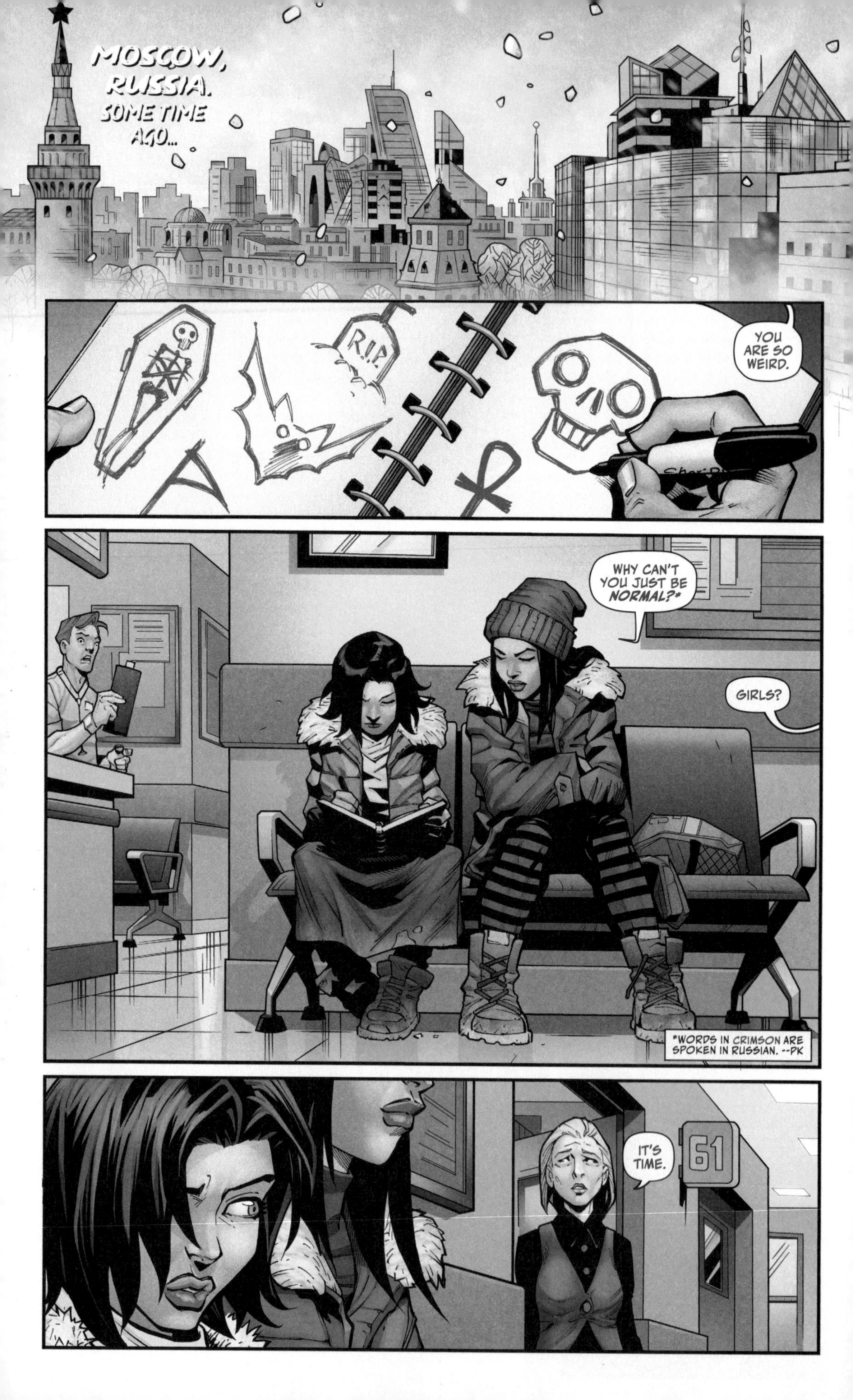
MOSCOW, RUSSIA. SOME TIME AGO...
YOU ARE SO WEIRD.
WHY CAN'T YOU JUST BE NORMAL?*
GIRLS?
*WORDS IN CRIMSON ARE SPOKEN IN RUSSIAN. --PK
IT'S TIME.
61

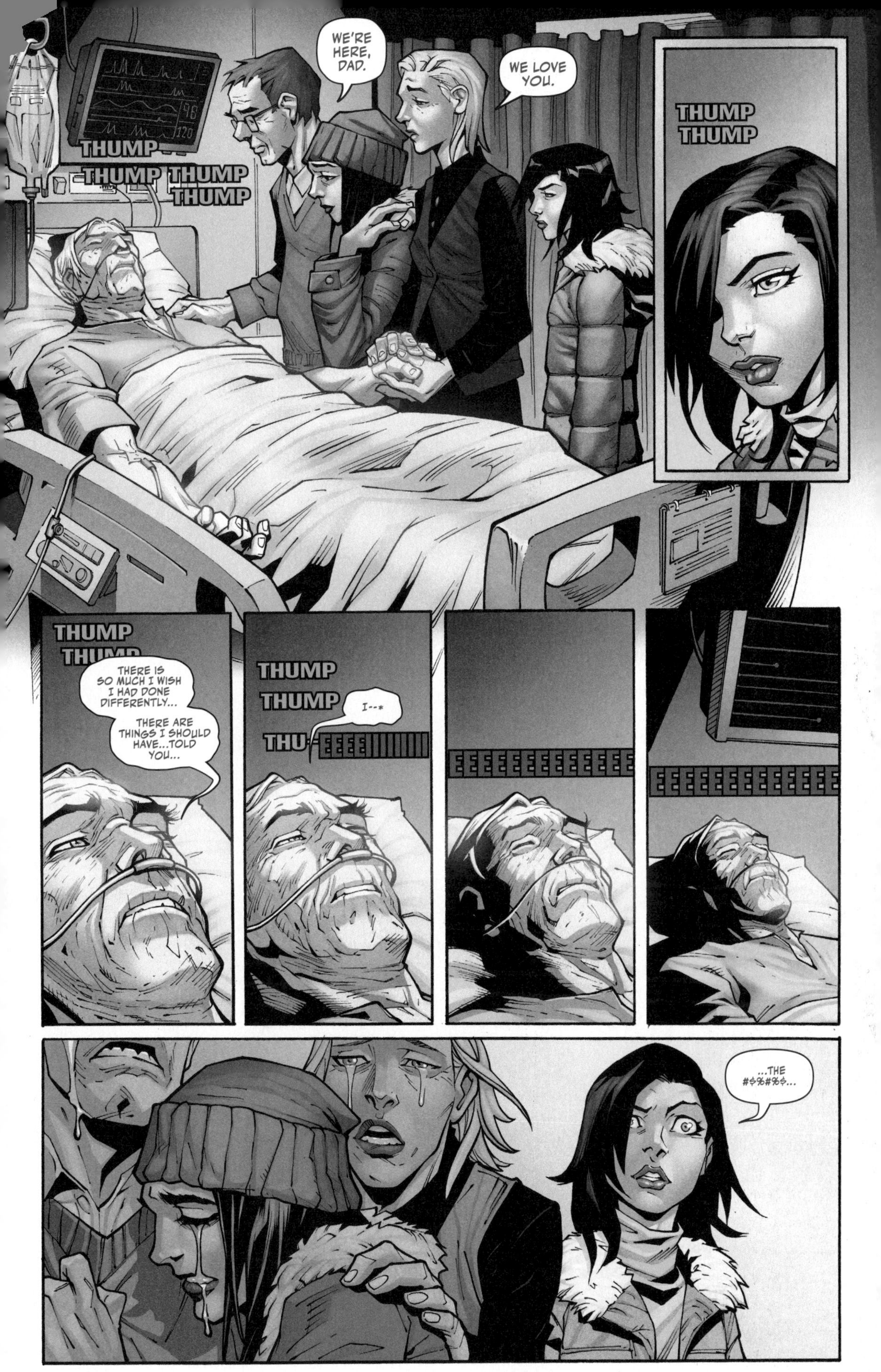
THUMP
THUMP THUMP
THUMP
WE'RE HERE, DAD.
WE LOVE YOU.
THUMP
THUMP
THUMP
THUMP
THERE IS SO MUCH I WISH I HAD DONE DIFFERENTLY...
THERE ARE THINGS I SHOULD HAVE...TOLD YOU...
THUMP
THUMP
THU-EEEE
I--*
EEEEEEEEEEEE
EEEEEEEEEEEE
...THE #$%#%$...

EEEEEEEEEEEEEEEEEEEEEEEEEEEEEEEEEEEEEEEEEEEEEEEEEEEEE

NNGH!

UH, DID YOU KNOW GRANDPA WAS A *SERIAL KILLER?*

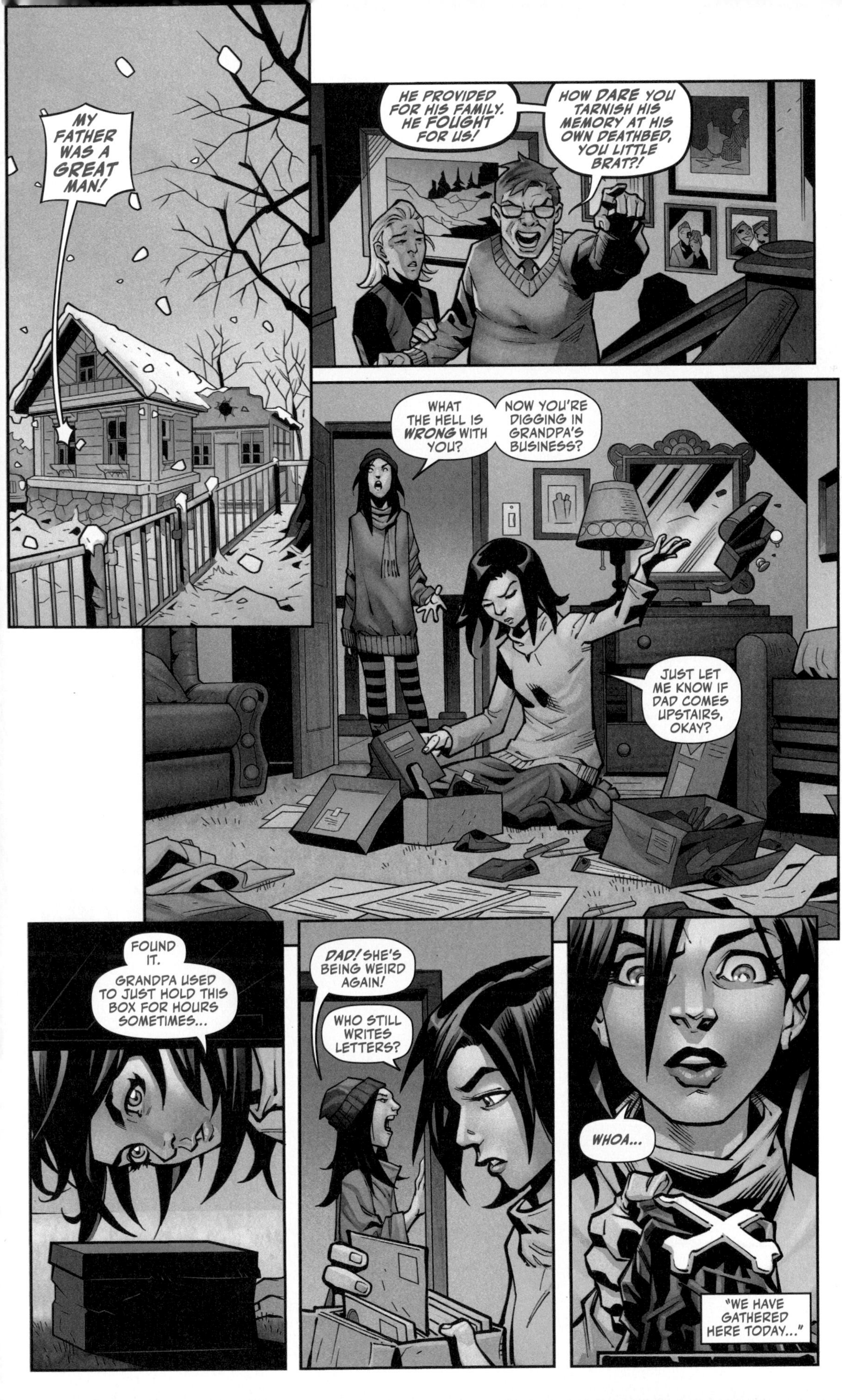
MY FATHER WAS A GREAT MAN!
HE PROVIDED FOR HIS FAMILY. HE FOUGHT FOR US!
HOW DARE YOU TARNISH HIS MEMORY AT HIS OWN DEATHBED, YOU LITTLE BRAT?!
WHAT THE HELL IS WRONG WITH YOU?
NOW YOU'RE DIGGING IN GRANDPA'S BUSINESS?
JUST LET ME KNOW IF DAD COMES UPSTAIRS, OKAY?
FOUND IT.
GRANDPA USED TO JUST HOLD THIS BOX FOR HOURS SOMETIMES...
DAD! SHE'S BEING WEIRD AGAIN!
WHO STILL WRITES LETTERS?
WHOA...
"WE HAVE GATHERED HERE TODAY..."

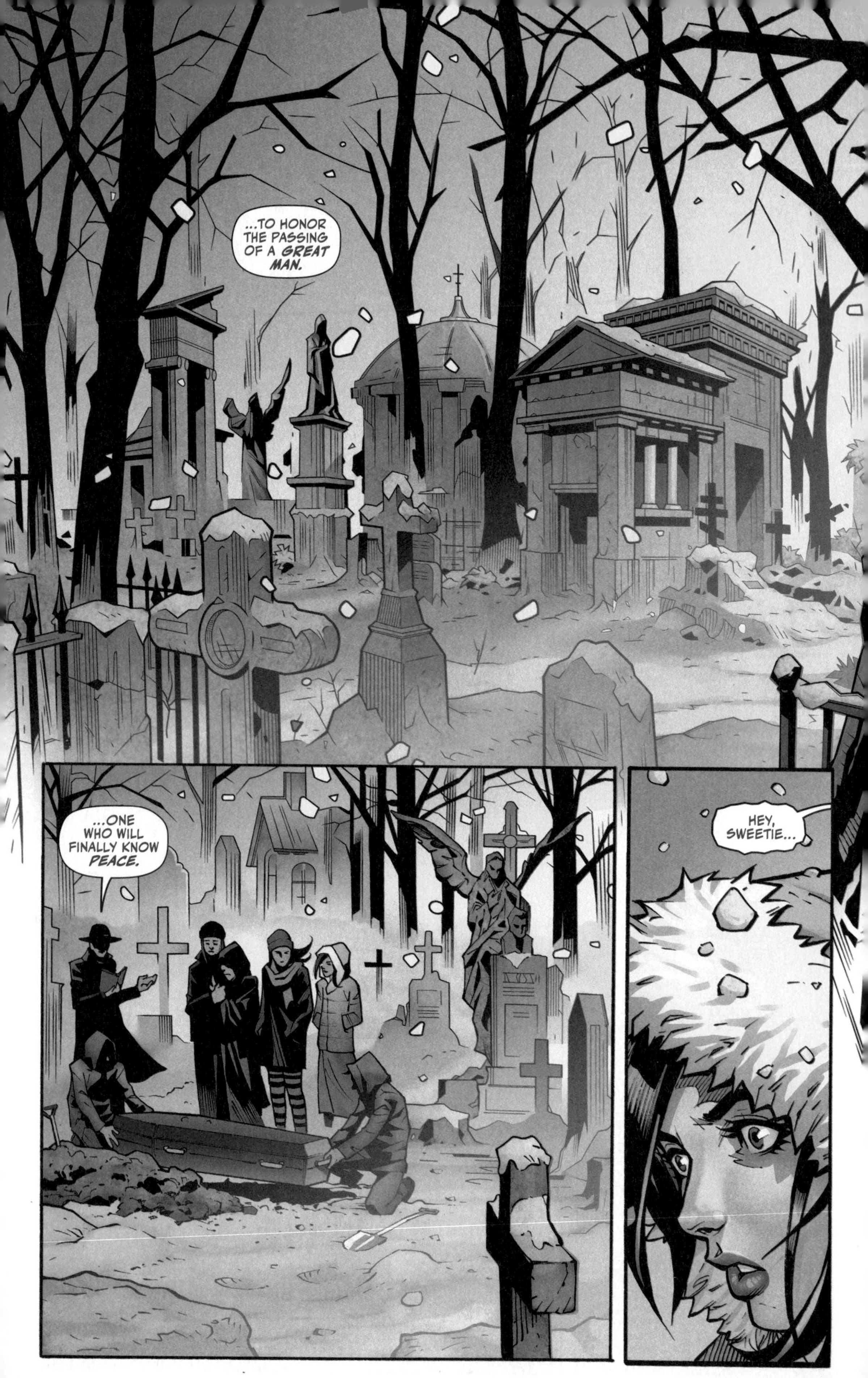
...TO HONOR THE PASSING OF A *GREAT MAN.*
...ONE WHO WILL FINALLY KNOW *PEACE.*
HEY, SWEETIE...

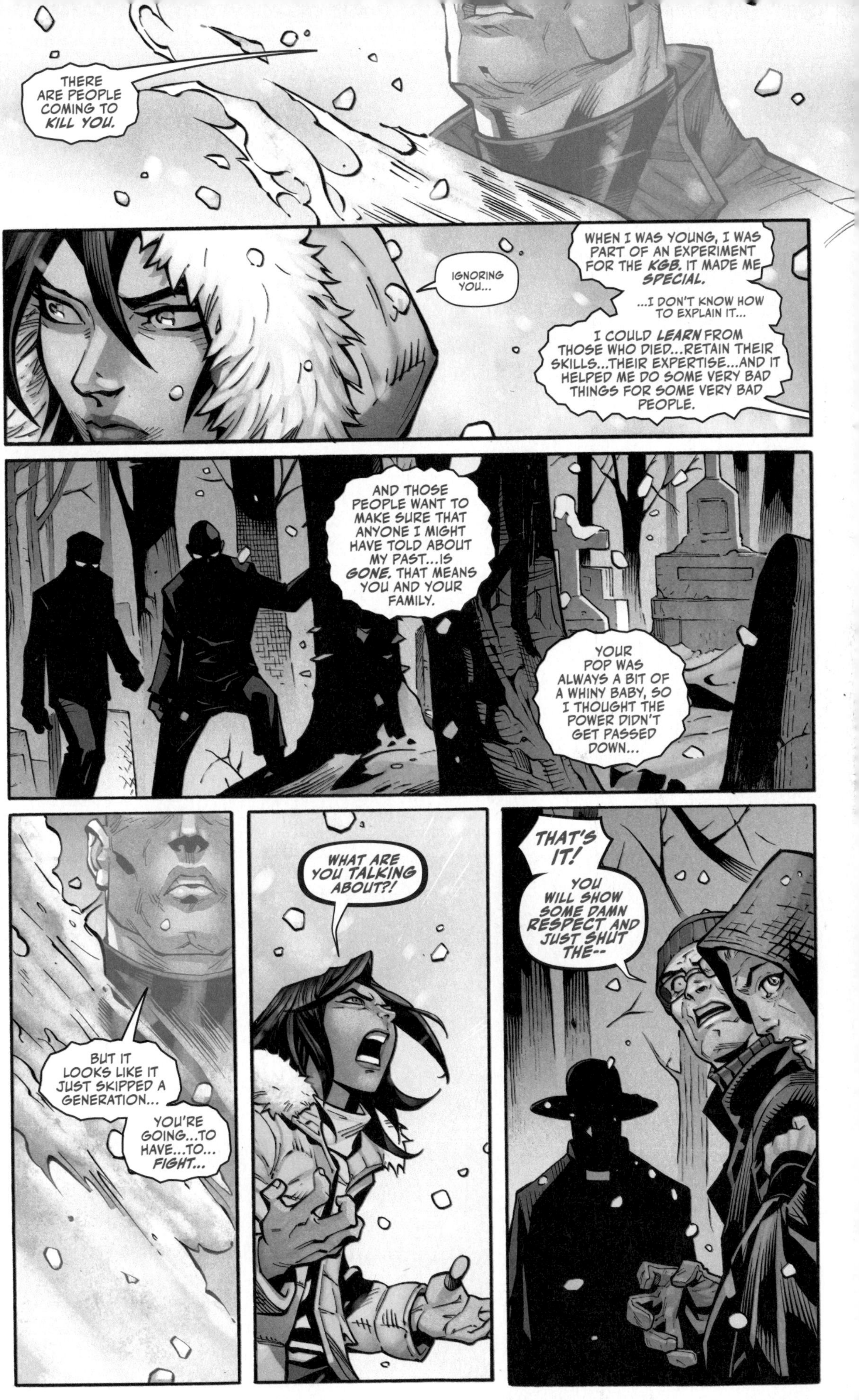
THERE ARE PEOPLE COMING TO KILL YOU.
IGNORING YOU...
WHEN I WAS YOUNG, I WAS PART OF AN EXPERIMENT FOR THE KGB. IT MADE ME SPECIAL.
...I DON'T KNOW HOW TO EXPLAIN IT...
I COULD LEARN FROM THOSE WHO DIED...RETAIN THEIR SKILLS...THEIR EXPERTISE...AND IT HELPED ME DO SOME VERY BAD THINGS FOR SOME VERY BAD PEOPLE.
AND THOSE PEOPLE WANT TO MAKE SURE THAT ANYONE I MIGHT HAVE TOLD ABOUT MY PAST...IS GONE. THAT MEANS YOU AND YOUR FAMILY.
YOUR POP WAS ALWAYS A BIT OF A WHINY BABY, SO I THOUGHT THE POWER DIDN'T GET PASSED DOWN...
BUT IT LOOKS LIKE IT JUST SKIPPED A GENERATION...
YOU'RE GOING...TO HAVE...TO... FIGHT...
WHAT ARE YOU TALKING ABOUT?!
THAT'S IT!
YOU WILL SHOW SOME DAMN RESPECT AND JUST SHUT THE--

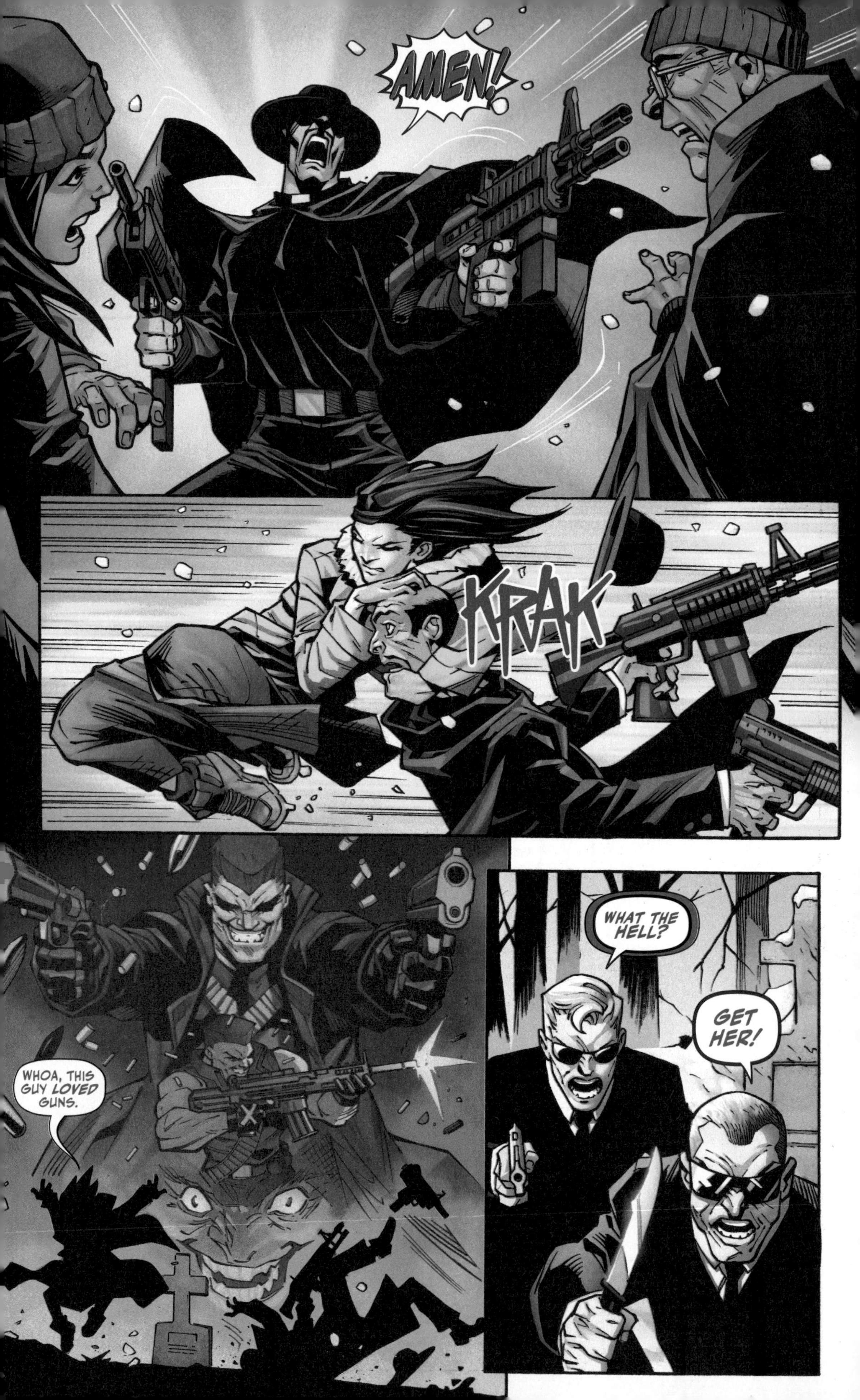
AMEN!
KRAK
WHOA, THIS GUY *LOVED* GUNS.
WHAT THE HELL?
GET HER!

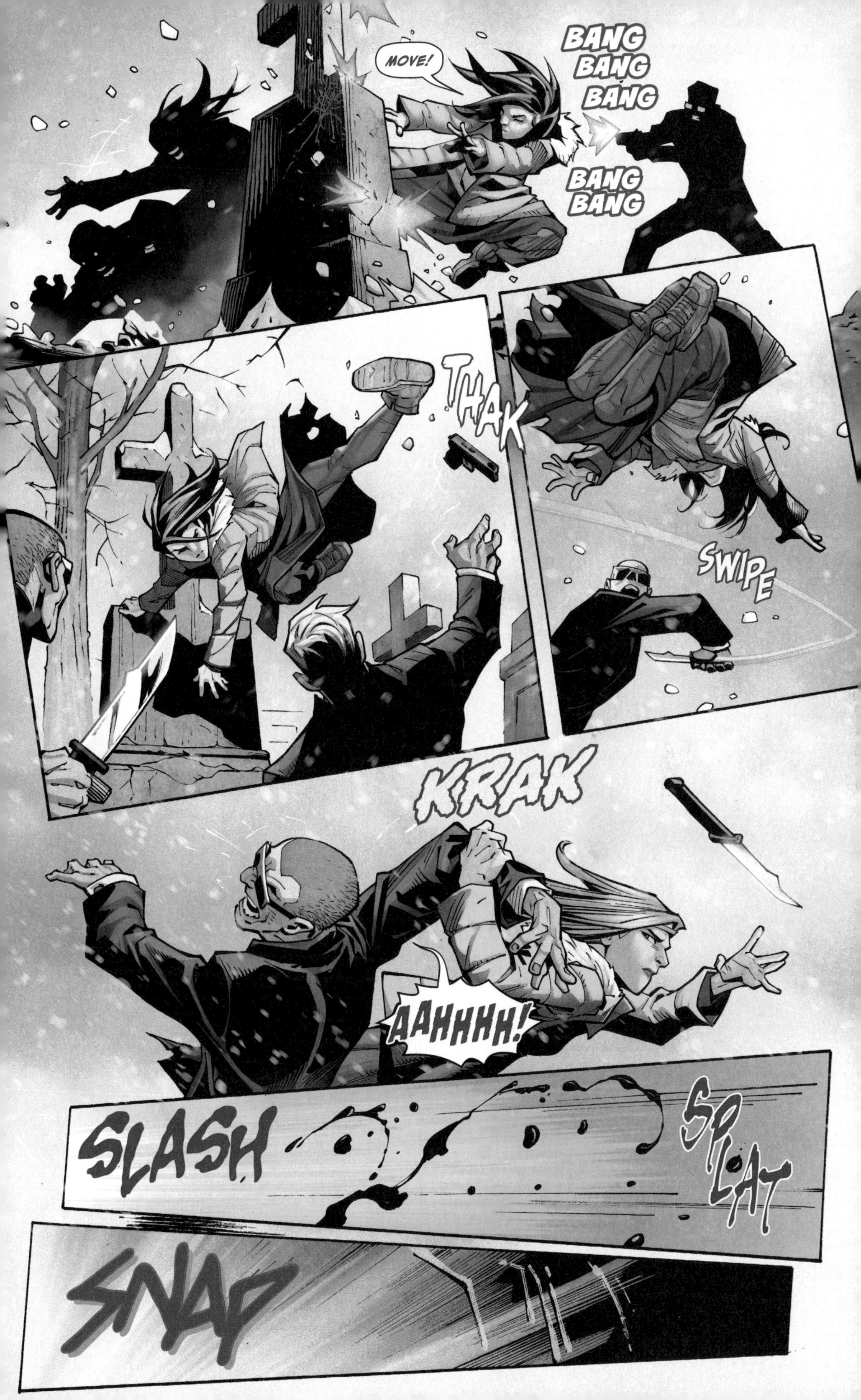
MOVE!
BANG
BANG
BANG
BANG
BANG
THAK
SWIPE
KRAK
AAHHHH!
SLASH
SPLAT
SNAP

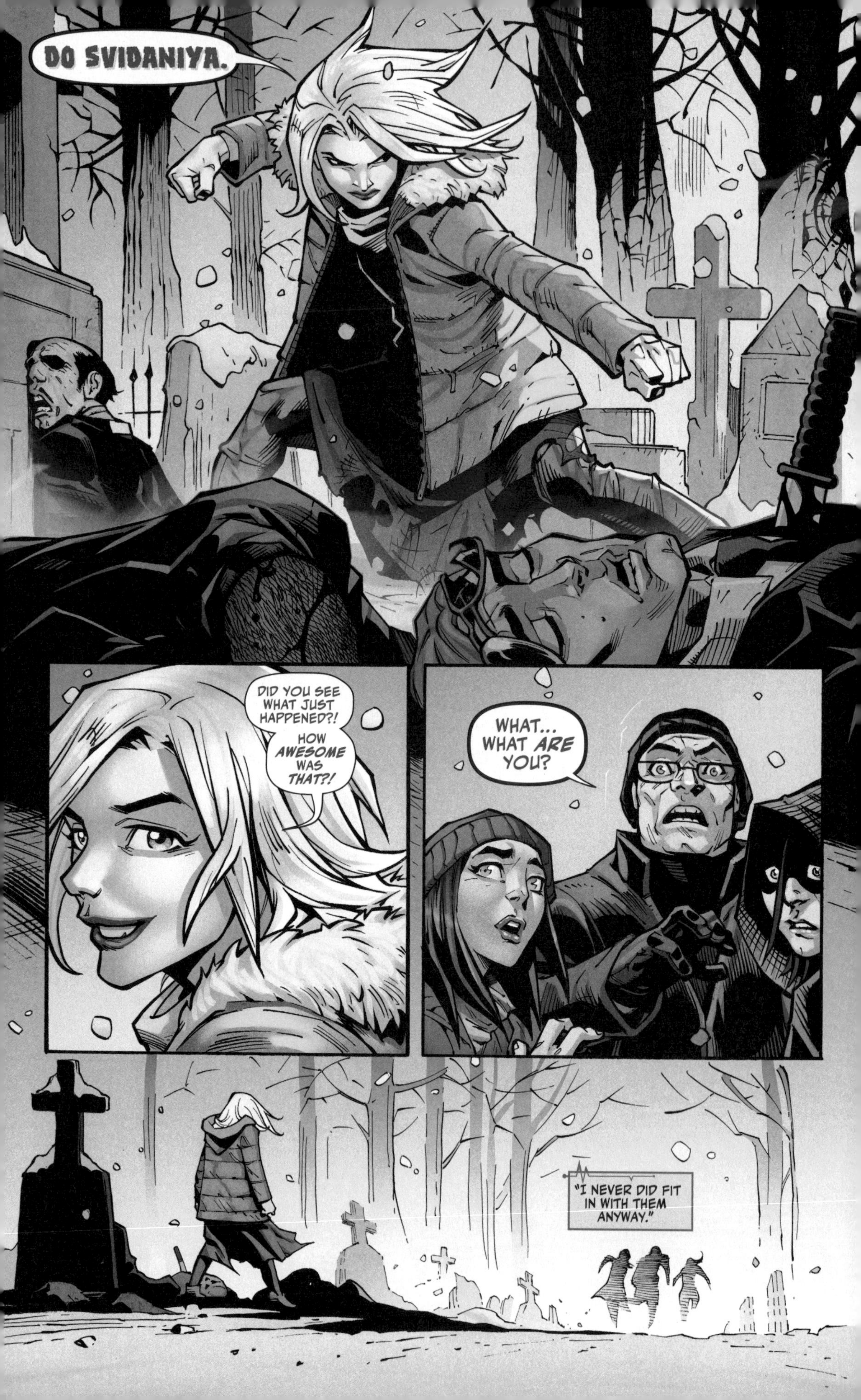
DO SVIDANIYA.
DID YOU SEE WHAT JUST HAPPENED?!
HOW AWESOME WAS THAT?!
WHAT... WHAT ARE YOU?
"I NEVER DID FIT IN WITH THEM ANYWAY."

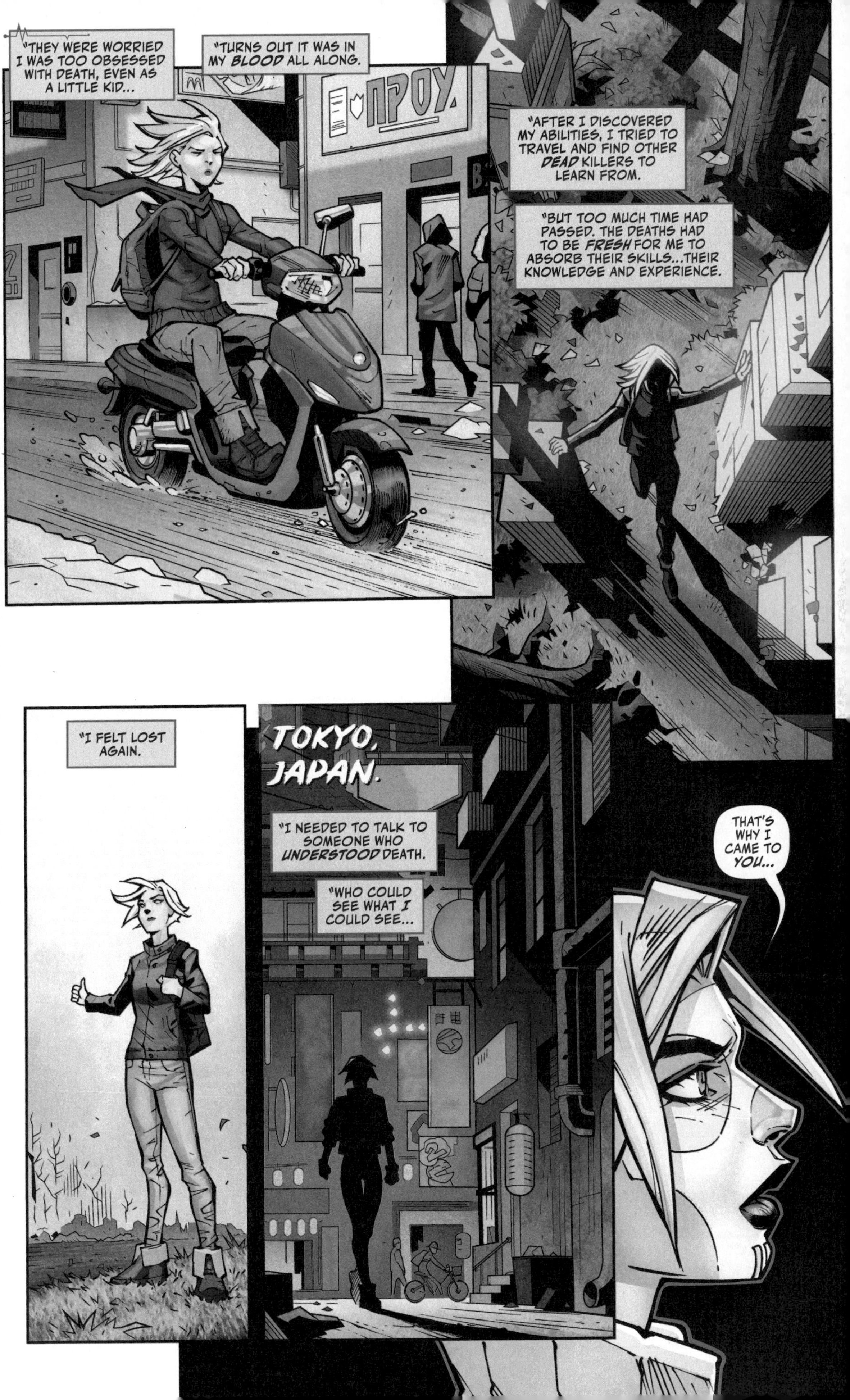
"THEY WERE WORRIED I WAS TOO OBSESSED WITH DEATH, EVEN AS A LITTLE KID...
"TURNS OUT IT WAS IN MY BLOOD ALL ALONG.
"AFTER I DISCOVERED MY ABILITIES, I TRIED TO TRAVEL AND FIND OTHER DEAD KILLERS TO LEARN FROM.
"BUT TOO MUCH TIME HAD PASSED. THE DEATHS HAD TO BE FRESH FOR ME TO ABSORB THEIR SKILLS...THEIR KNOWLEDGE AND EXPERIENCE.
"I FELT LOST AGAIN.
TOKYO, JAPAN.
"I NEEDED TO TALK TO SOMEONE WHO UNDERSTOOD DEATH.
"WHO COULD SEE WHAT I COULD SEE...
THAT'S WHY I CAME TO YOU...

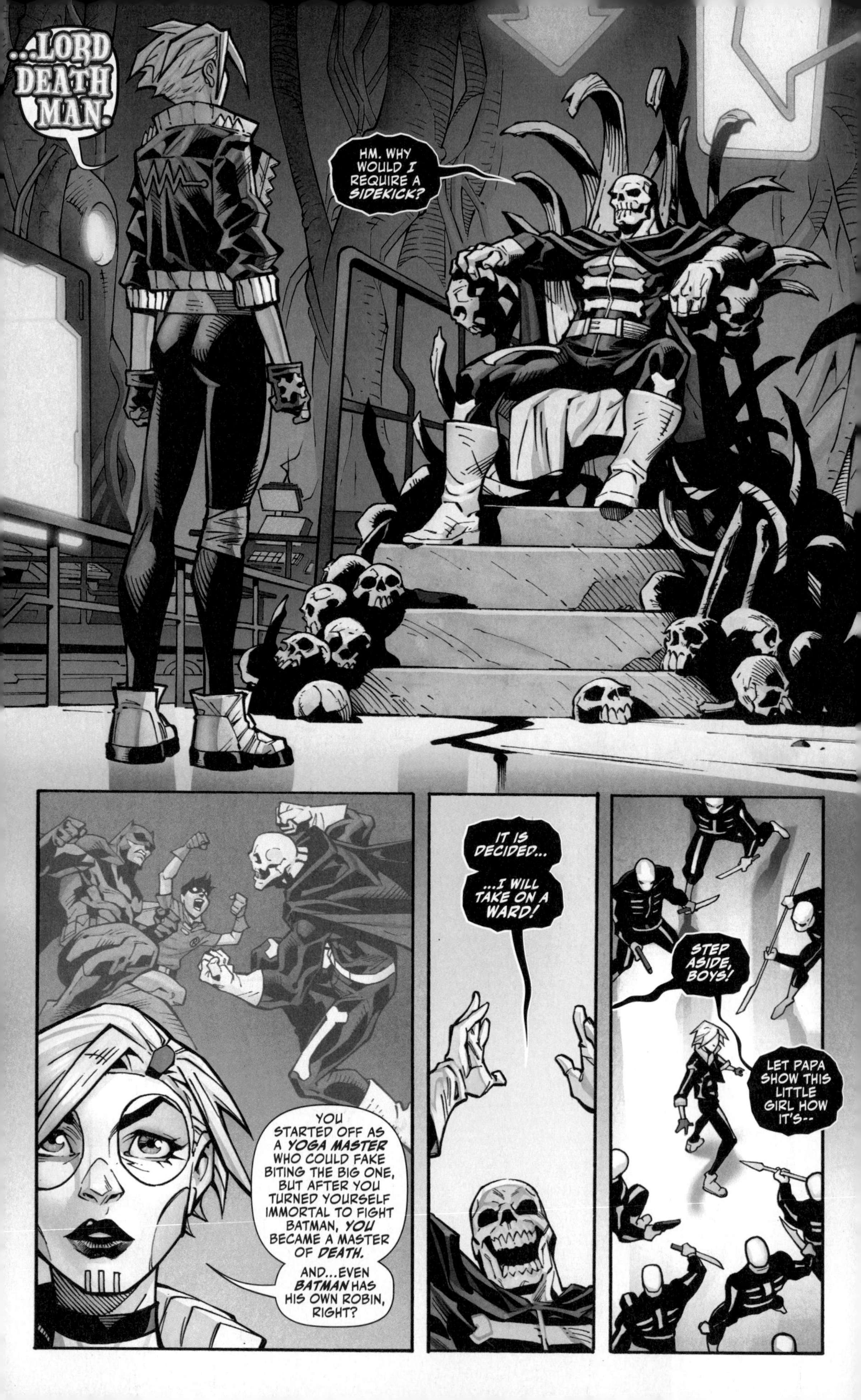
...LORD DEATH MAN.
HM. WHY WOULD I REQUIRE A SIDEKICK?
YOU STARTED OFF AS A YOGA MASTER WHO COULD FAKE BITING THE BIG ONE, BUT AFTER YOU TURNED YOURSELF IMMORTAL TO FIGHT BATMAN, YOU BECAME A MASTER OF DEATH.
AND...EVEN BATMAN HAS HIS OWN ROBIN, RIGHT?
IT IS DECIDED...
...I WILL TAKE ON A WARD!
STEP ASIDE, BOYS!
LET PAPA SHOW THIS LITTLE GIRL HOW IT'S--

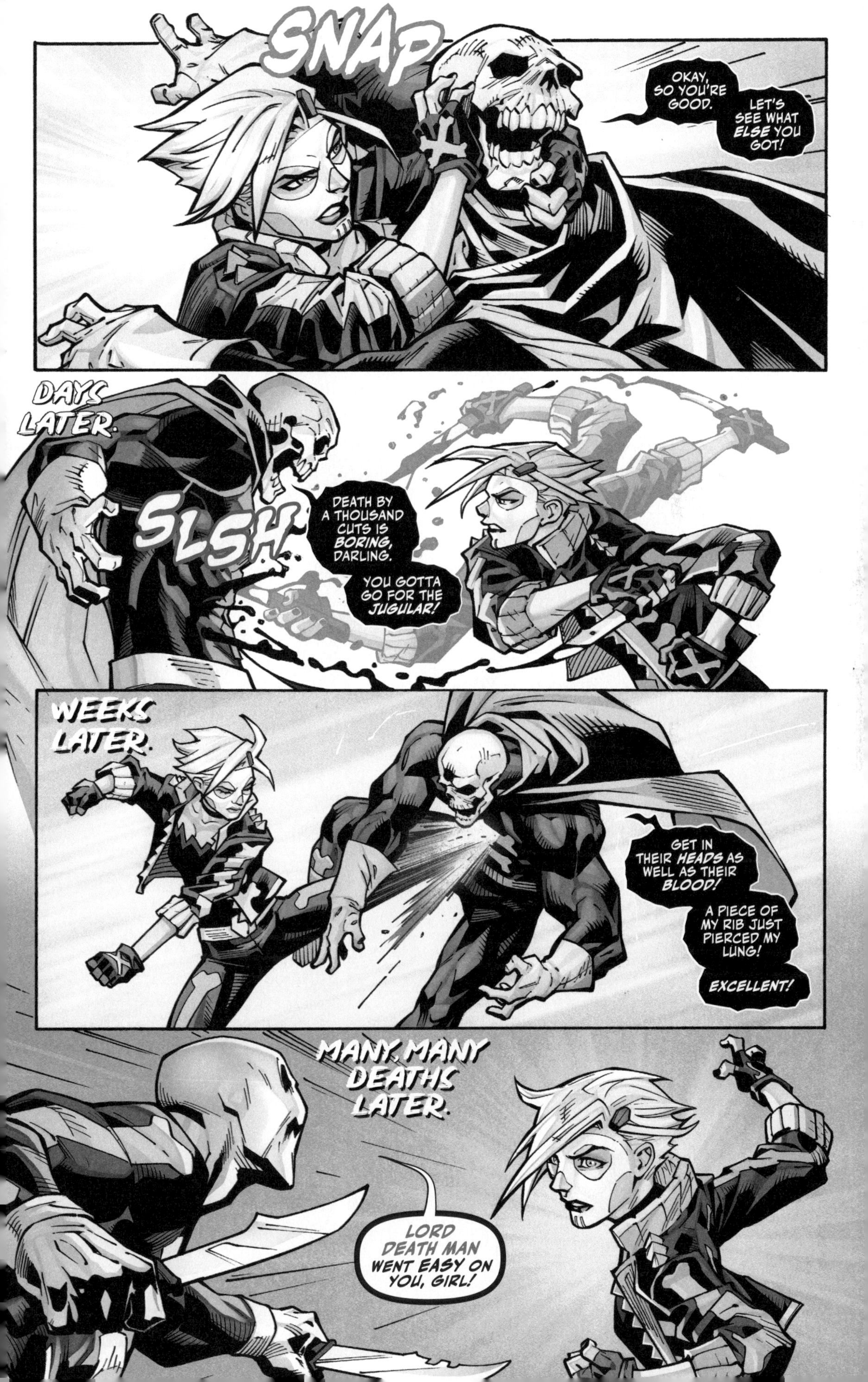
SNAP
OKAY, SO YOU'RE GOOD.
LET'S SEE WHAT ELSE YOU GOT!
DAYS LATER.
SLSH
DEATH BY A THOUSAND CUTS IS BORING, DARLING.
YOU GOTTA GO FOR THE JUGULAR!
WEEKS LATER.
GET IN THEIR HEADS AS WELL AS THEIR BLOOD!
A PIECE OF MY RIB JUST PIERCED MY LUNG!
EXCELLENT!
MANY, MANY DEATHS LATER.
LORD DEATH MAN WENT EASY ON YOU, GIRL!

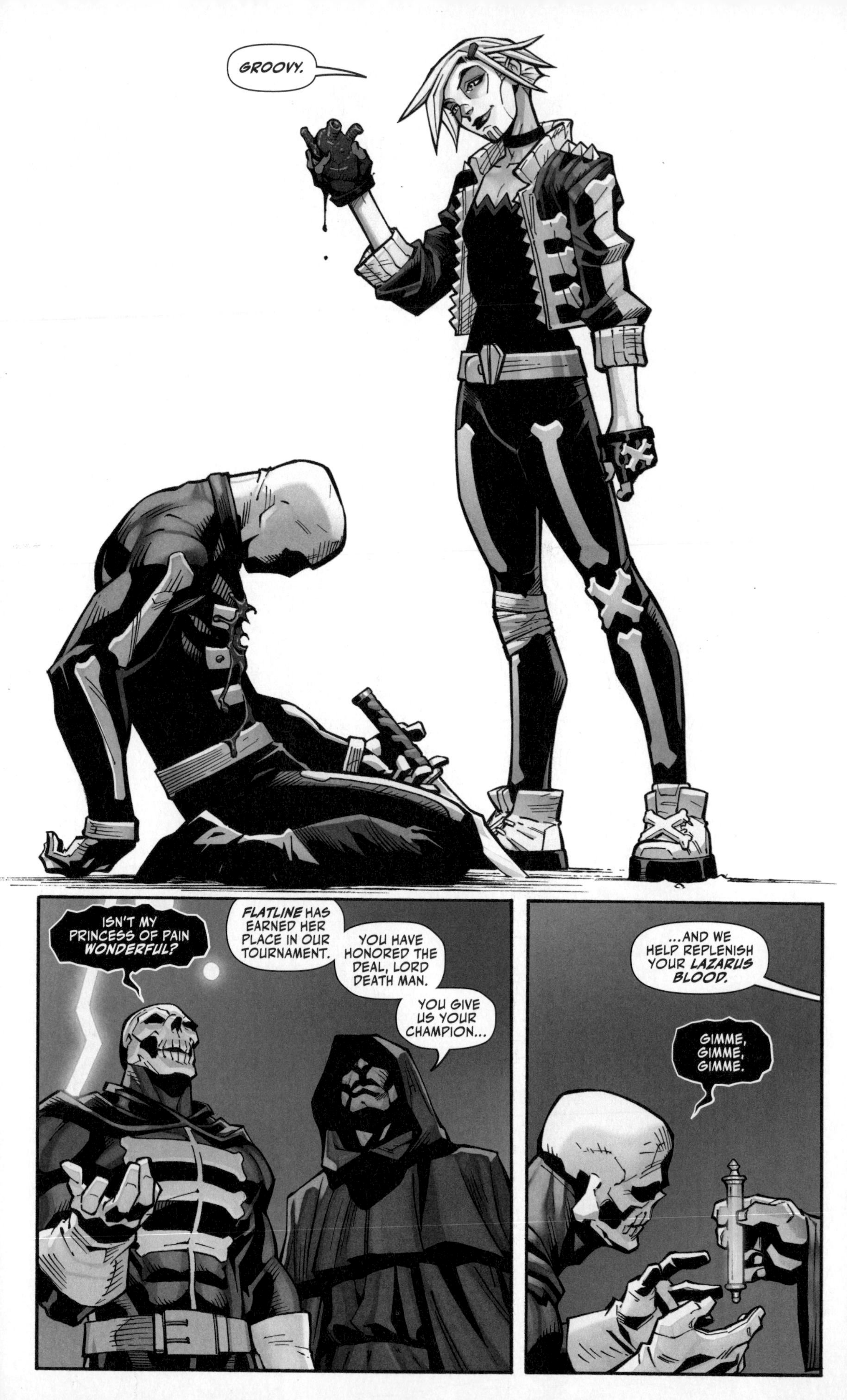
GROOVY.
ISN'T MY PRINCESS OF PAIN WONDERFUL?
FLATLINE HAS EARNED HER PLACE IN OUR TOURNAMENT.
YOU HAVE HONORED THE DEAL, LORD DEATH MAN.
YOU GIVE US YOUR CHAMPION...
...AND WE HELP REPLENISH YOUR LAZARUS BLOOD.
GIMME, GIMME, GIMME.

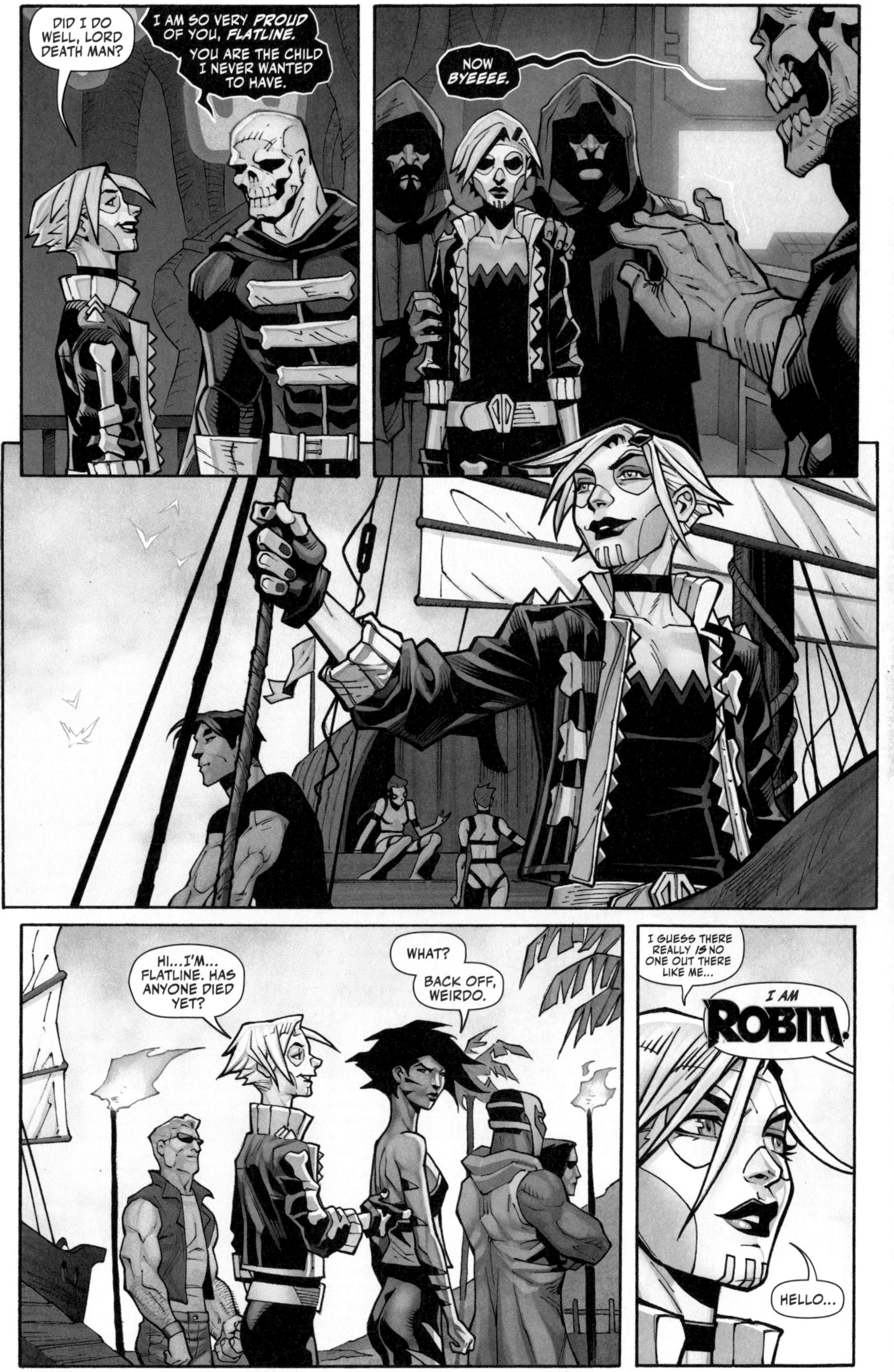
DID I DO WELL, LORD DEATH MAN?
I AM SO VERY PROUD OF YOU, FLATLINE.
YOU ARE THE CHILD I NEVER WANTED TO HAVE.
NOW BYEEEE.
HI...I'M... FLATLINE. HAS ANYONE DIED YET?
WHAT?
BACK OFF, WEIRDO.
I GUESS THERE REALLY IS NO ONE OUT THERE LIKE ME...
I AM ROBIN.
HELLO...

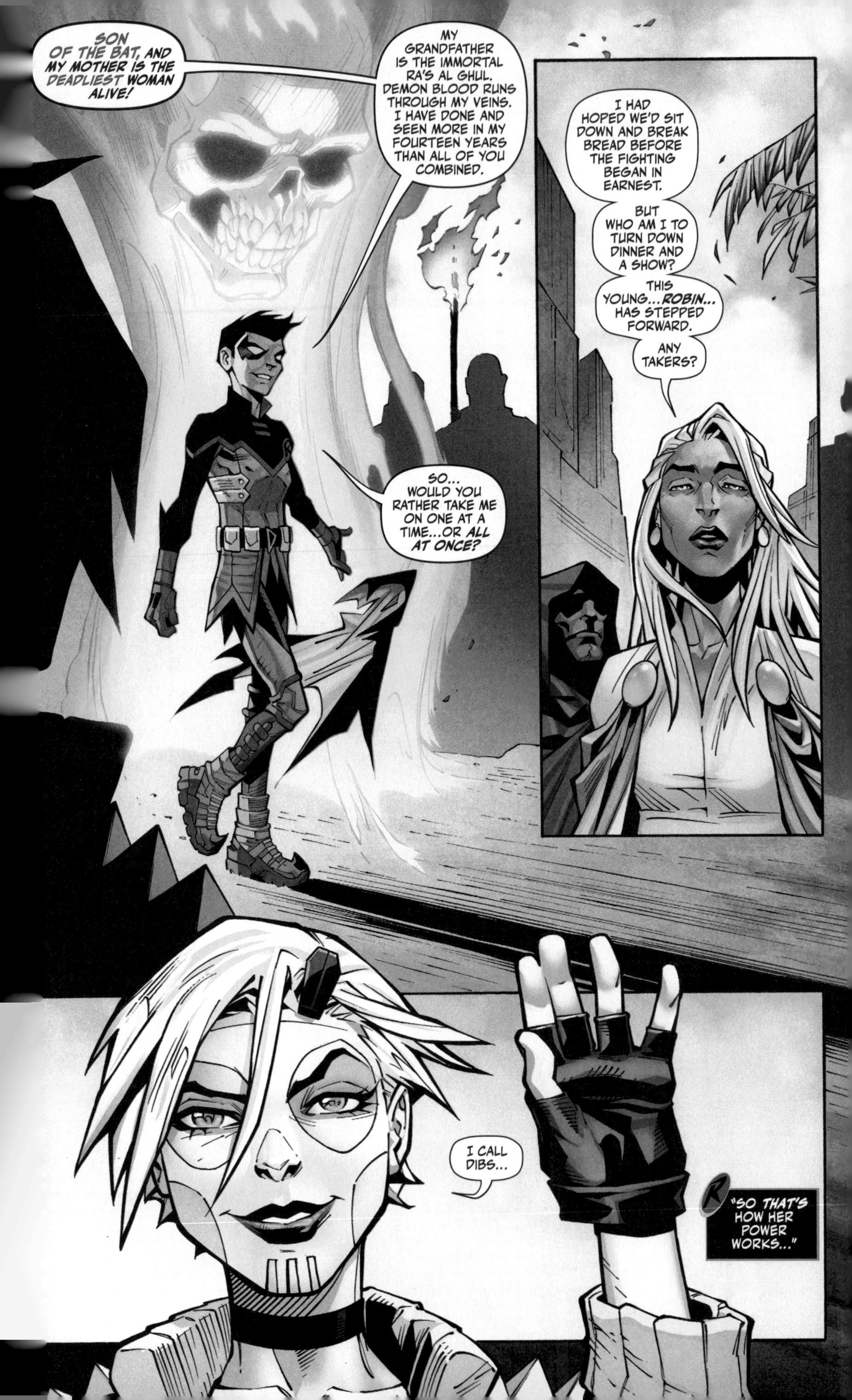
SON OF THE BAT, AND MY MOTHER IS THE DEADLIEST WOMAN ALIVE!
MY GRANDFATHER IS THE IMMORTAL RA'S AL GHUL. DEMON BLOOD RUNS THROUGH MY VEINS. I HAVE DONE AND SEEN MORE IN MY FOURTEEN YEARS THAN ALL OF YOU COMBINED.
SO... WOULD YOU RATHER TAKE ME ON ONE AT A TIME...OR ALL AT ONCE?
I HAD HOPED WE'D SIT DOWN AND BREAK BREAD BEFORE THE FIGHTING BEGAN IN EARNEST.
BUT WHO AM I TO TURN DOWN DINNER AND A SHOW?
THIS YOUNG...ROBIN... HAS STEPPED FORWARD.
ANY TAKERS?
I CALL DIBS...
"SO THAT'S HOW HER POWER WORKS..."

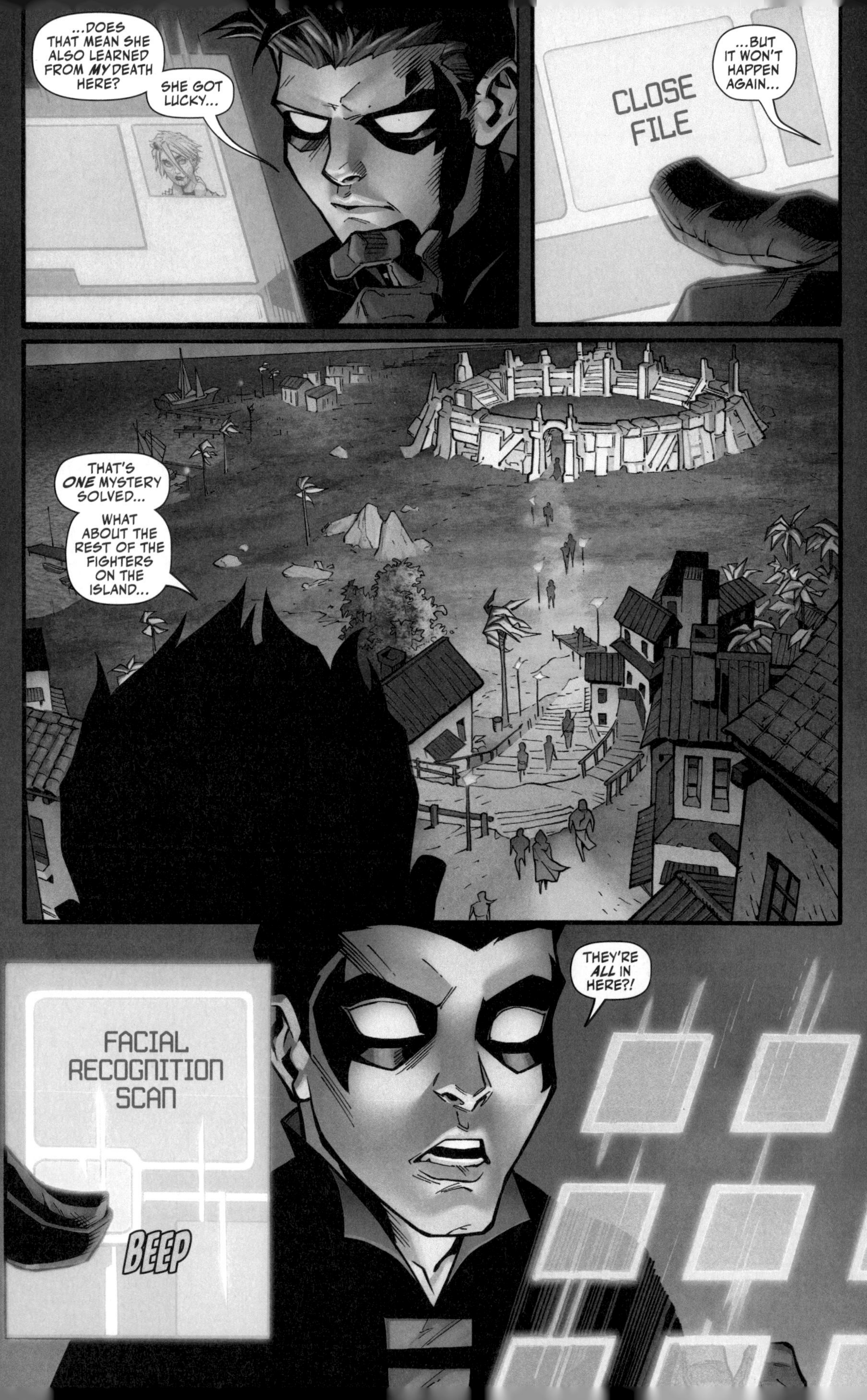
...DOES THAT MEAN SHE ALSO LEARNED FROM MY DEATH HERE?
SHE GOT LUCKY...
CLOSE FILE
...BUT IT WON'T HAPPEN AGAIN...
THAT'S ONE MYSTERY SOLVED...
WHAT ABOUT THE REST OF THE FIGHTERS ON THE ISLAND...
FACIAL RECOGNITION SCAN
BEEP
THEY'RE ALL IN HERE?!

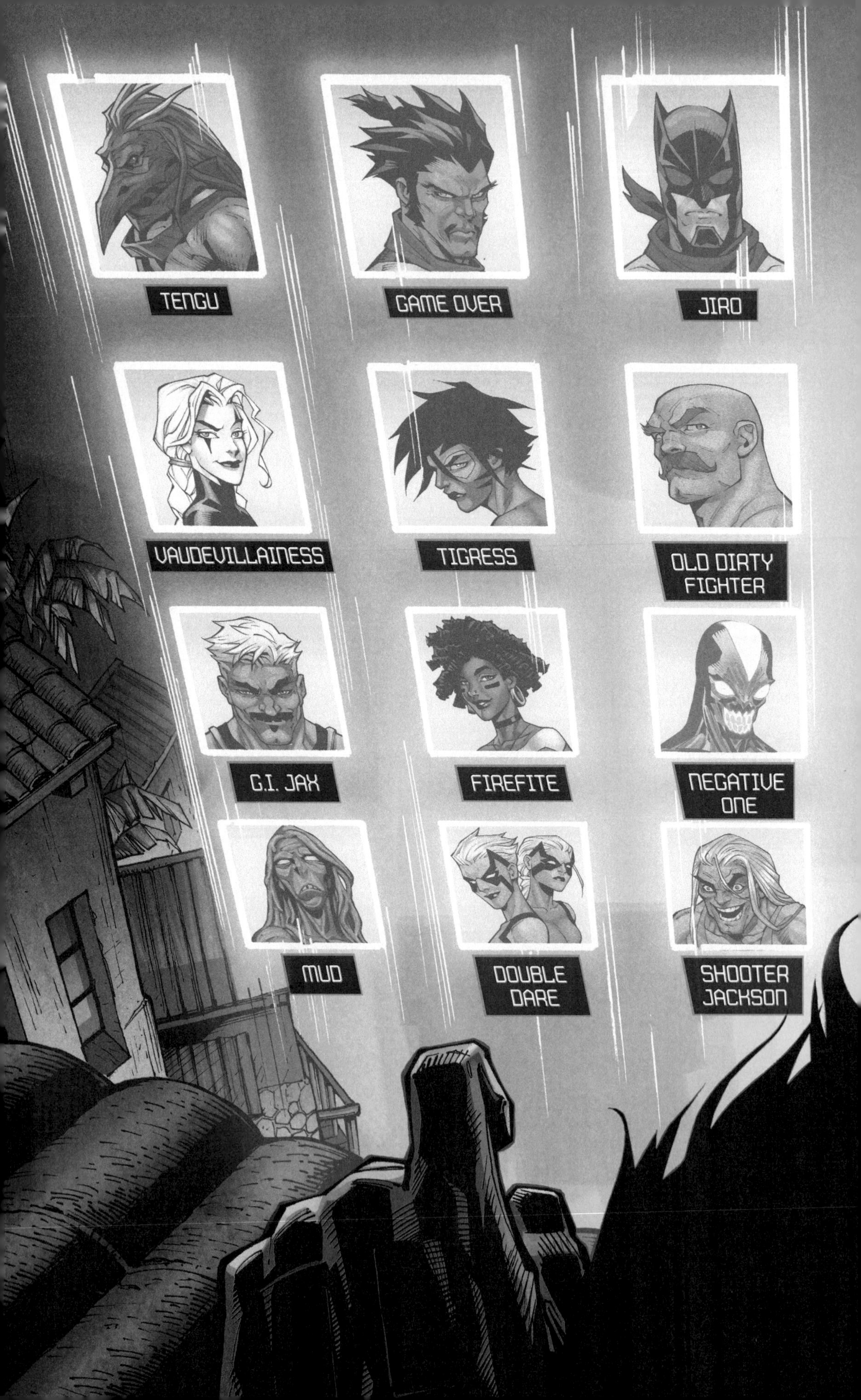
TENGU
GAME OVER
JIRO
VAUDEVILLAINESS
TIGRESS
OLD DIRTY FIGHTER
G.I. JAX
FIREFITE
NEGATIVE ONE
MUD
DOUBLE DARE
SHOOTER JACKSON

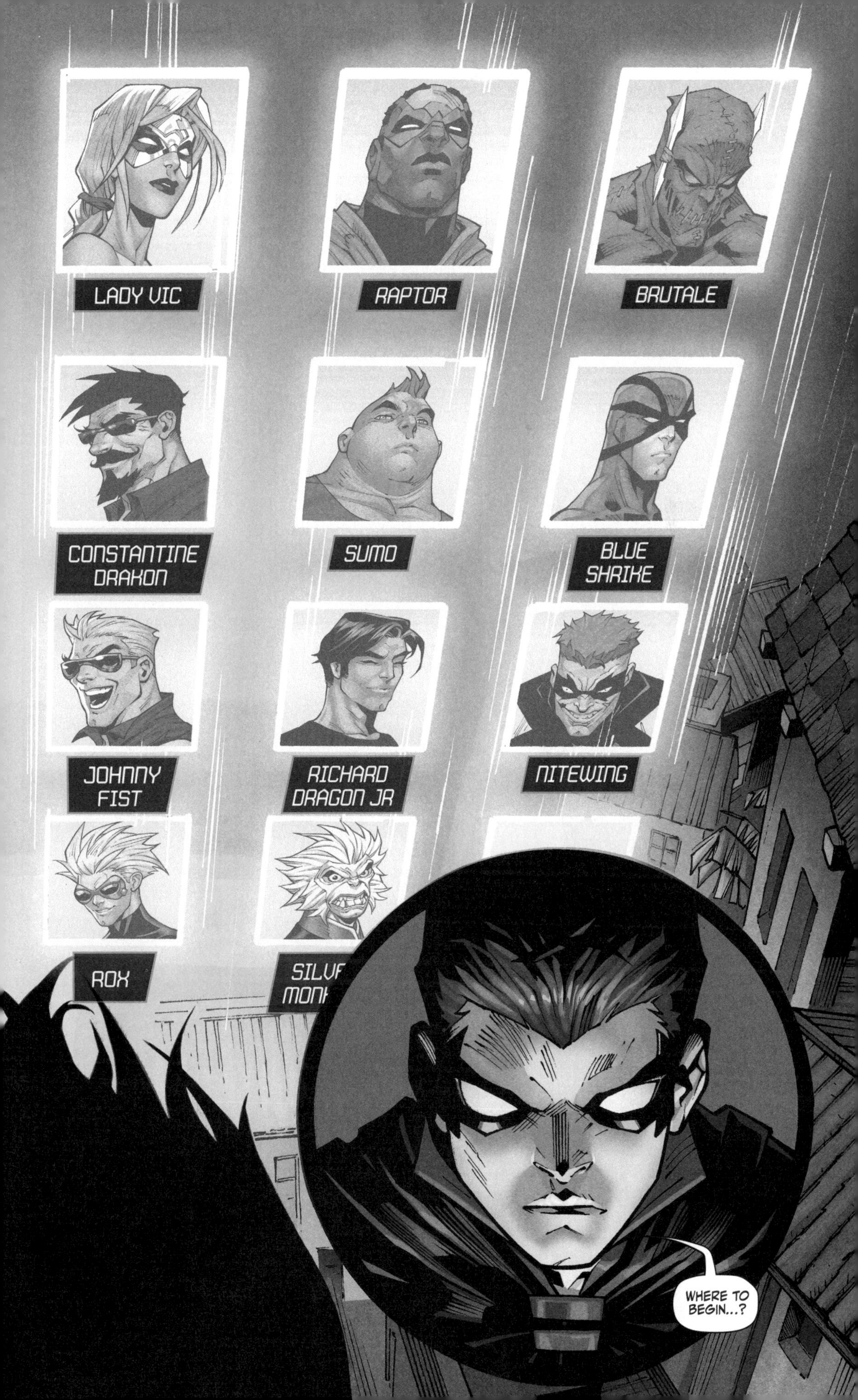
LADY VIC
RAPTOR
BRUTALE
CONSTANTINE DRAKON
SUMO
BLUE SHRIKE
JOHNNY FIST
RICHARD DRAGON JR
NITEWING
ROX
SILV
MONK
WHERE TO BEGIN...?

BLACK SWAN

BACKGROUND: Award-winning dancer, trained since birth. Lost control during a performance and killed everyone on stage.

ABILITIES: Enhanced agility, dexterity, and grace. Short temper. Kicks can kill.

CONFIRMED KILLS: 26.

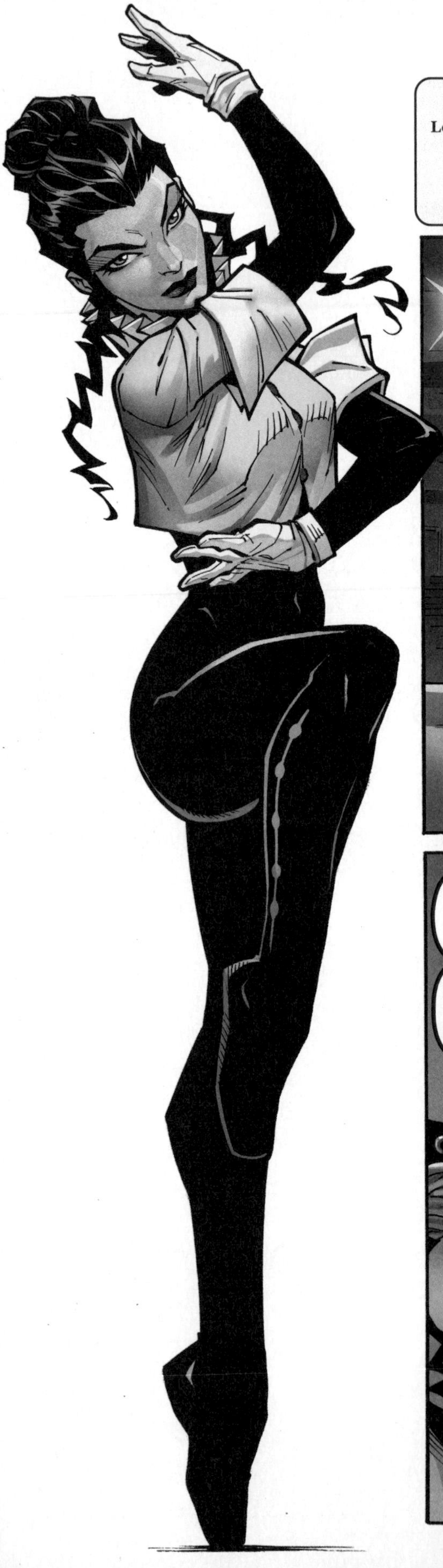

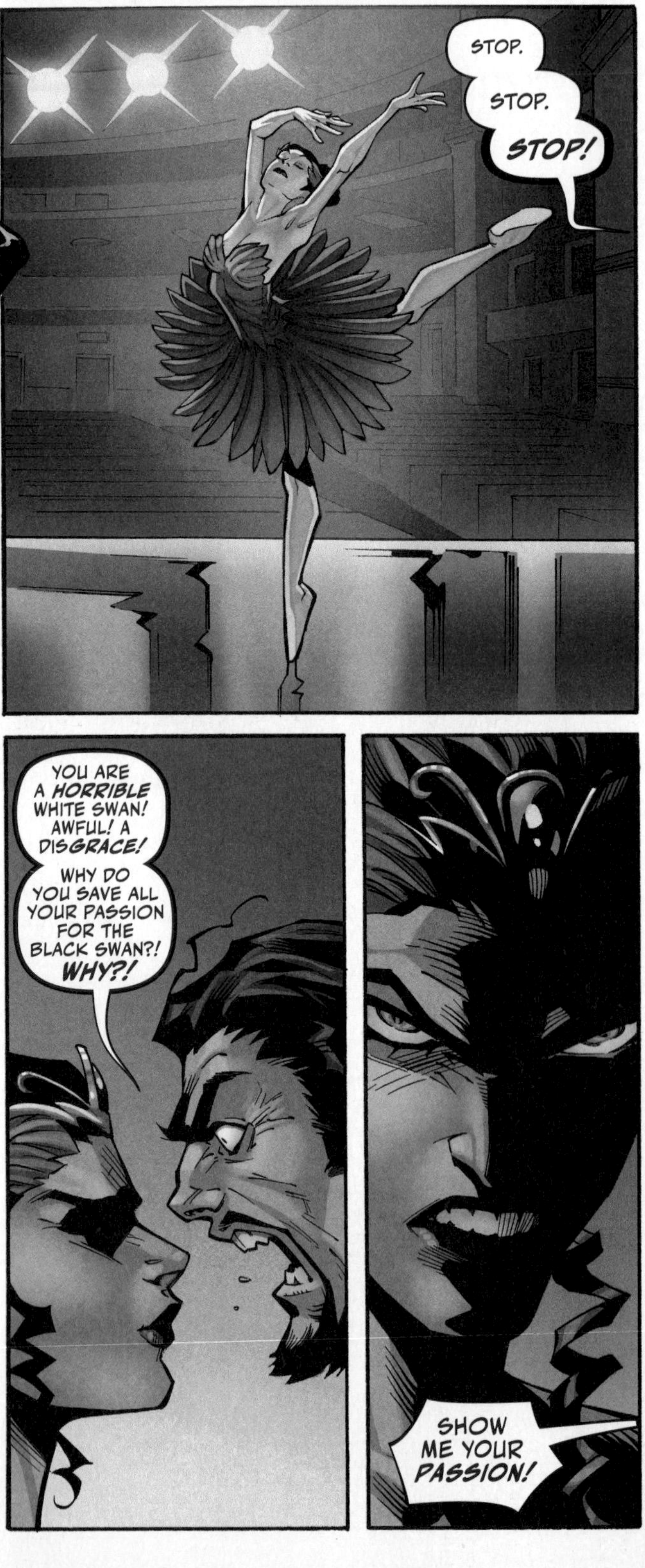
STOP.
STOP.
STOP!
YOU ARE A HORRIBLE WHITE SWAN! AWFUL! A DISGRACE!
WHY DO YOU SAVE ALL YOUR PASSION FOR THE BLACK SWAN?! WHY?!
SHOW ME YOUR PASSION!

XXL!

BACKGROUND: Ten years old. Overconfident and cocky. Fights for the rep, not the money.

ABILITIES: Unlimited wealth, titanium-laced gloves. Enthusiastic hype squad. Big feet for punting fools.

CONFIRMED KILLS: 14.

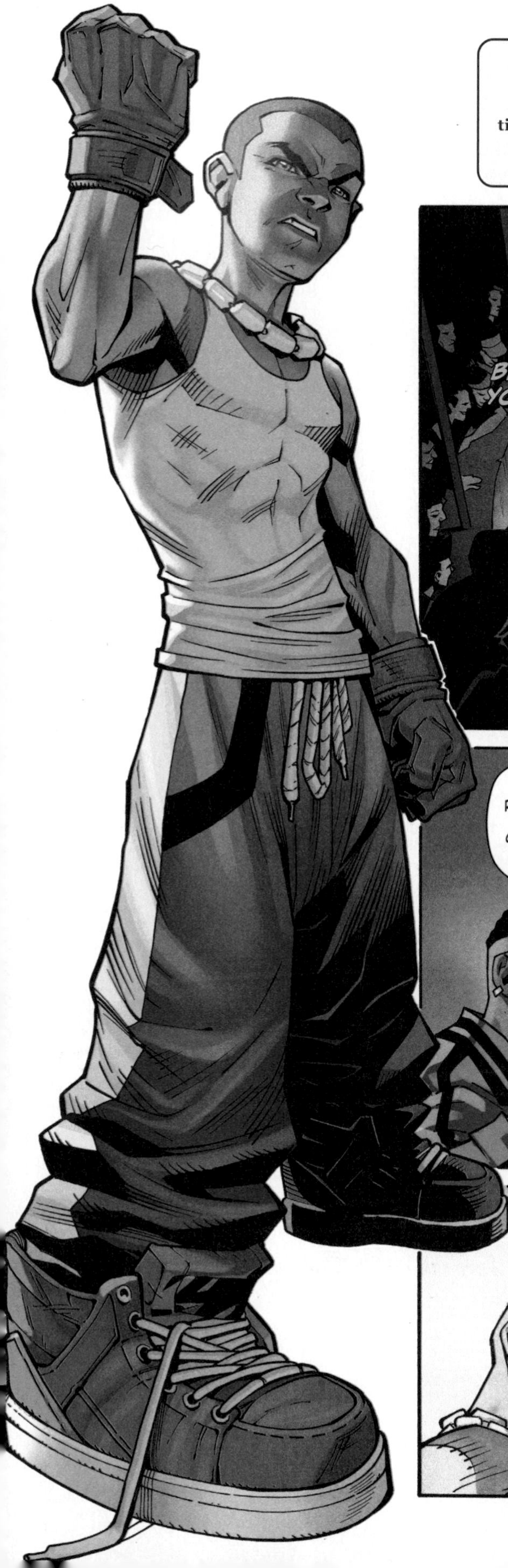

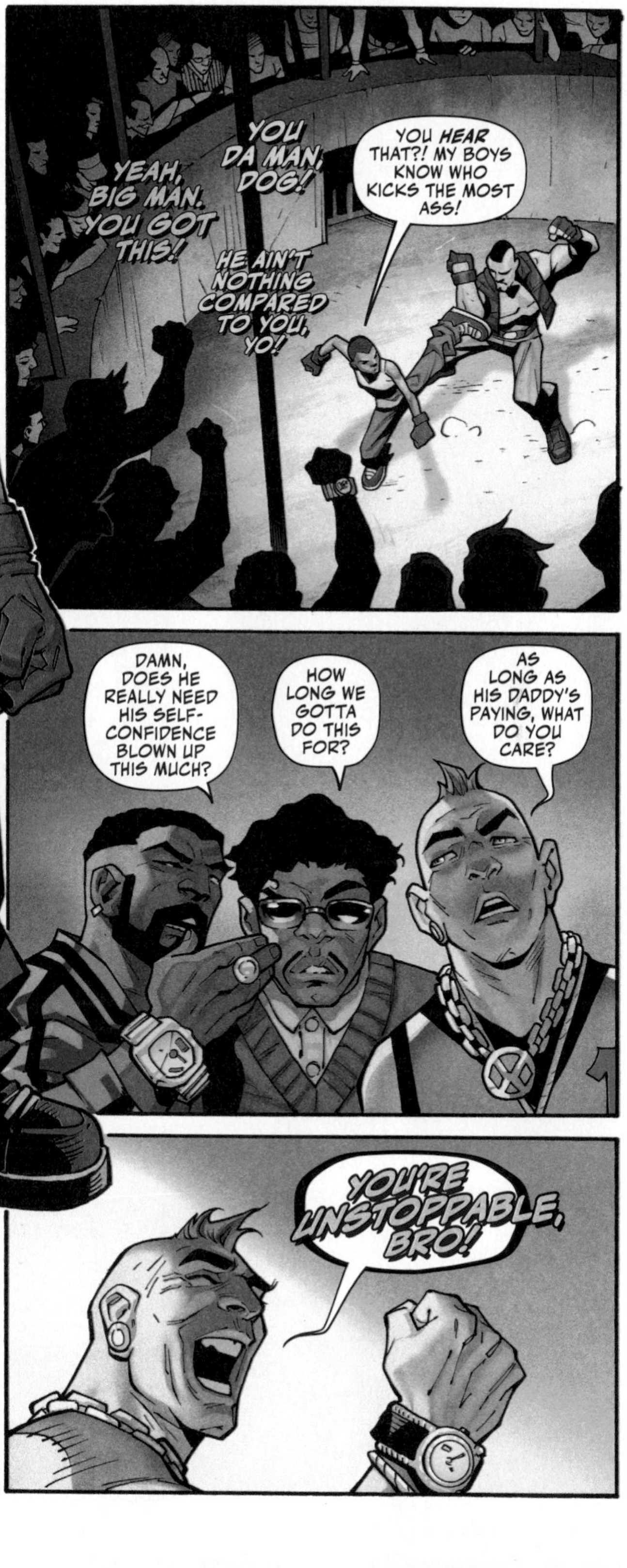
YEAH, BIG MAN. YOU GOT THIS!
YOU DA MAN, DOG!
HE AIN'T NOTHING COMPARED TO YOU, YO!
YOU HEAR THAT?! MY BOYS KNOW WHO KICKS THE MOST ASS!
DAMN, DOES HE REALLY NEED HIS SELF-CONFIDENCE BLOWN UP THIS MUCH?
HOW LONG WE GOTTA DO THIS FOR?
AS LONG AS HIS DADDY'S PAYING, WHAT DO YOU CARE?
YOU'RE UNSTOPPABLE, BRO!

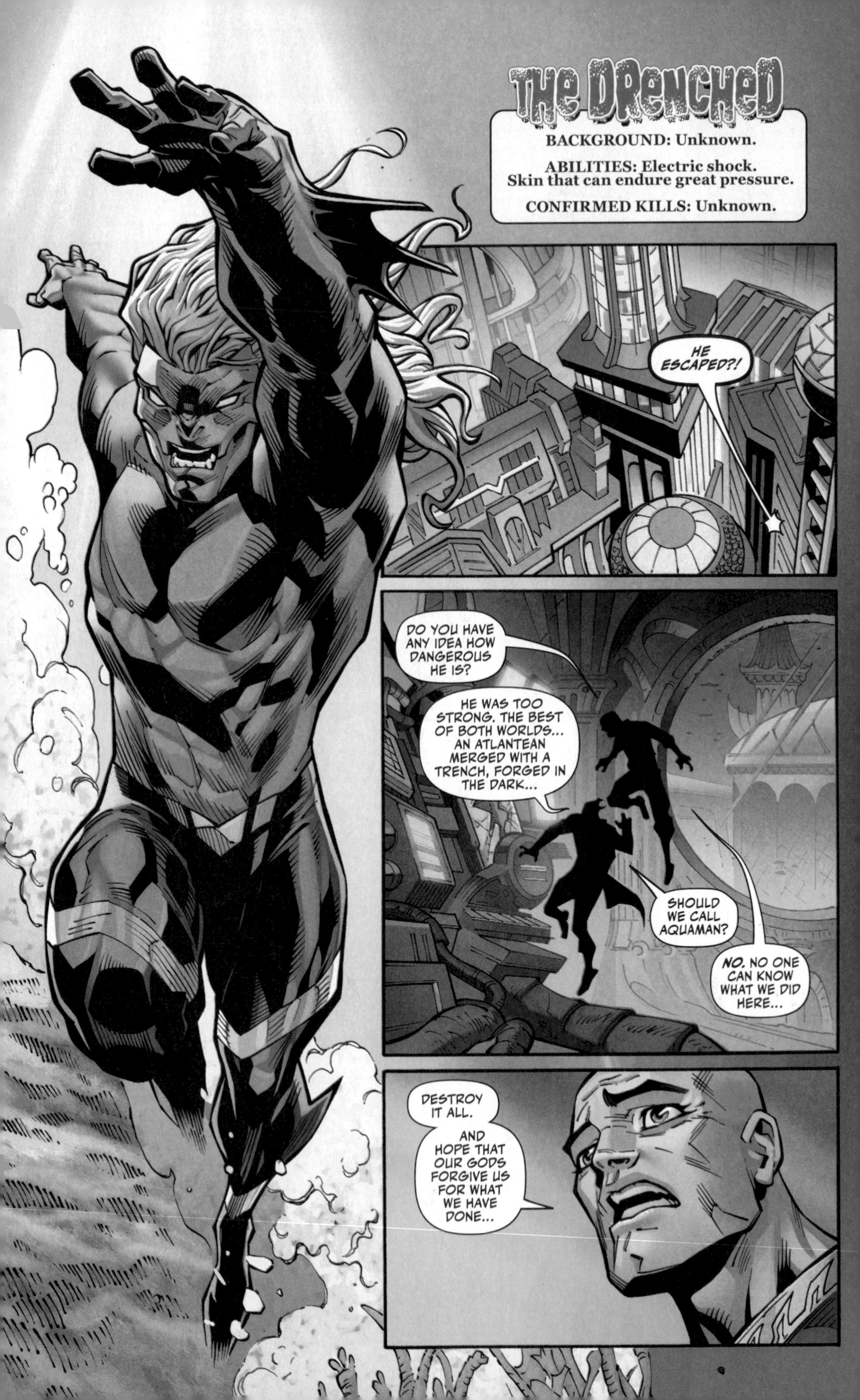
THE DRENCHED
BACKGROUND: Unknown.
ABILITIES: Electric shock. Skin that can endure great pressure.
CONFIRMED KILLS: Unknown.
HE ESCAPED?!
DO YOU HAVE ANY IDEA HOW DANGEROUS HE IS?
HE WAS TOO STRONG. THE BEST OF BOTH WORLDS... AN ATLANTEAN MERGED WITH A TRENCH, FORGED IN THE DARK...
SHOULD WE CALL AQUAMAN?
NO. NO ONE CAN KNOW WHAT WE DID HERE...
DESTROY IT ALL.
AND HOPE THAT OUR GODS FORGIVE US FOR WHAT WE HAVE DONE...

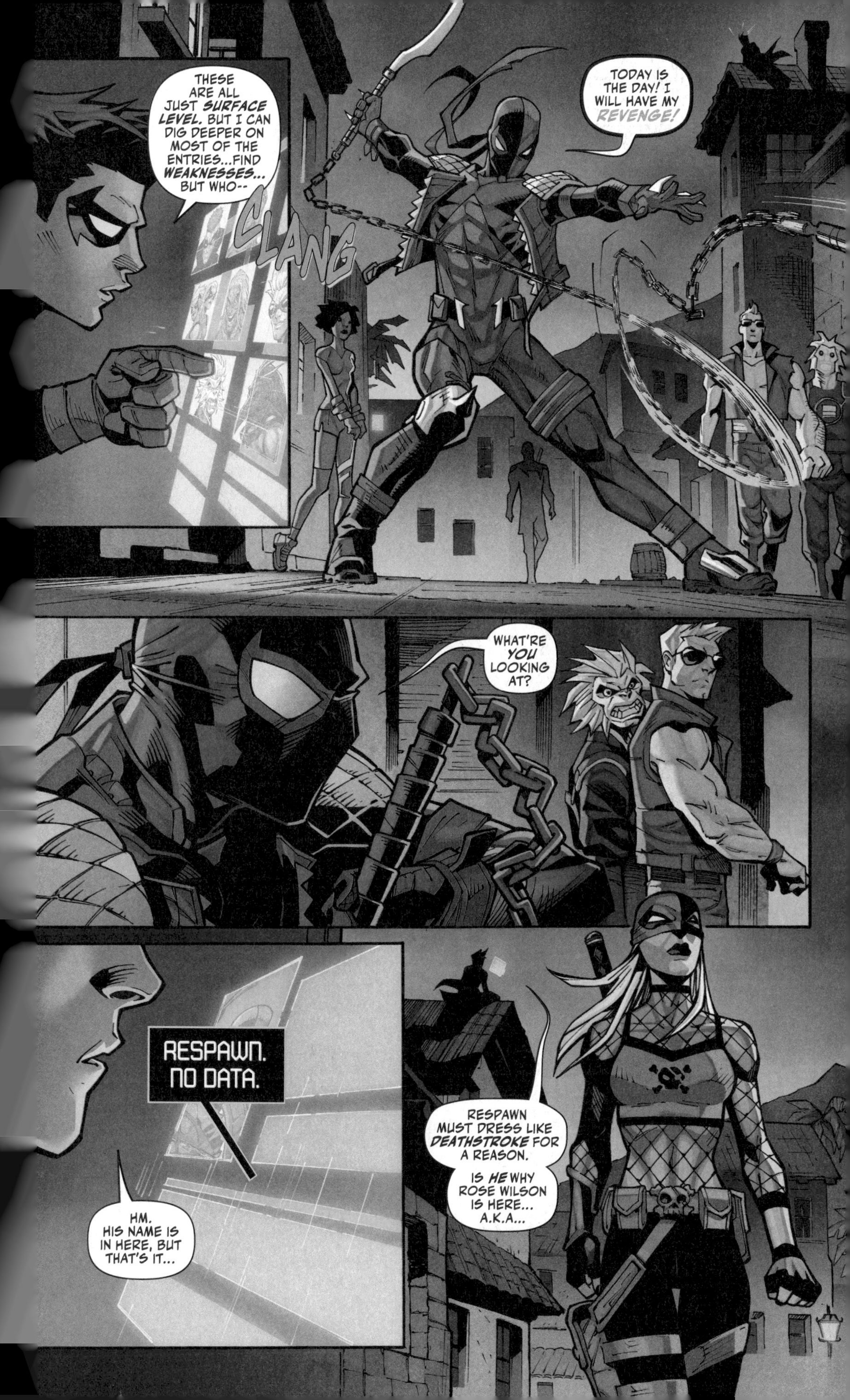

THESE ARE ALL JUST SURFACE LEVEL. BUT I CAN DIG DEEPER ON MOST OF THE ENTRIES...FIND WEAKNESSES... BUT WHO--
CLANG
TODAY IS THE DAY! I WILL HAVE MY REVENGE!
WHAT'RE YOU LOOKING AT?
RESPAWN. NO DATA.
HM. HIS NAME IS IN HERE, BUT THAT'S IT...
RESPAWN MUST DRESS LIKE DEATHSTROKE FOR A REASON.
IS HE WHY ROSE WILSON IS HERE... A.K.A...

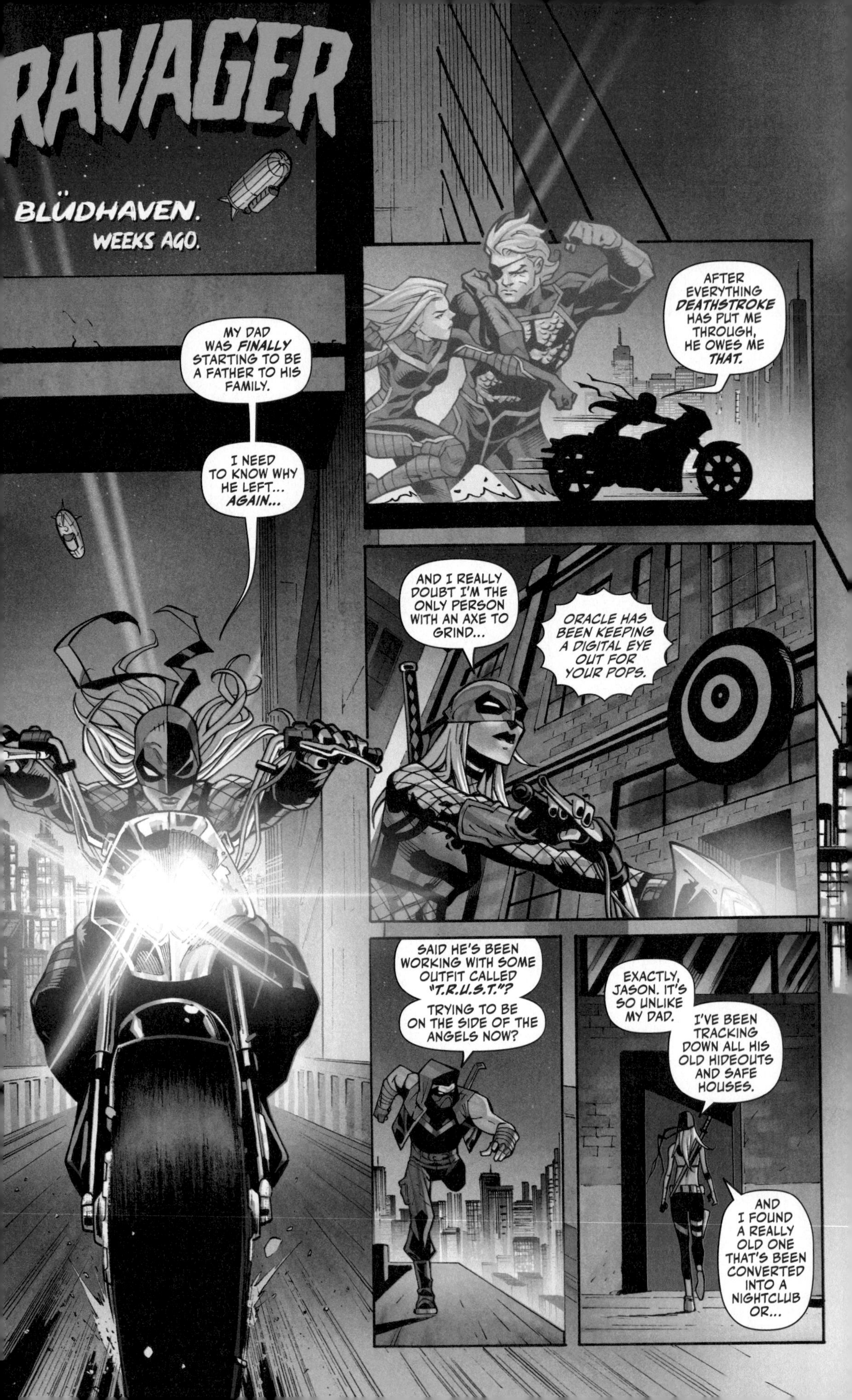
RAVAGER
BLÜDHAVEN.
WEEKS AGO.
MY DAD WAS FINALLY STARTING TO BE A FATHER TO HIS FAMILY.
I NEED TO KNOW WHY HE LEFT... AGAIN...
AFTER EVERYTHING DEATHSTROKE HAS PUT ME THROUGH, HE OWES ME THAT.
AND I REALLY DOUBT I'M THE ONLY PERSON WITH AN AXE TO GRIND...
ORACLE HAS BEEN KEEPING A DIGITAL EYE OUT FOR YOUR POPS.
SAID HE'S BEEN WORKING WITH SOME OUTFIT CALLED "T.R.U.S.T."?
TRYING TO BE ON THE SIDE OF THE ANGELS NOW?
EXACTLY, JASON. IT'S SO UNLIKE MY DAD.
I'VE BEEN TRACKING DOWN ALL HIS OLD HIDEOUTS AND SAFE HOUSES.
AND I FOUND A REALLY OLD ONE THAT'S BEEN CONVERTED INTO A NIGHTCLUB OR...

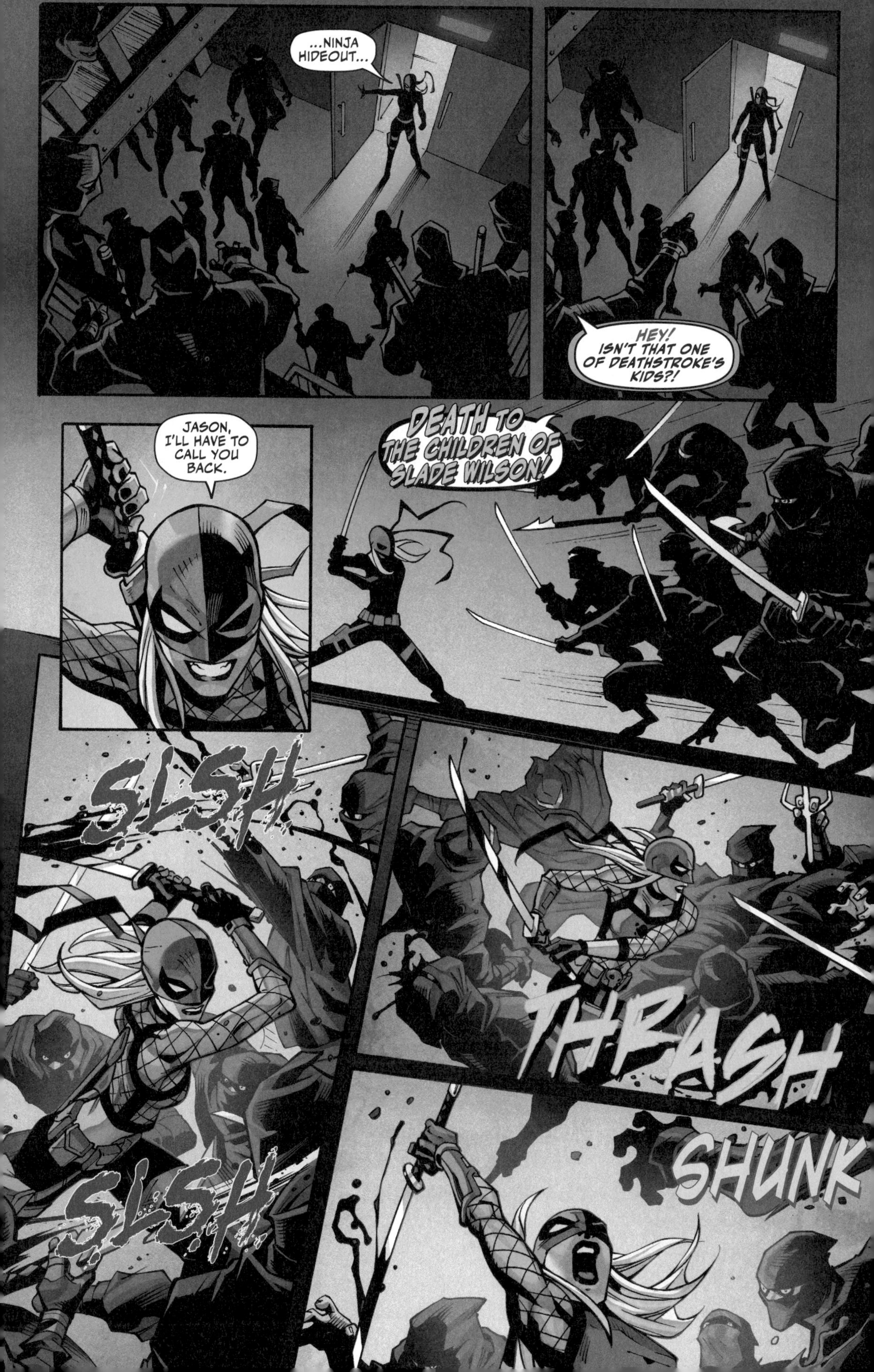
...NINJA HIDEOUT...
HEY! ISN'T THAT ONE OF DEATHSTROKE'S KIDS?!
JASON, I'LL HAVE TO CALL YOU BACK.
DEATH TO THE CHILDREN OF SLADE WILSON!
SLSH
SLSH
THRASH
SHUNK

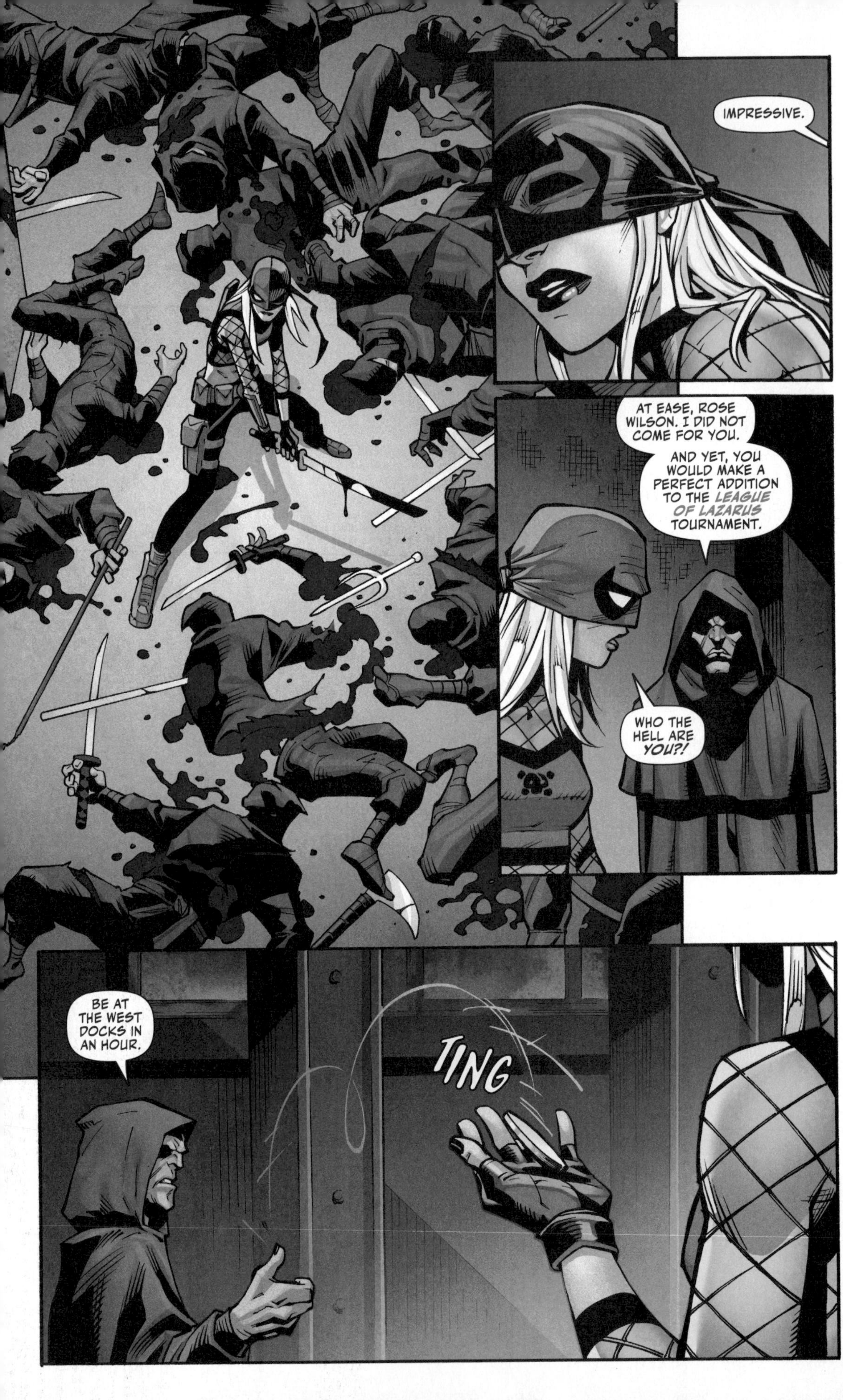
IMPRESSIVE.
AT EASE, ROSE WILSON. I DID NOT COME FOR YOU.
AND YET, YOU WOULD MAKE A PERFECT ADDITION TO THE LEAGUE OF LAZARUS TOURNAMENT.
WHO THE HELL ARE YOU?!
BE AT THE WEST DOCKS IN AN HOUR.
TING

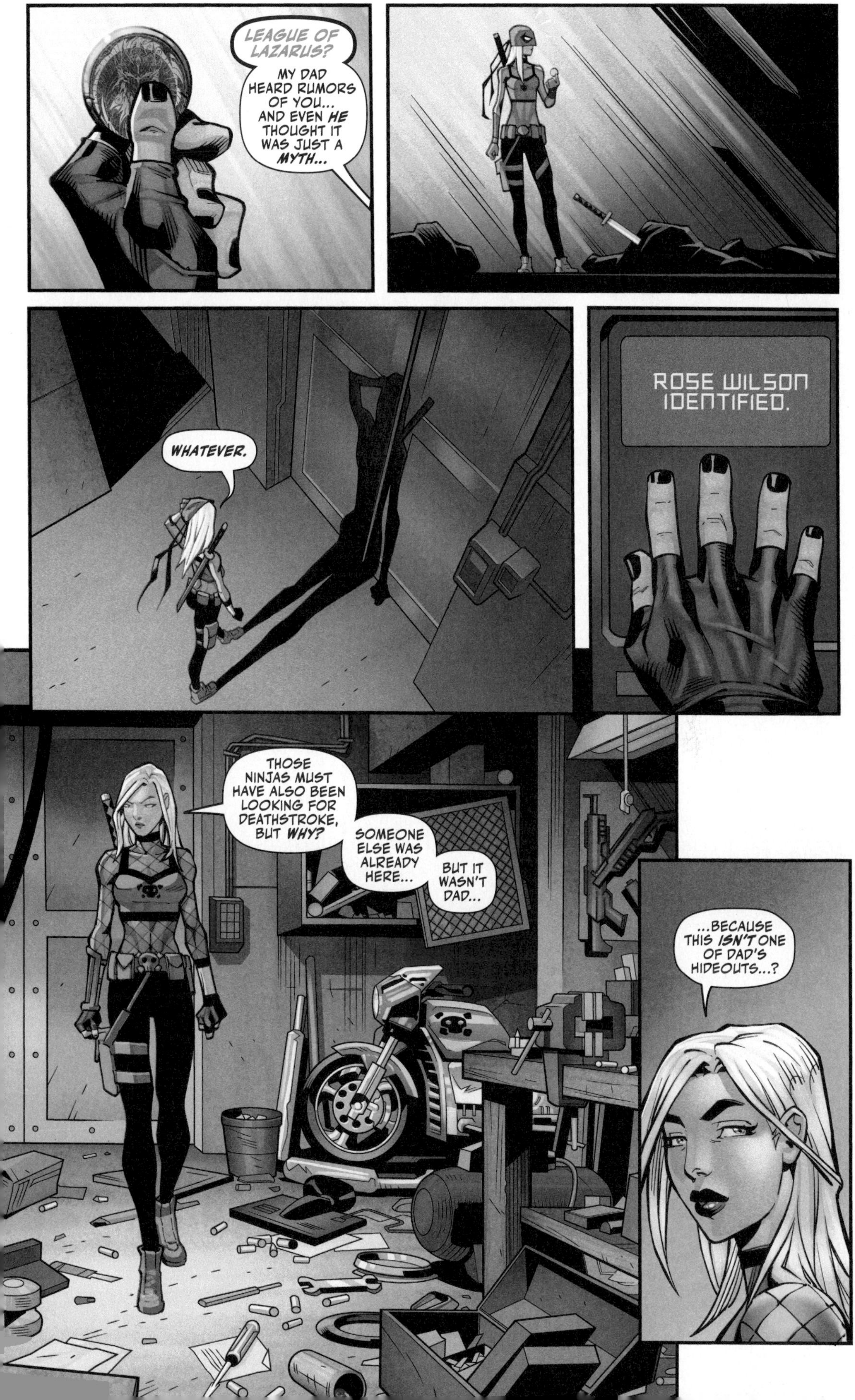
LEAGUE OF LAZARUS?
MY DAD HEARD RUMORS OF YOU... AND EVEN HE THOUGHT IT WAS JUST A MYTH...
WHATEVER.
ROSE WILSON IDENTIFIED.
THOSE NINJAS MUST HAVE ALSO BEEN LOOKING FOR DEATHSTROKE, BUT WHY?
SOMEONE ELSE WAS ALREADY HERE...
BUT IT WASN'T DAD...
...BECAUSE THIS ISN'T ONE OF DAD'S HIDEOUTS...?

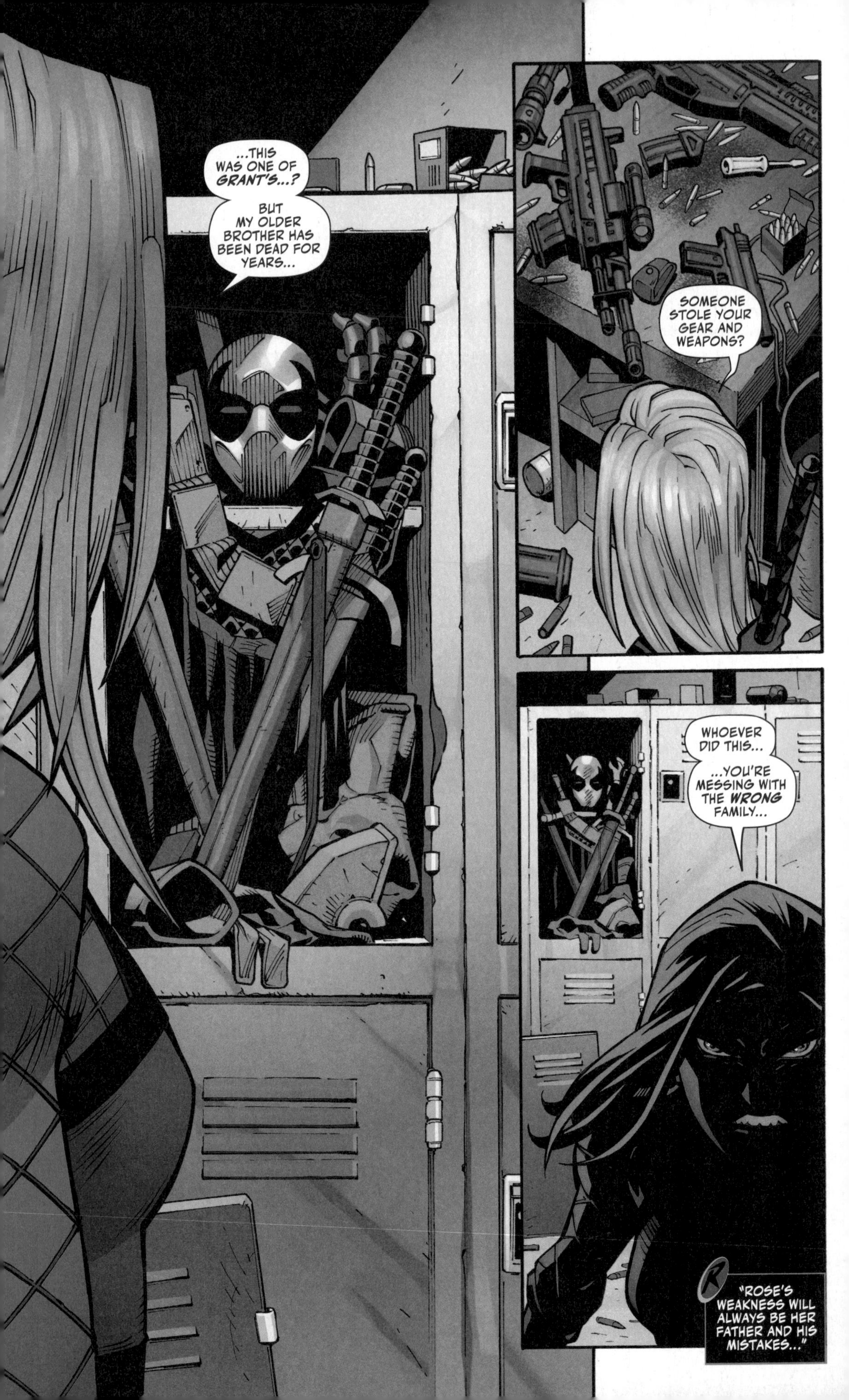
...THIS WAS ONE OF GRANT'S...?
BUT MY OLDER BROTHER HAS BEEN DEAD FOR YEARS...
SOMEONE STOLE YOUR GEAR AND WEAPONS?
WHOEVER DID THIS...
...YOU'RE MESSING WITH THE WRONG FAMILY...
"ROSE'S WEAKNESS WILL ALWAYS BE HER FATHER AND HIS MISTAKES..."

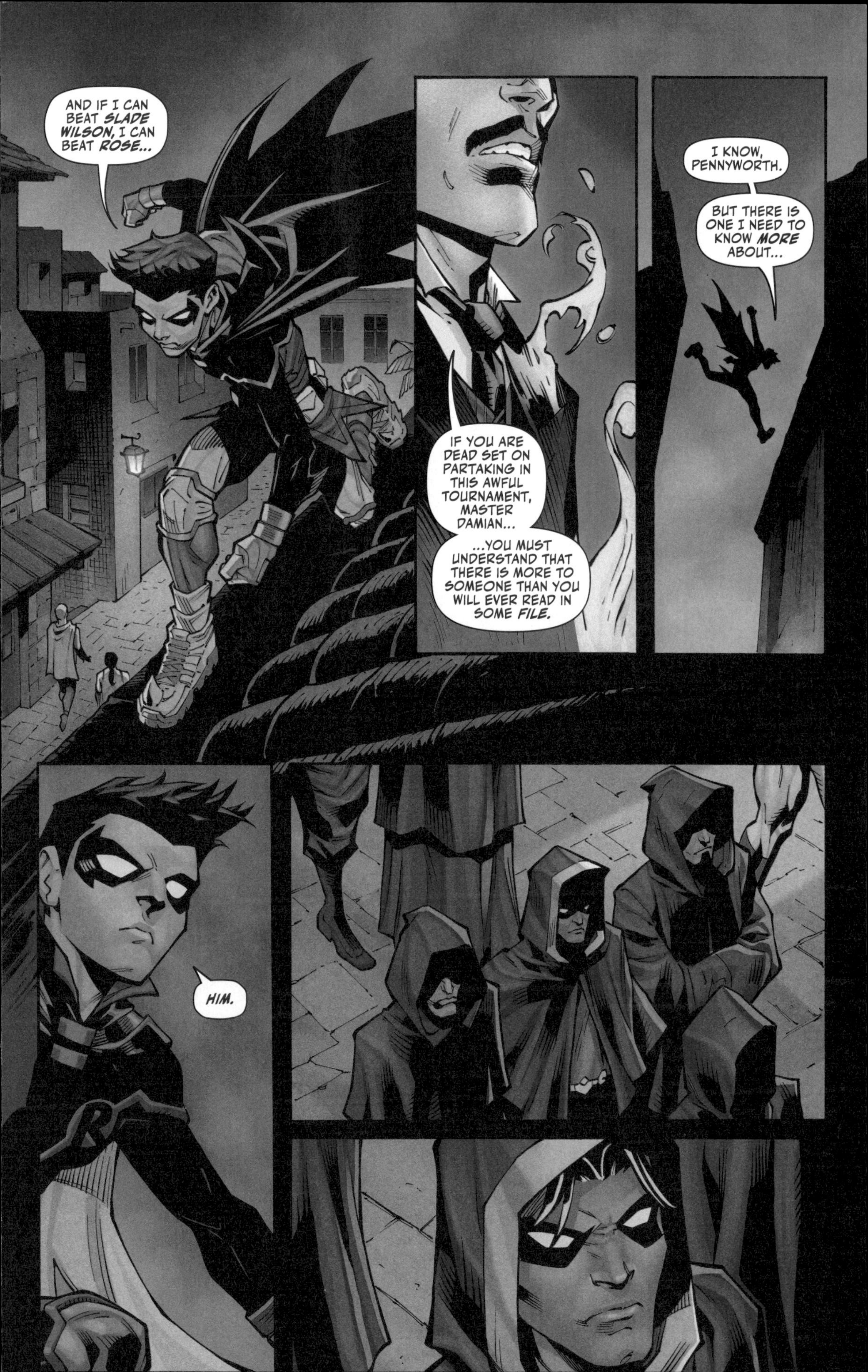
AND IF I CAN BEAT SLADE WILSON, I CAN BEAT ROSE...
IF YOU ARE DEAD SET ON PARTAKING IN THIS AWFUL TOURNAMENT, MASTER DAMIAN...
...YOU MUST UNDERSTAND THAT THERE IS MORE TO SOMEONE THAN YOU WILL EVER READ IN SOME FILE.
I KNOW, PENNYWORTH.
BUT THERE IS ONE I NEED TO KNOW MORE ABOUT...
HIM.

HAWKE

BACKGROUND: Son of Oliver Queen, a.k.a. Green Arrow, and Sandra Hawke. Raised in secret in an ashram. Current location unknown.

ABILITIES: Expert archer. Arguably the greatest hand-to-hand fighter in the world.

CONFIRMED KILLS: 1.

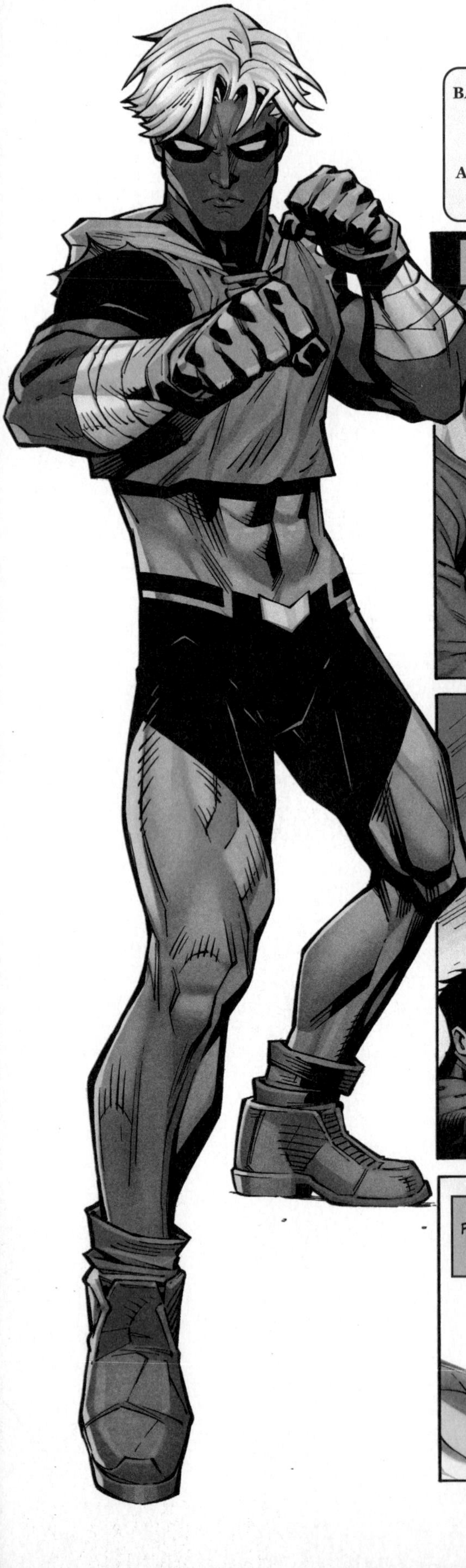

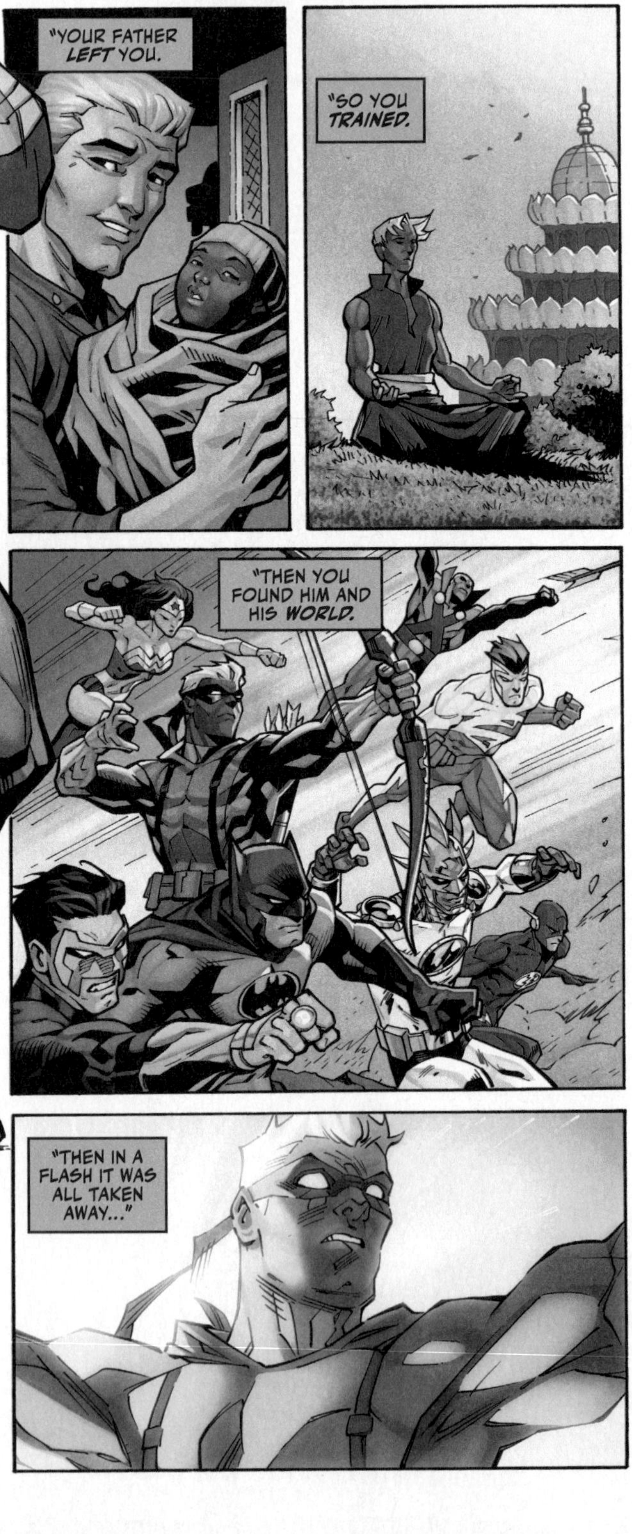
"YOUR FATHER LEFT YOU.
"SO YOU TRAINED.
"THEN YOU FOUND HIM AND HIS WORLD.
"THEN IN A FLASH IT WAS ALL TAKEN AWAY..."

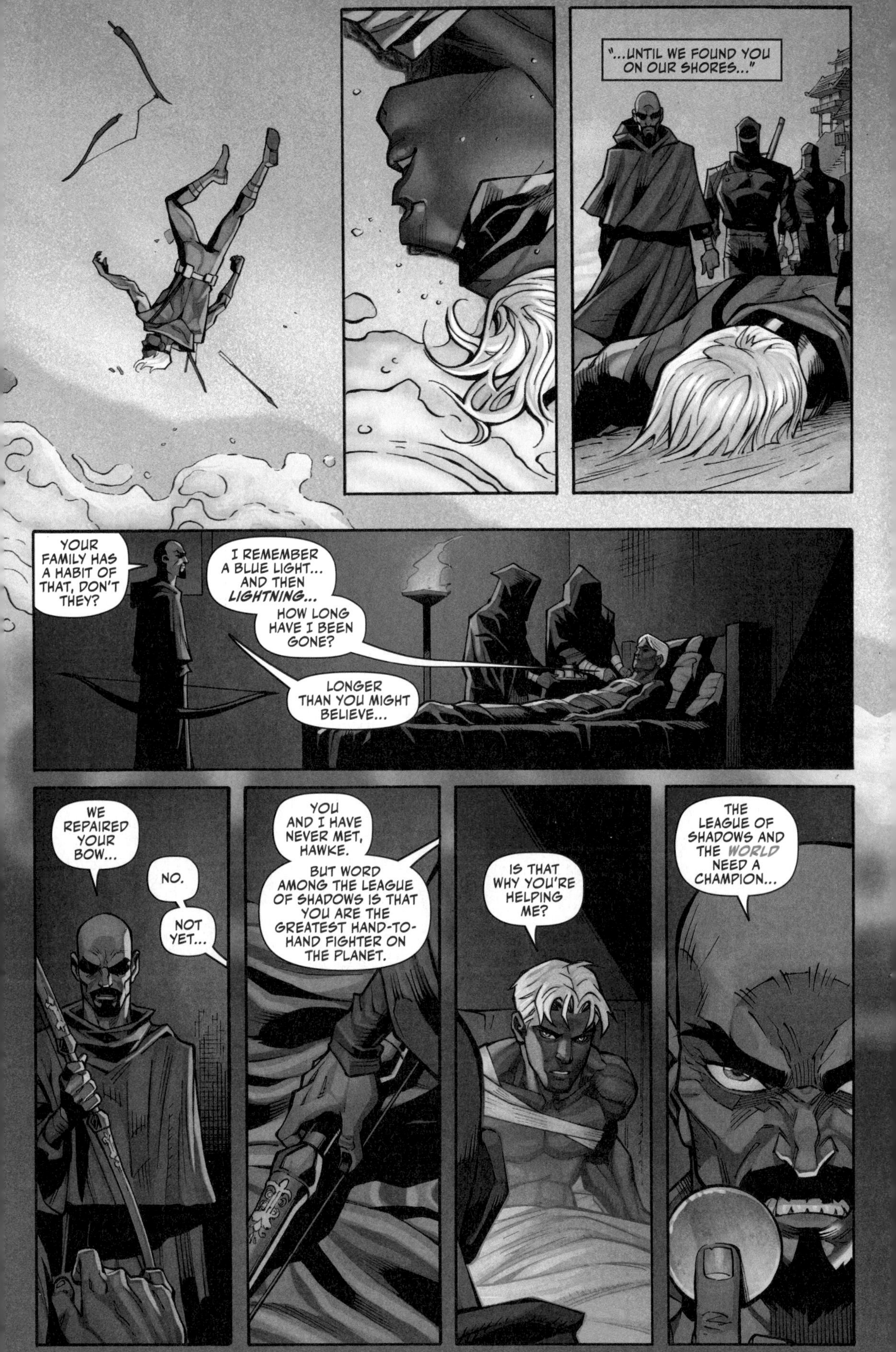
"...UNTIL WE FOUND YOU ON OUR SHORES..."
YOUR FAMILY HAS A HABIT OF THAT, DON'T THEY?
I REMEMBER A BLUE LIGHT... AND THEN LIGHTNING...
HOW LONG HAVE I BEEN GONE?
LONGER THAN YOU MIGHT BELIEVE...
WE REPAIRED YOUR BOW...
NO.
NOT YET...
YOU AND I HAVE NEVER MET, HAWKE.
BUT WORD AMONG THE LEAGUE OF SHADOWS IS THAT YOU ARE THE GREATEST HAND-TO-HAND FIGHTER ON THE PLANET.
IS THAT WHY YOU'RE HELPING ME?
THE LEAGUE OF SHADOWS AND THE WORLD NEED A CHAMPION...

HM.
HOW DID MY FATHER KNOW ALL THIS ABOUT THEM?
HE MUST HAVE EMPLOYED SPY TACTICS. USED HIS RESOURCES AND CONNECTIONS...
I CAN USE THAT TO WIN. I'D HAVE AN ADVANTAGE...
...WITH MY FATHER'S HELP...

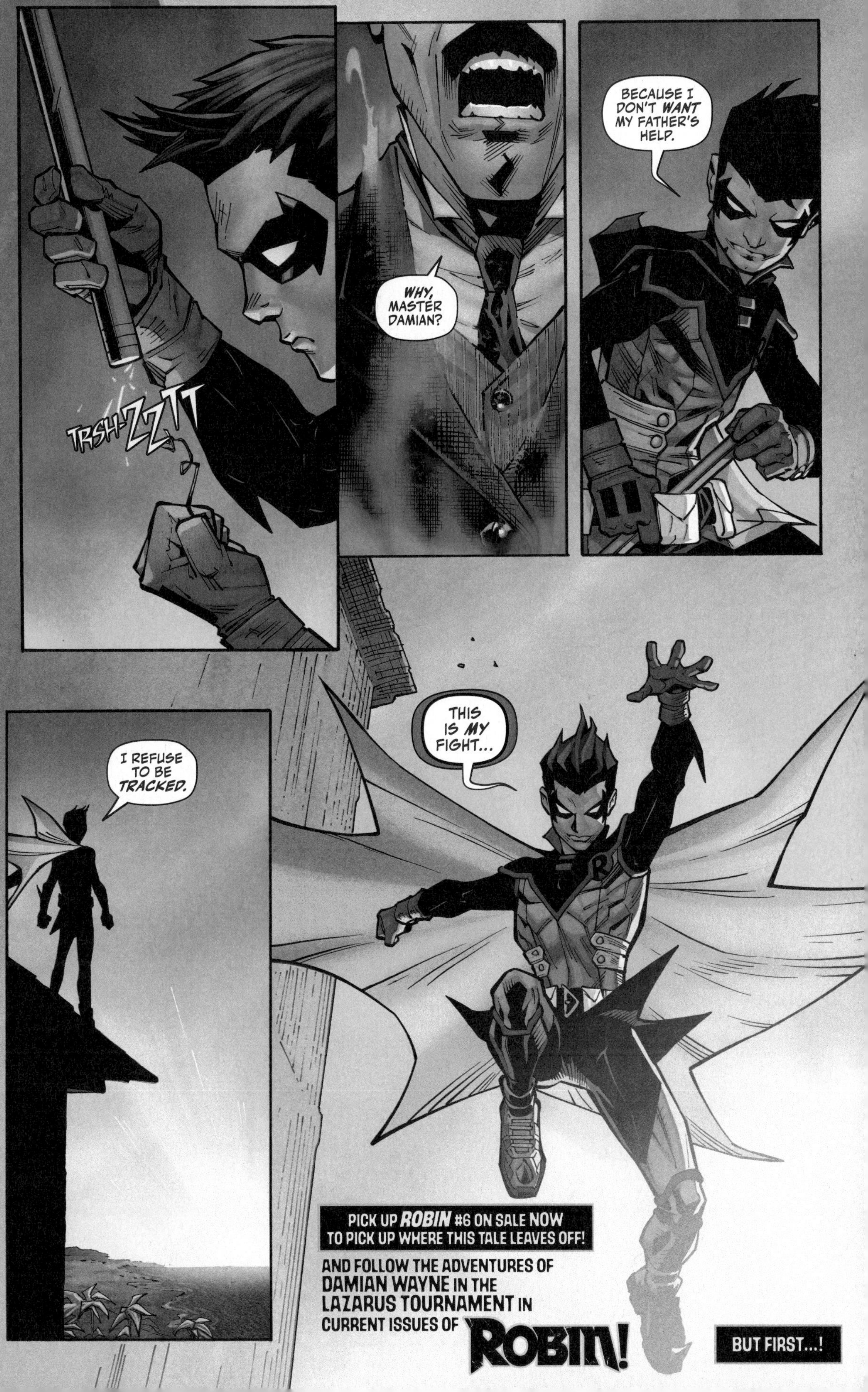

TRSH-ZZTT
WHY, MASTER DAMIAN?
BECAUSE I DON'T WANT MY FATHER'S HELP.
I REFUSE TO BE TRACKED.
THIS IS MY FIGHT...
PICK UP ROBIN #6 ON SALE NOW TO PICK UP WHERE THIS TALE LEAVES OFF!
AND FOLLOW THE ADVENTURES OF DAMIAN WAYNE IN THE LAZARUS TOURNAMENT IN CURRENT ISSUES OF ROBIN!
BUT FIRST...!

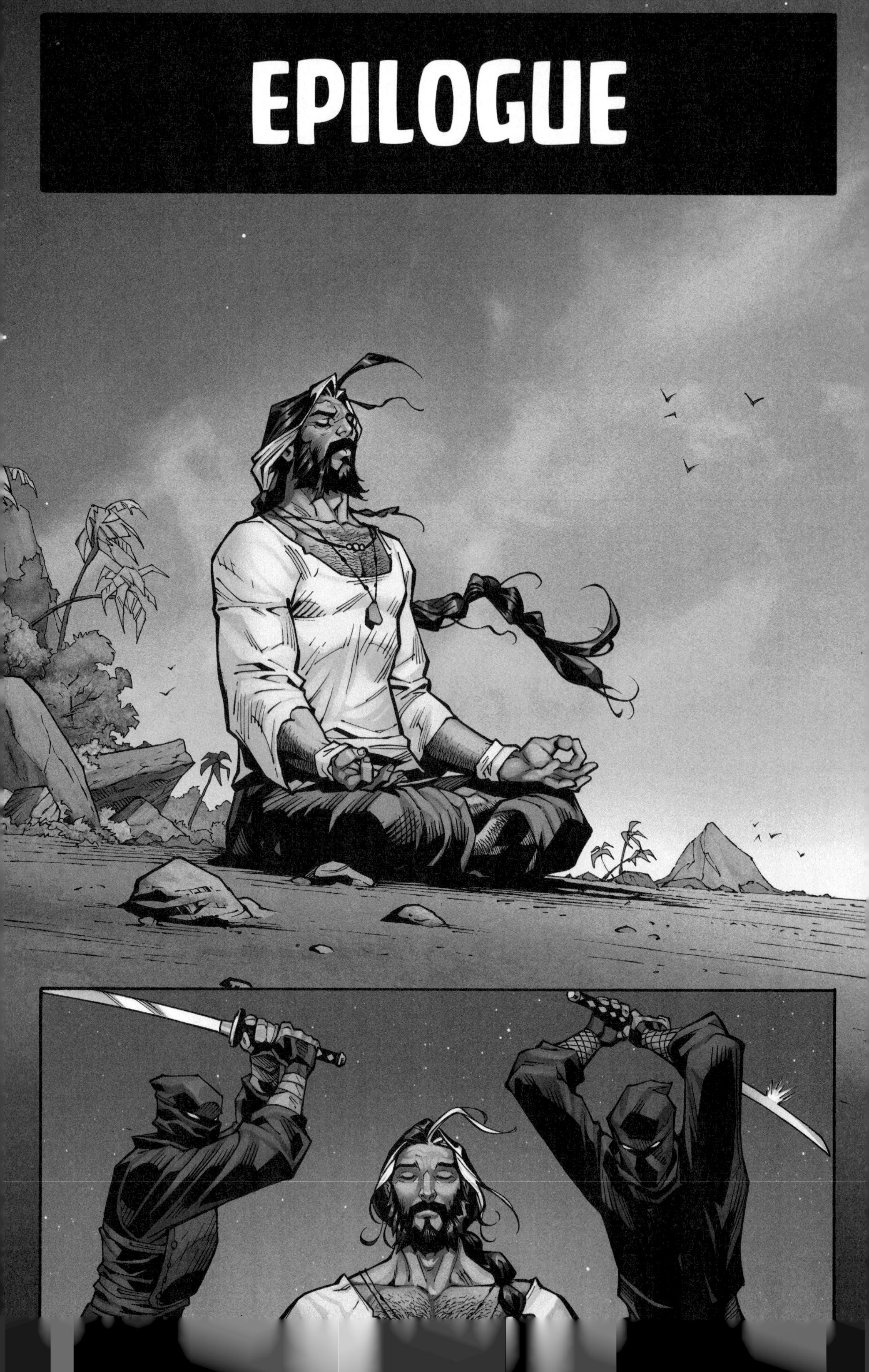
EPILOGUE

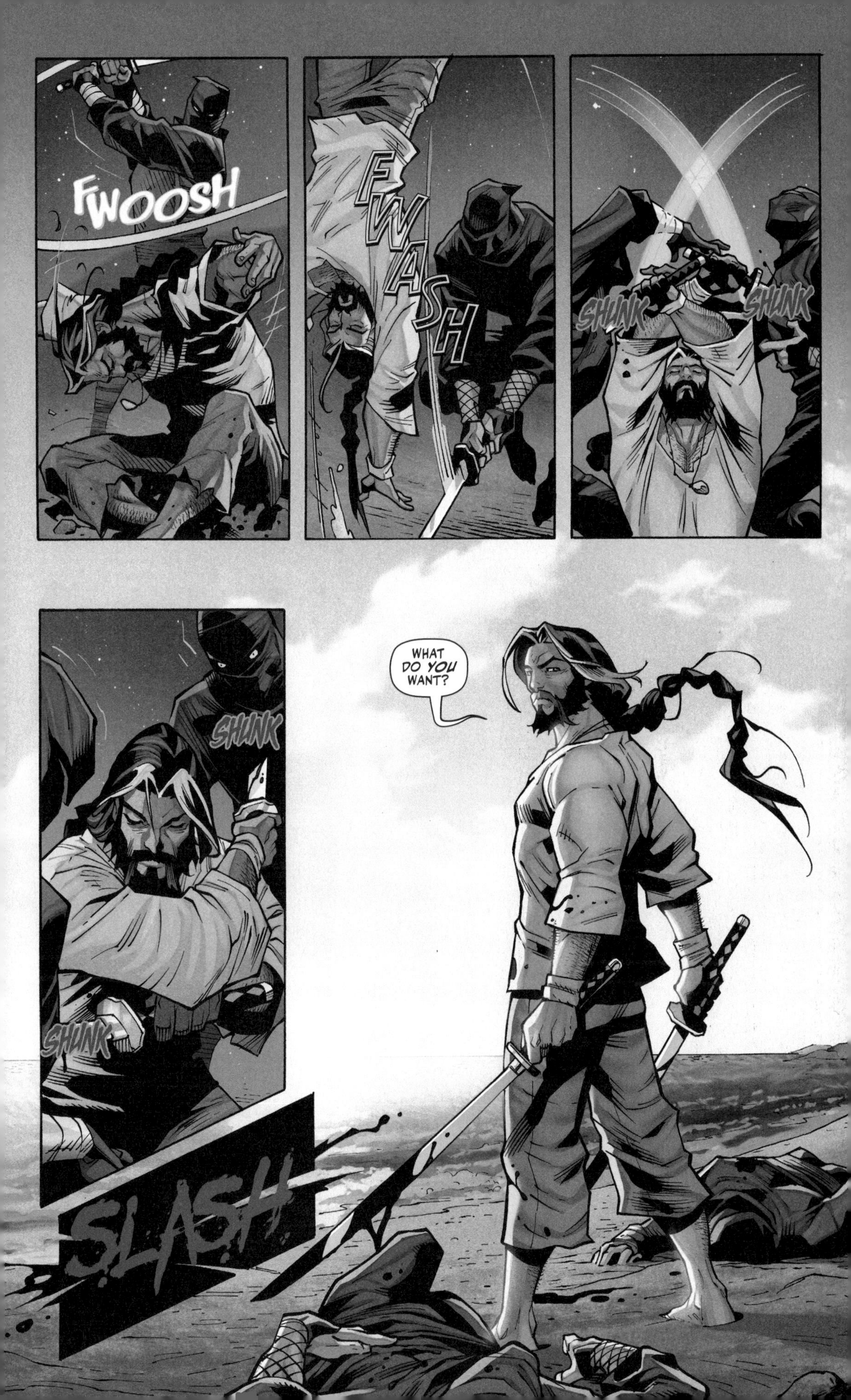
FWOOSH
FWASH
SHUNK
SHUNK
SHUNK
SHUNK
SLASH
WHAT DO YOU WANT?

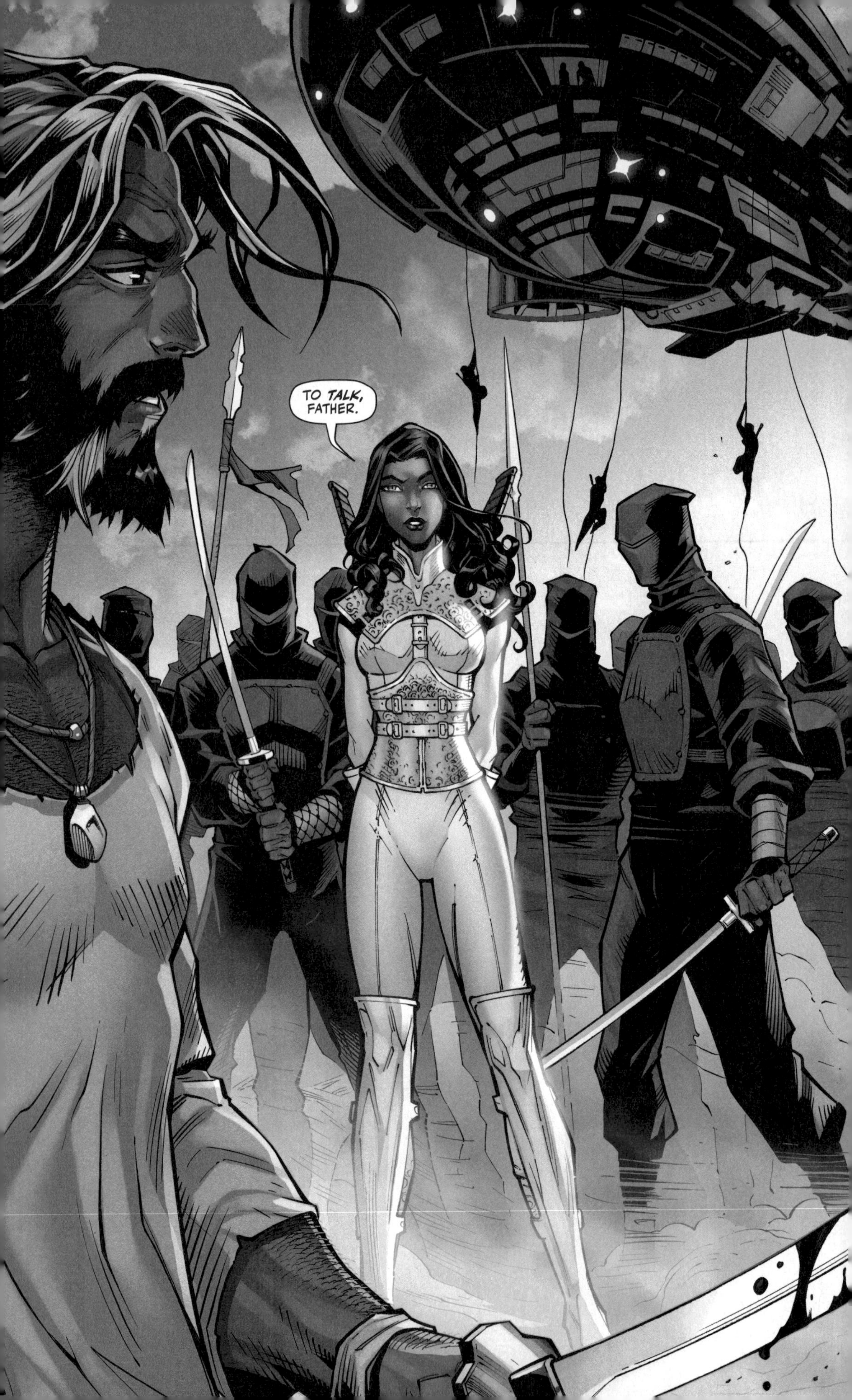
TO *TALK*, FATHER.

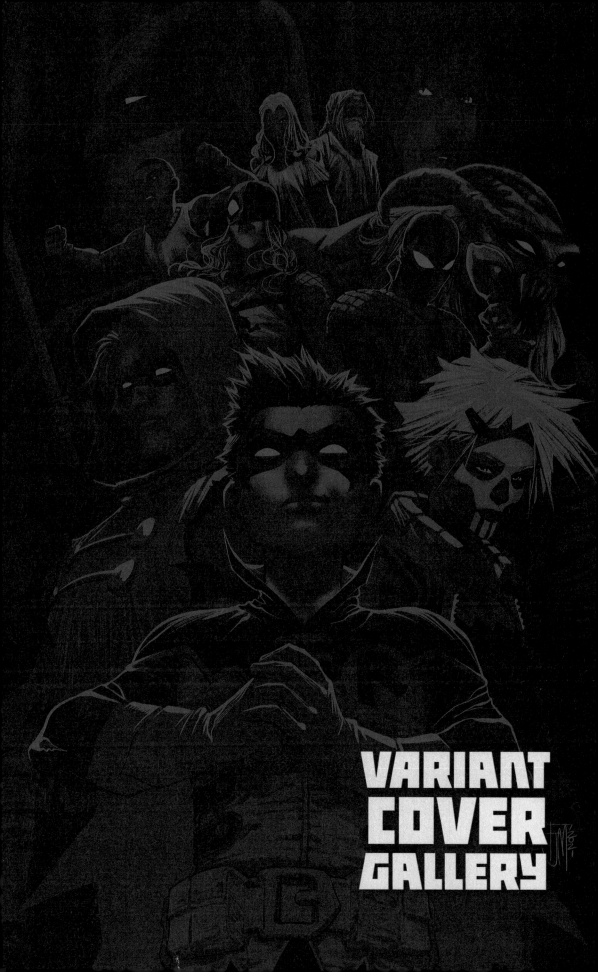

VARIANT
COVER
GALLERY

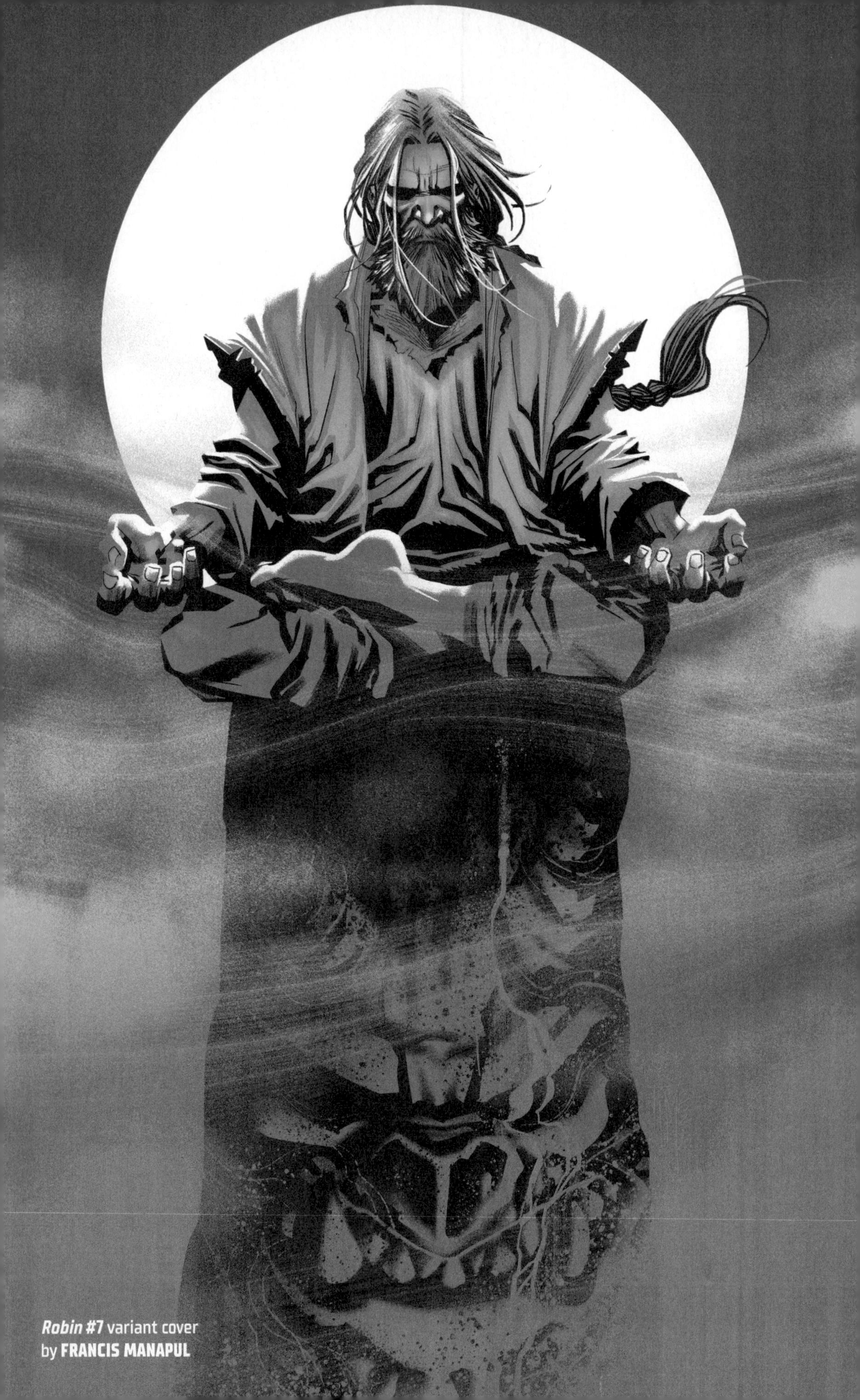

***Robin* #7** variant cover
by **FRANCIS MANAPUL**

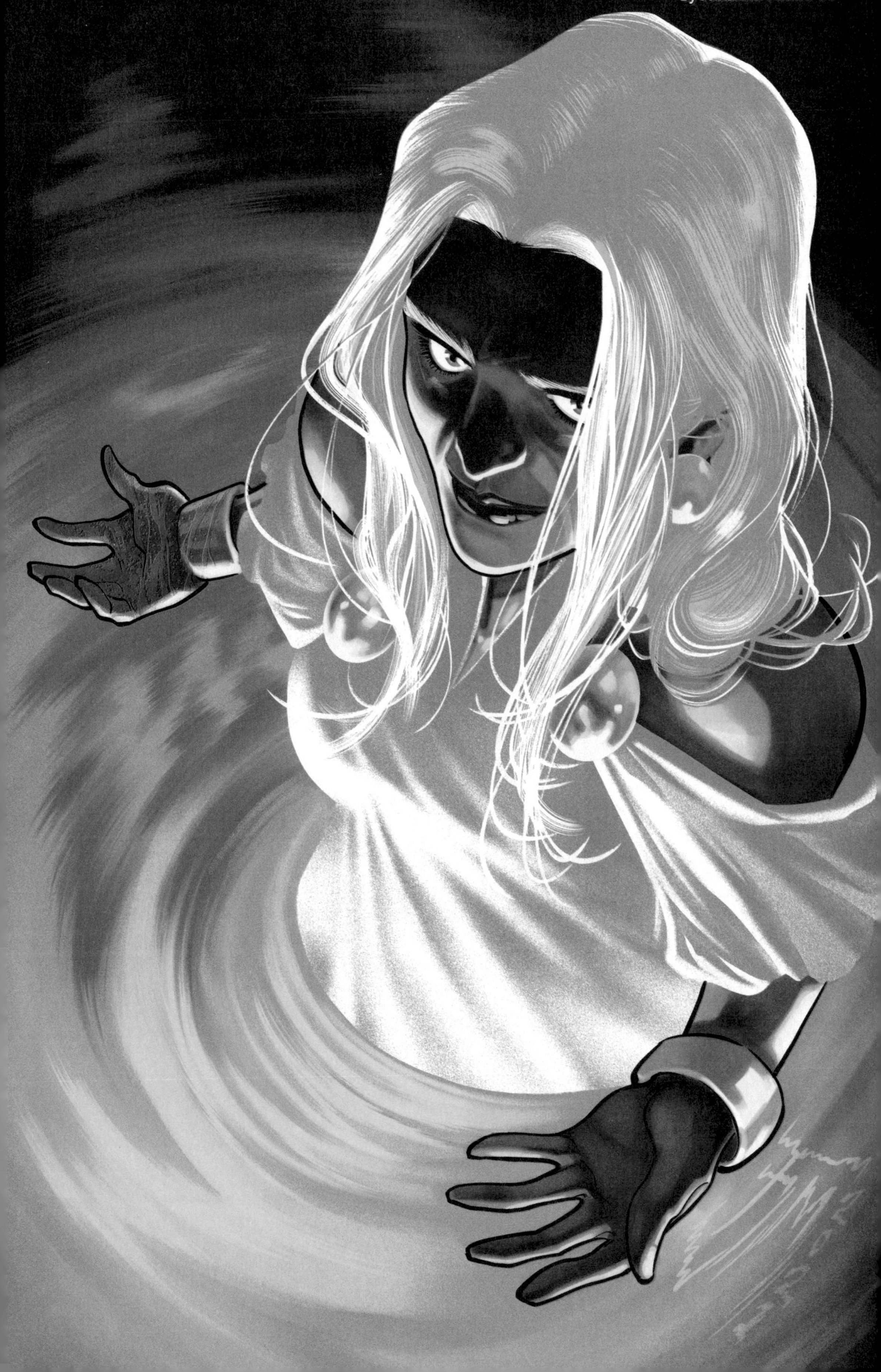

Robin **#8** variant cover
by **FRANCIS MANAPUL**

Robin **#9** variant cover
by **FRANCIS MANAPUL**

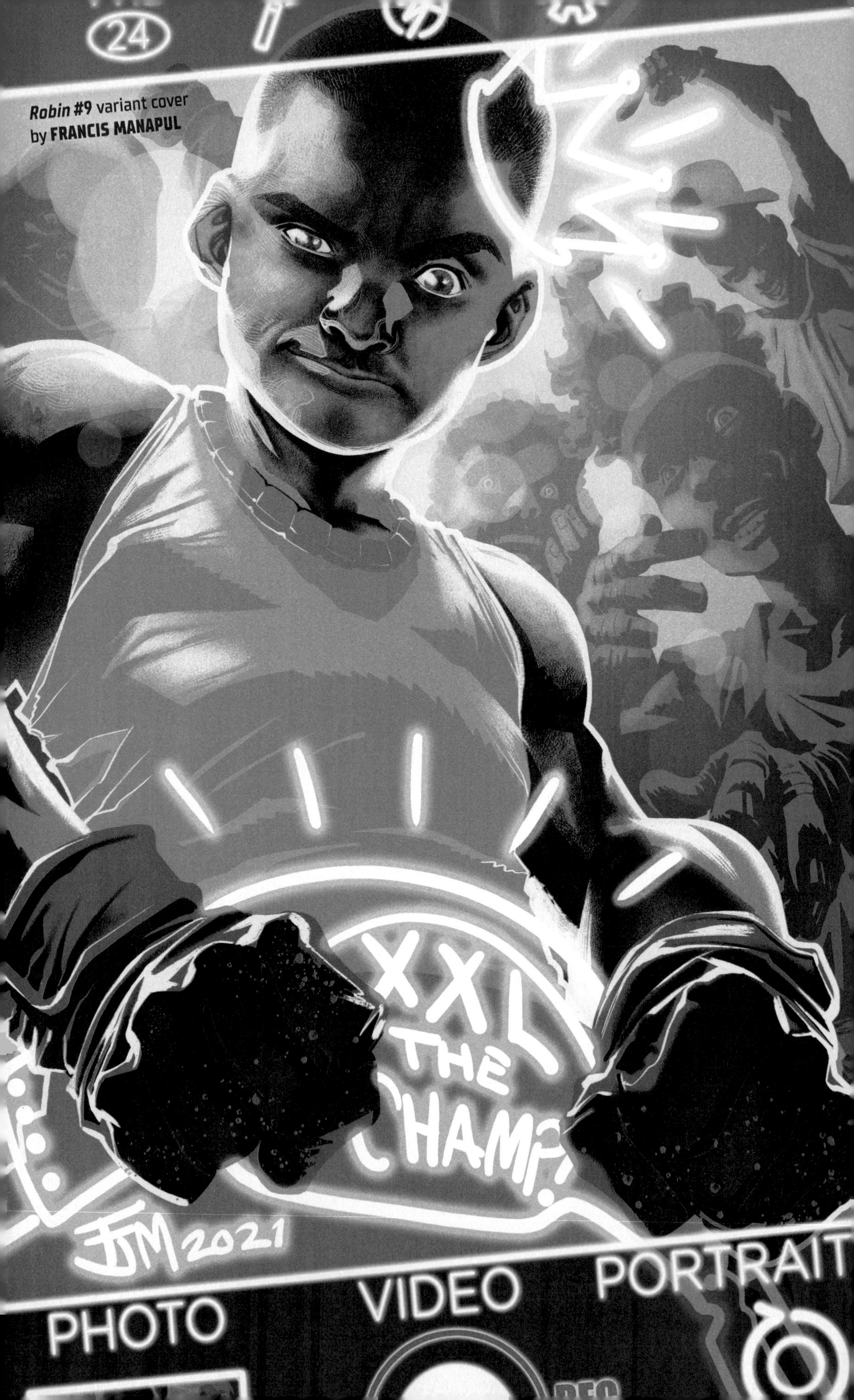
24
XXL
THE
CHAMP
FJM 2021
PHOTO
VIDEO
PORTRAIT

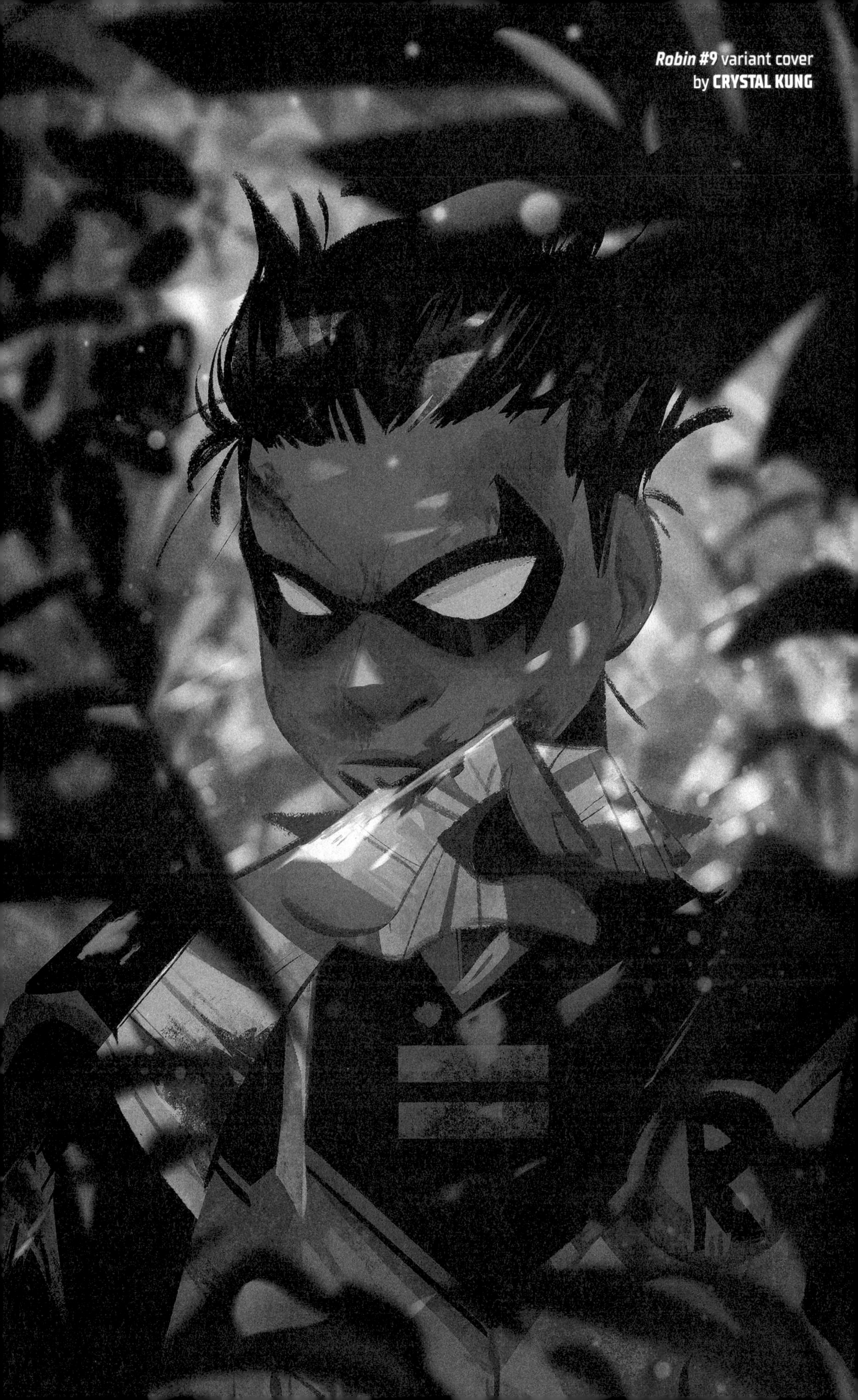

Robin **#9** variant cover
by **CRYSTAL KUNG**

Robin #10 variant cover
by **FRANCIS MANAPUL**

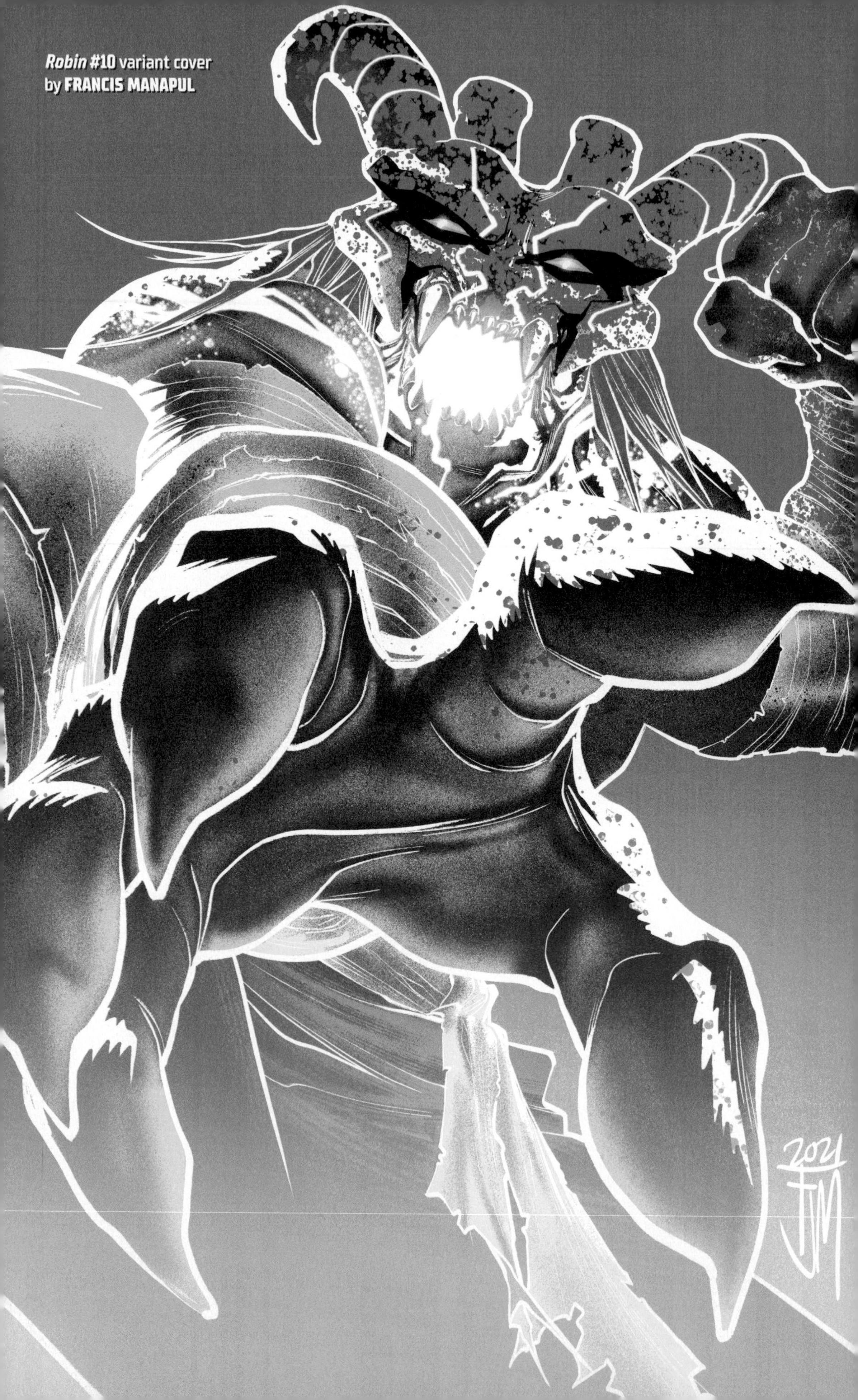
2021

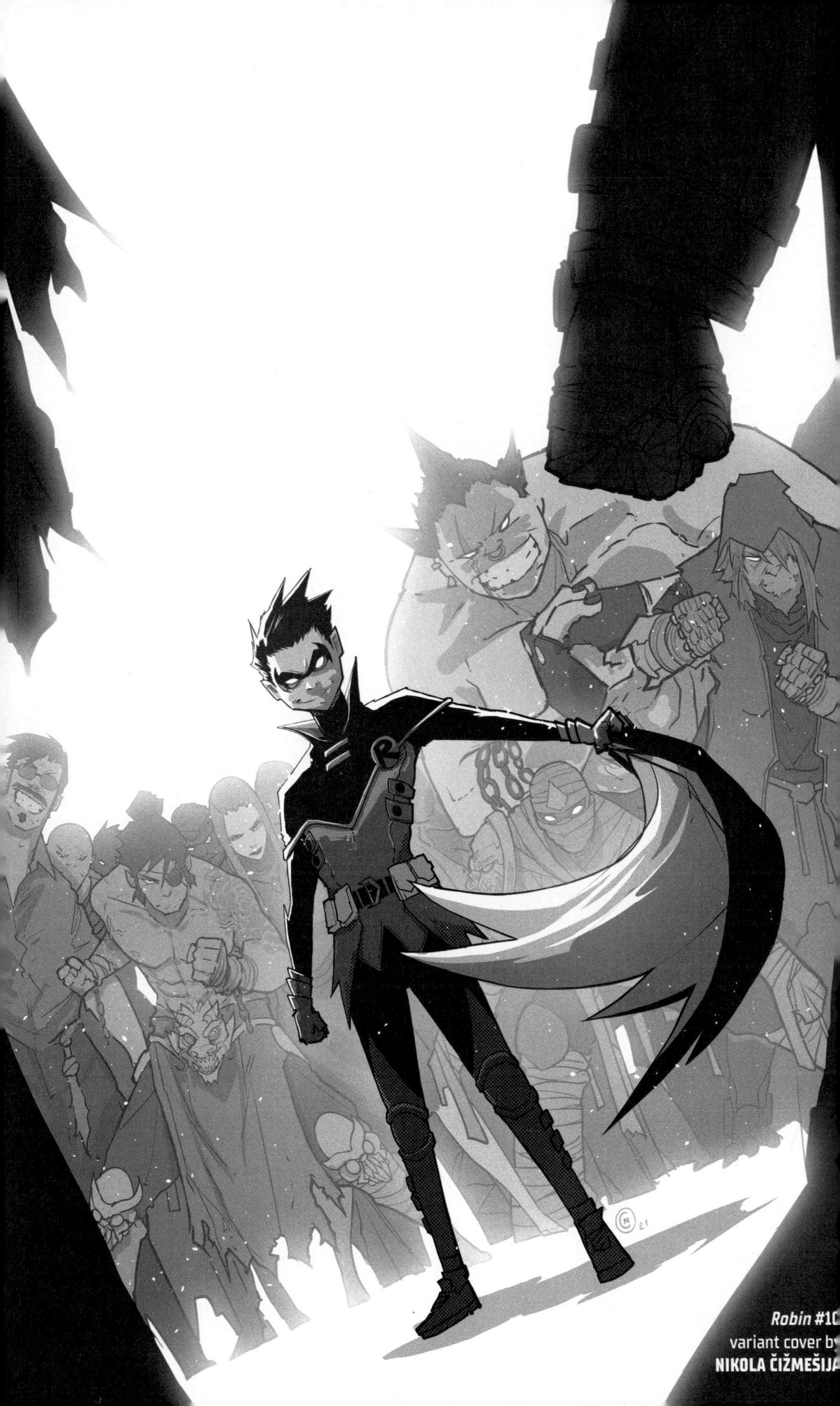

Robin #10
variant cover by
NIKOLA ČIŽMEŠIJA

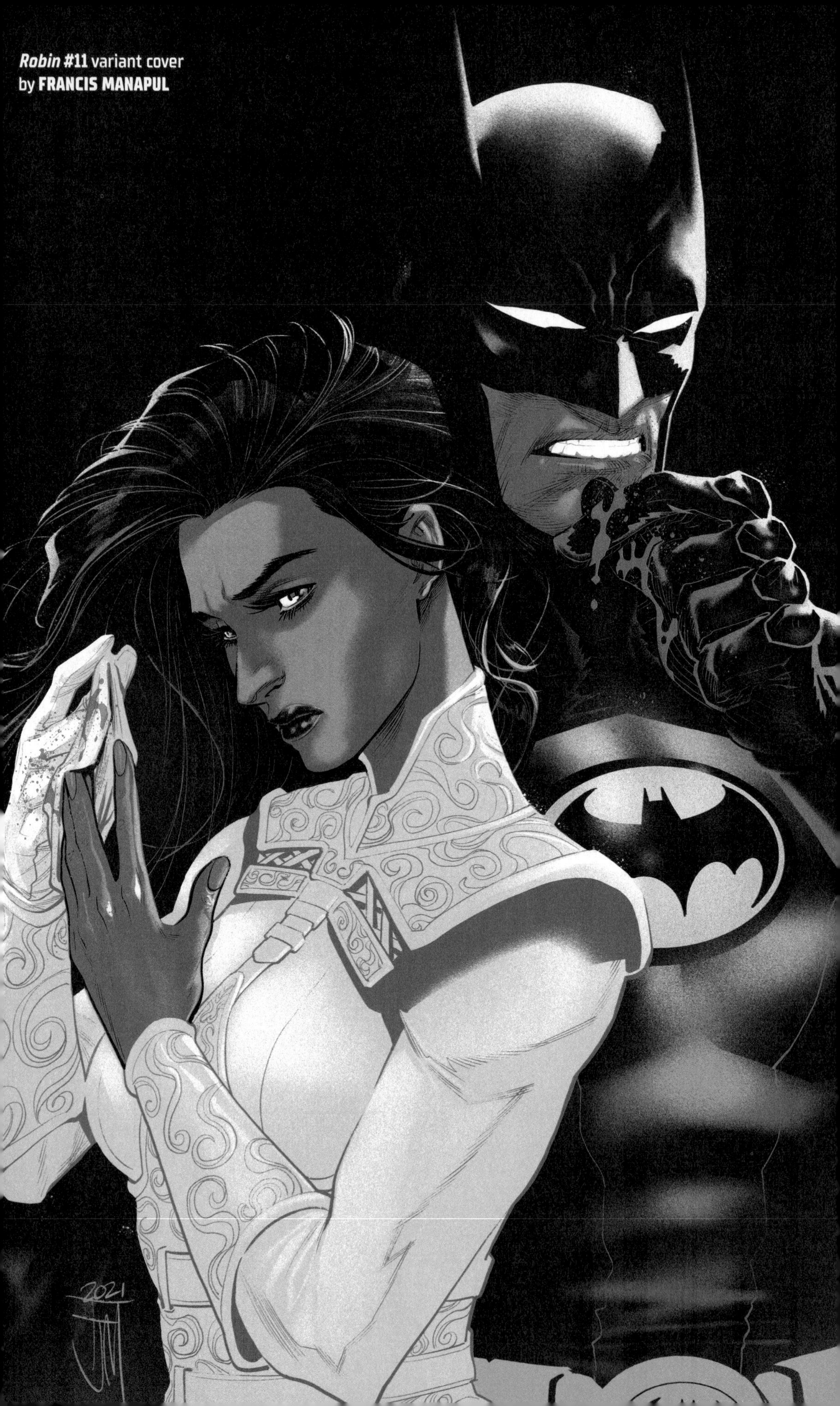

Robin **#11** variant cover
by **FRANCIS MANAPUL**

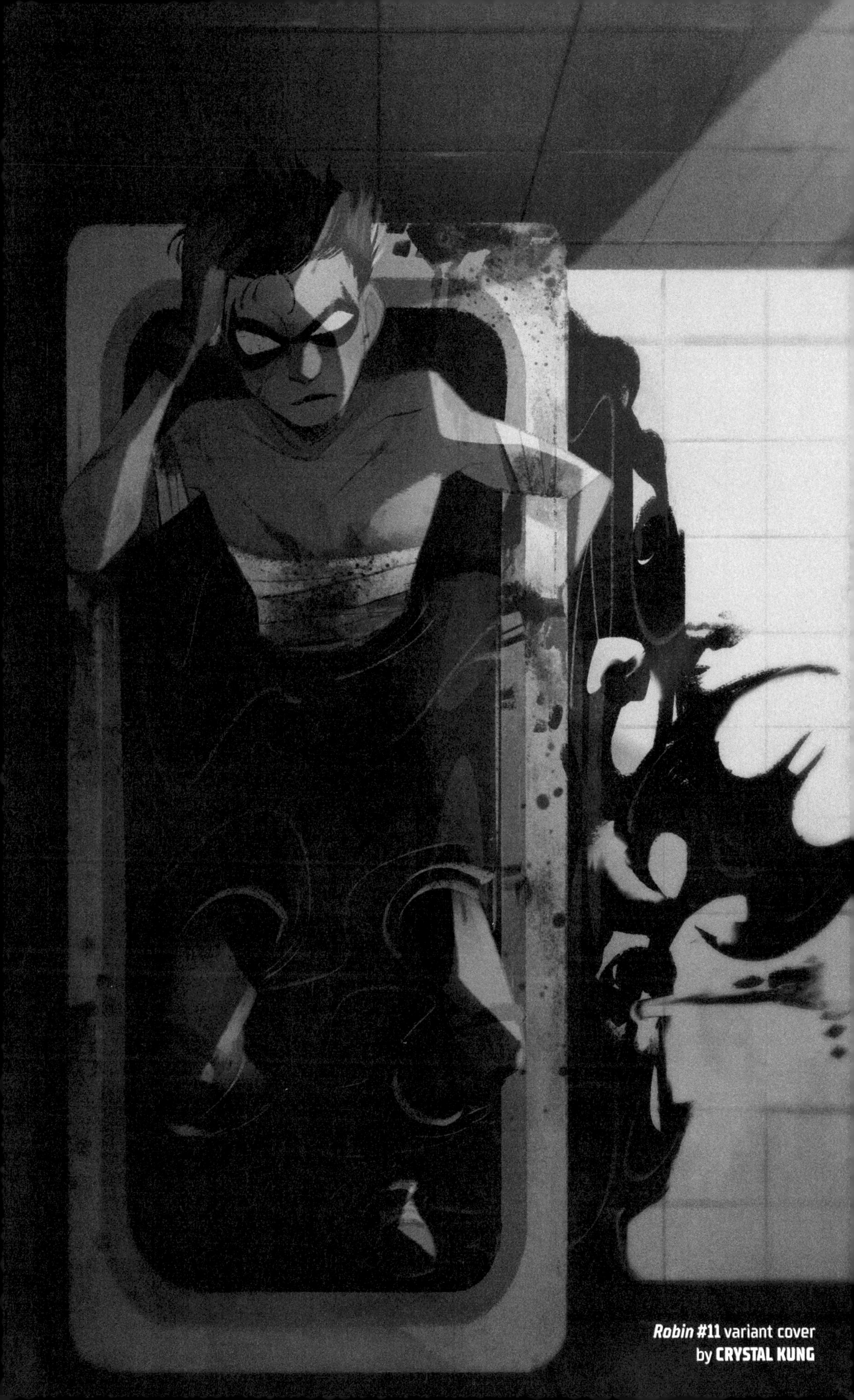

Robin #11 variant cover
by **CRYSTAL KUNG**

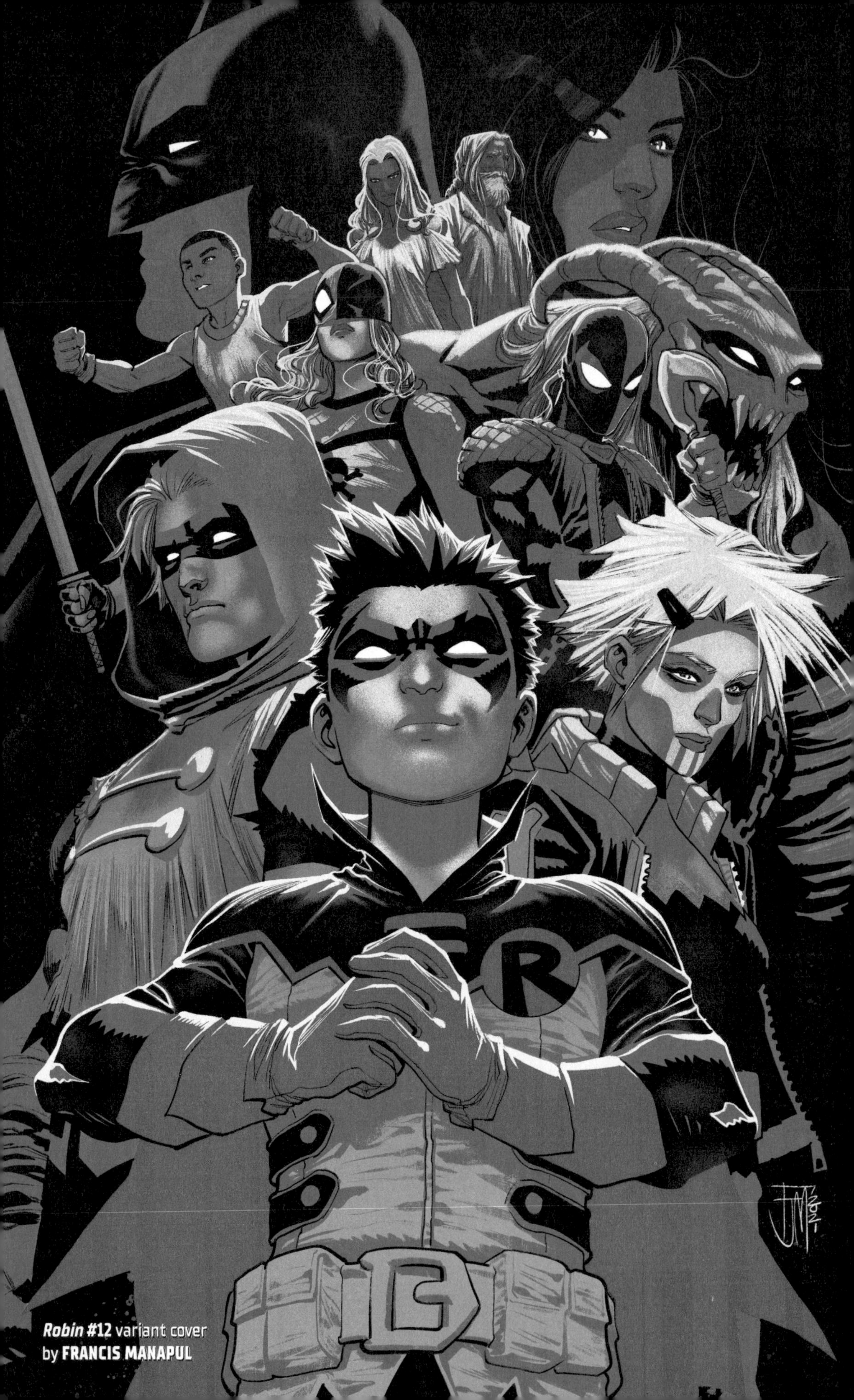

Robin **#12** variant cover
by **FRANCIS MANAPUL**

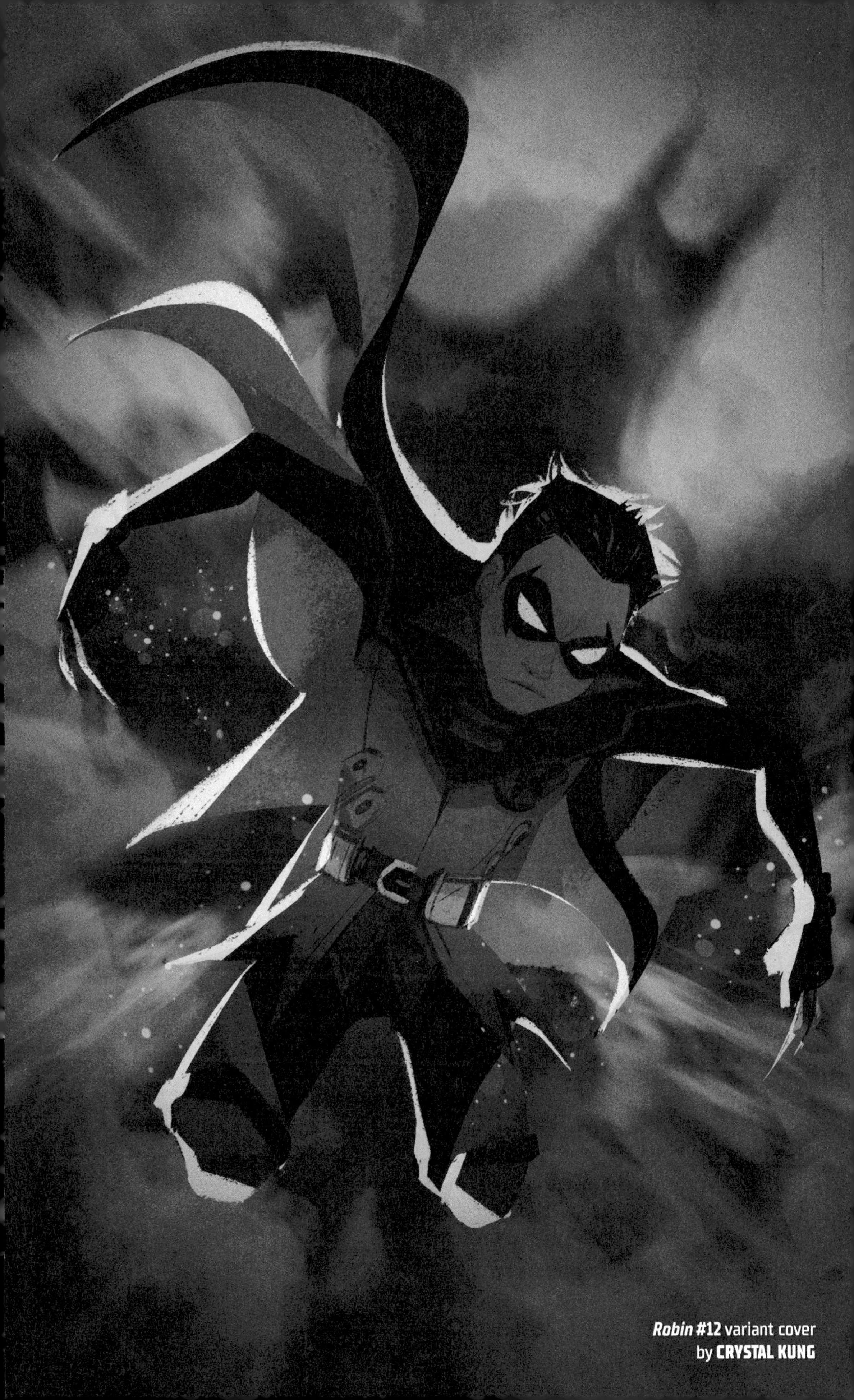

Robin **#12** variant cover
by **CRYSTAL KUNG**

Robin 2021 Annual **#1** variant cover
by **CRYSTAL KUNG**

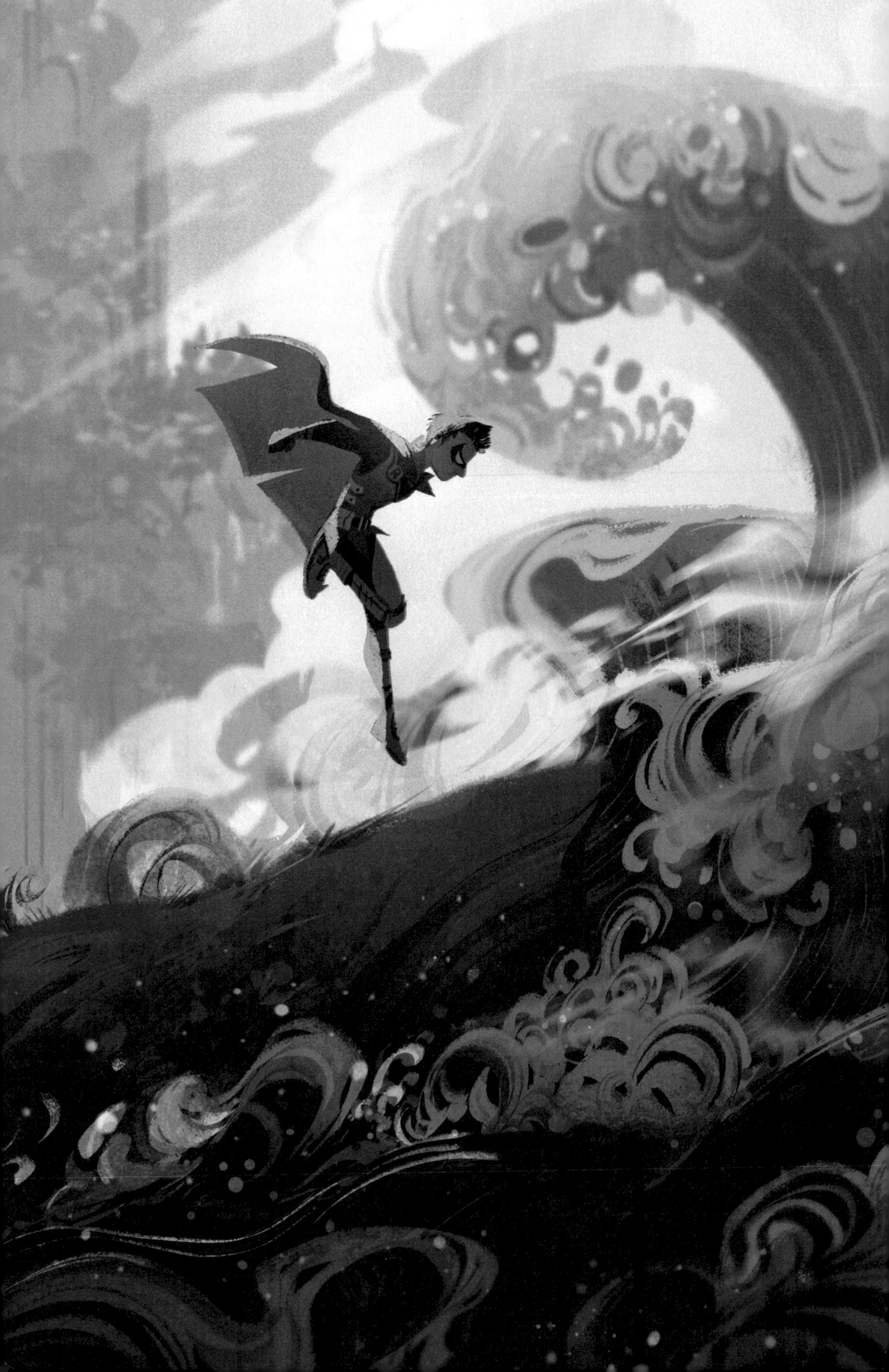

"Brilliantly executed."
–IGN

"Morrison and Quitely have the magic touch that makes any book they col-laborate on stand out from the rest."
–MTV's Splash Page

GRANT MORRISON
with FRANK QUITELY & PHILIP TAN

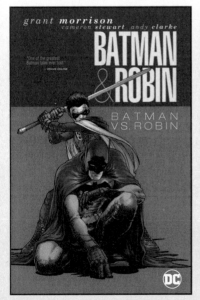

VOL. 2: BATMAN VS. ROBIN

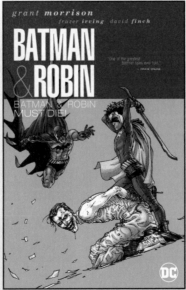

VOL. 3: BATMAN & ROBIN MUST DIE!

"Thrilling and invigorating... Gotham City that has never looked this good, felt this strange, or been this deadly."
–Comic Book Resources

"Rock solid."
– IGN

"This is the kind of Batman story I like to read: an actual mystery with an emotional hook."
– THE ONION / AV CLUB

THE NEW YORK TIMES BESTSELLER
THE NEW 52!
BATMAN AND ROBIN
VOLUME 1
BORN TO KILL
"PETER J. TOMASI AND PATRICK GLEASON ARE KNOCKING IT OUT ISSUE AFTER ISSUE."
– WIRED.COM
PETER J. TOMASI PATRICK GLEASON MICK GRAY

BATMAN & ROBIN

VOL. 1: BORN TO KILL

PETER J. TOMASI
with PATRICK GLEASON

THE NEW YORK TIMES BESTSELLER
THE NEW 52!
BATMAN AND ROBIN
VOLUME 2
PEARL
PETER J. TOMASI PATRICK GLEASON MICK GRAY

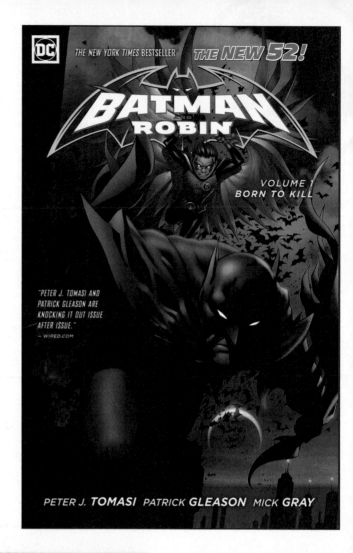

BATMAN & ROBIN VOL. 2: PEARL

THE NEW 52!
BATMAN AND ROBIN
VOLUME 3: DEATH OF THE FAMILY
PETER J. TOMASI PATRICK GLEASON MICK GRAY

BATMAN & ROBIN VOL. 3: DEATH OF THE FAMILY

READ THE ENTIRE EPIC!

BATMAN & ROBIN VOL. 4: REQUIEM FOR DAMIAN

BATMAN & ROBIN VOL. 5: THE BIG BURN

BATMAN & ROBIN VOL. 6: THE HUNT FOR ROBIN

BATMAN & ROBIN VOL. 7: ROBIN RISES

Get more DC graphic novels wherever comics and books are sold!

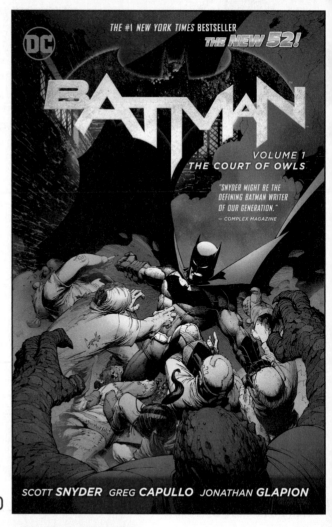
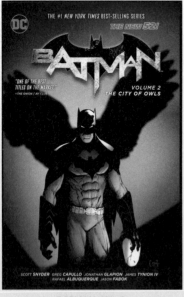
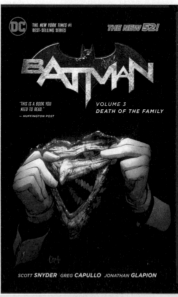

"An incredible story."
–NERDIST

"A clean, simple gateway into the Batman franchise."
–IGN

"King sets a new stage and tone for Batman and Gotham."
–POPMATTERS

DC UNIVERSE REBIRTH
BATMAN
FINCH 2016
VOL.1 I AM GOTHAM
TOM KING • DAVID FINCH

BATMAN
VOL. 1: I AM GOTHAM
TOM KING
DAVID FINCH

DC UNIVERSE REBIRTH
BATMAN
"The creative fusion between Tom King and Mikel Janin is a joy to behold." IGN
VOL.2 I AM SUICIDE
TOM KING • MIKEL JANÍN • MITCH GERADS • JUNE CHUNG

BATMAN: VOL. 2
I AM SUICIDE

DC UNIVERSE REBIRTH
BATMAN
"An incredible story." NERDIST
VOL.3 I AM BANE
TOM KING • DAVID FINCH • DANNY MIKI • JORDIE BELLAIRE

BATMAN: VOL. 3:
I AM BANE

READ THEM ALL!

BATMAN VOL. 4: THE WAR OF JOKES AND RIDDLES

BATMAN VOL. 5: RULES OF ENGAGEMENT

BATMAN VOL. 6: BRIDE OR BURGLAR?

Get more DC graphic novels wherever comics and books are sold!

"Tynion, Barrows and company have delivered the single strongest book of DC's Rebirth era."
–NEWSARAMA

"Dramatic, suspenseful, and full of gorgeously detailed artwork. What more could a Bat-fan ask for?" **–IGN**

DC UNIVERSE REBIRTH
BATMAN
DETECTIVE COMICS
VOL.1 RISE OF THE BATMEN
JAMES TYNION IV • EDDY BARROWS • ALVARO MARTINEZ • EBER FERREIRA • RAUL FERNANDEZ

BATMAN: DETECTIVE COMICS

VOL. 1: RISE OF THE BATMEN

JAMES TYNION IV,
EDDY BARROWS,
ALVARO MARTINEZ and more

DC UNIVERSE REBIRTH
BATMAN
DETECTIVE COMICS
VOL.2 THE VICTIM SYNDICATE
JAMES TYNION IV • ALVARO MARTINEZ • EDDY BARROWS • BEN OLIVER

BATMAN: DETECTIVE COMICS VOL. 2: THE VICTIM SYNDICATE

DC UNIVERSE REBIRTH
BATMAN
DETECTIVE COMICS
VOL.3 LEAGUE OF SHADOWS
JAMES TYNION IV • MARCIO TAKARA • CHRISTIAN DUCE

BATMAN: DETECTIVE COMICS VOL. 3: LEAGUE OF SHADOWS

READ THEM ALL!

BATMAN: DETECTIVE COMICS VOL. 4: DEUS EX MACHINA

BATMAN: DETECTIVE COMICS VOL. 5: A LONELY PLACE OF LIVING

BATMAN: DETECTIVE COMICS VOL. 6: FALL OF THE BATMEN

BATMAN: DETECTIVE COMICS VOL. 7: BATMEN ETERNAL

Get more DC graphic novels wherever comics and books are sold!

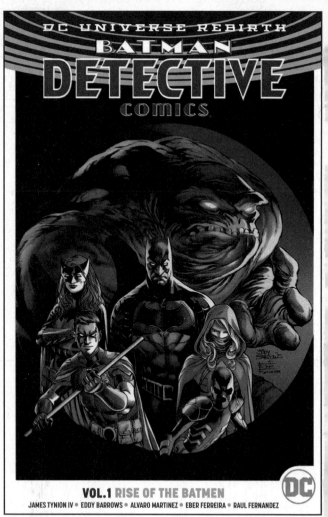

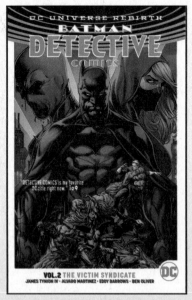